THE FATHERS
OF THE CHURCH

MEDIAEVAL CONTINUATION

VOLUME 14

THE FATHERS
OF THE CHURCH

MEDIAEVAL CONTINUATION

PETER THE VENERABLE

AGAINST THE INVETERATE OBDURACY OF THE JEWS

Translated by
IRVEN M. RESNICK

THE CATHOLIC UNIVERSITY OF AMERICA PRESS
Washington, D.C.

The paper used in this publication meets the minimum requirements
of the American National Standards for Information Science—
Permanence of Paper for Printed Library Materials,
ANSI z39.48-1984.
∞

LIBRARY OF CONGRESS CATALOGING-IN-PUBLICATION DATA
Peter, the Venerable, approximately 1092–1156.
[Adversus Iudeorum inveteratam duritiem. English]
Peter the venerable against the inveterate obduracy of the Jews / translated
by Irven M. Resnick.
pages cm. — (The fathers of the church mediaeval continuation ; v. 14)
Includes bibliographical references and index.
ISBN 978-0-8132-2129-8 (cloth : alk. paper)
ISBN 978-0-8132-2822-8 (pbk.)
1. Judaism—Controversial literature—Early works to 1800.
I. Resnick, Irven Michael.   II. Title.
BT1120.P4713 2013
239—dc23
2013003974

PUBLICATION OF THIS BOOK
IS SUPPORTED BY A GRANT FROM

Jewish Federation of Greater Hartford

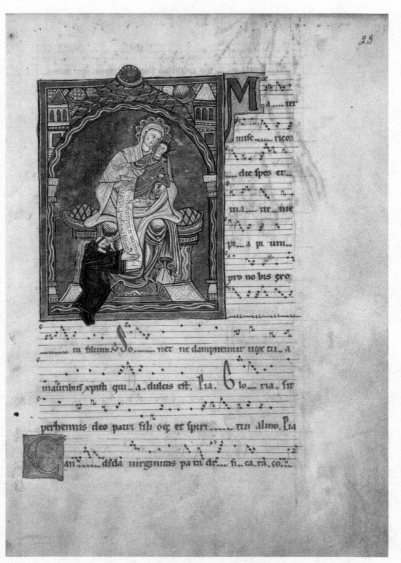

BnF 17716 fol. 23 (late 12th C.?), showing Peter the Venerable praying at the feet of the Virgin holding her child. The illustration follows the text of The Office of the Transfiguration (fols. 8r–22v) by Peter the Venerable.

CONTENTS

CONTENTS

CHAPTER FIVE

On the ridiculous and very foolish fables of

INDICES

ACKNOWLEDGMENTS

This project began in 2006 in London, while I was a Distinguished Visiting Fellow at Queen Mary College, University of London. I would like to express my appreciation to faculty and staff at Queen Mary, and to the staff at the British Library.

A very special note of thanks, however, is owed to Dr. Carole Burnett, staff editor at The Catholic University of America Press, who contributed helpful suggestions regarding the translation. For any errors that remain, I alone am responsible.

ABBREVIATIONS

B.T. Babylonian Talmud.

CC CM Corpus Christianorum Continuatio Mediaevalis.

CC SL Corpus Christianorum Series Latina.

Colon. Ed. *Sancti Doctoris Ecclesiae Alberti Magni Ordinis Fratrum Praedicatorum episcopi* Opera Omnia, *ad fidem codicum manuscriptorum edenda apparatu critico notis prolegomenis indicibus instruenda curavit. Institutum Alberti Magni Coloniense.* Ed. Bernhard Geyer (after vol. 37.2 [1978]: ed. Wilhelm Kübel). Monasterii Westfalorum: Aschendorff, 1951–.

CSEL Corpus Scriptorum Ecclesiasticorum Latinorum.

FOTC, MC Fathers of the Church, Mediaeval Continuation.

LXX Septuagint.

Mansi Mansi, Joannes Dominicus. *Sacrorum conciliorum nova et amplissima collectio.* New edition. 31 vols. Florence: Expensis Antonii Zatta, 1759–98.

MGH Monumenta Germaniae Historica.

QQ Geistesgesch. Quellen zur Geistesgeschichte des Mittelalters.

SS Scriptores.

Ovid *Met.* *Metamorphoses.*

PL Patrologiae Cursus Completus, Series Latina.

Vulg. Vulgate.

SELECT BIBLIOGRAPHY

Primary Sources

The Aberdeen Bestiary (Aberdeen University Library MS 24). Available: http://www.abdn.ac.uk/bestiary/bestiary.hti.

Albert of Aachen. *Historia Ierosolimitana*. Edited and translated by Susan B. Edgington. Oxford: Clarendon Press, 2007.

Albert the Great. *Albert the Great's Questions Concerning Aristotle's* On Animals. Translated by Irven M. Resnick and Kenneth F. Kitchell, Jr. FOTC, MC 9. Washington, DC: The Catholic University of America Press, 2008.

————. *De natura loci, De causis proprietatum elementorum, De generatione et corruptione*. In *Opera omnia Alberti Magni* 5.2. Edited by Paul Hossfeld. Monasterii Westf.: Aschendorff, 1980.

————. *Quaestiones super de animalibus*. In *Opera omnia Alberti Magni* 12. Edited by E. Filthaut. Monasterii Westf.: Aschendorff, 1955.

————. *Commentarii in III Sententiarum*. Edited by A. Borgnet, 28. Paris: L. Vivès, 1894.

Alexander of Hales. *Summa Theologica*. Quaracchi: Collegii S. Bonaventurae, 1930.

Andrew of Saint Victor. *Andreae de Sancto Victore Opera. VI: Expositionem in Ezechielem*. Edited by Michael Alan Singer. CC CM 53e. Turnholt: Brepols, 1991.

Anselm of Laon. *Anselms von Laon systematische Sentenzen*. Edited by Franz Pl. Bliemetzrieder. Beiträge zur Geschichte der Philosophie des Mittelalters 18, 2–3. Münster i. W.: Aschendorff, 1919.

Arnulf of Séez. *Invectiva in Girardum Engolismensem episcopum*. MGH, Libelli de lite, 3. Edited by J. Dieterich. Hanover, 1897.

Augustine. *Enarrationes in Psalmos*. Edited by Eligius Dekkers and J. Fraipont. CC SL 40. Turnholt: Brepols, 1956.

————. *De civitate dei*. Edited by Bernhard Dombart and Alfons Kalb. CC SL 47–48. Turnholt: Brepols, 1955.

————. *Contra Faustum*. Edited by Joseph Zycha. CSEL 25. Vienna: F. Tempsky, 1891.

Bartholomaeus Anglicus. *De rerum proprietatibus*. Frankfurt, 1601; reprint, Frankfurt on Main: Minerva, 1964.

Bede, the Venerable. *In Ezram et Neemiam libri iii*. Edited by D. Hurst. CC SL 119A. Turnholt: Brepols, 1969.

Bernard. *The Letters of St. Bernard of Clairvaux*. Translated by Bruno Scott James. Chicago: Henry Regnery Company, 1953.

————. *Epistola* 363. In *Sancti Bernardi Opera genuina*. Edited by the Monks of St. Benedict. 8 vols. Lyons and Paris: Perisse Frères, 1854. 8: 316.

Bruno of Segni. *Commentaria in Matthaeum*. PL 165: 71–314.

Fulbert of Chartres. *Tractatus contra Judaeos*. PL 141: 305–318.

Gilbert Crispin. *Disputatio iudaei et christiani; Disputatio christiani cum gentili de fide Christi*. Edited and translated by Karl Werner Wilhelm and Gerhard Wilhelmi. Freiburg im Breisgau: Herder, 2005.

————. *The Works of Gilbert Crispin, Abbot of Westminster*. Edited by Anna Sapir Abulafia and G. R. Evans. London and New York: Oxford University Press, 1986.

Guerric of Saint-Quentin. *Quaestiones de quolibet*. Edited by Walter H. Principe; rev. Jonathan Black. Studies and Texts 143. Toronto: Pontifical Institute of Mediaeval Studies, 2002.

Herman of Cologne. *A Short Account of His Own Conversion*. In *Conversion and Text: The Cases of Augustine of Hippo, Herman-Judah, and Constantine Tsatsos*. Translated by Karl F. Morrison. Charlottesville, VA: University of Virginia Press, 1992. Pp. 39–113.

———— [Hermannus Iudaeus]. *Opusculum de conversione sua*. Edited by Gerlinde Niemeyer. MGH, QQ Geistesgesch., 4. Weimar: H. Böhlaus, 1963.

Horace. *Carmina*. Translated by Richard F. Thomas. Cambridge: Cambridge University Press, 2011.

Isidore of Seville. *Etymologiae*. PL 82: 73–729.

Jerome. *Commentarii in Danielem*. Edited by F. Glorie. CC SL 75A. Turnholt: Brepols, 1964.

————. *Commentarii in Isaiam*. Edited by M. Adriaen. CC SL 73. Turnholt: Brepols, 1963.

————. *Liber interpretationis hebraicorum nominum*. Edited by P. de Lagarde, CC SL 72. Turnholt: Brepols, 1959.

————. *Liber quaestionum Hebraicarum in Genesim*. Edited by P. de Lagarde, CC SL 72. Turnholt: Brepols, 1959.

Joseph Kimhi. *The Book of the Covenant*. Translated by Frank Talmage. Toronto: Pontifical Institute of Mediaeval Studies Press, 1972.

Josephus. *Antiquitates, Books 16–17*. Translated by Ralph Marcus. Cambridge, MA: Harvard University Press, 1998.

————. *Antiquitates, Books 18–19*. Translated by Louis H. Feldman. Cambridge, MA: Harvard University Press, 1965.

————. *Antiquitates, Books 12–14*. Translated by Ralph Marcus. Cambridge, MA: Harvard University Press, 1957.

Linder, Amnon, editor. *The Jews in the Legal Sources of the Early Middle Ages*. Detroit: Wayne State University Press, 1997.

Maimonides. *Epistle to Yemen*. In *A Maimonides Reader*. Edited by Isidore Twersky. New York: Behrman House, Inc., 1972. Pp. 437–62.

Mühlhausen, Yom Tov Lippmann. *Disputatio adversus Christianos ad Jeremie, Eze-

chielis, Psalmorum et Danielis libros institute. Translated by M. Sebaldus Snellius. Altdorf: Typis Viduae Balthasaris Scherffi, 1645.

Odo of Tournai. *Two Theological Treatises of Odo of Tournai: On Original Sin, and a Debate with the Jew, Leo, Concerning the Advent of Christ, the Son of God.* Translated by Irven M. Resnick. Philadelphia: University of Pennsylvania Press, 1994.

Ovid. *Metamorphoses.* Translated by Frank Justus Miller. 2 vols. Cambridge, MA: Harvard University Press, 1951.

Paul Alvarez. *Epistola* 16. PL 121: 483D–491B.

Peter Abelard. *Collationes.* Edited and translated by John Marenbon and Giovanni Orlandi. Oxford: Clarendon Press, 2001.

————. *A Dialogue of a Philosopher with a Jew, and a Christian.* Translated by Pierre J. Payer. Toronto: Pontifical Institute of Mediaeval Studies, 1979.

Peter of Blois. *Contra perfidiam Judaeorum.* PL 207: 825–871.

Peter of Poitiers. *Capitula Petri Pictavensis ad domnum Petrum abbatem.* PL 189: 661A–662A.

Peter the Venerable. *De miraculis.* Edited by D. Bouthillier. CC CM 83. Turnholt: Brepols, 1988.

————. *Adversus Iudeorum inveteratam duritiem.* Edited by Yvonne Friedman. CC CM 58. Turnholt: Brepols, 1985.

————. *Schriften zum Islam.* Edited and translated [into German] by Reinhold Glei. Corpus Islamo-Christianum, Series Latina, 1. Altenberge: CIS-Verlag, 1985.

————. *Contra Petrobrusianos hereticos.* Edited by James Fearns. CC CM 10. Turnholt: Brepols, 1968.

————. *The Letters of Peter the Venerable.* Edited by Giles Constable. 2 vols. Cambridge, MA: Harvard University Press, 1967.

————. *De laude dominici sepulchri.* Edited by Giles Constable. In "Petri Venerabilis sermones tres." *Revue Bénédictine* 64 (1954): 232–54.

————. *Sermo de transfiguratione Domini.* PL 189: 953–972.

Petrus Alfonsi. *Dialogue Against the Jews.* Translated by Irven M. Resnick. FOTC, MC 8. Washington, DC: The Catholic University of America Press, 2006.

Pseudo Al-Kindi. *Exposición y refutación del islam: La versión latina de las epístolas de al-Hasimi y al-Kindi.* Edited by Fernando González Muñoz. A Coruña, Spain: Universidade da Coruña, 2005.

————. "Al-Kindi, Apologia del Cristianismo." Edited by Jose Muñoz Sendino. In *Miscellanea Comillas* 11–12 (1949): 337–460.

Pseudo Eliezer ben Hyrcanus. *Pirkê de Rabbi Eliezer.* Translated by Gerald Friedlander. New York: Hermon Press, 1916; reprint 1970.

Pseudo William of Champeaux. *Dialogus inter christianum et judaeum de fide catholica.* PL 163: 1045–1073.

Roger Frugard. *Chirurgia.* In *Anglo-Norman Medicine.* Edited by Tony Hunt. 2 vols. Cambridge: D. S. Brewer, 1994.

Sāwirus ibn al-Mukaffa. *History of the Patriarchs of the Egyptian Church.* Edited and translated by Y. Abd al-Massih and O. H. S. Khs. Burmester. 4 vols. Cairo: Société d'archéologie copte, 1943–74.

Simonsohn, Shlomo, editor. *The Apostolic See and the Jews. Documents: 492–1404.* 8 vols. Toronto: Pontifical Institute of Mediaeval Studies, 1988–90.

Thomas of Monmouth. *De vita et passione Sancti Willelmi Martyris Norwicensis. The Life and Miracles of St. William of Norwich by Thomas of Monmouth. Now First Edited from the Unique Manuscript, with an Introduction, Translation and Notes.* Edited and translated by Augustus Jessopp and M. R. James. Cambridge: University Press, 1896.

Vincent of Beauvais. *Speculum quadruplex, sive, Speculum maius: naturale, doctrinale, morale, historiale.* Graz, Austria: Duaci: Akademische Druck- u. Verlagsanstalt; ex officina typographica Baltazaris Belleri, 1964–1965.

White, T. H., editor and translator. *The Book of Beasts, being a Translation from a Latin Bestiary of the Twelfth Century.* New York: Dover Publications, 1984.

William of Malmesbury. *De gestis regum Anglorum.* Edited by William Stubbs. Rerum Britannicarum medii ævi scriptores. 2 vols. Wiesbaden: Kraus Reprint, 1964.

Secondary Sources

Abulafia, Anna Sapir. "Jewish-Christian Disputations and the Twelfth-Century Renaissance." In eadem, *Christians and Jews in Dispute: Disputational Literature and the Rise of Anti-Judaism in the West.* Aldershot: Ashgate Variorum, 1998. IX: 105–25.

————. "Theology and the Commercial Revolution." In eadem, *Christians and Jews in Dispute: Disputational Literature and the Rise of Anti-Judaism in the West.* Aldershot: Ashgate Variorum, 1998. XI: 23–40.

————. "Twelfth-Century Christian Expectations of Jewish Conversion: A Case Study of Peter of Blois." *Aschkenas* 8.1 (1998): 45–70.

————. "Twelfth-Century Renaissance Theology and the Jews." In *From Witness to Witchcraft: Jews and Judaism in Medieval Christian Thought.* Edited by Jeremy Cohen. Wolfenbütteler Mittelalter-Studien 11. Wiesbaden: Harrassowitz Verlag, 1996. Pp. 125–39.

————. "An Attempt by Gilbert Crispin, Abbot of Westminster, at Rational Argument in the Jewish-Christian Debate." *Studia Monastica* 26 (1984): 55–75.

Appleby, David F. "The Priority of Sight According to Peter the Venerable." *Mediaeval Studies* 60 (1998): 123–57.

Berger, David. "The Attitude of St. Bernard of Clairvaux Toward the Jews." In *Proceedings of the American Academy for Jewish Research* 40 (1972): 89–108.

Berry, Virginia. "Peter the Venerable and the Crusades." In *Petrus Venerabilis 1156–1956: Studies and Texts Commemorating the Eighth Centenary of His Death.* Edited by Giles Constable and James Kritzeck. Studia Anselmiana 40. Rome: Herder, 1956. Pp. 140–62.

Billet, Bernard. "Notes de mariologie. La dévotion mariale de Pierre le Vénérable (1092–1156)." *Esprit et vie* 87.37 (1977): 465–72.

Bishko, Charles Julian. "Liturgical Intercession at Cluny For the King-Emperors of Leon." *Studia Monastica* 7 (1961): 53–76.

————. "Peter the Venerable's Journey to Spain." In *Petrus Venerabilis 1156–1956: Studies and Texts Commemorating the Eighth Centenary of His Death.* Edited by Giles Constable and James Kritzeck. Studia Anselmiana 40. Rome: Herder, 1956. Pp. 163–75.

Burman, Thomas E. *Reading the Qur'ān in Latin Christendom, 1140–1560.* Philadelphia: University of Pennsylvania Press, 2007.

————. "'Tathlīth al-wahdānîyah' and the Twelfth-Century Andalusian-Christian Approach to Islam." In *Medieval Christian Perceptions of Islam.* Edited by John Victor Tolan. New York and London: Routledge, 1996. Pp. 109–28.

Burnett, Charles. "The Works of Petrus Alfonsi: Questions of Authenticity." *Medium Aevum* 66.1 (1997): 42–79.

Cahn, Walter B. "The 'Portrait' of Muhammad in the Toledan Collection." In *Reading Medieval Images. The Art Historian and the Object.* Edited by Elizabeth Sears and Thelma K. Thomas. Ann Arbor: University of Michigan Press, 2002. Pp. 51–60.

Callahan, Daniel. "The Cross, the Jews, and the Destruction of the Church of the Holy Sepulcher in the Writings of Ademar of Chabannes." In *Christian Attitudes toward Jews in the Middle Ages: A Casebook.* Edited by Michael Frassetto. New York: Routledge, 2007. Pp. 15–24.

Châtillon, Jean. "Pierre le Vénérable et les Pétrobrusiens." In *Pierre Abélard—Pierre le Vénérable: les courants philosophiques, littéraires et artistiques en Occident au milieu du XIIe siècle; [actes et mémoires du colloque international], Abbaye de Cluny, 2 au 9 juillet 1972, Colloques internationaux du Centre National de la Recherche Scientifique,* no. 546. Paris: Éditions du Centre national de la recherche scientifique, 1975. Pp. 165–76.

Chazan, Robert. "Undermining the Jewish Sense of Future." In *Christians, Muslims, and Jews in Medieval and Early Modern Spain: Interaction and Cultural Change.* Edited by Mark D. Meyerson and Edward D. English. Notre Dame Conferences in Medieval Studies, no. 8. Notre Dame, IN: University of Notre Dame Press, 2000. Pp. 179–94.

————. *Medieval Stereotypes and Modern Antisemitism.* Berkeley: University of California Press, 1997.

————. *European Jewry and the First Crusade.* Berkeley: University of California Press, 1996.

————. "Daniel 9: 24–27: Exegesis and Polemics." In *Contra Iudaeos. Ancient and Medieval Polemics Between Christians and Jews.* Edited by Ora Limor and Guy G. Stroumsa. Tübingen: J. C. B. Mohr, 1996. Pp. 143–59.

————. "Twelfth-Century Perceptions of the Jews: A Case Study of Bernard of Clairvaux and Peter the Venerable." In *From Witness to Witchcraft: Jews and Judaism in Medieval Christian Thought.* Edited by Jeremy Cohen. Wolfenbütteler Mittelalter-Studien 11. Wiesbaden: Harrassowitz Verlag, 1996. Pp. 187–201.

————. "The Christian Position in Jacob ben Reuben's *Milhamot Ha-Shem*." In *From Ancient Israel to Modern Judaism: Intellect in Quest of Understanding; Essays in Honor of Marvin Fox.* Edited by Jacob Neusner, Ernest S. Frerichs, and Nahum M. Sarna. 4 vols. Atlanta, GA: Scholars Press, 1989. 2: 157–70.

_____. *Daggers of Faith. Thirteenth-Century Missionizing and Jewish Response.* Berkeley, Los Angeles, London: University of California Press, 1989.

_____. *Medieval Jewry in Northern France: A Political and Social History.* Baltimore and London: Johns Hopkins University Press, 1973.

Cohen, Jeremy. *Sanctifying the Name of God: Jewish Martyrs and Jewish Memories of the First Crusade.* Philadelphia: University of Pennsylvania Press, 2004.

_____. "Christian Theology and Anti-Jewish Violence in the Middle Ages: Connections and Disjunctions." In *Religious Violence Between Christians and Jews: Medieval Roots, Modern Perspectives.* Edited by Anna Sapir Abulafia. New York: Palgrave, 2002. Pp. 44–60.

_____. *Living Letters of the Law: Ideas of the Jew in Medieval Christianity.* Berkeley: University of California Press, 1999.

_____. "The Muslim Connection or On the Changing Role of the Jew in High Medieval Theology." In *From Witness to Witchcraft: Jews and Judaism in Medieval Christian Thought.* Edited by Jeremy Cohen. Wolfenbütteler Mittelalter-Studien 11. Wiesbaden: Harrassowitz Verlag, 1996. Pp. 141–62.

Constable, Giles. "The Second Crusade as Seen by Contemporaries." *Traditio* 9 (1953): 213–79.

Cutler, Allan. "Peter the Venerable and Islam." *Journal of the American Oriental Society* 86 (1966): 184–98.

Cutler, Allan H., and Helen E. Cutler. *The Jew as Ally of the Muslim: Medieval Roots of Anti-Semitism.* Notre Dame, IN: University of Notre Dame Press, 1986.

d'Alverny, M. T. "Quelques manuscrits de la 'collectio Toletana.'" In *Petrus Venerabilis 1156–1956: Studies and Texts Commemorating the Eighth Centenary of His Death.* Edited by Giles Constable and James Kritzeck. Studia Anselmiana, philosophica, theologica, fasc. 40. Rome: Herder, 1956. Pp. 202–18.

Dahan, Gilbert. "La connaissance de l'exégèse Juive par les Chrétiens du XIIe au XIVe siècle." In *Rashi et la culture juive en France du Nord au moyen âge.* Edited by Gilbert Dahan, Gérard Nahon, and Elie Nicholas. Paris-Louvain: E. Peeters, 1997. Pp. 343–59.

Dan, Joseph. "Ben Sira, Alphabet of." In *Encyclopaedia Judaica.* Edited by Michael Berenbaum and Fred Skolnik. 2d ed. Detroit: Macmillan Reference USA, 2007. 3: 375–76.

Drouard-Ada, M. "Éléments historiques dans un traité de polémique anti-juive: 'L'Adversus Judaeos' de Pierre le Vénérable (Pierre de Cluny)." *Archives juives* 8 (1972): 1–6.

Eckert, Willehad Paul. "Die Universität Köln und die Juden im späten Mittelalter." In *Die Kölner Universität im Mittelalter. Geistige Wurzeln und soziale Wirklichkeit.* Edited by Albert Zimmermann. Berlin: Walter de Gruyter, 1989. Pp. 488–507.

Edwards, John, editor and translator. *The Jews in Western Europe 1400–1600.* Manchester and New York: Manchester University Press, 1994.

Evans, Michael. "The *Ysagoge in Theologiam* and the Commentaries Attributed to Bernard Silvestris." *Journal of the Warburg and Courtauld Institutes* 54 (1991): 1–42.

Fichtenau, Heinrich. *Heretics and Scholars in the High Middle Ages 1000–1200.*

Translated by Denise A. Kaiser. University Park, PA: Pennsylvania State University Press, 1998.

Fishbane, Michael. "'The Holy One Sits and Roars': Mythopoesis and the Midrashic Imagination." In *The Midrashic Imagination: Jewish Exegesis, Thought, and History*. Edited by Michael Fishbane. Albany: SUNY Press, 1993. Pp. 60–77.

Frassetto, Michael. "Heretics and Jews in the Early Eleventh Century: The Writings of Rodulfus Glaber and Ademar of Chabannes." In *Christian Attitudes toward Jews in the Middle Ages: A Casebook*. Edited by Michael Frassetto. New York: Routledge, 2007. Pp. 43–60.

Friedman, Yvonne. "Anti-Talmudic Invective from Peter the Venerable to Nicolas Donin (1144–1244)." In *Le brûlement du Talmud à Paris 1242–1244*. Edited by Gilbert Dahan. Paris: Les Éditions du Cerf, 1999. Pp. 171–90.

_____. "An Anatomy of Anti-Semitism: Peter the Venerable's Letter to Louis VII, King of France (1146)." *Bar-Ilan Studies in History* 1 (Ramat-Gan, 1978): 87–102.

Funkenstein, Amos. *Perceptions of Jewish History*. Berkeley, Los Angeles, Oxford: University of California Press, 1993.

Gandeul, Jean-Marie, and Robert Caspar. "Textes de la tradition musulmane concernant le tahrîf des écritures." *Islamochristiana* 6 (1980): 61–104.

Gaster, Moses. "Hebrew Visions of Hell and Paradise: The Revelation of R. Joshua ben Levi." In *Studies and Texts in Folklore, Magic, Mediaeval Romance, Hebrew Apocrypha and Samaritan Archaeology*. 3 vols. New York: KTAV, 1971. 1: 144–64.

Ginzberg, Louis. *The Legends of the Jews*. Translated by Henrietta Szold. 7 vols. Philadelphia: 1909–28; reprint Hildesheim: Georg Olms Verlag, 2000.

Golb, Norman. *The Jews in Medieval Normandy: A Social and Intellectual History*. Cambridge: Cambridge University Press, 1998.

_____. *Jewish Proselytism—a Phenomenon in the Religious History of Early Medieval Europe*. Tenth Annual Rabbi Louis Feinberg Memorial Lecture. Cincinnati: University of Cincinnati, 1988. Pp. 21–31.

_____. "The Messianic Pretender Solomon ibn al-Ruji and his Son Menahem (the so-called David al-Roy)." Acccessed at http://oi.uchicago.edu/pdf/false_messiah-1.pdf.

Gow, Andrew Colin. *The Red Jews: Antisemitism in an Apocalyptic Age 1200–1600*. Leiden: E. J. Brill, 1995.

Graboïs, Aryeh. "Une Principauté Juive dans la France du Midi à l'Époque Carolingienne." In idem, *Civilisation et société dans l'Occident mediéval*. London: Variorum, 1983. XV: 191–202.

_____. "Le Schisme de 1130 et la France." *Revue d'histoire ecclésiastique* 76 (1981): 593–612.

_____. "The *Hebraica veritas* and Jewish-Christian Intellectual Relations in the Twelfth Century." *Speculum* 50 (1975): 613–35.

_____. "La dynastie des 'rois juifs' de Narbonne (XIIe–XIIIe siècle)." In *Narbonne. Archéologie et histoire*. Vol. 2: *Narbonne au moyen âge*. Montpelier: Fédération historique du Languedoc méditerranéen et du Roussillon, 1973. Pp. 49–54.

Griffith, Sidney H. "Arguing from Scripture: The Bible in the Christian/Muslim Encounter in the Middle Ages." In *Scripture and Pluralism: Reading the Bible in the Religiously Plural Worlds of the Middle Ages and Renaissance.* Edited by Thomas Heffernan and Thomas Burman. Leiden: Brill, 2005. Pp. 29–58.

Guttman, J. "Alexandre de Hales et le Judaisme." *Revue des études juives* 19 (1889): 224–34.

Halm, Heinz. *The Empire of the Mahdi: The Rise of the Fatimids.* Translated by Michael Bonner. Leiden: Brill, 1996.

Hollengreen, Laura. "The Politics and Poetics of Possession: Saint Louis, the Jews, and Old Testament Violence." In *Between the Picture and the Word: Manuscript Studies from the Index of Christian Art.* Edited by Colum Hourihane. [Princeton, NJ]: Index of Christian Art, Dept. of Art and Archaeology, Princeton University, in association with Penn State University Press, 2005. Pp. 51–71; 90–115.

Hopkins, J. F. P. "Ibn Tūmart." In the *Encyclopaedia of Islam.* Edited by P. Bearman, Th. Bianquis, C. E. Bosworth, E. van Donzel, and W. P. Heinrichs. Brill, 2007. Accessed at Brill Online. Oxford University libraries. 30 August 2007. http://www.brillonline.nl/subscriber/entry?entry=islam_SIM-3395.

Hunt, Richard William. "The Disputation of Peter of Cornwall Against Symon the Jew." In *Studies in Medieval History Presented to Frederick Maurice Powicke.* Edited by R. W. Hunt, et al. Oxford: Clarendon Press, 1948. Pp. 143–56.

Iogna-Prat, Dominique. "The Creation of a Christian Armory Against Islam." In *Medieval Religion: New Approaches.* Edited by Constance Hoffman Berman. New York and London: Routledge, 2005. Pp. 325–46.

_____. *Order and Exclusion: Cluny and Christendom Face Heresy, Judaism, and Islam (1000–1150).* Translated by Graham Robert Edwards. Ithaca, NY: Cornell University Press, 2002.

Jestice, Phyllis G. "A Great Jewish Conspiracy? Worsening Jewish-Christian Relations and the Destruction of the Holy Sepulcher." In *Christian Attitudes toward Jews in the Middle Ages: A Casebook.* Edited by Michael Frassetto. New York: Routledge, 2007. Pp. 25–42.

Jordan, William C. "Marian Devotion and the Talmud Trial of 1240." In *Religionspräche im Mittelalter.* Edited by Bernard Lewis and Friedrich Niewöhner. Wiesbaden: Otto Harrassowitz, 1992. Pp. 61–76.

Katzir, Yael. "The Conquests of Jerusalem, 1099 and 1187: Historical Memory and Religious Typology." In *The Meeting of Two Worlds: Cultural Exchange between East and West during the Period of the Crusades.* Edited by Vladimir P. Goss and Christine Verzár Bornstein. Studies in Medieval Culture 21. Kalamazoo, MI: Medieval Institute Publications, 1986. Pp. 103–13.

Kedar, Benjamin Z. "Convergences of Oriental Christian, Muslim, and Frankish Worshippers: The Case of Saydnaya." In *De Sion exibit lex et verbum domini de Hierusalem: Essays on Medieval Law, Liturgy and Literature in Honour of Amnon Linder.* Edited by Yitzhak Hen. Turnholt: Brepols, 2001. Pp. 59–69.

Knight, Gillian. "Politics and Pastoral Care: Papal Schism in Some Letters of Peter the Venerable." *Revue Bénédictine* 109, no. 3–4 (1999): 359–90.

Koningsveld, P. Sj. Van. "La apologia de Al-Kindi en la España del siglo XII. Huellas toledanos de un 'Animal disputax.'" In *Estudios sobre Alfonso VI y la Reconquista de Toledo. Actes del II Congreso Internacional de Estudios Mozárabes (Toledo, 20–26 Mayo 1985)*. Series historica 5. Toledo: Instituto de Estudios Visigótico-Mozárabes, 1989. Pp. 107–29.

Kritzeck, James. *Peter the Venerable and Islam*. Princeton, NJ: Princeton University Press, 1964.

————. "Peter the Venerable and the Toledan Collection." In *Petrus Venerabilis 1156–1956: Studies and Texts Commemorating the Eighth Centenary of His Death*. Edited by Giles Constable and James Kritzeck. Studia Anselmiana, philosophica, theologica, fasc. 40. Rome: Herder, 1956. Pp. 176–201.

Kruger, Stephen F. "Medieval Christian (Dis) identifications: Muslims and Jews in Guibert of Nogent." *New Literary History* 29.2 (1997): 185–203.

Landes, Richard. "The Massacres of 1010: On the Origins of Popular Anti-Jewish Violence in Western Europe." In *From Witness to Witchcraft: Jews and Judaism in Medieval Christian Thought*. Edited by Jeremy Cohen. Wolfenbütteler Mittelalter-Studien 11. Wiesbaden: Harrassowitz Verlag, 1996. Pp. 79–111.

Langmuir, Gavin I. "The Faith of Christians and Hostility to Jews." In *Christianity and Judaism. Papers Read at the 1991 Summer Meeting and the 1992 Winter Meeting of the Ecclesiastical History Society*. Edited by Diana Wood. Cambridge, MA: Ecclesiastical History Society, 1992. Pp. 77–92.

————. "Thomas of Monmouth: Detector of Ritual Murder." *Speculum* 59 (1984): 820–46.

Lauzi, Egle. "Occidentali e Saraceni nel Medioevo Latino: Tracce di un incontro, II." *Rendiconti dell'Istituto Lombardo* 132 (1998): 485–502.

Le Goff, Jacques. *Your Money or Your Life: Economy and Religion in the Middle Ages*. Translated by Patricia Ranum. New York: Zone Books, 1988.

Lejbowicz, Max. "Développement autochtone assumé et acculturation dissimulée." In *Les relations culturelles entre chrétiens et musulmans au moyen âge: Quelles leçons en tirer de nos jours?* Colloque organisé à la Fondation Singer-Polignac le mercredi 20 octobre 2004 par Rencontres médiévales européennes. Edited by Max Lejbowicz. Turnholt: Brepols, 2005: 57–81.

Levy, Monique. "Massacre de juifs en France lors la deuxième croisade." *Archives juives* 28.2 (1995): 89–92.

Liere, Frans van. "Andrew of St. Victor, Jerome, and the Jews: Biblical Scholarship in the Twelfth-Century Renaissance." In *Scripture and Pluralism: Reading the Bible in the Religiously Plural Worlds of the Middle Ages and Renaissance*. Edited by Thomas Heffernan and Thomas Burman. Leiden: Brill, 2005. Pp. 59–75.

Lipton, Sara. *Images of Intolerance. The Representation of Jews and Judaism in the Bible moralisée*. Berkeley: University of California Press, 1999.

Little, Lester K. *Religious Poverty and the Profit Economy in Medieval Europe*. Ithaca, NY: Cornell University Press, 1978.

Lotter, Friedrich. "*Innocens virgo et martyr:* Thomas von Monmouth und die Verbreitung der Ritualmordlegende im Hochmittelalter." In *Die Legende vom Ritualmord: zur Geschichte der Blutbeschuldigung gegen Juden*. Edited by Rainer Erb. Berlin: Metropol, 1993. Pp. 25–72.

Maccoby, Hyam. *Judaism on Trial: Jewish-Christian Disputations in the Middle Ages.* London: Littman Library of Jewish Civilization, 1993.

Mansi, Joannes Dominicus. *Sacrorum conciliorum nova et amplissima collectio.* New edition, vol. 2. Florence: Expensis Antonii Zatta, 1759.

Marcus, Jacob Rader. *The Jew in the Medieval World: A Sourcebook, 315–1791.* Introduction by Marc Saperstein. Revised edition. Cincinnati: Hebrew Union College Press, 1999.

Marrow, James H. "*Circumdederunt me canes multi:* Christ's Tormentors in Northern European Art of the Late Middle Ages and Early Renaissance." *Art Bulletin* 59.2 (1977): 167–81.

Martínez Gázquez, José. "Trois traductions médiévales latines du Coran: Pierre le Vénérable-Robert de Ketton, Marc de Tolède et Jean de Segobia." *Revue des études latines* 80 (2003): 223–36.

McCulloh, John M. "Jewish Ritual Murder: William of Norwich, Thomas of Monmouth, and the Early Dissemination of the Myth." *Speculum* 72 (1997): 698–740.

Mews, Constant J. "Abelard and Heloise on Jews and *Hebraica Veritas.*" In *Christian Attitudes toward Jews in the Middle Ages: A Casebook.* Edited by Michael Frassetto. New York: Routledge, 2007. Pp. 83–108.

Momigliano, Arnaldo. "Sibylline Oracles." In *Encyclopedia of Religion.* Edited by Mircea Eliade. New York: MacMillan Publ. Co., 1987. 13: 305–8.

Moore, R. I. *The Birth of Popular Heresy.* Toronto: University of Toronto Press, 1995.

————. "Anti-Semitism and the Birth of Modern Europe." In *Christianity and Judaism. Papers Read at the 1991 Summer Meeting and the 1992 Winter Meeting of the Ecclesiastical History Society.* Edited by Diana Wood. Cambridge, MA: Ecclesiastical History Society, 1992. Pp. 33–58.

Nahon, Gérard. "From the *Rue aux Juifs* to the *Chemin du Roy:* The Classical Age of French Jewry, 1108–1223." In *Jews and Christians in Twelfth-Century Europe.* Edited by Michael A. Signer and John Van Engen. Notre Dame Conferences in Medieval Studies 10. Notre Dame, IN: University of Notre Dame Press, 2001. Pp. 311–39.

Ocker, Christopher. "Ritual Murder and the Subjectivity of Christ: A Choice in Medieval Christianity." *Harvard Theological Review* 91.2 (1998): 153–92.

Paulmier-Foucart, Monique, and Marie-Christine Duchenne. *Vincent de Beauvais et le Grand miroir du monde.* Turnhout: Brepols, 2004.

Resnick, Irven M. *Marks of Distinction: Christian Perceptions of Jews in the High Middle Ages.* Washington, DC: The Catholic University of America Press, 2012.

————. "Falsification of Scripture and Medieval Christian-Jewish Polemics." *Medieval Encounters* 2.3 (1996): 345–80.

Rosenthal, Erwin I. J. "Anti-Christian Polemic in Medieval Bible Commentaries." *Journal of Jewish Studies* 11 (1960): 116–35.

Roth, Norman. "Forgery and Abrogation of the Torah: A Theme in Muslim and Christian Polemic in Spain." *Proceedings of the American Academy for Jewish Research* 54 (1987): 203–36.

Saleh, Walid A. "A Fifteenth-Century Muslim Hebraist: Al-Biqā'ī and His Defense of Using the Bible to Interpret the Qur'ān." *Speculum* 83.3 (2008): 629–54.

Saltman, Avrom. "Gilbert Crispin as a Source of the Anti-Jewish Polemic of the *Ysagoge in Theologiam.*" *Bar-Ilan Studies in History* 7 (1984): 89–99.

Schatzmiller, Joseph. *La deuxième controverse de Paris. Un chapitre dans la polémique entre chrétiens et juifs au Moyen Age.* Paris and Louvain: Editions E. Peeters, 1994.

Schmitt, Jean-Claude. *The Conversion of Herman the Jew: Autobiography, History, and Fiction in the Twelfth Century.* Translated by Alex J. Novikoff. Philadelphia: University of Pennsylvania Press, 2010.

Schubert, Kurt. "Das christlich-jüdische Religionsgespräch am 12. und 13. Jahrhundert." In *Die Juden in ihrer mittelalterlichen Umwelt.* Edited by Alfred Ebenbauer and Klaus Zatloukal. Cologne: Böhlau, 1991. Pp. 223–50.

Signer, Michael. "Polemic and Exegesis: The Varieties of Twelfth-Century Hebraism." In *Hebraica Veritas? Christian Hebraists and the Study of Judaism in Early Modern Europe.* Edited by Allison P. Coudert and Jeffrey S. Shoulson. Philadelphia: University of Pennsylvania Press, 2004. Pp. 21–32.

Smalley, Beryl. *The Study of the Bible in the Middle Ages.* Oxford: Blackwell, 1952.

Smith, William, editor. *Dictionary of Greek and Roman Geography.* 2 vols. London: John Murray, 1878.

Southern, R. W. *Scholastic Humanism and the Unification of Europe.* 2 vols. Oxford: Blackwell, 1995.

————. "Peter of Blois: A Twelfth Century Humanist?" In idem, *Medieval Humanism.* New York: Harper and Row, 1970. Pp. 105–32.

Stacey, R. C. "Crusades, Martyrdoms, and the Jews of Norman England, 1096–1190." In *Juden und Christen zur Zeit der Kreuzzüge.* Edited by Alfred Haverkamp. Sigmaringen: Jan Thorbecke Verlag, 1999. Pp. 233–51.

————. "Jewish Lending and the Medieval English Economy." In *A Commercialising Economy: England 1086 to c. 1300.* Edited by R. H. Britnell and B. M. S. Campbell. Manchester and New York: Manchester University Press, 1995. Pp. 78–88.

Stern, David, and Mark Jay Mirsky, editors. *Rabbinic Fantasies: Imaginative Narratives from Classical Hebrew Literature.* Philadelphia and New York: Jewish Publication Society, 1990.

Stow, Kenneth R. *Jewish Dogs: An Image and Its Interpreters.* Stanford, CA: Stanford University Press, 2006.

————. "The Good of the Church, the Good of the State: The Popes and Jewish Money." In *Christianity and Judaism. Papers Read at the 1991 Summer Meeting and the 1992 Winter Meeting of the Ecclesiastical History Society.* Edited by Diana Wood. Cambridge, MA: Ecclesiastical History Society, 1992. Pp. 237–52.

Strickland, Debra Higgs. *Saracens, Demons, and Jews: Making Monsters in Medieval Art.* Princeton, NJ: Princeton University Press, 2003.

Stroll, Mary. *The Jewish Pope: Ideology and Politics in the Papal Schism of 1130.* Leiden: E. J. Brill, 1987.

Taitz, Emily. *The Jews of Medieval France: The Community of Champagne.* Westport, CT: Greenwood Press, 1994.

Tolan, John. *Saracens: Islam in the Medieval European Imagination.* New York: Columbia University Press, 2002.

_____. "Peter the Venerable on the 'Diabolical Heresy of the Saracens.'" In *The Devil, Heresy and Witchcraft in the Middle Ages: Essays in Honor of Jeffrey B. Russell.* Edited by Alberto Ferreiro. Leiden: Brill, 1998. Pp. 345–67.

_____. *Petrus Alfonsi and his Medieval Readers.* Gainesville, FL: University Press of Florida, 1993.

Torrell, Jean-Pierre. "Les juifs dans l'oeuvre de Pierre le Vénérable." *Cahiers de civilisation médiévale* 30.4 (1987): 331–46.

_____. "La notion de prophétie et la méthode apologétique dans la *Contra Saracenos* de Pierre le Vénérable." *Studia monastica* 17 (1975): 257–82.

Torrell, Jean-Pierre, and Denis Bouthillier. *Pierre le Vénérable et sa vision du monde.* Leuven: Spicilegium Sacrum Lovaniense, 1986.

Trautner-Kromann, Hanne. *Shield and Sword. Jewish Polemics Against Christianity and the Christians in France and Spain from 1100–1500.* Tübingen: J. C. B. Mohr, 1993.

Wilkinson, John, editor. *Jerusalem Pilgrims before the Crusades.* Warminster, England: Aris and Phillips Ltd., 2002.

_____, editor. *Jerusalem Pilgrimage 1099–1185.* London: The Hakluyt Society, 1988.

Zeitlin, Solomon. "Queen Salome and King Jannaeus Alexander: A Chapter in the History of the Second Jewish Commonwealth." *The Jewish Quarterly Review,* n.s. 51.1 (1960): 1–33.

INTRODUCTION

INTRODUCTION

PETER THE VENERABLE'S COMPOSITIONS

Peter the Venerable (Peter of Montboisser, b. 1092 or 1094), elected ninth abbot of Cluny in 1122, left behind a large collection of letters and polemical treatises. In his letters Peter expresses concern, among other issues, for the rigor and integrity of Benedictine life, as evidenced by repeated calls to avoid meat in the diet. At the same time he attempted to limit ascetic extremes—excesses in fasting, vigils, and acts of self-mortification—that might weaken the monk and prevent him from fulfilling his liturgical duties. He also was naturally concerned to protect and preserve Cluny's properties. *Letter* 164, addressed to Saint Bernard, concerns organizing the Second Crusade; *Letter* 58 shows him working to end the papal schism of 1130; and *Letter* 174 supports an appeal against some superstitious and rapacious canons. *Letters* 98 and 115 concern the affair of Peter Abelard, who found refuge at Cluny at the end of his life; *Letters* 158a and 158b provide insight into the state of Peter's health and frustrations with the medical advice he had received; while *Letter* 174 addresses judicial ordeals. As was not uncommon at this time, Peter's letters were written with an eye to publication.[1] His effort to recover original letters is sometimes mentioned (as in *Letter* 128) even though copies were likely made to be kept in books or registers at Cluny.

His letters appear in two collections. The first collection was likely assembled before 1142 by Peter and his *notarius* or sec-

1. For a discussion of the public nature of medieval letters in general at this time, and Peter's collection in particular, see *The Letters of Peter the Venerable*, ed. Giles Constable, 2 vols. (Cambridge, MA: Harvard University Press, 1967), 2: 1–44.

retary, Peter of Poitiers,[2] and includes his polemical attack on the Petrobrusians (*Tractatus contra Petrobrusianos haereticos*).[3] A second and larger collection was compiled perhaps just before or after Peter's death in 1156. Divided into six books, the latter collection contained 196 letters and several treatises. Between the two collections there are sometimes stylistic rather than substantive changes in the letters, suggesting that revisions were made, probably by Peter himself. But no two of the surviving manuscripts of Peter's letters are precisely the same in their contents. The first printed edition of the letters, published in 1522 and edited by the Cluniac monk Pierre de Montmartre, is based on a no longer extant manuscript probably from Cluny itself. This printed edition contains not only more letters than any other collection, but also the rare polemic *Against the Saracens* (*Contra sectam sive haeresim Saracenorum*).

Peter the Venerable's Polemical Treatises

In these collections Peter left behind not only correspondence and exhortations to contemporaries, but also lengthy polemical treatises that sought to refute significant contemporary challenges to Christian hegemony. These polemics include his *Against the Petrobrusians* (*Tractatus contra Petrobrusianos haereticos*),

2. Peter of Poitiers may have served as prior, perhaps even Grand Prior, of Cluny and then been elected abbot of St.-Martial at Limoges a few months before Peter the Venerable died in 1156. For Peter of Poitiers, see also *The Letters of Peter the Venerable*, ed. Giles Constable, 2: Appendix Q.

3. For the critical edition, see *Contra Petrobrusianos hereticos*, ed. James Fearns, CC CM 10 (Turnholt: Brepols, 1968). For discussion of the heresy, see Jean Châtillon, "Pierre le Vénérable et les Pétrobrusiens," in *Pierre Abélard—Pierre le Vénérable: Les courants philosophiques littéraires et artistiques en Occident au milieu du XIIe siècle. Abbaye de Cluny 2 au 9 juillet 1972* (Paris: Éditions du Centre national de la recherche scientifique, 1975), 165–76; Heinrich Fichtenau, *Heretics and Scholars in the High Middle Ages 1000–1200*, trans. Denise A. Kaiser (University Park, PA: Pennsylvania State University Press, 1998), 57–63. For more detailed discussion of the *Tractatus contra Petrobrusianos haereticos*, see especially Dominique Iogna-Prat, *Order and Exclusion: Cluny and Christendom Face Heresy, Judaism, and Islam (1000–1150)*, trans. Graham Robert Edwards (Ithaca, NY: Cornell University Press, 2002), part II, chap. 3; and Jean-Pierre Torrell and Denis Bouthillier, *Pierre le Vénérable et sa vision du monde* (Leuven: Spicilegium Sacrum Lovaniense, 1986), 162–71.

composed ca. 1137 and likely revised between 1139 and 1143. In early 1142, Peter had departed Cluny with a large entourage, leaving the care of all Cluniac monasteries during his absence to Archbishop Geoffrey of Bordeaux. His intent was to visit Cluniac monasteries in Spain, but also perhaps to go on pilgrimage to the shrine of Santiago de Compostella. In addition, he seems to have been invited to a meeting by Emperor Alfonso VII (d. 1157).[4] The emperor's father, Alfonso VI, had doubled his father Ferdinand's gift to Cluny and pledged an annual census donation of 2000 gold *metcales* or dinars.[5] Given Cluny's deteriorating financial condition and the fact that the donation was in arrears, Peter evidently hoped that the meeting would lead to an advantageous financial settlement. Although in a diploma of July 29, 1142, Alfonso VII ceded to Cluny the Castillian abbey of San Pedro de Cardeña, as well as certain minor properties near Burgos, Peter received only a small percentage of the funds owed the monastery and obtained only a pledge for a sharply reduced annual stipend from royal revenues. After he received reports that conditions at Cluny urgently required his presence, Peter began his return journey and arrived back at Cluny by summer 1143, at which time he likely completed a final revision to his *Against the Petrobrusians*. In this long refutation in five chapters, prefaced with a dedication to the archbishops of Arles and of Embrum and to the bishops of Die and of Gap, the abbot Peter attacks the heretical teachings of Peter of Bruis (as transmitted by Henry of Lausanne), providing the only source of precise historical details concerning him. Peter the Venerable identifies the Petrobrusians with three principal heretical theses: namely, that children who have not reached the age of reason cannot be saved by baptism; that Christians should tear

4. Bishko regards this as the most compelling factor to account for Peter's journey to Spain, which had been visited on two previous occasions by the Cluniac abbots Hugh I and Pontius. See Charles Julian Bishko, "Peter the Venerable's Journey to Spain," in *Petrus Venerabilis 1156–1956: Studies and Texts Commemorating the Eighth Centenary of His Death,* ed. Giles Constable and James Kritzeck, Studia Anselmiana 40 (Rome: Herder, 1956): 163–75.

5. For Cluny's relationship to Alfonso VI (d. 1109) and his father, Ferdinand I (d. 1065), see especially Charles Julian Bishko, "Liturgical Intercession at Cluny For the King-Emperors of Leon," *Studia Monastica* 7 (1961): 53–76.

down churches because they are unnecessary, since God hears prayers said anywhere; and that the holy cross should be burnt and destroyed, because the terrible instrument of Christ's death is undeserving of veneration. In addition, Peter adds that the Petrobrusians deny that the Eucharist is the body and blood of Christ and reject its offering, and they reject prayers and offerings on behalf of the dead, who, they claim, cannot be helped by such things.[6]

Although Peter of Bruis was killed in 1119 by the faithful of St. Gilles, who burned him in the flames of the very crosses he had set afire, Peter the Venerable expresses concern that his heretical views continue to spread, especially in regions ruled by the ecclesiastics to whom he has addressed his work. He therefore exhorts them to take action against this heresy and to root it out by preaching but also by force of arms if necessary. Nonetheless, "since conversion is better than extermination, Christian charity should be extended to them. They should be offered both authority and reason, and compelled to submit to authority if they wish to remain Christians, and to submit to reason if they are human."[7]

While *Against the Petrobrusians* was directed against a contemporary Christian heresy, Peter composed two other polemics to refute the doctrines of Islam: *Against the Saracens* (*Contra sectam sive haeresim Saracenorum*),[8] composed perhaps as late as 1155–

6. The date of this work remains in dispute, with some scholars suggesting that it was begun as early as 1134. The preface to the long polemic can be found in translation in R. I. Moore, *The Birth of Popular Heresy* (Toronto: University of Toronto Press, 1995), 60–62. For Peter's defense of the Eucharist against the Petrobrusians, see also David F. Appleby, "The Priority of Sight According to Peter the Venerable," *Mediaeval Studies* 60 (1998): 123–57.

7. "Sed quia maiorem operam eos conuertendi quam exterminandi adhibere Christianam caritatem decet, proferatur eis auctoritas, adhibeatur et ratio, ut, si Christiani permanere uolunt, auctoritati, si homines, rationi cedere compellantur." *Epist.*, cap. 2, in *Contra Petrobrusianos hereticos*, ed. James Fearns, CC CM 10 (Turnholt: Brepols, 1968), 4.

8. For the Latin text, see James Kritzeck, *Peter the Venerable and Islam* (Princeton, NJ: Princeton University Press, 1964). For criticism and corrections to Kritzeck's Latin text, see Jean-Pierre Torrell, "La notion de prophétie et la méthode apologétique dans le *Contra Saracenos* de Pierre le Vénérable," *Studia Monastica* 17 (1975), Appendix (pp. 281–82). For a useful review of Kritzeck's

1156, and the brief *Summary of the Complete Heresy and of the Dia-bolical Sect of the Saracens or Ishmaelites* (*Summa totius haeresis ac diabolicae sectae Sarracenorum sive Hismahelitarum*), [9] likely com-pleted soon after Peter's return to Cluny from Spain in 1143. These three polemics, then, address both internal and external threats to Christianity.

Even more important, however, will be Peter's longest po-lemical treatise, which he directed against a third enemy found both inside and outside Christendom, namely, the Jews. Pe-ter's *Against the Inveterate Obduracy of the Jews* (*Adversus Iudeorum inveteratam duritiem*),[10] in five chapters, was written between *Against the Saracens* and *Against the Petrobrusians*. According to the now widely held view of this treatise, *Against the Inveterate Obduracy of the Jews* was written in stages: Chapters One through the first third of Chapter Four can be dated to 1144, whereas the remainder of Chapter Four and Chapter Five were added later, perhaps in 1146, and then the entire work was "reissued" about 1147.[11]

Peter the Venerable's polemics seem to constitute a unified program, then, to defeat the most significant contemporary challenges to Christian faith and power. These polemical trea-tises were not incidental to Peter's concern, despite the many challenges he faced within his own monastery and the Church at large. Indeed, Peter of Poitiers, in a letter accompanying an account of the Islamic doctrines that he considered especially

---

arguments, see also Allan Cutler, "Peter the Venerable and Islam," *Journal of the American Oriental Society* 86 (1966): 184–98.

9. For a summary of their contents, see especially Kritzeck, *Peter the Venerable and Islam,* parts IV and V; cf. John Tolan, "Peter the Venerable on the 'Diaboli-cal Heresy of the Saracens,'" in *The Devil, Heresy and Witchcraft in the Middle Ages: Essays in Honor of Jeffrey B. Russell,* ed. Alberto Ferreiro (Leiden: Brill, 1998), 345–67; and Tolan, *Saracens: Islam in the Medieval European Imagination* (New York: Columbia University Press, 2002), 155–65. All of Peter the Venerable's writings against Islam have been edited and translated into German in a single volume: Petrus Venerabilis, *Schriften zum Islam,* ed. with German trans. and com-mentary by Reinhold Glei, Corpus Islamo-Christianum, Series Latina 1 (Alten-berge: CIS-Verlag, 1985).

10. Peter the Venerable, *Adversus Iudeorum inveteratam duritiem,* ed. Yvonne Friedman, CC CM 58 (Turnholt: Brepols, 1985).

11. For further discussion, see *infra,* pp. 30–31.

reprehensible, encourages his abbot Peter the Venerable to prevail over the Muslims' error. "I would like for you," he wrote, "to confound them just as you have confounded the Jews and the provincial heretics [the Petrobrusians]. For you alone in our times are the one who, with the sword of the divine Word, cut to pieces the three greatest enemies of holy Christianity: I mean the Jews and the heretics and the Saracens."[12]

During his visit to Spain, Peter had conceived his project to promote a study of Islam from original sources in order to refute its claims. Clearly, since the First Crusade at the end of the eleventh century, Christendom had become more and more preoccupied with a Muslim presence in the Holy Land. But Peter recognized that Muslims constituted not only a military threat, but also a religious one. Nonetheless, few European Christians outside Spain had the linguistic skills to study Islam through original source materials. In Spain, where Andalusian Christians were increasingly engaged in anti-Muslim polemic,[13] Peter had learned of a Christian book written in Arabic—the *Apology of [Ps.] Al-Kindi*[14]—that challenged or refuted Islamic doctrines, and he turned to Master Peter of Toledo to translate

12. "Volo autem quod sic isti confundantur a vobis, sicut confusi Judaei et provinciales haeretici. Solus enim vos estis nostris temporibus, qui tres maximos sanctae Christianitatis hostes, Judaeos dico et haereticos ac Saracenos divini verbi gladio trucidastis . . ." *Capitula Petri Pictavensis ad domnum Petrum abbatem,* PL 189: 661C.

13. See Thomas E. Burman, "'Tathlîth al-wahdânîyah' and the Twelfth-Century Andalusian-Christian Approach to Islam," in *Medieval Christian Perceptions of Islam,* ed. John Victor Tolan (New York and London: Routledge, 1996), 109–28.

14. The anti-Muslim polemic of pseudo-al-Kindi, the *Risālah (Apology)*, consists of two letters. The first purports to have been written to a Christian by a Muslim closely related to the caliph Al-Ma'mūn (r. 813–33), to encourage him to convert to the faith of Islam. The second is a much longer reply to the first, and was allegedly written by a Christian in the caliph's service. For the Latin translation, see José Muñoz Sendino, "Al-Kindi, Apologia del Cristianismo," in *Miscellanea Comillas* 11–12 (1949): 337–460. The Latin text itself appears on pp. 377–460. This edition is based on only two manuscripts, however: Oxford MS 184, Corpus Christi College, fols. 272–353; and Paris, MS Lat. 6064, Bibl. Nat., fols. 83–105; and it failed to take into account variant readings in MS 1162 of the Bibliothèque de l'Arsenal. For a new edition, see Fernando González Muñoz, *Exposición y refutación del islam: La versión latina de las epístolas de al-Hasimi y al-Kindi* (A Coruña, Spain: Universidade da Coruña, 2005).

it. But because Peter of Toledo did not know Latin as well as Arabic, Peter also assigned to the translator his own *notarius,* Peter of Poitiers, to polish Peter of Toledo's Latin.[15] Together they produced the *Letter of a Saracen with a Christian Response* (*Epistola Saraceni cum Rescripto Christiani*) from the *Apology of* [*Ps.*] *Al-Kindi.*

In addition to the *Letter of a Saracen with a Christian Response,* Peter commissioned the translation of other Arabic texts in Spain, relying on the skills of the Englishman Robert of Ketton, Herman of Dalmatia (or Carinthia), and a Muslim named Mohammad. These texts included the *Fables of the Saracens* (*Fabulae Saracenorum*), translated by Robert of Ketton and containing a potpourri of Islamic *hadith* traditions; the *Teaching of Mohammad* (*Doctrina Mahumet*) and a "life" of the prophet Mohammad (*Liber generationis Mahumet*), translated by Herman of Dalmatia;[16] and the whole of the Qur'an (*Lex Mahumet*), translated by Robert of Ketton.[17] Ultimately the translations, known as the

15. The identity of Peter of Toledo, evidently a convert to Christianity, remains controversial and much discussed. Most recently, it has been argued again that Peter of Toledo and Petrus Alfonsi, a Jewish convert to Christianity in Spain in 1106 who also composed a polemic against both Judaism and Islam, may have been one and the same. See especially P. Sj. van Koningsveld, "La apologia de Al-Kindi en la Espana del siglo XII. Huellas toledanos de un 'Animal disputax,'" in *Estudios sobre Alfonso VI y la Reconquista de Toledo. Actes del II Congreso Internacional de Estudios Mozárabes (Toledo, 20–26 Mayo 1985),* series historica 5 (Toledo: Instituto de Estudios Visigótico-Mozárabes, 1989): 107–29; Allan H. Cutler and Helen E. Cutler, *The Jew as Ally of the Muslim: Medieval Roots of Anti-Semitism* (Notre Dame, IN: University of Notre Dame Press, 1986), 52–80; cf. Charles Burnett, "The Works of Petrus Alfonsi: Questions of Authenticity," *Medium Aevum* 66.1 (1997): 49–50; John Tolan, *Petrus Alfonsi and his Medieval Readers* (Gainesville, FL: University Press of Florida, 1993), 210–11; and, for a summary of this controversy, see also the Introduction to Petrus Alfonsi, *Dialogue Against the Jews,* trans. Irven M. Resnick, Fathers of the Church, Mediaeval Continuation 8 (Washington, DC: The Catholic University of America Press, 2006), 22–24.

16. For Peter's treatment of Mohammad's status as a prophet, see J. P. Torrell, "La notion de prophétie et la méthode apologétique dans la *Contra Saracenos* de Pierre le Vénérable," *Studia monastica* 17 (1975): 257–82.

17. For discussion of Robert of Ketton's Latin translation of the Qur'an, completed in June or July 1143, see José Martínez Gázquez, "Trois traductions médiévales latines du Coran: Pierre le Vénérable-Robert de Ketton, Marc de Tolède et Jean de Segobia," *Revue des études latines* 80 (2003): 223–36. Very helpful to understanding Robert's work is also Thomas E. Burman, *Reading the*

Toledan Collection, were collected into a single volume,[18] perhaps with Peter of Poitiers as editor. The Toledan Collection, which contains the earliest medieval illumination to depict the prophet Mohammad,[19] provided Peter the Venerable with the materials necessary to construct a literary response that would assail and "cut to pieces" the threat of Islamic teaching.

About the same time that Peter completed his brief *Summary of the Complete Heresy and of the Diabolical Sect of the Saracens or Ishmaelites,* however, he began the much longer polemical work against the Jews, entitled *Against the Inveterate Obduracy of the Jews.*

POLEMIC AGAINST THE JEWS

Medieval Christendom perceived Muslims to be a genuine military and religious threat, justifying perhaps the energy that Peter the Venerable expended to refute and suppress the influence of Islamic doctrines in the West. European Jews, however, who were forbidden to bear arms,[20] represented no military threat to Christendom. Only in Christian eschatological fantasy

---

Qur'ān in Latin Christendom, 1140–1560 (Philadelphia: University of Pennsylvania Press, 2007), chaps. 3–4, pp. 60–123.

18. Max Lejbowicz remarks that the collection would perhaps be better known as the Cluniac Collection, since it had little significance in Spain. See Max Lejbowicz, "Développement autochtone assumé et acculturation dissimulée," in *Les relations culturelles entre chrétiens et musulmans au moyen âge: Quelles leçons en tirer de nos jours?* Colloque organisé à la Fondation Singer-Polignac le mercredi 20 octobre 2004 par Rencontres médiévales européennes, ed. Max Lejbowicz (Turnholt: Brepols, 2005), 57–81. For the Collection itself, see both James Kritzeck's *Peter the Venerable and Islam* and his earlier essay, "Peter the Venerable and the Toledan Collection," in *Petrus Venerabilis 1156–1956,* 176–201. In that same volume M. T. d'Alverny examines the rich manuscript tradition that contains the Toledan collection in "Quelques manuscrits de la 'collectio Toletana,'" 202–18.

19. See Walter B. Cahn, "The 'Portrait' of Muhammad in the Toledan Collection," in *Reading Medieval Images. The Art Historian and the Object,* ed. Elizabeth Sears and Thelma K. Thomas (Ann Arbor: University of Michigan Press, 2002): 51–60. The "portrait" of Mohammad appears in Bibliothèque de l'Arsenal, MS 1162, fol. 11r.

20. *Decretum* 13:108 of Bishop Ivo of Chartres (r. 1090–1116) explains that Jews have lost all dignity as warriors because they do not have the power to bear arms. For the text, see *The Jews in the Legal Sources of the Early Middle Ages,* ed. Amnon Linder (Detroit: Wayne State University Press, 1997), 668.

could Jews in the West be feared as a military danger.[21] Moreover, Jews, whose presence in Latin Christendom satisfied a Christian theological imperative, had lived there as a tolerated minority for centuries.[22] Although they observed different religious laws and customs and followed the authority of the rabbis of the Talmud rather than the Fathers of the Church, medieval Christian polemicists typically portrayed the material poverty, political weakness, and social inferiority of Jewish communities as a powerful refutation of the Jews' religious principles and as a sign of the triumph of Christianity.

Nonetheless, Peter the Venerable prepared his lengthiest and most vitriolic polemic against the Jews, not the Muslims. This can be explained in part by the fact that it was Jews, and not Muslims, who lived at the center of the European Christian world, both geographically and intellectually. Geographically, Jews lived in many of the important urban centers in twelfth-century Europe. Intellectually, that Jewish presence also represented an irritating challenge to Christian religious hegemony. In addition, allegations had appeared in the early eleventh century that Jews in the East had allied themselves with the Saracens, in opposition to Christian interests, as Latin accounts of the destruction of the Holy Sepulcher in Jerusalem by the Fatimid Caliph al-Hakim attest.[23] Later, Christian perceptions of

21. See Andrew Colin Gow, *The Red Jews: Antisemitism in an Apocalyptic Age 1200–1600* (Leiden, New York, Cologne: E. J. Brill, 1995). Although in general Latin writers dismissed contemporary Jews as an unwarlike and timid people, Albert of Aachen's account of the First Crusade (written between 1119 and 1130) indicates that the Jews of Haifa waged a spirited defense against the assault of Latin Crusaders before the Crusaders finally breached the city walls and slaughtered its inhabitants. See Albert of Aachen, *Historia Ierosolimitana* 7, 23–25, ed. and trans. Susan B. Edgington (Oxford: Clarendon Press, 2007), 517–21.

22. For patristic and early medieval theological foundations that established a basis for the toleration of European Jews in Christendom, see especially Jeremy Cohen, *Living Letters of the Law: Ideas of the Jews in Medieval Christianity* (Berkeley, Los Angeles, London: University of California Press, 1999).

23. See Richard Landes, "The Massacres of 1010: On the Origins of Popular Anti-Jewish Violence in Western Europe," in *From Witness to Witchcraft: Jews and Judaism in Medieval Christian Thought,* ed. Jeremy Cohen, Wolfenbütteler Mittelalter-Studien 11 (Wiesbaden: Harrassowitz Verlag, 1997): 79–112; Daniel Callahan, "The Cross, the Jews, and the Destruction of the Church of the Holy

Muslims encountered during the Crusades were informed from a dialectical relationship with the more familiar Jewish "Other."[24] That is, Muslims were dangerous because they were too much like the Jews, and vice versa. This supposed relationship may have exacerbated twelfth-century Christian fears of the Jew even before Muslims had successfully reversed some of the territorial gains achieved by the First Crusade, as when the Emir of Mosul took back the county of Edessa in 1144. Whereas Christian theologians long insisted that God had punished the Jews by depriving them of their own land, by the thirteenth century Jewish polemics had pointed to Muslim victories that reversed Christian territorial gains in the East as a sign that Christianity is a false religion.[25]

A more intense or passionate Christian relationship to the Holy Land and its sacred sites, then, aroused by the Crusades, rendered more volatile the relations between Latin Christians and Jews as well. Clearly, some Christians perceived that it was inconsistent to visit death upon the Muslims who hold the Holy Land, while allowing the Jews to live in the midst of Christendom. Such reasoning supported attacks upon Jewish communities, especially in the Rhineland, by crusading mobs at the end of the eleventh century and threatened them again in the twelfth and thirteenth.[26] By the thirteenth century, the

Sepulcher in the Writings of Ademar of Chabannes," in *Christian Attitudes toward Jews in the Middle Ages: A Casebook*, ed. Michael Frassetto (New York and London: Routledge, 2007): 15–24; Phyllis G. Jestice, "A Great Jewish Conspiracy? Worsening Jewish-Christian Relations and the Destruction of the Holy Sepulcher," in *Christian Attitudes toward Jews in the Middle Ages: A Casebook*, 25–42; Michael Frassetto, "Heretics and Jews in the Early Eleventh Century: The Writings of Rodulfus Glaber and Ademar of Chabannes," in *Christian Attitudes toward Jews in the Middle Ages: A Casebook*, 43–60.

24. On the relationship between Jews and Muslims in Christian perception, see Stephen F. Kruger, "Medieval Christian (Dis) identifications: Muslims and Jews in Guibert of Nogent," *New Literary History* 29.2 (1997): 185–203; Jeremy Cohen, "The Muslim Connection or On the Changing Role of the Jew in High Medieval Theology," in *From Witness to Witchcraft: Jews and Judaism in Medieval Christian Thought*, ed. Jeremy Cohen, 141–62.

25. See Joseph Schatzmiller, *La deuxième controverse de Paris. Un chapitre dans la polémique entre chrétiens et juifs au Moyen Age* (Paris and Louvain: Editions E. Peeters, 1994), 42–43.

26. For one Latin account of massacres of the Jews in Cologne and Mainz

argument was clearly presented (and rejected) in Alexander of Hales' *Summa Theologica* that if it is appropriate to slay Muslims because they insult Christ when they control Christian holy sites, how much more appropriate is it to slay the Jews within Christendom, who are guilty of rejecting and abusing the Redeemer each and every day?[27]

Although the Jew within Christendom never presented a real geopolitical threat, Peter the Venerable (and his contemporary Bernard of Clairvaux) clearly perceived the Jews as a growing economic threat that was nearly equivalent to the military threat posed by Muslims. Changing economic conditions—the growth of a profit economy—brought Christians more and more often into troubled financial relationships with Jews.[28] These relationships sometimes resulted in religious conversion, for example, in the case of the Jew Herman of Cologne, who allegedly converted to Christianity ca. 1128–29.[29] Herman explains

---

immediately before the First Crusade, see Albert of Aachen, *Historia Ierosolimitana*, 1.25, 29, pp. 49–53, 58–59. For a study of Crusader violence against Jewish communities during the First Crusade, see especially Robert Chazan, *European Jewry and the First Crusade* (Berkeley and Los Angeles: University of California Press, 1996); and Jeremy Cohen, *Sanctifying the Name of God: Jewish Martyrs and Jewish Memories of the First Crusade* (Philadelphia: University of Pennsylvania Press, 2004). Attacks against Jewish communities appeared at the time of the Second Crusade as well, especially at locations in France. See Monique Levy, "Massacre de juifs en France lors la deuxième croisade." *Archives juives* 28.2 (1995): 89–92.

27. Alexander of Hales, *Summa Theologica* 2, 2, Inq. 3, tr. 8, sect. 1, q. 1, tit. 2, membrum 1, cap. 1 (Quaracchi: Collegii S. Bonaventurae, 1930), 3: 729–30. For a discussion of Alexander's attitude toward Jews, see J. Guttman, "Alexandre de Hales et le Judaisme," *Revue des études juives* 19 (1889): 224–34.

28. A money economy, which encouraged the accumulation of moveable wealth, not only encouraged commercial life and the growth of towns and markets at the end of the eleventh century, but also challenged traditional religious values. Despite its usefulness, money itself might be dismissed as "filthy lucre," and those who profited from it (e.g., Jewish moneylenders) were debased by their association with it. For a helpful discussion, see especially Lester K. Little, *Religious Poverty and the Profit Economy in Medieval Europe* (Ithaca, NY: Cornell University Press, 1978).

29. Herman of Cologne identifies himself as "Herman, formerly known as Judas, of the Israelite race, from the Levitical tribe, from [his] father David and mother Sephora . . ." (*Hermannus quondam Iudas dictus, genere Israelita, tribu Levita, ex patre David et matre Sephora . . .*) See *Hermannus quondam Iudaeus, Opuscu-*

that he had arrived in Mainz to conduct business with various merchants when he encountered Bishop Egbert of Münster (r. 1127–1132), and there he arranged an unsecured loan for the impoverished bishop. Herman's parents rebuked their son because he received no collateral, and commanded him to remain near the bishop until the loan was repaid.[30] As a result of an imprudent financial transaction, then, Herman was brought into close contact with Christian teaching and soon after received baptism.

Other encounters did not bring about the Jew's conversion but instead challenged Christians to defend their beliefs, just as they challenged Jews to defend their own.[31] Pseudo-William of Champeaux, the author of the *Dialogue on the Catholic Faith between a Jew and a Christian (Dialogus inter christianum et judaeum de fide catholica)*, remarked that he made the acquaintance of a Jew from a certain business transaction, and this prompted the author to compose a defense of Christian faith.[32] Even though such

---

lum de conversione sua 1, ed. G. Niemeyer, MGH, Quellen zur Geistesgeschichte des Mittelalters (Weimar: H. Böhlaus Nachfolger, 1963), 70; for a translation and a discussion of the problems associated with this text, see Karl F. Morrison, *Conversion and Text: The Cases of Augustine of Hippo, Herman-Judah, and Constantine Tsatsos* (Charlottesville and London: University of Virginia Press, 1992), 39–113.

30. *Opusculum de conversione sua* 2, pp. 72–76.

31. In his *Milhamot ha-Shem (Wars of the Lord)*, written ca. 1170, Jacob ben Reuben explains that this anti-Christian polemic arose out of real contact with a Christian priest, learned in logic and theology, who sought his conversion. That encounter may have occurred while ben Reuben was a refugee in southern France after having fled from the Almohads in Spain ca. 1148. For a discussion of the author and his text, see Robert Chazan, "The Christian Position in Jacob ben Reuben's *Milhamot Ha-Shem*," in *From Ancient Israel to Modern Judaism: Intellect in Quest of Understanding; Essays in Honor of Marvin Fox*, ed. Jacob Neusner, Ernest S. Frerichs, and Nahum M. Sarna, 4 vols. (Atlanta, GA: Scholars Press, 1989), 2: 157–70; and Hanne Trautner-Kromann, *Shield and Sword. Jewish Polemics Against Christianity and the Christians in France and Spain from 1100–1500* (Tübingen: J. C. B. Mohr, 1993), 49–61.

32. This text is falsely attributed to William of Champeaux (ca. 1070–1121), a French scholastic philosopher who studied and taught in Paris. In 1109 William founded the monastic school of St. Victor, and from 1113 until his death he was the Bishop of Châlons-en-Champagne. Because the work is addressed to Alexander, the Bishop of Lincoln from 1123–1147, it is clear that it was written only after William's death. Anna Abulafia dates this text from 1128–43; see her

encounters might lead to the occasional conversion among the Jews, increasingly Christians despaired that this ardently desired outcome was obtained only at great risk to a sound faith. About the end of the twelfth century, the English Bishop Bartholomew of Exeter composed a *Dialogue against the Jews, Dispatched for Correction and Improvement* (*Dialogus contra Judaeos ad corrigendum et perficiendum destinatus*), addressed to Baldwin, Bishop of Worcester (1180–1184), which cautions Christians against arguing with Jews at all, since they impede every shared undertaking (*commune negotium*), like restless animals;[33] Peter of Blois (d. 1212) discourages Christians from engaging Jews in debate, since, even should one prevail over them with arguments, it is impossible to turn their hearts away from evil;[34] and similarly, before the middle of the thirteenth century, Guerric of Saint-Quentin (d. 1245) argues that because of the well-known malicious obstinacy of Jews, one should not even engage them in religious debate because of the risk such encounters present even to a sound faith.[35] Moreover, in his *Memoirs of Louis IX*, John de Joinville (d. 1318) records a revealing anecdote concerning France's king, Saint Louis IX (d. 1270). Although the king encouraged public disputations with the Jews, he conceded that a disputation at Cluny

---

"Jewish–Christian Disputations and the Twelfth-Century Renaissance," in *Christians and Jews in Dispute: Disputational Literature and the Rise of Anti-Judaism in the West* (Aldershot: Ashgate Variorum, 1998), IX: 108. At the very beginning of the text (PL 163: 1045A), the author remarks, "A certain Jew was known to me because of some business transaction . . ." (*Quidam mihi cum cognitus esset Judaeus cujusdam negotii causa . . .*).

33. See Richard William Hunt, "The Disputation of Peter of Cornwall Against Symon the Jew," in *Studies in Medieval History Presented to Frederick Maurice Powicke*, ed. R. W. Hunt et al. (Oxford: Clarendon Press, 1948), 148 (quoting from MS Bodley 482, fol. 1vb).

34. Peter of Blois. *Contra perfidiam Judaeorum* 1, PL 207: 827A. For Peter's life and career, see R. W. Southern, "Peter of Blois: A Twelfth-Century Humanist?" chap. 7 in his *Medieval Humanism* (New York: Harper and Row, 1970). Anna Sapir Abulafia identifies in Peter of Blois the growing internal tension among some twelfth-century Christian polemicists, who felt compelled to attempt the conversion of the Jews at the very moment when they grew more doubtful that any efforts could succeed. See her "Twelfth-Century Christian Expectations of Jewish Conversion: A Case Study of Peter of Blois," *Aschkenas* 8.1 (1998): 45–70.

35. Guerric of Saint-Quentin, *Quaestiones de quolibet* 3.3.63 (Toronto: Pontifical Institute of Mediaeval Studies Press, 2002), 223.

at which a Jew repudiated the Christian doctrine of the Virgin Birth could cast Christians astray, leading him to remark that "no one, unless he be a very learned clerk, should dispute with them [the Jews]; but a layman, when he hears the Christian law mis-said, should not defend the Christian law, unless it be with his sword, and with that he should pierce the mis-sayer in the midriff, so far as the sword will enter."[36] When rational discourse fails, it seems, the sword remains a potent argument. Christian-Jewish encounters, however, could hardly be avoided so long as medieval culture assigned to Jews the role of moneylenders or usurers.

Money as the Root of Their Evil

A need to borrow money was an inevitable but unexpected outcome of changes to the medieval economy. Even the Crusading movement relied upon a credit market, since frequently Crusaders had to pawn items of value or were compelled to mortgage vast estates to equip themselves for the journey to the East. Not only laymen—including kings and princes—but ecclesiastics and popes required credit, and they often turned to Jews rather than to Christian moneylenders to provide this service,[37] since in principle Christian theology forbade Christians

36. The text appears in Jacob Rader Marcus, *The Jew in the Medieval World: A Sourcebook, 315–1791*, intro. Marc Saperstein, rev. ed. (Cincinnati: Hebrew Union College Press, 1999), 46–47. Laura Hollengreen has pointed to "the clear visual cultivation of violence" in the Morgan Picture Bible (produced in Paris during Louis's reign) as a reflection of the king's policy against the Jews. See her "The Politics and Poetics of Possession: Saint Louis, the Jews, and Old Testament Violence," in *Between the Picture and the Word: Manuscript Studies from the Index of Christian Art,* ed. Colum Hourihane (Princeton, NJ: Index of Christian Art, Dept. of Art and Archaeology, Princeton University, in association with Penn State University Press, 2005), 51–71, 90–115.

37. For the relationship of the papacy of the high Middle Ages to Jewish moneylending, see especially Kenneth R. Stow, "The Good of the Church, the Good of the State: The Popes and Jewish Money," *Christianity and Judaism. Papers Read at the 1991 Summer Meeting and the 1992 Winter Meeting of the Ecclesiastical History Society,* ed. Diana Wood (Cambridge, MA: Ecclesiastical History Society, 1992): 237–52. For the problematic nature in general of usury for medieval society and the Church, see also Jacques Le Goff, *Your Money or Your Life: Economy and Religion in the Middle Ages,* trans. Patricia Ranum (New York: Zone Books, 1988).

to lend money at interest. This does not mean that there were not Christian usurers in the twelfth century; clearly there were, inasmuch as Guibert of Nogent[38] and others loudly condemned them. But usury was perceived to be more consonant with the carnal, material nature of Jews and therefore was condemned as a Jewish activity even when undertaken by Christians. Jewish apologetical literature from the second half of the twelfth century clearly demonstrates that Jews had to defend their practice of lending at interest before Christian criticism.[39] This practice had been forced upon Jews just as the need to borrow had been forced upon Christians by changes in the medieval economy.[40] Peter Abelard, who composed his *Dialogue of a Philosopher with a Jew, and a Christian* likely between CE 1129–1132, slightly more than a decade before Peter the Venerable wrote his own anti-Jewish polemic, had his Jewish interlocutor observe that since "we are allowed to possess neither fields nor vineyards nor any landed estates . . . the principal gain that is left for us is that we sustain our miserable lives here by lending money at interest to strangers; but this just makes us more hateful to them who think that they are being oppressed by it."[41] Indeed, some

38. For Guibert's attack on usury (and Jewish usurers), see Anna Sapir Abulafia, "Theology and the Commercial Revolution," in *Christians and Jews in Dispute*, XI: 23–40, but especially pp. 34–40. For the growing dependency of Jews in northern France on moneylending in the twelfth century, see Robert Chazan, *Medieval Jewry in Northern France: A Political and Social History* (Baltimore and London: Johns Hopkins University Press, 1973), 32–47.

39. See Joseph Kimhi, *The Book of the Covenant,* trans. Frank Talmage (Toronto: Pontifical Institute of Mediaeval Studies Press, 1972), 33–35. *The Book of the Covenant (Sefer ha-Berit)* was perhaps the first Jewish anti-Christian polemic composed in Europe, ca. 1160–1170. The author was, like Jacob ben Reuben, a refugee from Almohad persecution in Spain who settled in Provence. This text seems to have been prompted, too, by real encounters between Jews and Christians. For a discussion of the text, see also Hanne Trautner-Kromann, *Shield and Sword,* 61–72.

40. See R. I. Moore, "Anti-Semitism and the Birth of Modern Europe," in *Christianity and Judaism,* ed. Diana Wood, 33–58.

41. Peter Abelard, *A Dialogue of a Philosopher with a Jew, and a Christian,* trans. Pierre J. Payer (Toronto: Pontifical Institute of Mediaeval Studies, 1979), 31. The date of this work remains uncertain. Payer (see p. 7) defends a date between 1136–1139, rather than the older consensus of 1140–1141, whereas Constant Mews and John Marenbon have argued for an earlier date, with Marenbon

Christian theologians had identified profits derived from moneylending as a sort of theft,[42] and it was so clearly reprehensible in the eyes of many churchmen that it could only be a "Jewish" evil. So closely were Jews identified with usury that Bernard of Clairvaux attacked Christian moneylenders with the verb *judaizare,* "to judaize," a term that he invested with the meaning "to lend money at interest."[43] Nor is it a surprise that Jewish moneylenders will be cast, too, as villains responsible for any number of crimes. In Thomas of Monmouth's *Life and Miracles of St. William of Norwich,* which accuses the Jews of Norwich of ritually murdering in CE 1144 a Christian boy, William, the author identifies the Jew most directly responsible for the torture and death of the young boy as Eleazar, a moneylender.[44] The

---

urging the period between 1129–1132. See Peter Abelard, *Collationes,* ed. and trans. John Marenbon and Giovanni Orlandi (Oxford: Clarendon Press, 2001), xxxii. See also Constant J. Mews, "Abelard and Heloise on Jews and *Hebraica Veritas,*" in *Christian Attitudes toward Jews in the Middle Ages: A Casebook,* ed. Michael Frassetto (New York and London: Routledge, 2007), 86–87, where Mews seems to accept this dating as well.

42. See *Anselms von Laon systematische Sentenzen,* ed, Franz Pl. Bliemetzrieder, Beiträge zur Geschichte der Philosophie des Mittelalters 18, 2–3 (Münster i. W.: Aschendorff, 1919): "Sub furto comprehenditur usura," fol. 6oc, p. 98. Anselm of Laon (d. 1117) studied with Anselm of Canterbury at Bec, then taught in Paris with William of Champeaux. Later he returned to Laon to set up a theological school. Although Bliemetzrieder saw Anselm of Laon as the author of the works cited in this volume, it seems more likely that they were produced by a "school" at Laon influenced by him. For some discussion of Anselm of Laon and his "school," see R. W. Southern, *Scholastic Humanism and the Unification of Europe,* 2 vols. (Oxford: Blackwell, 1995–), 2: 32–51.

43. See, in *Sancti Bernardi Opera genuina, Epist.* 363.6, ed. Monks of St. Benedict, 8 vols. (Lyons and Paris: Perisse Frères, 1854), 8:316. This letter is addressed to the English people, and exhorts them to participate in the Second Crusade. It can be found in translation (as *Letter* 391), in *The Letters of St. Bernard of Clairvaux,* trans. Bruno Scott James (Chicago: Henry Regnery Company, 1953), 460–63. For Bernard's views on Judaism, see David Berger, "The Attitude of St. Bernard of Clairvaux Toward the Jews," in *Proceedings of the American Academy for Jewish Research* 40 (1972): 89–108.

44. Thomas of Monmouth, *De vita et passione Sancti Willelmi Martyris Norwicensis* 2.13, ed. and trans. A. Jessop and M. R. James (Cambridge, 1895), p. 97. For a discussion of this text and the spread of the ritual murder charge, see especially Gavin I. Langmuir, "Thomas of Monmouth: Detector of Ritual Murder," *Speculum* 59 (1984): 820–46; John McCulloh, "Jewish Ritual Murder: William

fact that some Jews clearly prospered from usury only increased Christian antipathy.[45] By the thirteenth century in Christian art the moneybag had become the most common symbol associated with Jews, suggesting their role in usury.[46]

Because usury was a sin (even a mortal sin) in Christian eyes, its practitioners represented a source of both spiritual and material impurity and carnality.[47] This may be seen clearly in the contested papal election of CE 1130, when Innocent II and Anaclet II (Petrus II Pierleoni) both claimed the papal throne. Innocent was forced to flee the city of Rome (whose population largely supported Anaclet II) and took refuge at Cluny, where he consecrated the great abbey church Cluny III that same year. A campaign of vilification against Anaclet II, however, largely centered in France, depicted him as a "Jewish pope" who had bought the papal office with wealth that his family, which had

of Norwich, Thomas of Monmouth, and the Early Dissemination of the Myth," *Speculum* 72 (1997): 698–740; and Friedrich Lotter, "Innocens Virgo et Martyr. Thomas von Monmouth und die Verbreitung der Ritualmordlegende im Hochmittelalter," in *Die Legende vom Ritualmord: zur Geschichte der Blutbeschuldigung gegen Juden,* ed. Rainer Erb (Berlin: Metropol-Verlag, 1993), 25–72.

45. A good example will be the Jewish community in England which, by 1130, had grown quite wealthy from moneylending. See R. C. Stacey, "Jewish Lending and the Medieval English Economy," in *A Commercialising Economy: England 1086 to c. 1300,* ed. R. H. Britnell and B. M. S. Campbell (Manchester and New York: Manchester University Press, 1995), 78–88; and R. C. Stacey, "Crusades, Martyrdoms, and the Jews of Norman England, 1096–1190," in *Juden und Christen zur Zeit der Kreuzzüge,* ed. Alfred Haverkamp (Sigmaringen: Jan Thorbecke Verlag, 1999), 233–51.

46. See Sara Lipton, *Images of Intolerance. The Representation of Jews and Judaism in the* Bible moralisée (Berkeley and Los Angeles: University of California Press, 1999), chap. 2; Debra Higgs Strickland, *Saracens, Demons, and Jews: Making Monsters in Medieval Art* (Princeton, NJ: Princeton University Press, 2003), 141–43.

47. A good summation of Christian arguments against usury will be found in the thirteenth-century work of the Dominican Vincent of Beauvais, *Speculum maius,* vol. 2: *Speculum doctrinale,* 10.120–25 (Graz: Akademische Druck-u. Verlagsanstalt, 1965), 969ff. For a discussion of his *Speculum,* see especially Monique Paulmier-Foucart and Marie-Christine Duchenne, *Vincent de Beauvais et le grand miroir du monde* (Turnholt: Brepols, 2004). See also the work of Vincent's contemporary, Albert the Great, *Commentarii in III Sententiarum,* Sent. 37, art. 13, ed. A. Borgnet, vol. 28 (Paris: L. Vivès, 1894), 705–7. See also Shlomo Simonsohn, *The Apostolic See and the Jews,* 8 vols. (Toronto: Pontifical Institute of Mediaeval Studies, 1991), 8: chap. 4.

converted to Christianity more than eighty years earlier, had acquired through usury.[48]

This anti-Jewish propaganda of the party of Innocent II did not leave Peter the Venerable unmoved. In his popular *On Miracles* (*De miraculis,* ca. 1135–1149?),[49] Peter the Venerable attacked Peter II Pierleoni, that is, Anaclet II, with a pun on his name, and dismissed him as that lion's whelp (*Leonis filius Petrus, et leonini catuli*) that raged against the Church, and as the Antichrist and chief of all schismatics.[50] Peter ignores the fact that Anaclet II had himself been a monk at Cluny, a fact of which Anaclet sought to remind the monastic community in a letter from CE 1130 in order to obtain its support.[51] Although Peter does not mention the family's connection to usury, it could not have been far from his mind. In the passage immediately above this one, Peter the Venerable praised Matthew of Albano, who had been named prior of Saint-Martin-des-Champs in 1117 by abbot Pontius of Cluny, because he forbade the monks there to enter further into financial transactions with Jews. When the monks complained that their monastery's poverty necessitated borrowing from Jews, Matthew insisted that there can be no relationship between Christ and Belial (cf. 2 Cor 6.15),[52] between

48. The most accessible treatment of this contested election can be found in Mary Stroll, *The Jewish Pope.* Also see Aryeh Grabois, "Le Schisme de 1130 et la France," *Revue d'histoire ecclésiastique* 76 (1981): 593–612. For claims of Jewish support found among Innocent's contemporaries, see especially pp. 609–10.

49. *De miraculis* was redacted in stages or various versions or collections, and the date of the parts of the work, as well as of the work as a whole, remains controversial. For a lengthy discussion, see especially Torrell and Bouthillier, *Pierre le Vénérable et sa vision du monde,* 107–35.

50. See his *De miraculis* 2.16, in CC CM 83, ed. D. Bouthillier (Turnholt: Brepols, 1988), 127. For a more charitable view of Peter's contribution to the campaign of vilification, see Gillian Knight, "Politics and Pastoral Care: Papal Schism in some Letters of Peter the Venerable," *Revue Bénédictine* 109, 3–4 (1999): 366–67.

51. PL 179: 696D–697A.

52. In the Hebrew Bible, "Belial" characterizes people who lie, deceive, conspire, or behave in a dissolute fashion. In the pseudepigrapha, however, "Belial" designates the Prince of Evil or Satan. See "Belial," *Encyclopedia Judaica,* 17 vols. (Jerusalem: Keter Publishing House, 1996), 4: 427–28. Arnulf of Seéz invoked the same text to condemn any contact with Anaclet II. See his *Invectiva in Girardum Engolismensem episcopum* 3, MGH, Libelli de lite, vol. 3, ed. J. Dieterich

light and darkness, between the faithful and the infidel. Matthew inquired:

How in [good] conscience shall I attempt to approach the altar of Christ the Savior, with what audacity shall I attempt to come to speak to his pious mother, when I shall have pandered to his blasphemous enemies? How will I be able to appease them, once I have befriended their worst enemies? How will I be able to invoke them, how will I dare to beseech them with the same mouth with which I have fawned upon them [the Jews] for the sake of funds or anything else? . . . Repay quickly whatever you owe them and, just as if established by an eternal law, refrain henceforth from all transactions with them.[53]

Clearly, the monastery's indebtedness to Jews was thought to jeopardize its essential function or holiness. How could he approach the altar of the most pure God, Matthew wondered, when his community was befouled by commerce with God's worst enemies? How could he invoke the Mother of God, the Blessed Virgin, with the same lips with which he must flatter the Jewish moneylender? Again, Matthew expressed a growing fear that contact with Jews corrupts the purity of the Roman Church. Because corruption stemming from usury was perceived to compromise the integrity of the Church, a later medieval inquisitorial text reminds us that an adult Jew cannot even be admitted to baptism until he has returned usurious loans.[54]

Peter likely composed this chapter in his *On Miracles* at about the same time that he was composing Chapter Four of his *Against the Inveterate Obduracy of the Jews,* that is, about CE 1144.[55] He was

---

(Munich, 1897), 96. Arnulf's *Invectiva in Girardum Engolismensem episcopum* is also found in MGH, SS, vol. 12 (Hanover, 1856; Kraus Reprint, 1963).

53. "qua conscientia, ad altare Saluatoris Christi accedere, qua fronte ad colloquium pie matris ipsius uenire temptabo cum blasfemis hostibus eius blanditus fuero? Quomodo pessimis inimicis ipsorum amicus effectus, ipsis placere ualebo? Quomodo illo ore quo pecuniarum uel cuiuslibet rei causa eis adulatus fuero, ipsos inuocare, uel deprecari audebo? . . . Soluite cito quicquid eis debetis, et uelut eterna lege prefixa, ab uniuersis eorum commertiis deinceps abstinete." *De miraculis* 2.15, p. 126.

54. See *The Jews in Western Europe 1400–1600,* ed. and trans. John Edwards (Manchester and New York: Manchester University Press, 1994), 36, citing a passage from *Le dictionnaire des inquisiteurs* (1494), ed. L. Sala-Molins (Paris and the Hague, 1981).

55. See Torrell and Bouthillier, *Pierre le Vénérable et sa vision du monde,* 128.

aware that the Jews reserved a special animus for the Christian cult of the Virgin,[56] and he seemed preoccupied with the role that Jews played in medieval France as moneylenders.[57] Although usury *per se* is not the focus of another important anti-Jewish text Peter produced just two years later, similar concerns come to the fore in his *Letter* 130 to King Louis VII (r. 1137–1180).[58] In that letter, Peter encourages the king to take up the Crusade so that, as one obedient to divine command, he may destroy the Saracens, the enemies of Christendom.[59] Nonetheless, he also reveals a link that exists between Saracens and Jews. Peter does not propose that like the Saracens the Jews should be the object of an armed crusade in defense of Christendom. Their lives are to be preserved in accord with the Augustinian doctrine of Jewish witness, which applied to the Jews Psalm 58.12 (Vulg.): "Slay them not, lest at any time my people forget. Scatter them by thy power; and bring them down, O Lord, my protector."[60]

Although this passage was instrumental for the formation of a doctrine that identified Jews as a tolerated and theologically necessary minority in Christendom, it also contained a justification for their oppression. In his anti-Jewish polemic, Peter remarks that for more than 1100 years Jews have been subject to

56. For Peter's own special devotion to the Virgin, see Bernard Billet, "Notes de mariologie. La dévotion mariale de Pierre le Vénérable (1092–1156)," *Esprit et vie* 87.37 (1977): 465–72. For the perception that Jews were the special enemies of the Virgin, see also William Chester Jordan, "Marian Devotion and the Talmud Trial of 1240," in *Religionsgespräche im Mittelalter,* ed. Bernard Lewis and Friedrich Niewöhner (Wiesbaden: Otto Harrassowitz, 1992), 61–76.

57. See Jean-Pierre Torrell, "Les juifs dans l'œuvre de Pierre le Vénérable," *Cahiers de civilisation médiévale* 30.4 (1987): 332.

58. For the Latin text, see *The Letters of Peter the Venerable,* ed. Giles Constable, 1: 327–30.

59. For Peter's own relationship to the Second Crusade, see Virginia Berry, "Peter the Venerable and the Crusades," in *Petrus Venerabilis 1156–1956,* 140–62. For Peter's *Letter* 130 to King Louis VII, see especially 148–50. See also Jeremy Cohen, "Christian Theology and Anti-Jewish Violence in the Middle Ages: Connections and Disjunctions," in *Religious Violence Between Christians and Jews: Medieval Roots, Modern Perspectives,* ed. Anna Sapir Abulafia (New York: Palgrave, 2002), 44–60, and esp. 48–53.

60. For Augustine's doctrine of Jewish witness, which established the parameters for toleration of the Jews in medieval Christendom, see especially Jeremy Cohen, *Living Letters of the Law,* 23–65.

the power of Christians, whom they hate more than any other people. The Jews, he adds, have become a mockery not only to Christians but even to the Saracens. Although in obedience to Ps 58.12 Christians allow Jews to live among them, it is only because God wants them to survive "as a spectacle for the world . . . like the fratricide, Cain." Like Cain, the Jews "will be cursed upon the earth" (Gn 4.11) and "will be a fugitive and wanderer upon it" (Gn 4.12).[61] Although Peter insists that the Jews are to be hated because they are even worse than the Muslims, and especially because—unlike Muslims—they do not even respect the Virgin Mary, nonetheless he proposes a very different punishment for them. Let them be preserved, Peter urges the king, in a life worse than death as an appropriate punishment for their guilt in the crucifixion. Moreover, let them be exploited and subjected to severe financial exaction in order to support the crusading efforts of this most Christian king.[62]

In this letter, Peter addressed a king that was sometimes criticized for having expanded Jewish settlements in France and for having conferred upon the Jews new freedoms, in return for gold.[63] He does not address usury directly, but he does allude to

61. *Adverus Iudaeorum* 5, p. 141, lns. 607, 610–11.
62. *Letter* 130.3–4. For the Latin text, see *The Letters of Peter the Venerable*, ed. Giles Constable, 1: 327–30.
For a discussion of this letter and for Peter the Venerable's understanding of Jews and Judaism, see Cohen, *Living Letters of the Law*, 246–54; Yvonne Friedman, "An Anatomy of Anti-Semitism: Peter the Venerable's Letter to Louis VII, King of France (1146)," in *Bar-Ilan Studies in History*, ed. Pinhas Artzi, 1 (Ramat-Gan, 1978): 87–102; Jean-Pierre Torrell, "Les juifs dans l'oeuvre de Pierre le Vénérable," *Cahiers de civilisation médiévale* 30.4 (1987): 339–46; and Robert Chazan, "Twelfth-Century Perceptions of the Jews: A Case Study of Bernard of Clairvaux and Peter the Venerable," in *From Witness to Witchcraft: Jews and Judaism in Medieval Christian Thought*, ed. Jeremy Cohen, Wolfenbütteler Mittelalter-Studien 11 (Wiesbaden: Harrassowitz Verlag, 1996), 187–201.
63. In the *Chronicle of the Abbey of Saint-Pierre-le-Vif de Sens*, Geoffroy of Courlon sums up, critically, Louis VII's urban achievements, noting, "He made new towns; and, driven by the thirst for gold, despite the respect he owed to the faith, he granted certain liberties to the Jews—leproseries, new synagogues, and cemeteries." Quoted in Gérard Nahon, "From the *Rue aux Juifs* to the *Chemin du Roy:* The Classical Age of French Jewry, 1108–1223," in *Jews and Christians in Twelfth-Century Europe*, ed. Michael A. Signer and John Van Engen, Notre Dame Conferences in Medieval Studies 10 (Notre Dame, IN: University of Notre Dame

various undesirable outcomes of the practice of moneylending: for example, that Christians steal sacred objects and then pawn them with Jewish moneylenders. Although, if apprehended, the Christian thieves are punished severely, the Jews, he protests, cannot be compelled to return the goods they received in pawn. In addition, Peter alludes to unspecified abuses that Jews are rumored to perpetrate against Christian sacred objects, such that they abuse indirectly and vicariously Christ himself. A growing emphasis upon love for the historical Jesus (and the holy sites of his ministry) ironically promoted a growing hatred and desire for vengeance against those thought to have insulted, abused, and slain him.[64]

Although *Letter* 130 was addressed to the king, Peter's letters were intended for a wider public, as already indicated. In addition, Peter's reputation and his position at the head of the largest and most distinguished Benedictine network in Europe insured that his opinions and views would circulate not only throughout the Cluniac order but even more widely in Christian society. Although he discouraged monks from taking up the Crusader's cross, he certainly encouraged medieval knights or *bellatores* to assume this task. What could be more appropriate, albeit impractical, than that the Jews should be despoiled of their allegedly ill-gotten gains to support the sacred purpose of the Christian King Louis VII to recover the holy places in the East?

Against the Inveterate Obduracy of the Jews

Unlike *Letter* 130, Peter's *Against the Inveterate Obduracy of the Jews* was not directly concerned with the crusading movement, even though its last chapters were written likely during the disastrous Second Crusade (CE 1146–1149).[65] It fits nonetheless

---

Press, 2001), 316. Similarly, the royal chronicler Rigord of St. Denis reprimanded Louis VII for improperly bestowing privileges upon the Jews. For discussion, see Kenneth Stow, *Jewish Dogs: An Image and Its Interpreters* (Palo Alto: Stanford University Press, 2006), 90–92; cf. Robert Chazan, *Medieval Stereotypes and Modern Antisemitism* (Berkeley: University of California Press, 1997), 52–53.

64. See Christopher Ocker, "Ritual Murder and the Subjectivity of Christ: A Choice in Medieval Christianity," *Harvard Theological Review* 91.2 (1998): 153–92.

65. For the contemporary source materials on the Second Crusade, see especially Giles Constable, "The Second Crusade as Seen by Contemporaries," *Tradi-*

within Peter's larger polemical program: the refutation of the enemies of Christendom. In his literary polemics Peter developed a formidable forensic arsenal[66] that paralleled the military effort of the Crusaders.[67] As the Crusades were intended to restore a divinely ordained order to the world, so Peter's polemics were meant to defend the spiritual order of Christendom against contemporary challengers. These challengers—Petrobrusians, Jews, and Muslims—all seemed to Peter more inclined toward this world than the next and challenged, as a result, the power that Christianity (and monasticism in particular) claimed for itself to open for its adherents the gates to heaven.

Yet Peter's anti-Jewish polemic stands within an *adversus Iudaeos* tradition more than 1000 years old. Just as the number of Christian anti-Jewish polemics expanded dramatically in the twelfth century, the tactics polemicists employed also began to evolve. As Amos Funkenstein observed, conservative polemicists from the twelfth and thirteenth centuries continued to follow a traditional pattern that entailed a laborious and tedious citation of scriptural proof texts in defense of Christian doctrine. In addition, however, by the beginning of the twelfth century, philosophical polemics appeared whose goal was to convict the Jews of error and to defend Christian truths by an almost exclusive appeal to reason. At the same time, although not always in the same texts, we begin to see accusations directed against the Talmud as a source of Jewish error and blasphemy.[68] It is largely

---

tio 9 (1953): 213–79; for the manner in which Christians attempted to interpret the military reverses in the East typologically or as punishment for their own sinfulness, see Yael Katzir, "The Conquests of Jerusalem, 1099 and 1187: Historical Memory and Religious Typology," in *The Meeting of Two Worlds: Cultural Exchange between East and West during the Period of the Crusades,* ed. Vladimir P. Goss and Christine Verzár Bornstein, Studies in Medieval Culture 21 (Kalamazoo, MI: Medieval Institute Publications, 1986), 103–13.

66. See Dominique Iogna-Prat, "The Creation of a Christian Armory Against Islam," in *Medieval Religion: New Approaches,* ed. Constance Hoffman Berman (New York and London: Routledge, 2005): 325–46 [an excerpt from his *Order and Exclusion*], and *Order and Exclusion,* 122.

67. Torrell and Bouthillier remark quite properly that for Peter "le dialogue est en réalité un autre forme de combat, la manière propre de se battre de ceux qui, comme lui, ne peuvent pas porter les armes." *Pierre le Vénérable et sa vision du monde,* 180.

68. See Amos Funkenstein, *Perceptions of Jewish History* (Berkeley, Los Ange-

for his attack upon the Talmud that Peter the Venerable's polemic stands out, and Robert Chazan remarks that for this reason it "heralds the new stance that will become the norm by
the 1240s."[69] Although Peter's attack upon the Talmud is not
especially creative, nonetheless it indicates a new awareness of
the Talmud's significance for contemporary Jewish communities and represents a limited effort to meet the Jews on their
own ground for the purposes of disputation.

Although Peter's polemics frequently turn to vulgar invective, nonetheless he sometimes expresses the view that the subjects of his attack—Muslims, Christian heretics, or Jews—might
be persuaded by rational argument. In his *Against the Saracens*
(*Contra sectam sive haeresim Saracenorum*), composed perhaps as
late as 1155–1156,[70] Peter explains that he will wage an assault
against them not with arms, as Christians often do, but with
words, not with force but with reason, not out of hate but with
love.[71] His attitude is dictated, he remarks, both by the example
of Christ, who instructed us to love our enemies, and by the
power of reason, which supports Christian authority. While it is
natural that every animal love its own kind,[72] this is true all the
more for human beings, who are led to love one another not
only by nature but by the dictates of reason.[73] In the same vein,

les, Oxford: University of California Press, 1993), especially chapter 6: "Polemics, Responses, and Self-Reflection" (pp. 169–219).

69. Robert Chazan, *Daggers of Faith. Thirteenth-Century Missionizing and Jewish
Response* (Berkeley, Los Angeles, London: University of California Press, 1989),
23.

70. Torrell and Bouthillier, *Pierre le Vénérable et sa vision du monde,* 181.

71. "Aggredior inquam vos, non ut nostri sepe faciunt armis sed verbis, non vi
sed ratione, non odio sed amore." *Liber contra sectam sive haeresim Saracenorum* 1, in
Kritzeck, *Peter the Venerable and Islam,* 231.

72. Cf. Albertus Magnus, *Quaestiones super de animalibus,* 8, q. 14: "Quare equus
maxime diligit suam speciem," in *Opera omnia Alberti Magni,* ed. E. Filthaut, vol.
12 (Monasterii Westf.: Aschendorff, 1955), 192–94. This text appears in translation in Albert the Great, *Questions Concerning Aristotle's* On Animals, trans. Irven
M. Resnick and Kenneth F. Kitchell, Jr., Fathers of the Church, Mediaeval Continuation 9 (Washington, DC: The Catholic University of America Press, 2008),
279–83.

73. *Liber contra sectam sive haeresim Saracenorum* 1, in Kritzeck, *Peter the Venerable and Islam,* 232.

even if disingenuously, he exhorts Muslims to follow the example of Christians, who enter patiently into discussion with the Jews and do not seek their deaths as blasphemers or enemies of the faith, but calmly respond to their arguments while seeking their conversion.[74] For every rational mind, Peter insists, desires to know the truth of things created, and pursues this understanding by argument and disputation, just as it does for an understanding of the uncreated truth.[75] This seemingly irenic tone may have been dictated by Peter's stated goal in *Against the Saracens,* namely, the conversion of the Muslims.[76] He even expressed a hope that this work might one day be translated into Arabic in order to achieve that.[77]

The tone of *Against the Saracens,* however, is markedly different from that of his earlier *Summary of the Complete Heresy and of the Diabolical Sect of the Saracens or Ishmaelites,* which Peter composed soon after his return from Spain in 1143 and before the loss of Edessa and the failed Second Crusade. That work was clearly intended for a Christian audience, and its purpose was to provide a brief summary or handbook of the Muslim's errors rather than to seek his conversion. As a result, Peter felt no need to restrain himself and depicted Mohammad and his followers as engaged in a diabolical conspiracy to prepare the way for the Antichrist and to destroy the Church.[78]

---

74. *Liber contra sectam sive haeresim Saracenorum* 1, in Kritzeck, *Peter the Venerable and Islam,* 244. Torrell suggests that this may be self-referential; indeed, in his *Adversus Iudeorum* Peter does remark that he had discussions with Jews concerning their interpretation of Gn 49.10.

75. *Liber contra sectam sive haeresim Saracenorum* 1, in Kritzeck, *Peter the Venerable and Islam,* 235.

76. "diligens vobis scribo, scribens, ad salutem invito." *Liber contra sectam sive haeresim Saracenorum* 1, in Kritzeck, *Peter the Venerable and Islam,* 232. It seems a mistake, however, to understand Peter as attempting to turn Christendom from violent conflict with Muslims to verbal disputation alone. Cf. Egle Lauzi, "Occidentali e Saraceni nel Medioevo Latino: Tracce di un incontro," II, *Istituto Lombardo* 132 (1998): 485–502, and especially 493–96.

77. *Liber contra sectam sive haeresim Saracenorum,* prol., in Kritzeck, *Peter the Venerable and Islam,* 229.

78. Following the First Crusade, it became common to identify Muslims as attendants of Antichrist. See Robert the Monk's *Historia Iherosolomitana,* and Ralph of Caen's *Gesta Tancredi,* in *Recueil des historiens des croisades. Historiens Occidentaux,*

Moreover, despite his appeals to reason, Peter himself does not promote the philosophical arguments in defense of Christianity introduced earlier by Anselm of Canterbury, Odo of Tournai, or Petrus Alfonsi. Peter the Venerable is more inclined to rely on scriptural revelation for his arguments. Consequently, essential to his approach was an attack upon the extra-biblical authoritative sources upon which Muslims or Jews relied but which Christians did not share, namely, the Qur'an and Hadith, and the Talmud. In this respect, his polemics are of great historical interest, for they reveal a growing awareness of these collections in Christian circles. But it is precisely an awareness of these additional religious authorities that tempers Peter's apparent optimism that rational argument can overcome the Jews' blindness, for example. For Peter, the Talmud not only contains anti-Christian blasphemies, but it also impedes the proper functioning of human reason in Jewish readers. He condemns it as a collection of lies and fables, by which rabbinic authorities have long misled Jewish communities. Despite this harsh criticism, Peter falls short of advocating that the Talmud be burned, a fate that will befall it in Paris before the middle of the thirteenth century.[79]

Peter the Venerable is the first Christian author to refer explicitly to the Talmud. The earlier polemicist Petrus Alfonsi, from whom Peter seems to have borrowed heavily, ridicules talmudic *aggadot*—that is, tales and folklore—in his own *Dialogue against the Jews* (composed about 1109) but refers to the Talmud not as such but as the "doctrine of the sages." Where Peter became acquainted with the name "Talmud" remains unknown; rather unhelpfully, Peter remarks that it was Christ himself who revealed to him the name "Talmud" and its secrets.[80] Clearly,

5 vols. (Paris: Academie des Inscriptions et Belles-Lettres, 1844–95), 3: 695 and 828. Cf. Iogna-Prat, *Order and Exclusion*, chap. 11: "Islam and Antichrist."

79. This despite the fact that in *Adversus Iudeorum* 5, p. 166, lns. 1444–46, Peter indicates that both the Talmud and its authors should be condemned to eternal fire. For Peter's influence upon thirteenth-century attacks on the Talmud, see Yvonne Friedman, "Anti-Talmudic Invective from Peter the Venerable to Nicolas Donin (1144–1244)," in *Le brûlement du Talmud à Paris 1242–1244*, ed. Gilbert Dahan (Paris: Les Éditions du Cerf, 1999), 171–90.

80. *Adversus Iudeorum* 5, p. 126, lns. 35–40.

he appears to have borrowed a great deal from Petrus Alfonsi's earlier citation of talmudic materials; yet Peter also includes talmudic materials not found in Alfonsi's *Dialogue,* as well as folklore drawn from other popular medieval Jewish sources like the *Alphabet of Ben Sira.*

It is of course possible that Peter learned the name and something about the content of the Talmud, particularly its *aggadot* or legends and folklore, during his visit to Spain, from a Jewish convert to Christianity,[81] or perhaps from Jews living near Cluny. Cluny's charters reveal an amiable relationship between the monastery and nearby Jews during the tenth and eleventh centuries. In 949 a Jew, Joshua, and his wife, Tensoretis, used their farm at Sennecé as security for a loan of 12 solidi from the abbey of Cluny. In the loan receipt, Joshua's name and that of his witness, Samuel, appear in Hebrew characters. In 1022 the Jew Solomon and the monks exchanged land parcels.[82] Peter the Venerable indicates that at one time he had had a conversation with Jews concerning biblical interpretation, but nowhere does he suggest that this was a frequent occurrence.[83] By the middle of the twelfth century, during Peter's abbacy, the apparently convivial earlier relationship between Cluny and neighboring Jews had been spoiled. It is unclear what precipitated the change. One factor, however, may have been that Jews were no longer indebted to Cluny, as was Joshua in the tenth century, but the other way around. As Cluny attempted to restructure its economy in the twelfth century, scholars have speculated that even under Peter the Venerable the monastery incurred burdensome debts to Jewish moneylenders. In his *Letter* 56, dated summer 1135, Peter alludes to a debt owed to the Jews of Mâcon, from whom he was able to recover certain sacred vessels they had held as collateral, thanks to financial assistance from his benefactor, Henry of Blois, Bishop of Winchester.[84] But even

81. Cf. Yvonne Friedman's introduction to *Adversus Iudeorum inveteratam duritiem,* xx; Dominique Iogna-Prat, *Order and Exclusion,* 302.

82. Dominique Iogna-Prat, *Order and Exclusion,* 278.

83. *Adversus Iudeorum* 4, pp. 68–69, lns. 29–31.

84. See *The Letters of Peter the Venerable,* 177. Peter had made his first visit to England in 1130; he completed a second visit at the end of 1155 or early

this inverted relationship cannot explain a pronounced shift in tone in the latter portion of Chapter Four and in Chapter Five of *Against the Inveterate Obduracy of the Jews*. The final chapter, indeed, is the most vituperative and vulgar in its attack on Jews and Judaism, and, as yet, there is no precise or specific explanation for the change. One can only assume that Peter's attitude toward the Jews grew harsher during the heightened atmosphere of the Second Crusade, when these later portions of the text were written.

Composition and Date of the Text

The date for Peter's *Against the Inveterate Obduracy of the Jews* has itself occasioned much debate. As already indicated, there are internal indicators that show that the work was completed in stages since, although the text consists of five chapters, in the first chapter Peter refers to its fourfold division.[85] Although at the beginning of the fourth chapter, Peter identifies that chapter as the penultimate "battle" to be waged with the Jews, the editor of the text suggests that the reference to a penultimate battle is a scribal interpolation, since other manuscripts identify that chapter as the final or last battle.[86] In addition, in the prologue Peter announces that he will address four errors of the Jews concerning the messiah: namely, "you do not believe that he is the Son of God, you deny that he is God, but you affirm that he will reign in time in the manner of other kings, and you affirm that he has not yet come but is still to come."[87] It is these four errors, he indicates, that dictate the fourfold division of the work that follows. The fifth chapter, then, would appear to have been conceived after the first chapter was begun, and likely even after Chapter Four was begun, although before Chapter Four had been completed. The editor of the text suggests that Chapter Four was originally intended to conclude much earlier, and

---

1156. It seems that on his second visit Peter helped Henry of Blois to transfer his considerable fortune to Cluny, where he took refuge temporarily after the accession of Henry II to the throne of England. See Jean-Pierre Torrell and Denis Bouthillier, *Pierre le Vénérable et sa vision du monde*, 56–58.

85. *Adversus Iudeorum* 1, p. 11, ln. 263.

86. *Adversus Iudeorum* 4, p. 68, ln. 5; cf. Friedman's introduction, p. lxv.

87. *Adversus Iudeorum*, prol., p. 3, lns. 74–76.

would have comprised only about one-third of its present length. Based on the topics and treatment in the latter portion of Chapter Four and in Chapter Five, she infers, "It seems, then, that the *Contra Iudaeos* was written as four short chapters and three supplements—'on the precepts,' 'on the miracles,' and 'against the Talmud.' The scope of these supplements exceeds the original framework. These supplements triple the size of the book as it was originally conceived . . ."[88] Since the discussion in the supplements "on the precepts" and "on the miracles" goes well beyond the questions Peter had said he would address in his prologue, it seems reasonable to conclude that these were added later to Chapter Four, while "against the Talmud" will form all of Chapter Five. These considerations seem sufficient to establish that the work was written in at least two stages.

The date of the text must likewise reflect, then, a composition completed in stages. Since the text quotes from the translation of the Qur'an that Peter had commissioned in Spain, it could not have been composed before summer 1143. In addition, early in Chapter Four Peter himself claims to be writing in the year 1144.[89] The supplements most probably were added later, and the whole of the work completed and "reissued," as Friedman suggests, by 1147.[90]

Formal Structure

Although Peter's *Against the Inveterate Obduracy of the Jews* stands in a long tradition of Christian anti-Jewish literature, it represents a departure from the dialogue form most commonly employed by Peter's contemporaries in the first half of the twelfth century to present the Jewish-Christian debate. These dialogues were certainly a popular literary convention, yet in some cases they may also have been based on real exchanges between Jews and Christians. Among these dialogues, we may include Gilbert Crispin's *Disputation between a Jew and a Christian*,[91]

88. Friedman, *Adversus Iudeorum*, p. lxvii. For her fuller discussion of the view that the work was produced in stages, see pp. lxiii–lxix.
89. *Adversus Iudeorum* 4, p. 73, lns. 193–95.
90. Friedman, *Adversus Iudeorum*, p. lxx.
91. For the text of the *Disputatio Iudei*, completed in the last decade of the

Petrus Alfonsi's already mentioned *Dialogue against the Jews,* Odo
of Tournai's *Disputation with the Jew, Leo, concerning the Advent of
Christ, the Son of God,*[92] Ps.-William of Champeaux's *Dialogue between a Christian and a Jew concerning the Catholic Faith,*[93] and Peter Abelard's *Dialogue of a Philosopher with a Jew, and a Christian.*[94]
By contrast, Peter the Venerable's *Against the Inveterate Obduracy
of the Jews* is a lengthy monologue, although in the early chapters Peter invites onto the stage Old Testament prophets as *dra-
matis personae* to address contemporary Jews. In fact, as Friedman notes, Peter constructed the first chapters of his polemic
around a series of appearances by the prophets reminiscent of
the twelfth-century liturgical drama, *Ordo Prophetarum.*[95] In this
way he transformed an often tedious theological discussion into
almost a dramatic performance. Peter seems to have been acquainted, then, with the life of the stage, although he disparages
contemporary stage-players or mimes. He promises to reveal
Jewish error to the reader and to lead the Jew like a "monstrous
beast out from its lair, and push it laughing onto the stage of the
whole world (*in theatro totius mundi*) . . ."[96]

---

eleventh century, see *The Works of Gilbert Crispin,* ed. Anna Sapir Abulafia and
G. R. Evans (London and New York: Oxford University Press, 1986). More recently, this work has appeared with Gilbert Crispin's *Disputatio christiani cum gentili de fide Christi* in a Latin edition with German translation, *Disputatio iudaei et
christiani; Disputatio christiani cum gentili de fide Christi,* trans. Karl Werner Wilhelm and Gerhard Wilhelmi (Freiburg im Breisgau: Herder, 2005). For a discussion of both works, see Anna Sapir Abulafia, "An Attempt by Gilbert Crispin,
Abbot of Westminster, at Rational Argument in the Jewish-Christian Debate,"
Studia Monastica 26 (1984): 55–75.

92. Cf. *Two Theological Treatises of Odo of Tournai: On Original Sin, and a Debate
with the Jew, Leo, Concerning the Advent of Christ, the Son of God,* trans. Irven M.
Resnick (Philadelphia: University of Pennsylvania Press, 1994), 85–97.

93. *Dialogus inter christianum et judaeum de fide catholica,* PL 163: 1045A–1072C.

94. See Abelard's *Collationes,* ed. and trans. John Marenbon and Giovanni
Orlandi.

95. Friedman, *Adversus Iudeorum,* p. xiii. The Limoges text of the *Ordo
Prophetarum* can be found in *Medieval Church Music-Dramas: A Repertory of Complete Plays,* ed. and trans. Fletcher Collins, Jr. (Charlottesville, VA: University
Press of Virginia, 1976), 165–88. For the medieval staging of the play, see Dun-
bar H. Ogden, *The Staging of Drama in the Medieval Church* (Newark, DE: University of Delaware Press, 2003), 133–35.

96. *Adversus Iudeorum* 5, p. 125, ln. 31.

Although Peter sometimes addresses his arguments to an (unnamed) individual Jew or to the Jews as a whole, in fact his audience is clearly the Christian community. Few Jews would have been able to read this Latin treatise,[97] and Peter does not express the wish that it be translated into Hebrew or into a vernacular Jews might read, as he hoped that *Against the Saracens* would be translated into Arabic for a Muslim audience. And while he does express the hope that his arguments will lead to the conversion of Jews, often he seems to despair that this outcome can be achieved. In Chapter Three he admits to doubts that the Jew can be persuaded by an appeal either to biblical authority or to the power of human reason, without which conversion seems impossible: "Surely I do not know," he remarks, "whether a Jew, who does not submit to human reason nor acquiesce to proof-texts that are both divine and his own, is a human. I do not know, I say, whether one is human from whose flesh a heart of stone has not yet been removed, to whom a heart of flesh has not yet been granted, within whom the divine spirit has not yet been placed,[98] without which a Jew can never be converted to Christ."[99] Despite their earlier exalted status as a chosen people, Peter laments, the Jews have become worse than pagans and worse even than demons.[100] Their willful ignorance, their "bovine intellect,"[101] and their peculiar form of "insanity,"[102] lead him to characterize Jews as more like devils or beasts than men.[103] By spreading the "lies" contained in the Talmud, "the Jew with his lies surpasses the prince of lies and makes the devil—who is not only a deceiver but is the father

97. Emily Taitz remarks that in Champagne "[b]oth R. Samuel (*Rashbam*) and R. Joseph Bekhor Shor of Orléans (ca. 1175) knew Latin as well as Hebrew and the local French dialect, and discoursed regularly with Christian clerics." Their knowledge of Latin was certainly exceptional, however. See her *The Jews of Medieval France: The Community of Champagne* (Westport, CT: Greenwood Press, 1994), 121.

98. Cf. Ezek 36.26.
99. *Adversus Iudeorum* 3, pp. 57–58, lns. 564–570.
100. *Adversus Iudeorum* 2, p. 41, lns. 874–75.
101. *Adversus Iudeorum* 3, p. 43, ln. 47.
102. *Adversus Iudeorum* 3, p. 43, ln. 54.
103. *Adversus Iudeorum* 3, p. 54, ln. 438.

and master of lies[104]—almost his son and disciple."[105] At other times Peter acknowledges the Jews' humanity but suggests that nonetheless they are the "dregs of the human race (*humani generis feces*)"[106] and make themselves like beasts by their recalcitrant rejection of Christian truths.[107] His doubts about the humanity and rationality of Jews notwithstanding, Peter insists that despite the warning in Mt 7.6 not to cast pearls before swine, he provides the arguments contained herein because "this text of mine might be beneficial, if not for all [Jews] and if not for many, at least for the few who we see are sometimes converted to God."[108] Such a modest outcome, however, would hardly seem to justify the effort required to write, let alone read, a text of this nature. It is instead more likely that Peter intended this work as a sort of textbook to provide Christians with responses to every Jewish challenge, and as an epitome of Christian teaching to strengthen and confirm Christian faith.

Distribution and Significance

Friedman identifies only four extant manuscript copies of Peter the Venerable's *Against the Inveterate Obduracy of the Jews,* although since none of the four was used as the basis for the first printed edition in the 1522 collection of Peter's works edited by Pierre de Montmartre, it is certain that at least one other copy has been lost. Three of these four extant manuscripts date from no more than a generation or two after Peter's death.[109] By comparison, Petrus Alfonsi's *Dialogue against the Jews* exists in more than eighty extant manuscript copies, suggesting that it enjoyed far greater popularity.[110] It is not only the larger number of manuscript copies that distinguishes the two works, however. Alfonsi's *Dialogue against the Jews,* written by a Jewish convert to Christianity, is a far more original and better informed

104. Cf. Jn 8.44.
105. *Adversus Iudeorum* 5, p. 183, lns. 2058–2060.
106. *Adversus Iudeorum* 3, p. 56, ln. 526.
107. *Adversus Iudeorum* 3, p. 63, lns. 766–72.
108. *Adversus Iudeorum* 5, p. 152, lns. 949–51.
109. Friedman, *Adversus Iudeorum,* p. xxviii.
110. See Introduction, Petrus Alfonsi, *Dialogue Against the Jews,* trans. Resnick, 26–28.

work, in part because it recognizes clearly that not only Jewish interpretations of biblical texts separate Jews from Christians, but even the Jewish text of the Bible itself. For this reason, Alfonsi concedes to his Jewish interlocutor, Moses,[111] that he will introduce to their discussion passages from the Old Testament only according to the "Hebrew truth" (*Hebraica veritas*).[112]

On the one hand, the *Hebraica veritas* can refer to Jewish canons of interpretation of the Hebrew text of the Bible; on the other hand, however, it can refer equally to the Hebrew *text* of the Old Testament as it was read in Jewish communities. Christian scholars of the twelfth century were increasingly aware that Jewish and Christian textual traditions of the Bible diverged, and in part this awareness stemmed from more frequent contacts between Latin scholars seeking from Jews insight into the Hebrew text and its interpretation.[113] In sum, then, twelfth-century Christian Hebraists[114] were increasingly aware that it was not only Jewish and Christian biblical *interpretations* that diverged, but even the Latin (Vulgate) and Hebrew texts them-

111. Moses is in fact Alfonsi's Jewish *alter ego,* since this is the name he bore before his conversion.

112. Petrus Alfonsi, *Dialogue Against the Jews,* trans. Resnick, 44, 182.

113. See especially Aryeh Grabois, "The *Hebraica veritas* and Jewish-Christian Intellectual Relations in the Twelfth Century," *Speculum* 50 (1975): 613–35. Constant Mews has discussed the familiarity with Hebrew of Peter Abelard and Heloise in "Abelard and Heloise on Jews and *Hebraica Veritas,*" in *Christian Attitudes toward Jews in the Middle Ages: A Casebook,* ed. Michael Frassetto (New York and London: Routledge, 2007), 83–108. For a broader but still useful discussion see also Beryl Smalley, *The Study of the Bible in the Middle Ages* (Oxford: Blackwell, 1952), 329–55. Also see Gilbert Dahan, "La connaissance de l'exégèse juive par les chrétiens du XIIe au XIVe siècle," in *Rashi et la culture juive en France du Nord au moyen âge,* ed. Gilbert Dahan, Gérard Nahon, and Elie Nicholas (Paris and Louvain: E. Peeters, 1997), 343–59.

114. For twelfth-century Christian Hebraism, see especially Michael Signer, "Polemic and Exegesis: The Varieties of Twelfth-Century Hebraism," in *Hebraica Veritas? Christian Hebraists and the Study of Judaism in Early Modern Europe,* ed. Allison P. Coudert and Jeffrey S. Shoulson (Philadelphia: University of Pennsylvania Press, 2004): 21–32. For an interesting examination of Hebrew study in the thirteenth and fourteenth centuries, see Willehad Paul Eckert, "Die Universität Köln und die Juden im späten Mittelalter," in *Mensch und Natur im Mittelalter,* ed. Albert Zimmermann in *Die Kölner Universität im Mittelalter. Geistige Wurzeln und soziale Wirklichkeit,* ed. Albert Zimmermann (Berlin: Walter de Gruyter, 1989), 488–507.

selves, hopelessly complicating, it seemed, efforts to convert the
Jews. This new awareness stemmed from efforts by scholars like
Andrew of St. Victor, whose contact with Jewish rabbis led to
a better understanding of discrepancies between the Vulgate
and Jewish readings of the text of the Old Testament.[115] The
Ysagoge in Theologiam, composed ca. 1135 as an introduction to
theology by an otherwise unknown scholar, Odo, and dedicated to Gilbert Foliot, prior of Cluny, displays a similar interest
in the *Hebraica veritas* and incorporates seventy-eight passages
from the Old Testament written out in Hebrew characters.[116]
Peter Abelard mentions listening to a Jew commenting on the
biblical text, and one of his disciples mentions that Abelard
often sought out Jews to discuss points of biblical interpretation.[117] While Petrus Alfonsi failed to do what he had promised,
namely, to discuss only according to the *Hebraica veritas* the Old
Testament passages that undergirded the Christian-Jewish debate, nonetheless his promise was an implicit recognition of
the importance of variant textual and exegetical traditions. In
addition, it reflected his understanding that until Christian po-

115. For Andrew of St. Victor's contact with Jewish scholars, see Michael
Signer's introduction to *Andreae de Sancto Victore Opera. VI: Expositionem in Ezechielem,* ed. Michael Alan Signer, CC CM 53e (Turnholt: Brepols, 1991), xiii,
xxxi. See also Frans van Liere, "Andrew of St. Victor, Jerome, and the Jews: Biblical Scholarship in the Twelfth-Century Renaissance," in *Scripture and Pluralism:
Reading the Bible in the Religiously Plural Worlds of the Middle Ages and Renaissance,*
ed. Thomas Heffernan and Thomas Burman (Leiden: Brill, 2005), 69.

116. For the Latin text, see Artur Landgraf, *Écrits théologiques de l'école
d'Abélard* (Louvain: Spicilegium sacrum lovaniense, 1934): 63–289. This singular work has survived in only one manuscript, and nothing more is known of
its author, although it seems that he was an Englishman who had studied in
France. A useful study of the text will be found in Michael Evans, "The *Ysagoge
in Theologiam* and the Commentaries Attributed to Bernard Silvestris," *Journal
of the Warburg and Courtauld Institutes* 54 (1991): 1–42. For the sources of the
Jewish polemic contained in this work, see Avrom Saltman, "Gilbert Crispin as a
Source of the Anti-Jewish Polemic of the *Ysagoge in Theologiam,*" *Bar-Ilan Studies
in History* 7 (1984): 89–99. It deserves special note that Odo did not take his
Hebrew passages from a Hebrew Bible, but rather *translated* passages from the
Latin Vulgate into Hebrew, because he recognized that one must be able to cite
the Bible in Hebrew to contend with the Jews.

117. For sources, see Peter Abelard, *Collationes,* ed. and trans. John Marenbon and Giovanni Orlandi, pp. xlvi–xlvii, and n.101.

lemicists acknowledged these variants, they could not hope to prevail in religious debate. It was for that purpose that Alfonsi agreed to introduce only the *Hebraica veritas* since, as he replied to Moses, "I desire greatly to slay you with your own sword."[118]

Some other Christian scholars, lacking Alfonsi's knowledge of Hebrew and lacking as well a more sophisticated understanding of the development of the biblical text, resorted instead to the explanation that where Jewish and Christian copies of the Old Testament diverge, it is because the Jews had intentionally falsified their Hebrew text in order to undermine the evidence that would otherwise demonstrate that Jesus is the messiah. Thus the ninth-century Christian Paul Alvarez alleged that "everyone knows that after the advent of Christ they [the Jews] falsified the Hebrew codices in order to suppress the clearest testimonies pertaining to Christ . . ."[119] Similarly, Bruno of Segni (d. 1123), an important commentator on Scripture, objected to the Jews' reading of Is 7.14 ("a virgin will conceive"), a passage Christians understood to foretell the birth of Jesus, and exhorted them to "[c]orrect therefore your books, Jews, which we do not doubt you have falsified out of envy."[120] Likewise, Peter of Blois alleges an ideal *Ur*-text that Jews corrupted to conceal the evidence for Christian truths.[121] At the same time, Christians were increasingly sensitive to Jewish complaints that the Vulgate Latin text was inferior to the Hebrew. In Gilbert Crispin's *Disputation of a Jew and a Christian*, the Jewish interlocutor attacks Christians for using the inferior, Latin translation of the Bible since it departs from the Hebrew text.[122] Similarly, the Jewish interlocutor in Joseph Kimhi's twelfth-century *Book of the Covenant* repeatedly upbraids the Christian for errors introduced into the Vulgate text by the translator, Jerome.[123]

Peter the Venerable, lacking any knowledge of Hebrew, could

---

118. Petrus Alfonsi, *Dialogue Against the Jews*, trans. Resnick, 44.

119. Paul Alvarez, *Epist.* 16 (PL 121: 486D).

120. *Commentaria in Matthaeum* 1 (PL 165: 75C).

121. See the argument of Peter of Blois, *Contra perfidiam Judaeorum* 4 (PL 207: 832C–34A).

122. *Disputatio Iudei* 128.1–11, in *The Works of Gilbert Crispin*, 43.

123. *Book of the Covenant*, pp. 29, 54, 58.

not, as Alfonsi did, truly appreciate the textual discrepancies that lay beneath differences in Christian and Jewish interpretations of Scripture. And yet, for another reason to be made clear below, he did not subscribe to the view that Jews had intentionally falsified or emended their own biblical codices to undermine Christian claims.[124] His unwillingness to allege a Jewish conspiracy of false emendation certainly did not stem from a positive view of Jews. Instead, it reflects his concern to oppose the allegation current in the Islamic world that both Jews *and* Christians had introduced corruption to their revealed texts. The Islamic doctrine of *tahrîf* mirrored the charge of false emendation that Christian authors alleged against Jews;[125] it asserted that Jews and Christians had intentionally falsified both Old and New Testaments in order to suppress prophetic passages that pointed to the coming of the prophet Mohammad. Although Peter the Venerable does not address this in his earlier *Summary of the Complete Heresy and of the Diabolical Sect of the Saracens or Ishmaelites,* it is an important concern in his *Against the Saracens,* written after his *Against the Inveterate Obduracy of the Jews.* In *Against the Saracens,* Peter defends the uncorrupted nature of the whole of the biblical text, and insists that if Muslims accept part of the Bible as an authoritative revelation, then they should accept it in its entirety. This defense demands, then, that Peter distance himself from the claim that Jews had corrupted their Hebrew codices in order to undermine Christian claims.[126]

124. For a discussion of the canard of false emendation, see my "Falsification of Scripture and Medieval Christian-Jewish Polemics," *Medieval Encounters* 2.3 (1996): 345–80.

125. See Jean-Marie Gandeul and Robert Caspar, "Textes de la tradition musulmane concernant le *tahrîf* des écritures," *Islamochristiana* 6 (1980): 61–104; for its role in medieval polemics, see also Norman Roth, "Forgery and Abrogation of the Torah: A Theme in Muslim and Christian Polemic in Spain," *Proceedings of the American Academy for Jewish Research* 54 (1987): 203–36; Sidney H. Griffith, "Arguing from Scripture: The Bible in the Christian/Muslim Encounter in the Middle Ages," in *Scripture and Pluralism: Reading the Bible in the Religiously Plural Worlds of the Middle Ages and Renaissance,* 29–58; and see my "Falsification of Scripture and Medieval Christian-Jewish Polemics," 368–70. Finally, for late medieval Muslim attitudes, see Walid A. Saleh, "A Fifteenth-Century Muslim Hebraist: Al-Biqā'ī and His Defense of Using the Bible to Interpret the Qur'ān," *Speculum* 83.3 (2008): 629–54.

126. Cf. *Contra sectam sive haeresim Saracenorum,* ed. James Kritzeck, 247–56.

Just as in *Against the Saracens* he was forced to defend the integrity of the Hebrew text in which Christian claims are rooted, so in his anti-Jewish polemic he defends the integrity of the Vulgate translation to establish its authority among the Jews. Peter is aware that the Old Testament was translated from Hebrew into Greek and Latin, but he assures his Jewish "audience" that the translations are reliable. Although he acknowledges that the Vulgate and the Septuagint (LXX) sometimes present different readings, he insists that this occurs only in passages where the Jewish translators of the LXX, who were unwilling to offend their idolatrous patron Ptolemy, sought a more politically correct way to express its underlying truths.[127] While he admits that there are textual discrepancies, then, that separate the LXX and Hebrew codices, nonetheless he insists upon the veracity of the Vulgate. The Hebrew text and the Latin do not differ in their essential meaning: "Only the languages are different, while the meaning of the languages is the same. There are two sounds, but only one meaning."[128] In Chapter Four he remarks that

we safeguard the [biblical] books intact, we guard them uncorrupted both as they were written by Moses and as they entered the languages of all the Gentiles, translated from the Hebrew and conserved, so to speak, by faithful translators; nothing is added to them, nothing is removed from them. I a Latin have, a Greek has, a Barbarian has, everything in those books that you have, O Jew. We copy what you copy, we read what you read, but on the whole we do not interpret the texts that were written or read in the way that you interpret them, nor on the whole do we understand them as you understand them. You sometimes follow in them the "letter that kills," whereas I always follow in them the "vivifying spirit."[129] You chew on the bark, whereas I eat the pith.[130]

And last, in Chapter Five, after commenting on the proper meaning of Ps 7.12, he advises the Jews: "Reread your Hebrew language text, and you will discover (if Jewish blindness does not prevent it) that this is the meaning of this text. Now even though we are Latin readers, nonetheless nothing could con-

127. *Adversus Iudeorum* 2, pp. 26–27, lns. 356–66.
128. *Adversus Iudeorum* 2, p. 21, lns. 170–71.
129. Cf. 2 Cor 3.6.
130. *Adversus Iudeorum* 4, p. 99, lns. 1093–1102.

ceal from us the truth of your Scriptures, in which the abundant erudition of many men skilled in both languages has instructed us."[131]

For a Christian audience, Peter's stubborn defense may have mitigated a growing insecurity concerning the integrity of their Old Testament text, an insecurity that resulted in numerous efforts in the twelfth and thirteenth centuries to produce a corrected edition especially of the Old Testament.[132] In part, then, because Peter is unable to acknowledge the textual differences that distinguish the Hebrew and Latin Scriptures, he must find other explanations for the fact that Jews and Christians understand them so differently. Since he insists that Christian teachings are reasonably deduced from the shared text of the Old Testament, Peter only seems able to explain Jewish exegetical traditions as the result of "obduracy," stubbornness, folly, irrationality, and perversity. Even after the giving of the Mosaic Law, human reason had been "put to sleep" and could not be restored, Peter alleges, except by Christ himself.[133] Therefore, the alleged blindness and inherent hostility of the Jews toward Christians[134] make it all but impossible for them to appreciate Peter's "rational" arguments. Moreover, lacking Christian faith, Jews are unable to acknowledge the authority of the Church and tradition, which provide a sure guide for the Christian community. As a result, Peter's treatise could hardly expect to achieve any positive outcome with a Jewish audience.

Reason and authority are not the only factors that Peter understands may lead to religious conversion. In *Against the Inveterate Obduracy of the Jews,* Peter claims that there are five causes that can result in error or, conversely, result in religious con-

131. *Adversus Iudeorum* 5, pp. 144–45, lns. 718–23.
132. See my "Falsification of Scripture and Medieval Christian-Jewish Polemics," 367–68.
133. Cf. *Adversus Iudeorum* 4, p. 108, lns. 1432–36.
134. *Adversus Iudeorum* 5, p. 141, lns. 600–601. This hatred, Chazan remarks, was a present reality for Peter, for whom "the traditional sense of historic Jewish enmity was transformed into something more immediate: Jews were perceived as exploiting every opportunity to vent their age-old hatred of Christianity in their contemporary setting." Robert Chazan, *Medieval Stereotypes and Modern Antisemitism* (Berkeley: University of California Press, 1997), 51.

version: authority, reason, miracles, power, and pleasure.[135] Jews cannot be persuaded by an appeal to authority, because they do not receive the New Testament or recognize the Church; they cannot be persuaded by reason, both because they are said to be blinded and benighted and because, Peter concedes, "faith does not derive merit where human reason provides proof."[136] Moreover, Jews cannot be compelled by the power of the State or Church to submit to Christian baptism. As already noted, Peter reluctantly invokes the Augustinian theology of Jewish witness that established a basis for the toleration of Jews in Christendom: "since for 1100 years already you [Jews] have moaned in sorrow under the feet of Christians, whom you hate above all others, having been made a mockery not only to them but also even to the Saracens and to all races and demons at one and the same time, what will restrain our hand from spilling your blood if not the commandment of the one who cast you off and elected us, the commandment of God saying through your prophet: 'Slay them not'?"[137] (Ps 58.12) Thus Peter does acknowledge that Jews are not to be killed even though he does not explore the further boundaries of their tolerated status laid out more than 500 years earlier in Pope Gregory I's *Sicut Iudaeis*.[138] Instead, Peter reminds his reader, in the early Church not only were the Gentiles not compelled by the power of the State to accept Christianity, they were actively persecuted for their faith, and yet Christianity spread nonetheless. Therefore, worldly power cannot explain the appeal of Christianity for the convert, nor justify the Jews' error,[139] nor effect their conversion. Neither can the Jews be persuaded by an appeal to material inducement or carnal pleasure because Christianity, for Peter, entails an ascetic spirituality and the renunciation of pleasures of the world. He inquires, "What pleasure is there, O Jew, in the

---

135. *Adversus Iudeorum* 4, p. 110, lns. 1498–1500.
136. *Adversus Iudeorum* 4, p. 112, lns. 1585–87.
137. *Adversus Iudeorum* 5, p. 141, lns. 600–605.
138. For the text of *Sicut Iudaeis,* see Simonsohn, *The Apostolic See and the Jews. Documents 492–1404,* no.19, 1: 15–16. For discussion of this important bull, see Cohen, *Living Letters of the Law,* 74–79.
139. Needless to say, Peter ignores the dramatic change in the material conditions of the Christian community after the Christianization of the Roman Empire.

religion of Christ? Did he himself not say to his own [disciples]: 'In the world you shall have distress'? (Jn 16.33) Did not his apostle say: 'And all that desire to live godly in Christ Jesus, will suffer persecution'? (2 Tm 3.12) Does not the Christian sword cut off everywhere whatever it can that pertains to pleasure?"[140]

Having dismissed authority, reason, power, and pleasure as effective agents for conversion, "Therefore miracles remain," Peter concludes. Thus,

> If it is true that a race can only be forced or enticed to embrace what is new and unfamiliar by authority or reason or miracles or power or pleasure, then it is certain that the Christian world could only be enticed or forced to embrace the religion (*lex*) of Christ, which is new and unfamiliar to it, by one of these causes. . . . But again it has been proved that it was not converted to Christ by authority, nor by reason, power, or pleasure. It is clear, then, that only by miracles was it challenged to accept the faith of Christ, by the grace alone of the Spirit.[141]

Torrell and Bouthillier have argued that Peter composed this addition to Chapter Four about the time he was completing revisions to his *On Miracles* and, for that reason, Chapter Four should be read with *On Miracles* as its companion piece.[142] Peter's contention that the world could only have been drawn to Christian faith miraculously through the power that miracles exercise over the mind—a power not only exercised by Jesus but also conferred by him upon his disciples and even upon contemporary saints—allows him to pursue an important theme in Chapter Four. The very spread of Christianity and its representation throughout the world (even as a minority culture in lands not ruled by Christians) are itself miraculous, he suggests, since the "wisdom of the world"[143] could not otherwise have been drawn to the "foolishness" of Christian teaching. In response to his putative Jewish interlocutor's claim that Islam has spread across the world as well, without attributing miraculous power to the prophet Mohammad,[144] Peter replies that while Islam has spread

140. *Adversus Iudeorum* 4, p. 113, lns. 1622–26.
141. *Adversus Iudeorum* 4, p. 114, lns. 1659–71.
142. *Pierre le Vénérable et sa vision du monde*, 180.
143. Cf. 1 Cor 1.20–21.
144. Peter places in the mouth of a Jew the question "How is it that when five hundred years after Christ had passed, the Mohammedan heresy arose, and

like a shadow over parts of the earth, still, "even though the heathens (*gentiles*) or the Saracens exercise dominion over some
parts of it, even though the Jews lurk among the Christians and
the heathens (*ethnici*), there is still no part of the earth, not even
a small part, neither the islands of the Tyrrhenian sea nor even
of the most distant ocean, that is not inhabited by Christians who
either rule or are subjects there . . ."[145] Like a plague, Islam, just
as other heresies, has infected a part of the body of the world,
but it cannot, like a corrupt humor, act upon the whole. By contrast, Christianity is a healthful balm working to heal the entire
body of the world.

Peter also anticipates another Jewish criticism. He condemns
the Jews for accepting reports of miracles performed by the
prophets of the Old Testament, while rejecting the claims found
in the New Testament that Jesus performed miracles and that he
conferred upon his disciples "power over unclean spirits, to cast
them out, and to heal all disease, and all infirmity" (Mt 10.1).[146]
Equally, he attacks Jewish polemical responses that sought to
dismiss the miracles of Jesus and the disciples as magic, rather
than the work of God.[147] Magic, he insists, is learned only after
a long period of study, whereas Jesus conferred a power to perform miracles upon his unlettered disciples in an instant. Furthermore, "magical portents . . . deceive human senses . . . by
demonic administration."[148] Magic tricks the senses to see what
is not there—like ephemeral phantasms of human shapes, or flying animals, and so on—to no good purpose. By contrast, Peter
insists, all of Jesus' miracles worked for the good and had lasting
effect. As if in summary, then, he adds:

If you place your faith in your Scriptures, then accede to authority.
If you would be rational or reasonable, then acquiesce to argument
(*ratio*). If you are still anxious, then believe the miracles that confirm

---

that without any miracles a sect as nefarious as this was produced that infected
such large parts of the world?" *Adversus Iudeorum* 4, p. 108, lns. 1449–52.

145. *Adversus Iudeorum* 4, p. 109, lns. 1467–71.

146. *Adversus Iudeorum* 4, pp. 115–16, lns. 1708–10.

147. *Adversus Iudeorum* 4, p. 115ff. For the charge that Jesus' miracles were
rather acts of diabolical magic, see Petrus Alfonsi, *Dialogue Against the Jews,* trans.
Resnick, 106, 232–36.

148. *Adversus Iudeorum* 4, p. 116, lns. 1729–31.

all these things, because, according to our apostle, "The Jews require signs."[149] . . . Do not glory in the miracles performed in the era of your Law, nor prefer it to the Gospel of Christ for that reason or for some other reason. The miracles of the Jewish law were many and great, but the deeds of Christian faith are far greater and incomparably more wondrous.[150]

These miraculous deeds did not come to an end, according to Peter, in the New Testament era; he has himself witnessed miraculous cures, he claims. He also draws attention to the miracle alleged to occur annually at the Holy Sepulcher, when the candles at the tomb are miraculously illuminated on the Sabbath before Easter.[151] Peter contends that this contemporary and "divine and public act of Christ"[152] has not only been recognized by Christians the world over, but even by heathens and Saracens. Since he accuses Jews alone of repudiating it, the Jews alone, it seems, reject not only the conclusions of reason but even the testimony of the senses, which Peter is able to explain only by invoking the Jews' implacable hostility for Christ and the Christian Church.

149. 1 Cor 1.22.

150. *Adversus Iudeorum* 4, p. 83, lns. 536–45.

151. As early as the second half of the ninth century, Bernard the monk, a Christian pilgrim to Jerusalem, mentioned this Easter miracle at the Holy Sepulcher. See his "A Journey to the Holy Places and Babylon," in *Jerusalem Pilgrims before the Crusades,* ed. John Wilkinson (Warminster, England: Aris and Phillips Ltd., 2002), 266. It appears that the Caliph al-Hakim ordered the Church of the Holy Sepulcher destroyed in 1009 precisely because he viewed the Easter miracle of Holy Fire as a fraud, but it survived in later Christian accounts, e.g., Theodoric's *Guide to the Holy Land,* composed ca. CE 1172. For this text, see *Jerusalem Pilgrimage 1099–1185,* ed. John Wilkinson (London: The Hakluyt Society, 1988), 283.

152. *Adversus Iudeorum* 4, p. 122, lns. 1955–56. Peter also explores this Easter miracle at the Holy Sepulcher in his sermon *De laude dominici sepulchri,* ed. Giles Constable in "Petri Venerabili sermones tres," *Revue Bénédictine* 64 (1954): 232–54, and esp. 249–52. There is also some justification for Peter's claim that—at least until 1009—Muslims also recognized the Easter miracle of the lights. See Benjamin Z. Kedar, "Convergences of Oriental Christian, Muslim, and Frankish Worshippers: The Case of Saydnaya," in *De Sion exibit lex et verbum domini de Hierusalem: Essays on Medieval Law, Liturgy and Literature in Honour of Amnon Linder,* ed. Yitzhak Hen (Turnholt: Brepols, 2001), 60–61.

CONCLUSION

Although Peter's treatise *Against the Inveterate Obduracy of the Jews* neither enjoyed the popularity of Petrus Alfonsi's *Dialogue against the Jews* nor exhibited its more sophisticated treatment, nonetheless Peter the Venerable's anti-Jewish polemic—never before translated into English—written by one of the most influential men from the world of Christian monasticism, holds significant historical interest. It presents a portrait of medieval Jews that all but strips them of their humanity, just as it expresses doubt concerning their rationality.[153] It seems to indicate that there is found in Jews some essential defect that alone can account for their diabolical rejection of Christian truths. The text also suggests that the Talmud, containing within itself a web of lies and offenses against God, not only gives expression to this defective nature but also supports and confirms that defect. Moreover, it does seem to be the case that, as Amos Funkenstein first argued[154] and as Jeremy Cohen has more recently conceded,[155] Peter's text breaks new ground with its treatment of the Talmud. Peter seems less inclined than other medieval theologians to safeguard the normative Augustinian conception that proposed that Jews fulfill a positive theological purpose in Christendom as "living letters" or guardians of the law of the Old Testament. Instead, Peter appears to hold that the Jews have increasingly abandoned the Old Testament and replaced it with the Talmud, thereby undermining a traditional argu-

153. See Kurt Schubert, "Das christlich-jüdische Religionsgespräch am 12. und 13. Jahrhundert," in *Die Juden in ihrer mittelalterlichen Umwelt*, ed. Alfred Ebenbauer and Klaus Zatloukal (Cologne: Böhlau, 1991), 224–25; Anna Sapir Abulafia, "Twelfth-Century Renaissance Theology and the Jews," in *From Witness to Witchcraft: Jews and Judaism in Medieval Christian Thought*, ed. Jeremy Cohen, 135–38; Gavin I. Langmuir, "The Faith of Christians and Hostility to Jews," in *Christianity and Judaism: Papers Read at the 1991 Summer Meeting and the 1992 Winter Meeting of the Ecclesiastical History Society*, ed. Diana Wood, 85.

154. Funkenstein concluded that "Peter the Venerable took present Judaism out of the framework of the Church doctrine of conditional tolerance because, as he thought, Jews did change and hold today to the Old Testament only outwardly." *Perceptions of Jewish History* (Berkeley, Los Angeles, Oxford: University of California Press, 1993), 193.

155. Cohen, *Living Letters of the Law,* 264.

ment for tolerating Jewish communities within Christendom. With his extra-biblical traditions "the Jew," Peter remarked, "has so completely consecrated himself to lies that are more than diabolical that no one trusts him in any way whatsoever."[156] While he may not have characterized Jews as heretics, Peter suggests that the Jews also nourished Mohammad's heresy on the milk of the Talmud.[157] And while Peter still admitted that it was not permitted to slay the Jews (although it was permissible to kill the Muslims in the East in the course of a holy war), this admission grants to the Jews of his age little more than protection for their lives.

156. *Adversus Iudeorum* 5, p. 184, lns. 2076–77.
157. *Adversus Iudeorum* 5, p. 184, lns. 2087–88.

AGAINST THE INVETERATE
OBDURACY OF THE JEWS

Here Begins the Book of Lord Peter the Venerable, Abbot of Cluny, *Against the Inveterate Obduracy of the Jews.*[1]

PROLOGUE

APPROACH YOU, O Jews—you, I say, who even to this day deny the Son of God. How long, wretches, will you fail to believe the truth? How long will you reject God? How long will you fail to soften [your] iron hearts? Behold that since antiquity almost the entire world has acknowledged Christ, while you alone do not acknowledge him; while all peoples submit to him, you alone do not listen to him; every tongue confesses him, while you alone deny him; others see him, hear him, understand him, but you alone remain blind, deaf, like stones. Clearly your eyes are blind, your ears are deaf, your hearts are stone.

Nor is this something new for you. Everywhere this world reads and recites in frequent readings what God says about you to Moses: "I see that this people is stiff-necked: Let me alone, that my wrath may be kindled against them, and that I may destroy them."[2] And again he says to you: "You are a stiff-necked people; once I shall come down in your midst, I shall destroy you."[3] [The world] also reads of your Moses, or rather ours, arguing against you in this manner: "I know your obstinacy," he says, "and your most stiff neck. While I am yet living, and going in with you, you have always been rebellious against the Lord: how much more when I shall be dead?"[4] It also reads Isaiah,

1. *Petri Venerabilis adversus Iudeorum inveteratam duritiem*, ed. Yvonne Friedman, CC CM 58 (Turnholt: Brepols, 1985).

2. Ex 32.9–10.   3. Ex 33.5.
4. Dt 31.27.

a prophet of singular excellence, to whom God said of you: "Blind the heart of this people," he said, "and make their ears heavy, and shut their eyes, lest they see with their eyes, and hear with their ears, and understand with their heart, and be converted and I heal them."[5] It reads and hears its own Stephen, whom your stones, O stone-like race, made the first witness to Christ after Christ.[6] It reads and surely it hears him, filled with the Holy Spirit, upbraiding in you the spirit of most wicked stubbornness: You, "uncircumcised in hearts and ears," you traitors and murderers, "you have always resisted the Holy Spirit even as your fathers did."[7]

But will you always do so? Will you always make of yourselves a public spectacle throughout all the lands of the world because of such great obduracy? Come to your senses, now at last come to your senses; "return to the heart, O transgressors," as one prophet says to you. "Return to the heart"[8] now, at least, when by the just judgment of the Most High you have fallen not only from heavenly glory but even from the earthly glory that alone you loved. Observe that those very things have been fulfilled among you that the Christ, whom you deny, spoke to your fathers and predicted for you if you did not come to your senses: "The kingdom of God will be taken away from you and given to a people yielding its fruit."[9] Having lost, then, the heavenly kingdom, and now having lost a very long time ago even an earthly kingdom, acknowledge that this has happened to you because of this impiety. Acknowledge that the cause of your very harsh condemnation is this: that you did not recognize, did not receive, did not worship the messiah once he came, the one that for such a long time you sang, read, and preached would come, but instead you spurned him, mocked him, slew him, in your detestable fashion.

But what else? If you decide to convert, you need not fear that you have slain him. He is not intent upon avenging his death, if the correct outcome of your conversion follows. Previously, while hanging from the cross as the man that he had assumed, he prayed for the very ones who crucified him, and he did not

5. Is 6.10.   6. Cf. Acts 6.5; 7.55.
7. Acts 7.51.   8. Is 46.8.
9. Mt 21.43.

pray only while he suffered[10] but even later, after he had risen from the dead, he granted his favor to those who repented and converted.[11] He was not unmindful that he had suffered death for the sake of the life of men and, once they had converted, he received those whom he regarded as mockers and murderers with that very evident and truly bountiful divine compassion which is upon every man. This same infinite bounty will not be lacking for you, nor will that bounty that embraces almost the entire world reject your small number from among the number of the saved, if you do not reject it.

Believe, then, your law, and not another's; believe your prophets and not those of others; believe your own Scriptures and not those of others. Why does this barely move you? Why does it not move you that the entire strength of the Christian faith, that the entire hope for human salvation, originates in your texts? Why does it not move you that we have received the patriarchs, the prophets, the harbingers, the apostolic preachers, the highest and supercelestial Virgin mother of Christ, and Christ himself, the author of our salvation—who was called the "expectation of the nations"[12] by your own prophet—not from the barbarous races, not from just any nations whatsoever, but from your race, as descendants from the great stock of Abraham? I refer you, then, to men of your own race, I refer you to your own Scriptures that you received from God, and I offer testimonies from them to which, however often there is a Jewish disputation, it will be compelled to surrender.

Moreover, I am not ignorant of the fact that you agree with us in some respect, whereas for the most part pertinaciously you disagree with us. You agree with us in that you assert that the messiah was foretold by the prophets many times and in various ways. You disagree in that you do not believe that he is the Son of God, you deny that he is God, but you affirm that he will reign in time in the manner of other kings, and you affirm that he has not yet come but is still to come. Therefore, the chapters already mentioned must be followed through in the order in which we have proposed them against you.

10. Cf. Lk 23.34.   11. Cf. Lk 24.47.
12. Gn 49.10.

CHAPTER ONE

That the Messiah (*Christus*) is the Son of God

ISTEN THEN, O Jews, and know from your own Scriptures that Christ, or the Messiah as you would have it, is the Son of God. Come, then, propose your claims again in the first place to the most excellent of the prophets, Isaiah, and to a people, one neither from your time nor from ours, that believes the truth. Tell us what God said of the eternal generation of his Son: "Shall not I that make others to bring forth children, myself bring forth, said the Lord? Shall I, that give generation to others, be barren? said the Lord."[1] What clearer proof is there, O Jews, of the generation of the Son of God? Indeed, if God has borne [a son], then necessarily he is a father with respect to the one he bore, and necessarily he is a son and the Son of God with respect to the one who bore him. But I am unwilling to believe—indeed, I do not believe—that you are so foolish, that you are so senselessly lacking in understanding as to attempt to compare the eternal generation of the deity to a carnal generation, or to do so with some weak analogy. Far be it from you, far be it from every intelligence, for the mind to be so asinine as to compare in any way whatsoever the eternal, ineffable, incomprehensible generation of the Father omnipotent—[that is] the nativity of the omnipotent Son—to some earthly or customary generation[2] or birth. Nonetheless, if anything at all can be derived concerning something so ineffable from some analogy, apart from analogies to corporeal

1. Is 66.9.
2. "Customary generation": i.e., one that follows the customary or usual course of nature.

52

generations, then it is said that the Son of God is begotten from God just as is light from light, a ray from the sun, splendor from fire.[3] I mention this briefly, O Jews, lest you understand or think that we understand the nativity of the Son of God in an insipid or bestial fashion. Therefore, this prophetic testimony[4] compels you to understand and to confess that Christ is the Son of God, not insofar as he is a man but insofar as he is God. In fact, it is inappropriate for any man, for any angel, for any creature either to be thought to be begotten from God or to be the Son of God, so far as pertains to the nature of the deity. Thus, if this does not befit any creature insofar as it is a creature, then it is only appropriate for that one who, insofar as he is God, is born from God. But even more lucid examples follow the testimony offered and more clearly make evident that Christ alone is the Son of God.

Tell me, O David, prophet of God, at one time king of the people of God, father according to the flesh of the Son of God, tell me if you think that Christ is the Son of God. He said, "I am appointed king by him over Zion his holy mountain."[5] Tell me, too, what follows: "The Lord said to me: You are my son; today I have begotten you."[6] How do Jews respond to these things? Behold, speaking in the person of Christ when he said that he was established as a king by God, he confessed Christ, he preached the anointed one, he affirmed the man. When he added that God said, "You are my son; today I have begotten you,"[7] he indicated his deity through which he is naturally the Son of God. But you deny this, you mock it. You say that these words pertain neither to Christ nor to someone else, but pertain only to David himself, who was made a king by God some time ago on your Mount Zion, upon that holy mountain at Jerusalem some time ago. You say that this same David was called a son by God, that he was called a begotten one, not because he was truly the son

---

3. Cf. The Nicene Creed, *Symbolum Nicaenum* (Mansi 2, p. 667).
4. Is 66.1, *supra*, p. 52.
5. Ps 2.6. The Psalm numbering in this volume corresponds to the Vulgate, not to modern versions.
6. Ps 2.7.
7. Ibid.

of God or was begotten by God, but because he deserved to be honored with this title because he was pleasing [to God] on account of his saintly customs and his many virtues.

But, O Jews, that meaning does not escape us, that understanding does not escape us in which elsewhere, even if not here, we read that men are often called sons by God. We know that this was said to Pharaoh concerning your fathers: "Israel is my firstborn son; release my son so that he may sacrifice to me."[8] And according to a certain one of the prophets: And "Israel is my child and I have loved him and I have called my son out of Egypt."[9] Although this was more properly said in the prophetic voice concerning our Lord, who, when fleeing Herod in the manner of men, was called by God the Father through an angel at the appropriate time,[10] nevertheless this is understood also to refer to that people from which you take your origin according to the flesh. In time past in Egypt that people expanded from a few fathers into a great people, dwelled there a long time, was severely oppressed, was heard crying out to God,[11] and then, after having been called forth from there it was honored by God with the name of "son." And according to Isaiah, this is appropriately said about you: "I have begotten children, and exalted them: but they have despised me."[12]

It does not escape us, moreover, the understanding does not escape us that not only men are called either sons of God or begotten by God by virtue of some grace or some merit, but in addition that even insensible things can be designated with names of this sort. Thus it is that: "Who is the father of the rain, or who has begotten the drops of dew?" And again, "Out of whose womb came the ice, and the frost from heaven, who has begotten it?"[13]

Do not, O Jews, do not think, then, that the Church of God has been unable to see such clear examples. It sees this, it acknowledges this, it discerns this. It discerns that similar names have to be understood differently in things that are dissimilar; nor does it discern that even though they sound the same, it is

8. Ex 4.22–23.   9. Hos 11.1.
10. Cf. Mt 2.13–15.   11. Cf. Ex 3.7.
12. Is 1.2.   13. Jb 38.28–29.

necessary for them to be understood in only one and the same way. You have this in innumerable examples from your Scriptures—you have the same names not always signifying the same things. And when could these be presented one after another? But, for the sake of an example, let some be presented so that many may be easily gathered up from these few cases. Clearly head, eye, ear, hand, arm, and foot are names properly signifying some parts of the body, which nonetheless not only designate the parts themselves but are often extended to other, different things. To stand, to sit, lie down, sleep, wake, walk, and fly are words properly designating something that happens (*accidens aliquod*), which nonetheless [not only designate themselves but] are also introduced to designate other, different things. And because these things are clear to those who have been instructed even in a mediocre fashion, they do not need other examples. Therefore, in this same way the noun "generation," when it is understood in God, does not always designate the same thing, but sometimes very different things. These prophetic testimonies that I have set forth show clearly the manner in which generation is taught to signify very different things. Does not that generation, O Jews, of which it is written: "I have begotten children, and exalted them: but they have despised me,"[14] seem different to you from that type of generation of which it is said: "Who is the father of the rain, or who has begotten the drops of dew?"[15] or different from the one where one reads: "Out of whose womb came the ice, and the frost from heaven, who has begotten it?"[16] I do not think that you have become so deaf and so void of understanding that what is clear to everyone else should be obscure to you alone, that what is light for all should be darkness for you alone. For it is clear to all that a great and not a small, a sure and not a dubious difference is present in what was expressed under the noun, "generation." Actually, God is said to beget (*generare*) men by loving them, by cherishing them, by leading them, by saving them; he is said to beget the rain, the drops of dew, the ice, and the frost, by willing, creating, producing, and constituting it. Just as, then,

14. Is 1.2.   15. Jb 38.28.
16. Jb 38.29.

I think you see now that quite different and discrete things are signified by this one noun, "generation," so too I think you will see something else far more sublime in the same noun, once the old blindness has been washed from your eyes. You can perceive it, I say, only with God revealing it; see it in those very words that you read: "The Lord said to me: You are my son; today I have begotten you,"[17] and understand that this is nei-ther the latter nor the former [type of] generation that was set forth but a natural birth of the Son of God from the essence of the Father. For just as the all-powerful Creator is said to be the father of the rain, just as he is said to have begotten the drops of dew while producing ice and frost, just as he is said to be the father of Israel, just as he is said to have begotten sons by cherishing them, so too is it written that he is the father of his only-begotten Son, so is it foretold that he begot him, not from something else, not *ex nihilo,* but by bringing him forth from his own substance. Although only the Spirit of the same Father and Son can bring you to believe this, O Jews, if you carry the sacred Scriptures, as is appropriate, if you do not reject them pertina-ciously, if you do not reject them in your Jewish manner, you will at least submit to the argument that follows.

What follows next? "Ask of me, and I will give you the nations (*gentes*) for your inheritance, and the utmost parts of the earth for your possession."[18] Look: apply this, if you can, to David, who once reigned among the Jews. He was enjoined to request that the nations be given to him as an inheritance and the ends of the earth as a possession. And because it was enjoined, one must not think that he did not obey. Therefore he requested, and as had been promised, the nations were given to him as an inheritance and the ends of the earth as a possession. But which nations? Perhaps, according to you, the Philistines of whom this was written: "David took the bridle of tribute out of the hand of the Philistines."[19] Perhaps your opinion is that it can be ap-plied to Syria Damascus, of which one reads: "[And David put garrisons] in Syria of Damascus: and Syria served David under tribute."[20] Perhaps, according to your tortured interpretation,

17. Ps 2.7.   18. Ps 2.8.
19. 2 Kgs 8.1.   20. 2 Kgs 8.6.

it applied to the children of Ammon or to some surrounding nations that it is written that he overcame in war. But reread, carefully scrutinize your Malachi, and you will find that David restrained the Philistines but did not subjugate them, that Syria Damascus served him for a period of time, but that before very much time had passed, it rebelled, and that immediately afterward there followed proud and the most powerful kings in that very same Damascus. [Read] that the children of Ammon or the rest that he had conquered immediately revived[21] and, for the entire time that the Jewish race had kings, they had their own kings up until the Babylonian migration of your fathers. Therefore, these words of God were not made for David, because neither these nations nor others except the Jews were given to him as an inheritance.

But what will you say about the last words of this divine passage? For after he said: "I will give to you the nations as your inheritance,"[22] he immediately added: "and the ends of the earth as your possession." He said "the ends of the earth." What are the ends of the earth? Is this not where the earth is bounded, where human habitation ends? Were, then, these ends of the earth given to David as a possession? If these ends of the earth were given to David as a possession, then all the lands of the world also were given to him as a possession. If this is the case, then the [lands] of the Indians, Persians, Gauls, Germans, Scythians (*Scitae*),[23] Africans, and, last, every nation that the world contains, was given to him as a possession. Do you see yet how remarkable and absurd this is, how unsuitable even for herd animals! Why, O wretches, do you not understand that, according to the words of our apostle, the letter is killing you?[24] Why do you almost alone not follow the vivifying spirit in the world? Did David, whose kingdom was adequately bounded by a small part of Syria, have dominion over the lands of the world? Look then, look for another for whom these words of God were formed and

21. Cf. 2 Sm 17.27; 2 Chr 20.1 and 27.5.
22. Ps 2.8.
23. For *Scitae,* see Albertus Magnus, *De natura loci* 3.2 (Colon Ed. 5.2, p. 32, ln. 26).
24. Cf. 2 Cor 3.6.

to whom the nations were given as an inheritance, to whom the ends of the earth were given as a possession. And whom else will you be able to find but Christ? Whom else but him whom, up until now, you have denied to be the Son of God? Clearly it is he, that Christ, that Son of God, that Jesus in whose name, willy-nilly, "every knee of heaven, earth, and places below"[25] bends, he who says: "All power in heaven and on earth is given to me,"[26] to whom the voice of the Father was formed: "You are my son, today I have begotten you."[27]

But let the discourse proceed to others that are clearer even than these cases, and let what David himself thinks about this Son of God be heard again. In fact, he introduces a lord speaking to a certain lord and saying, among other things: "in the splendor of the saints I begot you from the womb before I begot the day star (*Lucifer*)."[28] Who is this lord that another lord begot before the day star? Run, O Jews, think, busy yourselves, exert yourselves, chew your nails, and pervert this statement if you can, and, in your customary way, apply a passage so divine and admirable to one and then another. Here surely it is necessary to plant your feet, to set your hands with us; here it is necessary either to respond with something rationally or to remain silent, as in the past your fathers were silent when the beginning of this psalm was proposed to them [to refer] to Christ. As I said, they were silent concerning the first verse of the psalm that had been proposed [to refer] to him; now you, being perhaps wiser than your fathers in this respect, respond if you can to our verse: "I begot you from the womb before I begot the day star."[29] Who is this lord of David who was begotten by another lord of his before the day star? Show me, show me that lord of David that is begotten, as is said, from another lord and before the day star. Show me at the time when these words were said any king, any prophet, any great man who is lord to so great a king besides God, and, in order to include many men in a brief phrase, [show me one] from the first Adam to the last, who will be born at the end of the age from the sons of Adam.

25. Phil 2.10.   26. Mt 28.18.
27. Ps 2.7.   28. Ps 109.3.
29. Ibid.

If you like, investigate the heavens themselves and find David's lord for me among the various orders of the saints' spirits, who are called angels by a more customary name! For even though some of the earlier fathers called the angels that appeared to them "lords,"[30] nonetheless the angels are not lords of men nor are they subordinated, with respect to the dignity of nature, to the sovereignty of those who were created equal to the angels.[31] It is clear in this regard, then, that if no angel has dominion over any man, then none of the angels was called "lord" by David. And neither did God beget angels from a womb; instead he created them, just as he did other creatures, by his all-powerful will. Whereas this [passage] does not say that he created but rather affirms that he begot from a womb. Since, then, David's lord cannot be found here among angelic spirits nor in the human race but only in God, either deny that your psalm is divine or present to us someone that reason compels us to believe is David's lord.

He says, "Before the day star I begot you."[32] Once more difficulties, or once more a snare, or once more a pit has been prepared for you into which your insane blindness will fall. It is plainly clear that none of you is released from there unless you are released by the one who releases the prisoner from the prison cell,[33] "who opens, and no one shuts, shuts and no one opens."[34] "Before the day star I begot you."[35] Who is the day star (*Lucifer*) here? If you say that it is a star, that it shines more brightly than the other stars except the principal [ones], and that for this reason it is called the day star just like one that bears a greater light,[36] I reply: no man was created before that day star. Now you know that that star was created on the fourth day with the other stars, since Moses indicates as much.[37] Man, however, was made later, that is, on the sixth day.[38] Therefore God did not say to any human being,

---

30. Cf. Gn 18.3; 19.2.
31. Cf. Ps 8.5–6; cf. Augustine, *De civ. Dei* 11.13.16 (CC SL 48, pp. 334, 336); 11.9 (pp. 328–29).

32. Ps 109.3.	33. Cf. Is 42.7; Acts 5.19.
34. Rv 3.7.	35. Ps 109.3.

36. "bears a greater light": *maiorem ferens lucem,* suggesting then an etymology for Lucifer from *ferens lucem.* Cf. Isidore of Seville, *Etym.* 3.71.18 (PL 82: 180C).

37. Cf. Gn 1.16.	38. Cf. Gn 1.26–27.

"Before the day star I begot you."[39] Neither was this said to any
of the angels, since, for the compelling reason already indicated,
this was said only to the Lord.[40] Therefore, for the same reason,
none of the angels is David's lord. It follows, then, that "before
the day star I begot you"[41] does not refer to any of the angels. But
if you say that the day star is the apostate archangel to whom the
prophet Isaiah spoke under the name of the Babylonian king,
having adopted a metaphor from this star: "How have you fallen
from heaven, Lucifer, [you] who will rise in the morning?"[42] I reply that not only was no man formed before that day star (*Lucifer*), but neither had any angel been created then. In fact, in the
same way divine words are related to Job concerning him: "He is
himself the beginning of the ways of God."[43] But if he is the beginning of God's ways—that is, works—then none of God's works
was created before him. But if none of God's works was created
before him, then God did not say, "Before the day star I begot
you,"[44] to any man or to any angel. Now, I do not think that you
are so mindless (*amentes*) as to understand that "Before the day
star I begot you"[45] was spoken by God to refer to the Babylonian
king, who was indicated by the name Lucifer. Nor indeed will the
divine expression (*sermo*) refer to some magnate if, as everyone
knew, David spoke before the Babylonian king was begotten.
How is it then, O you most wretched race of men, that you do
not perceive something so transparent, you do not see something
that is so clear? Open your eyes at last, lay open your ears, and
blush to appear as the only blind ones in the world, blush to remain the only ones among mortals that are deaf. Finally, do not
become a spectacle for all the world, do not put yourselves on
display as a false tale for all the ages. Observe that David's lord
could only have been God, acknowledge that David himself only
called his lord, God. And because he said "lord" first, and then
immediately afterward he named another lord, understand that
both the one and the other can only be the Father and the Son.
Therefore, he introduced the Lord there at the beginning of the

39. Ps 109.3.   40. Cf. Ps 109.1.
41. Ps 109.3.   42. Is 14.12.
43. Jb 40.14.   44. Ps 109.3.
45. Ibid.

already cited psalm as the Father speaking to the Lord the Son, when he said: "The Lord said to my Lord."[46] Now according to the preceding [arguments] that David's lord is not to be found among creatures, it is necessary that only his Creator be called Lord. And because the name of the Creator and the name of God signify one and the same thing, David's lord is the Creator, David's lord is God. Therefore another lord, by all means himself the Creator, by all means God, is speaking to this lord of David, to this Creator, to this God.

What does he say? "Sit at my right side."[47] To whom was God able to say this if not to God? To whom, I say, was God able to say, "Sit at my right side,"[48] if not to one who is of such great dignity that God could say to him: "Sit at my right side"?[49] And where will so great a dignity be found that could be worthy of sitting beside the deity? Clearly, what nature will have such great dignity that it will be able to deserve the throne of the deity? Certainly none, O Jew, except one divine and human that, owing to the divine nature, deserved this in Christ alone. But if your choice can establish another on God's chair other than God, whether from among heavenly or earthly creatures, then indicate it, offer it, reveal it. But it [your choice] will be unable to do so, it will not prevail, because deity enjoys no equal but God, the throne of deity accepts none but God, none but the Son of God is equal to God the Father, and God himself is with him. And surely the Spirit of both is equal to the Father and the Son, but the Father's voice is not directed to the Spirit, because it is not begotten of the Father. Whereas to the one to whom was said, "Sit at my right side,"[50] this was added: "I begot you from the womb before the day star."[51] "From the womb," he says, so that you will know that he is born from God's own essence and not from another's. He said, "Before the day star," so that you would observe that his birth is eternal, prior to every creature's. He said, "I begot you," so that you would understand that he was not made from any material, nor created *ex nihilo*, but rather that he was begotten eternally from the Father.

46. Ps 109.1.
47. Ibid.
48. Ibid.
49. Ibid.
50. Ibid.
51. Ps 109.3.

See, then, that I proposed to prove in the first part of this
four-part [chapter] division nothing except that Christ is the
Son of God; now, O Jews, I have even proved that he is God, by
virtue of this divine psalm.

But you will say: the psalm that you have invoked against us,
and which you have adduced publicly in order to prove the deity of your lord, does not work on your behalf, nor does it support your premise. In fact, it was not offered in David's persona, but rather it was written by David for the person of Eliezer,
Abraham's servant. The real meaning of the psalm is this: "The
Lord"—that is, God—"said to my lord"—Abraham—"Sit on my
right hand."[52] Even as you do, O Jews, we concede Abraham's
great merit before God and Abraham's great and manifold
prerogatives before him. We concede his great merit because
"Abraham believed in God"[53] with a great grace, because "it was
reckoned to him as justice." We concede his great merit because,
when God commanded, "he extended his hand and seized a
sword to slay his son."[54] We concede his great grace when, after
he was prevented from slaying his son, it was said to him: "I have
sworn by myself, the Lord says: because you have done this thing
and you have not spared your only-begotten son for my sake,
I will bless you and multiply you like the stars of the heavens
and like the sands that are on the shore of the sea."[55] Abraham's
great merit before God was not merely simple but manifold, or
rather the excellence of [his] singular grace was great and greater than all the gifts God gathered for him, [grace] by which he
promised to him: "All peoples will be blessed in your seed."[56] But
was it so great that God enjoined him to "Sit at my right side"?[57]
Was it so great that, just as was said not much earlier, what is

52. This text was often cited in Jewish and Christian disputations. Cf. Rashi,
ad loc.; B.T. *Nedarim* 32b. In Joseph Kimhi's *The Book of the Covenant*, written perhaps a generation after Peter the Venerable's text, a Jewish respondent insists
that Jerome's Vulg. translation has corrupted the meaning of this passage intended by the Hebrew, leading Christians astray. See *The Book of the Covenant*,
trans. Frank Talmage, 58–59; cf. Erwin I. J. Rosenthal, "Anti-Christian Polemic
in Medieval Bible Commentaries," *Journal of Jewish Studies* 11 (1960): 116–35,
and especially 129ff.

53. Gn 15.6; Rom 4.3.   54. Gn 22.10.
55. Gn 22.16–17.   56. Gn 22.18.
57. Ps 109.1.

specific to God would be shared by man and God together? I say
only by man, as we know that Abraham was a man, and not by
man and God at the same time, as we know that Christ was. Did
God say this, then, to one who was naught but a man, "Sit at my
right side"?[58] Where is that which the Jewish heart alone holds
back lest the Jew believe in Christ: the contemplation of human
humility, that unworthy consort (as you believe) of divine majesty?[59] Where indeed is that zeal for God, "but not according to
knowledge"[60] as our apostle states. Was it not on account of these
words that you ascribe to Abraham that you stoned Stephen our
first martyr, shutting up your ears as if to blasphemy and hissing
through [your] teeth as if for vengeance, you men who are always avid for sacred blood?[61] What did Stephen say about Christ?
"I see the heavens opened and Jesus standing at the right hand"
of God.[62] What does the Jew say of Abraham? "The Lord"—that
is, God—"said to my lord"—Abraham—"Sit on my right hand."
How is it that you were unable to endure, then, to hear even
once that Jesus stands at the right side of the power of God, and
yet now every day you can hear with equanimity that Abraham
sits at the right side of God? Do not, do not, I beg you, give God
a consort who is other than God; do not establish anyone on
the divine throne except God. If you concede what previously
you were never wont to deny, [then] the words offered in the
person of Eliezer are false: "The Lord"—that is, God—"said to
my lord"—Abraham—"Sit on my right hand." Not only do the
things already said show them to be false, but the entire sequence of the psalm clearly declares the same thing. For whom
is the next sequence of verses [that God speaks]: "Until I place
your enemies as a footstool for your feet; sit"?[63] According to
you, God says, O Abraham, "at my right side, until I place your
enemies as a footstool for your feet"—that is, until your enemies
are placed beneath your feet. And what enemies did Abraham
have when he lived? Examine, Jew, the entire text of your sacred

58. Ibid.
59. That is, Peter implies that Jews fail to appreciate the humble human
condition, whose humble condition, they believe, can even sit at the right hand
of God.
60. Rom 10.2.   61. Cf. Acts 7.54.
62. Acts 7.56.   63. Ps 109.1.

canon, and unless I am mistaken you will be unable to find that Abraham had, I do not say many, but even one enemy. In fact, although he tarried in the land of the Gentiles, nevertheless he was a just man in his religion, in his sobriety, in his wisdom, and so too he was a good man among the wicked, and he was a peace-loving man as well among those who hated peace. For this reason, neither Christian nor Jew has been able or will be able to read in the Hebrew canon that he had any enemy at all. If you say that he fought with 318 retainers against the kings who had conquered the Sodomites[64] and who had captured Lot, the son of his brother, and that he overcame the thieves, freed Lot, and carried off many spoils from the enemies, I reply: The kings did not go forth to do battle because of Abraham, nor did they capture Lot, the son of his brother, because of Abraham. Scripture reports the reason why the kings were roused to do battle against kings—to wit, four against five—that is, because the five kings had served the four kings for some time, and then they were unwilling to serve when they came to consider the terms of service to be shameful.[65] This was the reason why Lot was found captured by the victors among the conquered, and Lot himself was the reason why Abraham was arrayed in battle against the thieves already mentioned. It is clear, then, that in this manner a Jew will be unable to find Abraham's enemies, of whom he can imagine that God said to him: "until I place your enemies as a footstool for your feet."[66]

But if you are unable to find Abraham's enemies, then neither will you be able to explicate the third verse of the psalm so that it pertains to him, that is: "The Lord will send forth the rod of your power from Zion,"[67] nor that God said to him: "to rule in the midst of your enemies."[68] Now, because when speaking to Jews I am prevented from touching the marrow, which they disdain, of the sacred psalm and I am compelled to tarry over the useless shell of the letter that alone they are accustomed to chew over like cattle, tell me, according to your brute intellect, tell me why God would say to this kindly man, to this quiet

64. Cf. Gn 14.12–15.   65. Cf. Gn 14.1–9.
66. Ps 109.1.   67. Ps 109.2.
68. Ibid.

man, to this peace-loving man who one almost always reads was unarmed, "The Lord will send forth the rod of your power from Zion."[69] How was the rod of Abraham's power, which was unnecessary to him for battle, sent forth by the Lord? How "from Zion," which did not exist yet? How did the Lord say to him: "to rule in the midst of your enemies,"[70] when there were none?

But I will turn now to the fourth [verse]: "With you is the principality."[71] What principality is with Abraham? Was there a principality of heaven and earth with Abraham? Or was there a principality of other creatures with Abraham? "In the day of your strength."[72] What is the day of Abraham's strength? What is the day when the principality is joined to Abraham's strength? "In the splendor of the saints I begot you from the womb before the day star."[73] What are these splendors of the saints, O Jew, in which splendors Abraham was begotten from the womb before the day star? But I do not tarry over these almost ineffable matters, because they do not have to be explicated by the Christian so as to refer to Christ, but by the Jew so as to refer Abraham, if he is able to do so.

And what follows next? "The Lord swore, and he will not repent him."[74] What is it that the Lord swore? What is it that he swore that he will not repent? He said, "You are a priest for ever according to the order of Melchizedech."[75] Was Abraham a priest? Was Abraham a priest forever? Was there a priest forever and according to the order of Melchizedech? Now if Abraham was "a priest according to the order of Melchizedech,"[76] why, since each one would be equal in office, equal in order, equal in dignity, did he proclaim that he was blessed by him, why did he [that is, Melchizedech] offer bread and wine, why did he give him the tithes from all that he had seized?[77] Explicate all these things, Jew, if you can, as referring to Abraham. But I believe, rather I know, rather I affirm, that neither you nor the entire synagogue of Satan when gathered together will be able to explicate these words so sacred, so divine, so surpassing every hu-

69. Ibid.
71. Ps 109.3.
73. Ibid.
75. Ibid.
77. Cf. Gn 14.18–20.

70. Ibid.
72. Ibid.
74. Ps 109.4.
76. Ibid.

man, as referring either to the man Abraham or even to any man whatsoever. Therefore, that Jewish exposition that pretends that God said these words concerning Abraham is false, and the Christian exposition that affirms that God said these words not as referring to any human but to Jesus Christ, at once God and man, is true. To God, I say, and man. And let me shake up the Jew more and more, if not to make him believe, at least to make him angry by saying repeatedly what he shrinks to hear, [that this is said] not only to man and God, but, as has often been said, to man and God and at the same time to the Son of God.

And why does the Jew so completely shrink from the name of the Son of God when the pagan freely and constantly confesses it? Was not Nebuchadnezzar a pagan? And what does he say while approaching the door of his furnace? He said, "Did we not send three shackled men into the midst of the fire? Behold," he says, "the form of the fourth is like the Son of God."[78] Look, the heathen king foretells the Son of God, and the Jew denies him. The king that is without God's law confesses the Son of God, and the man educated and instructed in the law of God disavows and casts aside the Son of God. But that Son of God who saved the boys that confess [his name] from that Babylonian furnace—without a doubt, the furnace of hell—will endlessly torment his deniers, the Jews. On the basis of the proof texts set forth, Christ is God, and Christ is the Son of God, whether the Jew denies or confesses him.

But after the ones that have already been set forth, hear in addition one more testimony, a testimony from your Solomon concerning the Son of God. In fact, he says in Proverbs: "Who has ascended into heaven and descended? Who has held the spirit in his hands? Who has gathered up the waters as if in a garment? Who has raised all the ends of the earth?"[79] To whom can these words be understood to apply, O Jews, if not to God? And indeed to ascend into heaven and to descend seems able to fit either the holy angels or certain blessed spirits of the saints. But the words that follow those already cited prove that they are not said of the angels, nor are they said of the spirits of the

78. Dn 3.91–92.
79. Prv 30.4.

saints. The words that follow prove, I say, that this was said neither about any spirit nor was it said of any creature, but only of God himself, the Creator of all spirits—rather, the Creator of all things—when is added: "Who has held the spirit in his hands?"[80] Now, who contains "the spirit in his hands"—that is, in his power—if not the one of whom Job says: "Has not he whom you have wished to teach made the spirit?"[81] Certainly, to whom can one apply: "Who has gathered up the waters as if in a garment," if not to the one of whom one reads in the same Book of Job: "When God blows there comes frost, and again the waters are poured out abundantly"?[82] Of whom could it be said: "Who has raised up all the ends of the earth,"[83] unless of that one of whom the psalm sings: "You have created all the ends of the earth, summer and spring you have formed them"?[84] Therefore, your Solomon did not perceive that these things referred to anyone but God, nor did he proclaim them about anyone other than God. Hear, then, the following: "What is his name or what is the name of his son, if you know it?"[85] What do you do, Jews? See, Solomon demands to know the name of God, just as he demands to know the ineffable name of the Son of God. Clearly, that wise man would never demand to know the name of a God that has a Son, if he did not believe that he is a Father. He would never investigate into the name of his Son, if he did not perceive that there is a Son of God. Therefore, Solomon perceived what so far you have not perceived, he confessed what so far you have denied, and he attests that God is a Father who has a Son, and that his Son is the one who is professed to be a Son under the investigation of the name of God. What is clearer than these words? What is more splendid than this light? Is it not necessary then, O Jews, for you to confess that there is a Son of God, not only according to this single testimony of Solomon's but even according to other, more remote testimonies in Scripture that urge you to do so? For nowhere is there available to you a byway (*angulus*) to lay an ambush, from which you may undertake to pervert the singular noun, the Son of God, with the plural, sons

80. Ibid.
82. Jb 37.10.
84. Ps 73.17.

81. Jb 26.4. Cf. *infra* 5, pp. 218, 225.
83. Prv 30.4.
85. Prv 30.4.

of God. An examination of the name of God, and an examination of the name of the Son of God, which Scripture seems
to set forth, excludes the plural, sons of God.[86] For neither the
holy angels nor the just men whom, as was said above, Holy
Scripture calls sons of God because of some excellent grace
lacked their own proper names when it was necessary, or those
that had previously been imposed like coverings (*tecta*),[87] so that
Solomon especially wondered about them, and while wonder-
ing was believed to investigate them with such great diligence as
to say: "What is his name or what is the name of his son, if you
know it?"[88] But neither does any reason allow [this], as when
after that which he proclaimed so solemnly about God, he said:
"What is his name?" so that what follows would be perceived to
have been said of any man or any angel: "or what is the name
of his son if you know it?"[89] Indeed, now an angelic or human
name would seem to be made equal to the divine name, now
the name of a creature be said to equal that of the Creator. The
name of God, however, is above every name, as you know, and
is no less ineffable or less incomprehensible than God himself.
Nor is God one thing and his name another, but he is himself
just like his name; that is, the same simple and highest God is
preferred to all his works. From this [it is clear] that this Scripture that states: "What is the name of his son if you know it" not
only proclaims the Son of God but also demonstrates that he is
the same God. The only reason that the name of God's son will
be inquired after with equal diligence as the name of God is to
show that the Son of God is himself also God. Therefore, the
fact that the name of the Father and the name of the Son are inquired after with equal sublimity, teaches that they are endowed
with equal deity. Or then present to me with a sure proof-text or
argument (*ratio*) someone else, O Jews, that I will be forced to
believe and confess is not among the plural number of the sons
of God but is the Son of God in a unique sense, or accept our
Christ, who has been proved to be God and the Son of God with
so many proof-texts and so many arguments.

86. Cf. *supra*, p. 54.

87. Perhaps a reference to Rom 4.7: "Blessed are they whose iniquities are
forgiven, and whose sins are covered (*tecta*)."

88. Prv 30.4.   89. Ibid.

CHAPTER TWO

In which Christ is shown specifically to be God

UT AFTER CHRIST has been proved to be God and the Son of God on the authority of your texts, O Jews, perhaps, with your customary depravity, you will still insist and demand that his divinity be shown to you more clearly with other examples. And how, I ask, can it be shown more clearly? Among things of the world, what is clearer than the light, what is more resplendent than the sun? Nonetheless, even the light is a night for the blind, and the sun is darkness. The clarity of the sacred Scriptures shines so brightly on you, shines so plainly on you, that those that illuminate others cannot shine on you, those that are resplendent for others become dark for you. Except for you, for whom will the lucid testimony of the divine psalm that has been set forth fail to suffice to prove the deity of Christ: "The Lord said to my Lord: Sit at my right side,"[1] and the rest? Other than for you, for whom will Solomon's splendid statement fail to suffice to prove the deity of Christ, by which, inquiring after the name of God's son as well as the name of God himself, he shows that Christ is not only the Son of God but also is God? Other than for you, for whom will that argument alone fail to suffice with which, because Christ has been proved by sacred proof-texts to be the Son of God, he is also proved to be God?

And how is this? Listen: If he is the Son of God, he is the Son of God either according to nature (*naturaliter*) or only metaphorically (*vocaliter*). But as I showed above, some angels have been called sons of God just as some men have been called sons

1. Ps 109.1.

of God, but only metaphorically (either because of some grace or from some merit) and not according to nature. Some of the angels [have been called sons of God] as in the Book of Job: "On a certain day when the sons of God came to stand before the Lord."[2] Some men [have been called sons of God], as when through Ezekiel God said: "I took them and they have borne me sons and daughters."[3] Because Christ was shown above to have been begotten before every creature from the very essence of the Father, he is the Son of God according to nature. But if he is the Son of God according to nature, then certainly he is not different from the Father. The Father, however, is God. Therefore, the Son cannot be anything but God. Now, to take an example from a carnal generation, although it is very dissimilar, just as a man is nothing other than a man if begotten from a man, and just as a bird is nothing other than a bird if begotten from a bird, just as light is nothing other than light if kindled from light, so God is nothing other than God born from God. Or does this argument by itself not suffice for you? Then let the other arguments and other examples from your sacred Scriptures succeed and let testimony be offered up as evidence to prove the true deity of Christ from your very own lawgiver, Moses.

I say approach, then, holy Moses, you singular friend of God,[4] you whom God himself says that he knew by name,[5] you who were given to the Jews in a veil but who were revealed to us,[6] approach a people that no longer belongs to God, but come arrayed against the enemies of God, and expose to them just as to us the deity of the Son of God: "The Lord," he says, "rained down brimstone and fire upon Sodom and Gomorrah from the Lord out of heaven."[7] Who is the Lord, O Jews, who rained down brimstone and fire out of heaven from another Lord? You have already heard David saying: "The Lord said to [my] Lord," so listen as well to Moses saying: "The Lord rained down from the Lord."

---

2. Jb 1.6.

3. Ezek 23.4.

4. Cf. Ex 33.11.

5. Cf. Ex 33.17.

6. Cf. Ex 34.33–34; cf. 2 Cor 3.14–16.

7. Gn 19.24.

Do not take refuge in the angels who had arrived earlier, who had come to Sodom in the evening,[8] who in the morning led Lot away from Sodom with his wife and daughters.[9] They had already gone, they had already departed, they had already fulfilled the purpose for which they had been sent. Neither of them can be called Lord, because each is called an angel, each is called a messenger, because neither one is called Lord but rather a minister [of the Lord]. They were sent in attendance upon him, to lead away Lot, a just man, to separate him from the impious, but not to assume the name of the deity or of a ruling power that did not belong to them.[10] Nor does the fact that Lot called them lords, that he worshiped them, that he supplicated them, persuade us. For it is a human custom that sometimes peers are called lords honorifically by those equal in rank, and sometimes the greater are called lords by their inferiors. It was an ancient custom, and it remains a modern custom, for supplicants to worship either with the entire body prostrate or partly prostrate, except for that singular cult of worship by which the deity honors humans with a kind of reciprocal veneration. It is a common custom, hidden from no one, by which humans often repeat prayers to each other, for whatever purposes, and grant to each other what they ask for. Often, one reads that the saintly men did this and either honored each other with such rites, or honored the angels who appeared to them. In this way, in this usual rite of human veneration, Lot worshiped the angels, called them lords, and prayed to them, but not, I say, in the manner in which divinity is worshiped. For their own words declared to Lot that they were angels and not God, not lords, but ministers [of the Lord]. They said, "We will destroy this place because their cry has grown loud before the God who sent us to slay them."[11] Therefore, those who were sent to destroy the place were certainly not lords but ministers of the Lord who sent them, although not only good angels but even wicked angels are read to have brought injuries and various wounds upon men. This was demonstrated for Job himself,[12] and it was dem-

---

8. Cf. Gn 19.1.   9. Cf. Gn 19.15–17.
10. Cf. Gn 19.1–2, 18.   11. Gn 19.13.
12. Cf. Jb 1.6; 4.18.

onstrated for those of whom it is written: "He sent the wrath of his indignation against them, wrath and indignation and trouble, which he sent by wicked angels."[13] Nor is it persuasive that one of the angels who appeared said: "Behold also in this, I have heard your prayers, not to destroy the city for which you have spoken."[14] Now here, like one surpassing the measure of an angel, he seems to adopt for himself God's persona, like the one that the same text in Genesis introduced speaking to Abraham, saying: "Behold, an angel of the Lord called out from heaven: Abraham, Abraham."[15] And in the intervening verse:[16] "Now I know that you fear God and you have not spared your only-begotten son on account of me."[17] Scripture clearly named him as an angel, whereas now the same angel says: "You have not spared your only-begotten son on account of me."[18] Nevertheless, Abraham did not spare his son, not for an angel's sake but for God's sake. Therefore, with these words it seems that the same angel had assumed for himself the persona of God, or that God had spoken in the angel. So perhaps it is the same even in this case. But whether this is the case or not, the angels appearing to Lot were angels, as was said, not God; they were ministers and not Lords, serving and not commanding, beseeching and not ruling. From these passages it is clear that "the Lord rained down from the Lord"[19] was not said about any of them. For the angels are not called lords, the "spirits of the administrator"[20] are not called lords, but he alone, he truly, he perfectly is called Lord who said through Moses, O Jews, to your fathers: "Hear, O Israel, the Lord your God the Lord is one."[21] Surely he is the one God, he is the one Lord of whom our apostle, even though you do not believe him, said: "One God the Father from whom are all things and One Lord Jesus Christ through whom are all things."[22] Your Scripture, when it says, "The Lord rained down

---

13. Ps 77.49.   14. Gn 19.21.
15. Gn 22.11.
16. Note that Peter seems to confuse the order of these two verses.
17. Gn 22.12.   18. Ibid.
19. Gn 19.24.
20. Heb 1.14. Note the Vulg. reads *administratorii spiritus,* the ministering spirits.
21. Dt 6.4; cf. Mk 12.29.   22. Cf. 1 Cor 8.6.

from the Lord,"[23] says this about this Lord the Father, about this Lord the Son. Plainly the Lord rained down from the Lord, the Son from the Father, God from God, who, just as it has to be the case that God exists from God, just as it has to be the case that the Lord exists from the Lord, so too he has to exist from him essentially, to recompense the just, punish sinners, glorify the good, and condemn the profane. He did this even then when "he rained brimstone and fire from the Lord of heaven upon Sodom and Gomorrah."[24] For the words "to rain," "to shower," "to thunder," and the like are not appropriate for any creature but indicate only the Author of creation, who produces them when he wills and produces them as he wills. The words of the Book of Kings also suggest this: "The Lord sent thunder (*voces*) and rains on that day."[25] And one reads in the text of the Psalms too: "The Lord thundered from heaven and the Most High gave his voice (*vox*)."[26] And in Exodus: "The whole people saw the thunder (*voces*) and lamps and the sound of the trumpet and the smoking mountain."[27] Observe then, O Jews, that Christ is called Lord and God in your Scriptures. Do not deny that he is Lord, do not deny that he is also God, lest perhaps he rain down brimstone and fire from the Lord from heaven upon you blasphemers just as upon the impious, and fulfill in you what one reads in the psalm: "He will rain snares upon sinners; fire, brimstone, and storms of winds will be the portion of their cup."[28]

But perhaps you will say: you affirm that Christ is indeed called Lord, as appears to you to be the case from the Scriptures, and on that basis you want to compel us to confess that he is also God. But after having put aside for some considerable period of time this name of Lord [you say], demonstrate clearly that he is also called God from the same Scriptures. And I would do this surely if I thought that you are people who listen, or rather if I thought that you are people capable of understanding, which is the whole matter. Hear, then, once again your David—or, much more so, ours—who has been oft named

23. Gn 19.24.
25. 1 Sm 12.18.
27. Ex 20.18.

24. Gn 19.4.
26. Ps 17.14.
28. Ps 10.7.

and who ought to be called upon often. "Your throne, O God," he said, "is forever and ever; the scepter of your kingdom is a scepter of uprightness. You have loved justice, and hated iniquity; therefore, God your God has anointed you with the oil of gladness above your fellows."[29] Who is speaking? According to us, it is God the Father; according to you, it is David himself. To whom is he speaking? According to us, God the Father is speaking to his Son; according to you, David himself is speaking to his son, the king. For the moment, having put aside our understanding of it, let your psalm be interpreted in that way. Let us see whether these words can be appropriate to King Solomon or to someone else from his lineage, that is, to anyone at all other than Christ. As was said, I say that according to you David speaks to his son Solomon or to someone else, based on the following: "Your throne, O God, is forever."[30] And surely you can pervert the words of the psalm that precede or follow this and, in your fashion, perhaps twist them into this meaning or that. But what about these words? In what sense, with what cunning, by what overly strained interpretation will you be able to apply these sacred words to any mortal being but Christ? "Your throne," he said, "O God." For what reason, with what boldness is a man called God by the prophet?

But you will say, God said to Moses: "I have appointed you the god of Pharaoh."[31] And you will add that it is written in the Psalms that "God has stood in the congregation of gods, and being in the midst of them he judges gods."[32] Nor will you omit this: "I have said: You are gods."[33] And we have known these [passages], O Jews. They are clear, they are manifest, they could not be hidden from us. They are not called gods because some deity existed in them, but rather they were preferred by God over certain others because of some preeminence, some dignity or holiness. You yourselves know this as well, that they were not called gods by God because they *were* gods, but because God preferred them to others because of some excellent grace. But the one to whom David spoke is not called "God" in this sense

29. Ps 44.7–8.   30. Ps 44.7.
31. Ex 7.1.   32. Ps 81.1.
33. Ps 81.6.

by him. What follows indicates this: "Forever. Your throne," he said, "O God, is forever."[34] No throne of a king or an earthly prince will remain forever. Contradict this if you can and show me the throne of any mortal whatsoever that can last forever. But you cannot. Nature opposes this, the world contradicts it, and every person denies this. Therefore, it is necessary for you to confess that this cannot be the throne of any king whatsoever, but only of God himself. Moreover, the God whom it concerns is none other than Christ himself.

And what follows in this verse declares this. For it is not a different person that says to the same God: "The scepter of your kingdom is a scepter of uprightness."[35] And immediately after that: "You have loved justice, and hated iniquity; therefore God, your God, has anointed you with the oil of gladness."[36] If this God is anointed, then certainly Christ is God. In fact, we proclaim that the one that is anointed, whom you call the messiah but whom we just as clearly as you call the Christ, is Christ.[37] Only the languages are different, while the meaning of the languages is the same. There are two sounds, but only one meaning. Therefore, the God who is anointed is Christ, and the anointed, that is, Christ, is God. "He has anointed you," he said, "God your God."[38] Pay attention, Jews! Not merely once does he call him God. Previously he had called him God, when he said: "Your throne, O God."[39] Now he calls him God again when he says: "God has anointed you."[40] In fact what follows, "Your God," is already in a different case. Actually, when he said God the first time, it was in the vocative case, while in the second instance it is a nominative case.[41] As if to say: "O God, God has anointed

34. Ps 44.7.   35. Ibid.
36. Ps 44.8.

37. Peter plays on the terms "messiah" and *Christus,* which both mean "anointed one."

38. Ps 44.8.   39. Ps 44.7.
40. Ps 44.8.

41. In fact, in Latin the vocative singular of the noun *Deus* is *Deus,* and is indistinguishable from the nominative case. Only in the plural (*di*) would it have a different form. Peter relies on the repetition "God your God," with the addition of the possessive pronoun, to support the inference that the first "God" is a vocative, and then a nominative singular second declension noun.

you." Do you see yet that not only once but twice in two con-
nected verses Christ is so transparently, so clearly called God
by the great prophet? Now, with what animus, with what boldness will you dare to deny that Christ is God? Therefore confess,
confess, even if somewhat late, that Christ is God, whom the
greatest of your prophets so splendidly proclaims to be God.
Whose "throne," according to the same prophet, is not of any
sort whatsoever but is such that it "remains forever."[42] But who is
the God by whom this God has been anointed? Actually, I read
it this way: "O God, your God has anointed you."[43] You have acknowledged that God has anointed; acknowledge then also that
God has been anointed! See, if nevertheless it has been granted
to you [to do so], what previously you were unable to see. Observe at last that it is necessary for there to be one who anoints,
and another who is anointed. Nonetheless, your prophet calls
both the one and the other God. In fact, both the one who is
anointed is called God, and the one who anoints is called God.
Why do you struggle? There is no escape. It is your Scripture
that is recited; it is your prophet who speaks, or, rather, they
are God's words that he speaks. Be silent, therefore, and now at
least understand that, constrained on all sides by divine power,
God and [your] God can be none other than the Father and
the Son. That it is the Father who, as is proved in other places
of Scripture, says to the Son: "Today I have begotten you," and
"before the day star I begot you."[44] It is the Son that called upon
the same Father, as the Father himself says elsewhere concerning this same Son: "He will call out to me: You are my Father."[45]
God the Son has been anointed by this God the Father, Christ
has been anointed, not insofar as he is God but insofar as he is
man. God the Father can add nothing to God the Son insofar
as it pertains to the nature of God. Insofar as concerns the same
divine essence, God the Father, who conferred all things upon
him at once by generating him eternally and ineffably, was able

42. Ps 44.7.
43. That is, Peter inserts a comma after "O God," which is not present in the
Vulg., in order to underscore the distinction between vocative and nominative
forms.
44. Ps 2.7; Heb 1.5; 5.5; Ps 109.3.
45. Ps 88.27.

to confer nothing by bestowing it upon him. But truly he conferred many things; truly he granted many things to the human nature that was assumed by his Son, through which nature, as an intermediary, the man who had been cast away from before God, evicted from God's paradise, transformed from a servant into God's worst enemy, was once again restored to and united to God. Therefore, insofar as he is human, God the Christ was anointed by God the Father with oil—not that oil with which kings were once anointed among you—but with the "oil of gladness,"[46] with the oil of grace, by which even that human [nature], once it had been assumed by God, was deified by that same assumption, and the entire world was reconciled to God, glorified, and saved. So then, read, understand, and explain in the Christian fashion and not in Jewish error, "Your throne O God is forever,"[47] and, "God your God has anointed you with the oil of gladness"![48]

And even though these are sufficient to prove Christ's deity, even for dull minds, nonetheless let there come into [our] midst either a prophet or a prophetic man, Baruch, the prophet Jeremiah's secretary or colleague. Let him come and, although drawing the spirit from the heart of another, from the prophetic heart of Jeremiah, let him reveal what he understands concerning Christ's deity, not through shadows but openly and clearly, just as one dedicated to prophecy. Surely he adds here, after he had set forth many things that have to do with God: "Here," he said, "is our God, and no other will be accounted like him. He found out all the way of knowledge, and gave it to Jacob his servant and to Israel his beloved. Afterwards he was seen upon earth, and conversed with men."[49] What is clearer? What is more fully revealed? He calls [him] God. Whom? He who "found out all the way of knowledge."[50] What way? The one, namely, that he "gave to Jacob his servant and to Israel his beloved."[51] And what way of knowledge did God give to Jacob or Israel other than the precepts that he handed down to your first ancestors, other than the law that he gave through Moses? Plainly this God, who

46. Ps 44.8.
48. Ps 44.8.
50. Bar 3.37.

47. Ps 44.7.
49. Bar 3.36–38.
51. Ibid.

found every way of knowledge, who gave it through the fathers, who gave it to Israel particularly through Moses, "was seen on earth, and conversed with men."[52] Analyze this, unravel this, explain in some other way, if you can, how the God who gave the law to Israel through Moses was seen on earth, explain how he conversed with men.

But perhaps you will respond: God was seen by Jacob, God conversed with Jacob when, as is said in Scripture, a certain "man wrestled with him until morning,"[53] and about whom Jacob himself said: "I have seen the Lord face to face, and my soul has been saved."[54] Perhaps you will say that God was seen on earth in this manner by many people. You will add, so I think, that "God was seen by men and conversed with men"[55] at the time when Moses ascended the mountain and was with God for forty days,[56] [and] when God sounded from Mount Sinai in a loud corporeal or audible noise to the people arrayed below.[57]

But, in order to overturn your objections briefly, neither Jacob nor Moses nor the people nor anyone whatsoever was able to see God, as God himself attests. Remember that God spoke thus to Moses: "No man will see me and live."[58] When, therefore, they still lived in the flesh, they could not see God. But I believe that you will agree that those whom this passage concerns lived in the flesh. Therefore, it is necessary that you concede that none of them could see God. But, in truth, they saw some images representing God's persona, [and] they heard some noises and a corporeal sound offered up not from God's essence but by God's command. Now, it is not merely the passage that I set forth—"no man will see me and live"—that proves the fact that they did not see God himself, that they did not hear the sound (*vox*) of his divine and uncircumscribed essence, but also what one reads in Exodus concerning the people of Israel: "Go down," God said to Moses, "and charge the people, lest they should have a mind to pass the limits to see the Lord, and a very great multitude of them should perish."[59] And

52. Cf. Bar 3.38.
54. Gn 32.30.
56. Cf. Gn 24.18.
58. Ex 33.20.

53. Gn 32.24.
55. Bar 3.38.
57. Cf. Gn 19.17–20.
59. Ex 19.21.

a little after that: "Moreover, let not the priests and the people pass the limits, nor come up to the Lord, lest he kill them."[60] How will you be able to say, O Jew, that God was seen on earth and conversed with men at that time, when he forbade them to cross the limits to see him, when he threatened transgressors with death, when he said not only with reference to the people but also to the priests: "let them not pass the limits, nor come up to the Lord, lest he kill them"?[61] Therefore, he was not seen on earth then nor did he converse with men. Then when? When, if not at the time when, according to our Gospel, "the Word was made flesh and dwelled among us,"[62] and when, according to Wisdom's words, which your Solomon wrote down, which said, "My delights were to be with the children of men,"[63] the Wisdom of God, having put on flesh, conversed with the children of men? Therefore, only then, truly only then, and not before and not afterward, your God, who found every way of knowledge and who had given it to Jacob his servant and to Israel his beloved through Moses, was seen on earth and conversed with men. Nonetheless, the passage noted above remains: "No man will see me and live."[64] In fact, God, who, according to our Apostle, "was in Christ, reconciling the world to himself,"[65] was not invisible to mortal man, was seen on earth, but, according to the man he had put on, with whom he had cloaked his immense majesty, truly and without a doubt was seen on earth and conversed with men. Thus the one plainly seen by men, who conversed among men, that prophetic man calls God, not a foreign God but his own, your God, the God of all the Jews, when he says: "This is our God, and no other will be accounted like him."[66]

What more do you want? Do not so many divine testimonies now completely satisfy you that the Christ whom we worship, whom we preach, is our God, is your God, is the God of all? Or do you want still more testimonies to be presented? Indeed, they are infinite and cannot be expounded in a short text but

60. Ex 19.24.
62. Jn 1.14.
64. Ex 33.20.
66. Bar 3.36.

61. Ibid.
63. Prv 8.31.
65. 2 Cor 5.19.

would require many more volumes. But even though the proposed brevity should suffer, after the others you have already
heard listen not only to a prophetic man but to the greatest of
the prophets, Isaiah.

Return to us then, great Isaiah, and the one you had reported to be the Christ, the Son of God from eternity, declare also
to the Jews to be God that is born on earth from a virgin. Indeed, they are Jews, [but] they are stones, just as you experienced yourself, and they do not listen to the prophets but they
are their persecutors and murderers.[67] Nonetheless talk, speak,
do what you must, so that the Jews will either believe you and
be converted or, if they are unwilling to believe, "let them be
turned back and confounded," according to their psalm.[68] Nor
will your instruction, which unlocks divine secrets, be able to fail
to achieve the best outcome for the world, to which, if the Jew
has scorned it, the Christian will listen, which, if a few of those
incapable of believing have cast it aside, the infinite expanse
of the lands of the world will accept and venerate. He said, "A
child is born to us, a son is given to us."[69] What else? This is common. In fact, many children are born to men, many sons are
given to men by God. "The government is upon his shoulder."[70]
And this too can be said about many. For many have ruled and
do rule on the earth. "And his name will be called wonderful."[71]
Now with this the child you mentioned, the son you named, is
distinguished from the ruler common to others. "Counselor."[72]
And here again he implies something great and unique. But
there follows: "God."[73] Do you hear, Jews? That a "child is born,"
that a "son is given," of whom it is said that "the government is
upon his shoulder,"[74] and of whom it is written that he is "marvelous," who is called "counselor," and is even called "God" by
the prophet. What more do you want? Or what will you be able
to grumble about? Be ashamed, wretches, be ashamed and acquiesce to a truth so lucid, so splendid that even you perceive
that you cannot refute it. The great man Isaiah, a great prophet,

67. Cf. Heb 11.37.   68. Ps 34.4.
69. Is 9.6.   70. Ibid.
71. Ibid.   72. Ibid.
73. Ibid.   74. Ibid.

filled with God, a friend of God, known to you, known to the world, said this: "The name" of the child "will be called wonderful, counselor, God."[75] But attend to what follows as well: "Mighty." Now it is clear to everyone that the one who is "God" is also "mighty," that he is both the source of might and the Lord of hosts.[76] But what else? "Father of the world to come."[77]

Who is speaking? The prophet. When is he speaking? Certainly in this life and surely in this world. Then to what does "Father of the world to come"[78] refer? Clearly not to that world in which he lived, in which he spoke. For that world was present. Therefore, he did not speak of the present world but of some other: "Father of the world to come."[79] And what world is that? Surely, one that is invisible to mortals, surely one that is everlasting. And who can be the father of that world other than God? Now since only God can properly be called the father of this visible and transitory world, how much less can anyone other than God alone be called the father of this invisible and eternal world? Therefore, it is necessary that the one who is called the father of the world to come also be believed to be God. But if perhaps with Jewish cunning you should say that that child is called the father of that world, when he is said to be its father, because he was going to rule it, because it did not yet exist and certainly was to be in the future, neither will this explanation prevail nor can this Jewish interpretation stand. In fact, the things that came before overturn this understanding. How so? Because he is called "God."[80] You yourselves profess, however, that no earthly king, no temporal prince could be God, or can be God. Whence, moreover, it follows from your understanding that the one who is called God is not said to be a temporal king or prince of this world by the prophet. If this is true, then "Father of the world to come"[81] is not said of this present world. "Prince of Peace."[82] Neither can this be understood of anyone other than God. Now, any man can be called a peace-lover, a friend of peace, a follower of peace, a son of peace, and things

75. Ibid.
77. Is 9.6.
79. Ibid.
81. Ibid.

76. Cf. Ps 23.10.
78. Ibid.
80. Ibid.
82. Ibid.

like these. But only God can be understood to be the "Prince of Peace," the father of peace, the source of peace. Turn the sacred pages and, if I am not mistaken, you will see that these names are only applied to God. Because this is true, only God is called the prince of peace by the prophet. Plainly he, surely he is called the prince of peace who governs peace in such a way as to say that it is his, so that he who was about to suffer and die would bestow it, just as if it were his own property, upon his disciples, saying: "My peace I give unto you, peace I leave unto you."[83] Here is truly, I say, the "prince of peace,"[84] who also after he rose from the dead, appearing to the disciples, solemnly used this same word, peace, in his first utterance, saying: "Peace be with you."[85] It is not hidden from us—which perhaps you do not know—that in the past the seventy translators who your Josephus reports were directed by the priest Eleazar to translate the sacred Scriptures from the Hebrew language into Greek for Ptolemy,[86] the king of the Egyptians, kept silent regarding those six sublime names of the child that was born, and translated in their place "angel of great counsel."[87] But they did this, as your authorities as well as ours report, in order not to scandalize the king, who already worshiped one God,[88] or so that objections concerning the deity of the human Christ not disturb once more rather than instruct one that had recently cast aside the worship of idols, while he was still unable to penetrate the summit of so great a mystery. But whether they did this for this reason or with some other intention, what is it to you? If the Greek books do not have these names, the Hebrew books do. If a Greek does not have them, a Hebrew does. But read Isaiah again, reexamine those passages, and believe your texts rather than my words, and rather than believe foreign books, admit your own.

Now that these things have been presented, proceed to the

83. Cf. Jn 14.27.   84. Is 9.6.
85. Jn 20.19, 21; Lk 24.36.
86. Josephus, *Antiquitates, Books 12–14*, 12.2.5–8, 11, trans. Ralph Marcus (Cambridge, MA: Harvard University Press, 1957), 23–28, 42–46.
87. Is 9.6 LXX.
88. Cf. Jerome, *Commentarii in Isaiam* 9.6/7, ed. M. Adriaen, CC SL 73 (Turnholt: Brepols, 1963), 127; B.T. *Megillah* 9a.

following: "His empire will be multiplied."[89] Whose empire?
That of the aforementioned child. What follows? "And there
will be no end to peace."[90] And halt your step here, Jews. What
is this empire that is so multiplied, that it is written that its peace
will have no end? Who is that child, who is that son, whose empire is not only proclaimed to be very long-lasting, not only everlasting, but even is called eternal? Untie this knot if you can;
explain the link of this question: "His empire will be multiplied
and his peace will have no end."[91] And what, or rather whose,
is the throne of an empire as great as this? He said, "Upon the
throne of David and upon his kingdom."[92]

Run through and enumerate all the kings from David's stock,
from David himself or his son Solomon to the very last kings of
the Davidic line, I mean Joachim and Zedekiah, of whom the
former, after having voluntarily put aside his kingdom, surren-
dered to the Babylonians, while the latter, after having been captured by them by force of war, was led as a captive to Babylon,
once his eyes had been plucked out.[93] See whether this passage
suits either of them. It certainly does not suit either of them, as
you perceive, as is perfectly clear, nor are these sacred passages
that have been presented appropriate to that good king Josiah,
to whom some of you, as I once heard, like dreamers argue that
they apply.[94] But is Josiah "God"?[95] Is he "the father of the world
to come"?[96] Is he the "prince of peace"?[97] Did not the end of
his kingdom follow very quickly upon peace? Was not he, who
reigned but a very brief time, slain on the field of Megiddo by
Neco, king of the Egyptians?[98] And, once he was slain, did not
the peace of his empire come to an end with his own life? In
fact, after a few years elapsed, there followed the destruction
of your city,[99] the burning of God's temple, the captivity of the
Jews, and their migration to Babylon. Therefore, it is particularly erroneous and very foolish to apply these prophetic pas-

89. Is 9.7.   90. Ibid.
91. Ibid.   92. Ibid.
93. Cf. 2 Kgs 25.7.
94. Cf. Rashi, ad Thren. 4, 20 acc. to B.T. Taanith 22b.
95. Is 9.6.   96. Ibid.
97. Ibid.   98. Cf. 2 Chr 35.22–24.
99. I.e., Jerusalem.

sages to Josiah. Actually, it is ridiculous, not to be tolerated by human ears, to think that these passages, which can only be applied to God and to the God Christ, can be applied to Josiah or to any king of the Jews or of any other people. He said, "Upon the throne of David and upon his kingdom."[100] What about the end? "To confirm it and strengthen it in judgment and justice now and forever."[101] And to whom but to God, I say, to whom but to God do these words apply? Who can surely confirm the throne of any kingdom, who can strengthen it "in judgment and justice now and forever"?[102] Can a man? But can one who is not eternal confirm the throne of his kingdom forever? Is it not clear, is it not transparent even to the blind that something can be confirmed forever only by one who is everlasting? Because they cannot oppose this, then, because neither any Jew nor heathen nor Satan will prevail contrariwise against such obvious truth,[103] it is certain that the child who is designated by the divine utterances as God is none other than our Christ. Therefore, it follows that Christ is the everlasting and true God.

Now, you will either give me another child or give me another son of whom all these things can be understood; or, if you cannot (which in fact you cannot), necessarily you will be compelled to understand that that child, that son, of whom so many divine things are written, is none other than Christ our Lord. He is a child in terms of the stages of human life; in terms of being born, he is born in a wondrous and unique fashion, the son of a virgin, perpetually united to deity with respect to the nature of the humanity he assumed; he is "wonderful," he is "counselor," he is "God," he is "mighty," he is the "prince of peace," he is the "father of the world to come."[104] His empire is multiplied unceasingly by an infinite number of all peoples; the peace of his kingdom never ends; his throne is confirmed and strengthened not merely for many years like that of mortal kings, but forevermore, like that of an eternal king.[105]

But I know, O Jew, that you can be overcome when pressed by so many powerful proof-texts, you can be overwhelmed,

---

100. Is 9.7.
102. Ibid.
104. Is 9.6.

101. Ibid.
103. Reading *contrarie* for *contraire*.
105. Cf. Is 9.7.

but perhaps still you cannot believe. Why is this? Because you are confounded to believe in the God-man, you are ashamed to confess the God-man. In your mind, the human condition is vile; you think that it is unworthy of the name or honor of divine majesty. If you contemplate its humble character, you will perceive its sublimity.[106] It seems to you that things so high cannot befit those so humble, that things so sublime cannot befit those so abject, that is, things divine cannot befit humans. Surely this is the entire reason why you remain incredulous, why you resist God, why you do not believe your own Scriptures, which proclaim everywhere, over and over, that Christ is God. And do you think, O fool, that the understanding of divine sublimity and of human humility will have escaped Christian wisdom? In truth, I say, the Christian is struck dumb by a work of God that is so sublime and ineffable, nor is it sufficient to marvel at so singular a miracle of the deity. But it is one thing to marvel and believe, and another to marvel and condemn. The Christian marvels and is illuminated; the Jew marvels and is made blind. The Christian marvels and praises God in a singular fashion for a solitary miracle, while the Jew marvels and blasphemes. Nor, when marveling at something so great, does the Jew follow the prudence of his prophets, who, knowing and foretelling things future, did not spurn them, but trembled even while marveling at them and foretelling them.

These are the words of one of them: "O Lord, I have heard your hearing, and I was afraid. I have considered your works, and I have trembled."[107] What did he fear, why did he tremble? Listen: "O Lord, your work." What work? Was it perhaps the formation of the world? But the words that follow contradict this view. He said, "In the midst of years bring it to life."[108] And surely the work of heaven or earth (that is, of those things that are in them) had already been created a long time ago and had already been brought to life with respect to the appropriate differences of the parts. Therefore, it is another work that

106. Or, possibly: If you contemplate his humble character, you will perceive his sublimity.
107. Hab 3.2 LXX.
108. Hab 3.2.

he fears here, another at which he trembles, another which he
pleads be brought to life in the midst of years, that he not only
pleads be brought to life but even foretells that it will have to be
known when he adds: "In the midst of the years you will make it
known."[109] Investigate, O Jew, what work this can be that Habak-
kuk the prophet marveled at and that he prayed be completely
fulfilled. Surely all of the miracles or wondrous acts performed
among the Jews had already occurred before this prophet. Nor
were there any remaining of those that you read about in your
canon, at which you are wont to marvel. Therefore, either show
me another work so marvelous (whether fulfilled or to be fulfilled) by which the prophet ought to be shaken by God, or,
if you cannot, acknowledge that the work so to be feared, so
much to be wished for, was consummated in the Son of God
when he assumed the nature of man for the salvation of men.
Because the prophet saw that this work is more excellent than
all of God's works, he both marveled at it and feared it. And
lest one think that he feared it by denying or fleeing from it,
he also pleaded that it be fulfilled. This is surely the work about
which Isaiah, who most frequently unlocked the secret works
to be accomplished by God, was not silent, [saying] that the
work is strange to God and yet is God himself. "That he may
do his work," he said, "his strange work. That he may perform
his work, his work is strange to him."[110] For what work of God
was stranger to God than that one in which a human was per-
sonally united to God? That "heaven, earth, the sea, and what
are contained in them"[111] were created by him was not a work
strange to God. But neither were lesser nor even the greatest
miracles that he performed at any time works strange to God.
That truly the lowest human was united to the highest God:
then in truth, only then was there a work that was strange to
him. This is what Jeremiah spoke of: "How long will you be dissolute in deliciousness, O wandering daughter? for the Lord
will create a new thing upon the earth."[112] What new thing?
How is there anything new on earth? For Solomon said: "There
is nothing new on the earth, nor will anyone be able to say, Be-

109. Ibid.   110. Is 28.21.
111. Cf. Ex 20.11.   112. Jer 31.22.

hold, this is new."[113] What, then, is this new thing? "Woman," he
said, "will compass a man."[114] Explain this in a Jewish fashion,
if you can, O Jew! How can a woman compass a man so that it
will be new? If with her hands or arms, this is not new. If she
is said to compass in her maternal body the infant whom she
bears in the womb, this is not new either. Actually, there is no
new way in which a woman is said to be able to compass a man.
Nonetheless, it is necessary for you to see some woman compass
a man in a manner that can be new, if the prophetic words are
to be safeguarded. But because you are unable to find that in
human practice, it is necessary for you to flee to the divine. It is
necessary, I say, that you flee to the divine and that you confess
together with me the one whom the Virgin carried, compassing
him in the virginal womb, conceiving by the Holy Spirit only,
[and] called Emmanuel, which in Latin means "God with us,"
that is, God made man.[115] For what purpose? So that you cease
to blaspheme and cease to be incredulous when looking upon
Christians, when you perceive that God's prophets were afraid,
marveled at, [and] revered this singular act of God by which
God, on account of his highness, deigned to be made man for
the sake of men. Neither should you draw away from the faith
nor turn back from the hope of your salvation, which is a great
reality that is upon you, one that is ineffable and incomprehensible. Now, just as you heard from your prophets, for God to be
made man was a work strange to God, so far as it pertains to the
difference of natures, but it was not strange to [his] mercy. But
the aforementioned prophet added to the words already indicated above, that God had to show mercy to man by assuming
the human into himself. In fact, after saying, "You will make it
known in the midst of years,"[116] he added: "When you are angry, you will recall your mercy."[117] Why, then, does it surprise
you so far as to unbelief, if God has mercy upon man through
the man that he assumed? See and reconsider that this work of
God, so strange and so foreign for him, did not turn those great
men away from faith in God nor urge them to blasphemy, but

113. Eccl 1.10.   114. Jer 31.22.
115. Cf. Mt 1.23.   116. Hab 3.2.
117. Ibid.

it supported them in admiration, it moved them to devotion. They understood that for a greater grace God had to be loved more, had to be glorified more. They did not know that the more guilty men are, the more they had to be scandalized by that, nor that the greater their debt, the more they had to rush ahead to cause injury. What was lacking to divine praise other than the assumption of human humility? It was certain that he is highest, that he is greatest, that he is almighty; no one except those great prophets believed that he would deign to become a humble man. Who could think, who could suspect, that one so great would receive the least, the greatest receive the small, the eternal receive the mortal, that immense majesty would receive into itself that human worm, so to speak, and bring it into God? This work of his must not be mocked, must not be blasphemed, because it surpasses all his works, but rather it ought to have drawn you thenceforth in a more sublime fashion to admire, to praise, and to glorify him above all his works. It is surprising that, as was said, Jew, although this work of his is the most excellent and chief among all his works, it provoked in you such obstinate unbelief.

Now why did the fact that God wished to speak to men through a man provoke scandal in man? Reread Exodus, and you will find that God conversed with Moses from a bramble-bush or from the flame of a bush.[118] Leaf through the books that follow, and you will find that from the golden propitiatory that was between the two cherubim [God] often presented replies to those seeking his counsel.[119] Nor should it slip your mind that God frequently appeared to and often spoke to the fathers by means of the airy bodies of angels. But neither the bush, nor its flame, nor that golden tablet of the propitiatory, nor an airy body temporarily assumed by angels, are equal to a man. As you know, man surpasses these as well as all [other] earthly creations, nor can he, for whose sake all things were created and to whom all things were subjected by God, become

118. Cf. Ex 3.2–4.
119. "Golden propitiatory": a covering for the ark of the covenant, upon which the Lord was supposed to rest his feet, and from which he showed mercy. Cf. Ex 25.17–22; Heb 9.5.

CHAPTER TWO   89

inferior or equal to them in any way whatsoever. But if he is not less than nor equal, then certainly he is greater. So, do you believe that God was able to speak to men from or through a lesser creation, but you do not believe that he wanted to speak to the same men through one greater than they? If he is believed to have provided responses to mortals from a bush, from the propitiatory, from insensible air, why is it denied that he spoke to mortals through the rational soul and sensible flesh he assumed? And although he did not assume those bodies with which or through which he spoke in the same way that he assumed the human [nature], he did not unite [those bodies] with himself for eternity as he did the human nature, nor did he deify it like the human [nature] that was assumed, nonetheless the one who was heard through a bush or the propitiatory, who spoke through an airy body, who appeared himself to men through an earthly, sensible, and animated body, thundered at men with a physical and audible sound. Therefore, be a Jew now, O Jew, not in perfidious obstinacy but with a true confession, so that the God who spoke to your fathers from inferior or by means of inferior creations you will confess to be the same God who appeared and spoke with men through the greater nature that was assumed, that is, a human nature.

But perhaps you still experience scandal, and, in order not to be compelled to think that God was encompassed in or polluted by the filth of a human body, you flee from confessing that he was incarnate or born of a virgin. You are afraid that if you confess that he is incarnate, you will also be compelled to confess that he was polluted from the flesh he received, or was defiled, so to speak, by the physical or spiritual uncleanness of sin. You also fear that you will be seen to be a blasphemer if you profess, if you believe, if you perceive that God labored, hungered, thirsted, wept, that, finally, he suffered, died, and was buried. But here your fear is foolish, and this fear or your suspicion is actually in vain. The Christian eye is not so blind, Jew, nor is Christian wisdom so foolish as to believe that one who cannot be contaminated is defiled either by the filth of human flesh, or by the crimes of the human soul, or that the impassible suffers, or that the immortal dies, or that he, who is the resurrection of all the dead, is buried in the fashion common to all men, in the way that you think. It knows and confesses with a mouth (*os*) shared by its Christians that God, insofar as it pertains to divine majesty, is not defiled by the filth (*feces*) of the flesh, nor polluted by human sins, neither can he be afflicted with the pains or miseries of a condemned nature. And let me show this to you very clearly with an analogy drawn from visible things: Can the light of the stars or the everlasting light of the sun or the nocturnal light of the moon, which is either cast in shadow by the clouds opposite it or shines brightly with rays that have been released from them, be defiled when it shines on very filthy places or places that cause filth? Or, can it be injured or wounded if it seems to be cut a thousand times by swords or daggers, with tremendous effort, or to be struck in vain with blows? Or can it be made filthy by contact with a filthy thing, or can it suffer pain from the cut of some blade? The Christian "with the heart, believes unto justice, and with the mouth, makes confession unto salvation"[120] that the essence of the deity absolutely never can be defiled, absolutely never can be wounded, absolutely never can suffer torment or pain in such a manner. This is why he proclaims that the Son of God, who assumed human flesh united to a soul from a virgin womb, and afterwards, conversing among men in that very human substance, not only could not have been polluted by any filth of flesh or spirit, but [the Christian] even confirms that the very nature that [the Son of God] assumed and the Virgin from whom he assumed that nature actually had been cleansed by him from every remnant (*faex*) of sin. This is why he understands and confesses that when God hungered with a flesh that hungered, or thirsted with a flesh that thirsted, or wept with a flesh that wept, or suffered with a flesh that suffered, or died with a flesh that died, or was buried with a flesh that was buried, this does not pertain to the unity of the one person from different substances so much as it pertains to a property of one of these substances.

Remove scandal of foolishness from your heart, then, O Jew, exclude a bestial understanding from your mind, because the

120. Rom 10.10.

true reception of human flesh does not preclude the true deity of Christ, because God is not defiled, God does not suffer, God is not humiliated on account of the man that was assumed, but instead man is cleansed, glorified, and exalted on account of the God who assumes, purifies, and even deifies him.

Now indeed the things that have already been presented to show that Christ is true God can suffice for every human being except one hard as a rock. But nonetheless, in order not only to crush but even to bury the wicked head of the serpent[121] with an even greater collection of statements, let Micah also approach and say what he thinks about the deity of Christ.[122] He was not afraid of the impious king, Ahab, nor from fear of him nor because of [the king's] favor (*gratia*) did he remain silent concerning the truth. Let him act thus now against the impious Jews, let him not dread either those stones with which stony men are wont to rush forth against the prophets: "And you," he said, "Bethlehem Effrata, are you a little one among the thousands of Judah? Out of you will come to me the one who will be the ruler of Israel."[123] Behold, O holy prophet, you say that the ruler of Israel will come forth out of Bethlehem, that is, he will be born in Bethlehem and will go forth from there. But there were many rulers of Israel, and there can be still. Express this more openly, and differentiate this ruler of Israel from the other rulers of Israel. He said, "And his going forth [is] from the beginning, from the days of eternity."[124] What are you doing, Jews? Is there one you can find among all your kings, from among all the rulers of Israel, whose going forth can be "from the beginning, from the days of eternity"? In fact, whose going forth can be said to be from the beginning, other than God's, whose days can be said to be the days of eternity, except God's? Without a doubt his going forth is from the beginning, his coming forth is from the days of eternity, whose temporal birth was in Bethlehem from a virgin mother and whose everlasting ori-

---

121. Cf. Gn 3.15.
122. Cf. 1 Kgs 22.8–28; but cf. Mi 1.1. The editor of the text remarks that Peter has confused the prophet Micah the Morasthite with Micaiah the son of Jemla.
123. Mi 5.2.
124. Ibid.

gin came from God the Father before every creature. Plainly it
is his going forth from the days of eternity that is mentioned under Wisdom's name, in the Book of Wisdom: "I was set up from
eternity, and of old before the earth was made. The depths were
not as yet, and I had already been conceived. Neither had the
fountains of waters as yet sprung out. The mountains with their
huge bulk had not as yet been established. I was born before the
hills. He had not yet made the earth, or the rivers, or the poles
of the world."[125] Therefore, the going forth of this wisdom, the
going forth of this Son of God, who was born according to the
flesh in Bethlehem but born according to deity from the Father
from the beginning, is from the days of eternity. Bring forth
some other, O Jews, if you have one, of whom these things can
be said! You do not have one. Therefore, if you believe your
prophet, it is necessary for you to accept this one.

After him, let David return, he who at the time "was seen" to
have withdrawn "with a strong hand," [126] and whom none of his
enemies could resist; let him conquer completely the Jews, who
have now become his enemies. The Philistine failed and perished from the stone that he threw; let the Jewish enemy, worse
than the Philistine, fall and perish by the sacred words that he
hurled.[127]

He said, "God, give your judgment to the king and your justice to the son of the king."[128] Who is speaking, Jews? You reply: David. To whom is he speaking? To God. Of whom does he
speak? Of a king and a king's son. And who is the king, and the
king's son? You reply: Solomon. And you add: The title of the
psalm that you propose, which is "A Psalm of David on Solomon,"[129] indicates as much. Therefore, according to you David
is speaking of his son Solomon in this psalm. Let us see, then, if
everything in this psalm fits Solomon. And answer in what sense
you will apply to Solomon the things I introduce that it seems
are able to be applied in some manner to Solomon according
to a Jewish interpretation: "And he will continue with the sun,
and before the moon, throughout all the generations."[130] How

125. Prv 8.23–26.   126. Cf. Bar 3.38.
127. Cf. 1 Sm 17.49–51.   128. Ps 71.2.
129. Ps 71.1.   130. Ps 71.5.

could one who reigned only forty years remain with the sun? Do you not observe the sun in the heaven every day? Do you not know that Solomon died 2,000 years ago? Open your eyes then, open your eyes and, as I said, look upon the sun in the heaven and remember that Solomon is placed in a grave. How, then, has Solomon continued, or how could he continue with the sun? Pay attention, too, to "before the moon."[131] Is this not even more absurd? Was not the moon created not only before Solomon but before every human being? And was not Solomon, David's son, not only born after his father but even after many generations of mortal men? How, then, has he continued or does he continue with the sun, how has he continued or does he continue before the moon, throughout all generations when, as already was mentioned, he died many ages earlier with the sun still continuing, and he was born many ages after the moon had already existed? But one must not tarry any longer over things that are so clear. Run through the psalm and read the verse contained there: "Justice and an abundance of peace will arise in his days."[132] But, according to you, in some way this can stand. But how will what follows stand: "Until the moon be taken away"?[133] Does not the moon still continue, and did not the "abundance of peace," which existed during Solomon's age only in the kingdom of the Jews, die out once he had died? Pay attention: both of these are true! Pay attention to your Scripture that says in the third book of Kings: "In the fifth year of the reign of Rehoboam, Shishak the king of the Egyptians came up against Jerusalem and he took away the treasures of the house of the Lord, and the king's treasures, and carried all off. Also the shields of gold that Solomon had made, and King Rehoboam made shields of brass instead of them."[134] And so as not to seem to provide only one witness from your canon concerning this matter, reread your *Debreiamin*,[135] and if your jealous eye should find anything there different from what I have proposed, then

131. Ibid.　　　　132. Ps 71.7.
133. Ibid.　　　　134. 1 Kgs 14.25–27.
135. Peter refers here to First and Second Chronicles, which in Hebrew are known as *Dibre Haijamim*. Cf. Petrus Alfonsi, *Dialogue Against the Jews*, trans. Resnick, 193.

convict me of deception. Each book already mentioned reports that "in the fifth year of the reign of Rehoboam"[136] "the abundance of the peace"[137] of Solomon was extinguished. Extinguished, I say, by Shishak the king of Egypt "with 2,000 chariots and 60,000 horsemen and a people beyond number"[138] falling upon Judea, extinguished by him when he seized "the strongest cities of Judah with an army of Libyan Trogodites and Ethiopians,"[139] extinguished, or to speak more gently, breached, "having taken away the treasures of the house of the Lord, and the king's treasures,"[140] and all the other things written of above, while granting a rich booty to his own kingdom. But if these things occurred in the fifth year of King Rehoboam, son of Solomon, then what you want to apply to Solomon, from psalms that are truthful, is false: "Justice and an abundance of peace will arise in his days until the moon be taken away."[141] Now, on the one hand, justice arose before him, and it arose especially after him, and the abundance of peace that charmed the Jews so very seductively in his days was extinguished in the fifth year [of the reign] of his son Rehoboam, as was already established. I remain silent concerning the loss of the ten tribes by Rehoboam. I remain silent concerning the almost continuous war between the two kingdoms, which from a single kingdom had been made into two, that is, Judah and Israel, as the Jews' sins deserved.[142] It was continuous or almost continuous from Rehoboam, namely, the king of Judah, until Shalmaneser, king of the Assyrians. Under him, lest the daily strife drag out too long, it happened that ten tribes were captured from the twelve tribes of the Hebrew stock.[143] If these things are true—and they are so true that no Jewish perversity can deny them—then it is clear to those who see, it is transparent even to the blind, that the prophetic spirit did not say of your Solomon, "Justice and an abundance of peace will arise in his days."[144]

Read the next verse, and it is transparent that it cannot be

136. 2 Chr 12.2.
137. Ps 71.7.
138. Cf. 2 Chr 12.2–4.
139. Cf. ibid.
140. Cf. 1 Kgs 14.26.
141. Ps 71.7.
142. Cf. 1 Kgs 12.15–19.
143. Cf. 2 Kgs 17.6; 18.9–12.
144. Ps 71.7.

applied to Solomon: "And he will rule from sea to sea and from the river to the ends of the earth."[145] Now, who does not see that this cannot refer to Solomon?[146] From what sea to what sea did he rule, when his kingdom was bounded by the short borders of Syria? But if you say that he reigned from the Dead Sea (*lacus Asphalticus*),[147] which is called a sea in your language's idiom, "unto the sea" that is said to be at the western side of Palestine and is called by us the Tyrrhenian or Mediterranean Sea, then you will limit his kingdom to a space less than it occupied. Moreover, the lake is in the middle of the Galilee,[148] and Solomon is said to have ruled from the river of Egypt, which flows out of that lake intermittently,[149] as far as places that are located near the Mediterranean Sea.[150] Therefore, the boundary of his kingdom was not "from sea to sea." Neither was it "from the river to the ends of the earth."[151] In fact, the ends of the earth are said to be where the earth ends. But it is known to every people that Solomon not only had not ruled as far as the ends of the earth, but that he ruled a much smaller expanse of the earth than many kings of the earth. Actually, there were innumerable kings in the past that, although they did not rule over all the earth, surpassed the limits of Solomon's kingdom with the great expanse of their own kingdoms. Therefore, it is apparent to all that Solomon did not rule from sea to sea nor from the river to the ends of the earth. Proceed from this and read a third verse, after only two intervening verses: "And all kings will worship him, all nations will serve him."[152] Does this refer to Solomon? The earth cries out, No, No, No. I do not say that a few [kings]

145. Ps 71.8.

146. Indeed, *Pirkê de Rabbi Eliezer* 11, trans. Gerald Friedlander (New York: Hermon Press, 1916; repr. 1970), 83, treats this passage from Ps 71.8 as yet to be fulfilled at the time of the coming of the messiah whom Jews await.

147. The Dead Sea was also known as the *lacus Asphalticus* because of bituminous deposits in the area.

148. "Lake": i.e., the *lacus Asphalticus* or Dead Sea. The editor notes that Peter seems to have confused the Dead Sea with the lake of Genesareth (cf. Lk 5.1), i.e., the Sea of Galilee.

149. "Intermittently": lit., with a period of some days intervening.

150. Cf. 1 Kgs 4.21; 2 Chr 9.26.   151. Ps 71.8.

152. Ps 71.11.

did so, but we do not read that any kings at all worshiped Solomon. It is clearer than the sun that one need not oppose the
statement that all the nations served him, because in fact they
did not serve him.

Examine the psalm and either read or hear what follows a few
verses later: "Let his name be blessed forever."[153] Whose name?
According to you, Solomon's name. Reread the entire collection
of Holy Scriptures, and rarely or actually never will you find this
verse, "Let his name be blessed forever,"[154] or the like, spoken
with reference to the name of any man at all. Scripture is wont
to say this of God alone, to say this only concerning the name of
God, as does this passage: "Blessed be the name of his majesty
forever."[155] And: "We who live bless the Lord."[156] And: "Blessed
be the Lord God of Israel, who alone does wonderful things."[157]
And many others like these. This is why when it is said: "Let his
name be blessed forever,"[158] necessarily this is understood to refer no more to that man Solomon than to any other man. What
follows indicates this very clearly: "His name continues before
the sun."[159] That is, "Let his name," which "continues before the
sun," "be blessed forever."[160] Did Solomon's name continue before the sun? Did Solomon precede the sun? Was the sun not
created before him? Was it not given a name before him? Do
you see now not only how impious but how blasphemous it is
to think something like this about Solomon? Nor should the
following verse escape your attention: "And all the tribes of the
earth will be blessed in him."[161] In whom? In Solomon? It is not
suitable to delay any longer over things that are so very apparent, which are so very easy for me to prove to be utterly false
that every disputant remains silent. What next? "All nations will
magnify him."[162] Whom? Solomon? Everyone knows that this age
neither is, nor has been, nor will be fulfilled.

Look then, O Jews, look for another to whom all these things
can be understood to refer, about whom that divine psalm can
clearly be proved to have been written. And whom will you

153. Ps 71.17.   154. Ibid.
155. Ps 71.19.   156. Ps 113.26.
157. Ps 71.18.   158. Ps 71.17.
159. Ibid.   160. Ibid.
161. Ibid.   162. Ibid.

be able to find? None other, surely none other, plainly none other—not even if you could fly to the stars on wings—than Christ our Lord, our God, and, like it or not, your Lord too, your God.[163] These things are written, they are meant, they are proclaimed about him. How so? Because they can be applied to no one else but to a God-Man. Not to man alone nor to God alone but, as was said, to one that is at one and the same time the God-Man, not each one separately. Christ alone, however, can be found to be at one and the same time God and Man. But the words of the psalm written above can fit no one else but the God-Man. Therefore, they were proclaimed concerning no one other than Christ. And this must be demonstrated. "God," it says, "give your judgment to a king, and to the king's son your justice."[164] Therefore, even you confess that this king's son is certainly a man. And, for both the king and the king's son we understand our Christ, who, insofar as he is called a son, is the Only-begotten Son of God the Father, and insofar as he has received judgment and justice from God, he is the Son of man.

But for the moment I grant your interpretation, and I concede that this was written of the son of David. Now, if it was said of the son of David, then certainly it was said about a man. But it has already been proved that the subsequent verses of the psalm that have been set forth cannot be understood to apply either to Solomon or to any of David's sons who succeeded him in the kingdom, in a temporal sense. Therefore, it is necessary to find someone else who, according to your interpretation, will be the son of David concerning whom you expound the first verse of this psalm, but concerning whom not only part but the whole of the psalm can be expounded. But do not struggle, do not vex your heart in vain by seeking false alternatives (*diverticula*). It is our Christ; our Christ alone is, I say, a son of David according to

163. For a similar christological interpretation of Ps 71, see Ps. William of Champeaux, *Dialogus inter christianum et judaeum de fide catholica* (PL 163: 1059BC) written between 1128–43, i.e., immediately before Peter the Venerable's text. For a Jewish response to this christological interpretation of Ps 71.17, see Joseph Kimhi's *The Book of the Covenant*, p. 61, in which it becomes clear that the fact that Jews and Muslims do not serve and magnify Jesus is invoked as evidence that he cannot be the subject of this text.

164. Ps 71.2.

the flesh, that is, from David's stock. In fact, in the same way you do not call sons only those that have been begotten from their fathers, but also those that arise from their lineage several generations later. Therefore, in this way Christ is the son of David, that is, son of the man, and the already cited verse was written about him with respect to humanity. There are others as well that were written concerning him in the series of passages from this same psalm with respect to the fact that he is man. Since, as was said above, you struggle to apply these already cited testimonies to Solomon, they prevent you, they keep you from this interpretation. Because they cannot be understood to apply wholly to any man whatsoever, they force you to accept that they are about Christ, who is man and God. In fact truly, insofar as he is God, "he continues with the sun,"[165] because he has no end. He continues also "before the moon"[166] because he precedes every creature and there is nothing prior to him. "Justice has arisen in his days"[167] because he justifies all those believing in him. "And an abundance of peace,"[168] by which he unites the sons of peace to the peace to come. And this, "until the moon be taken away,"[169] that is, until human mutability is brought to an end, and an eternity of blessed peace takes its place. "He rules from sea to sea,"[170] because he rules either completely or in part over all languages and all nations within the ocean's sphere, by which the entire earth is girded, not only through the power of deity but even through the Christian faith. You yourselves perceive this; you yourselves prove this with your eyes and ears. "And from the river,"[171] which is certainly none other than the Jordan, whence, beginning his baptism and spreading it among all nations, he reached as far as the furthest ends of the earth, to rule it. "All the kings of the earth worship him"—who are either understood to be "all" by synecdoche[172] for the largest part,

---

165. Ps 71.5.   166. Ibid.
167. Ps 71.7.   168. Ibid.
169. Ibid.   170. Ps 71.8.
171. Ibid.

172. Synecdoche: a figure of speech whereby the part stands for the whole. Peter's acknowledgment that the kings of the earth worship Christ by synecdoche would address the later complaint in Kimhi's *The Book of the Covenant* (p. 61), that this passage cannot be applied to Christ since "Ishmaelite" [kings] have not worshiped or served him.

or because even the heathen kings revere him as the greatest of all, after God. "All the nations will serve him"[173] because, except for you, whom the prophet excluded from this reference to the nations, all nations believe in him either universally or partially, serve him, and render obeisance to him. "His name is blessed forever,"[174] like God's name, like the Redeemer's name, like the Savior's name, which even you hear repeated daily, continuously blessed, and assiduously celebrated by every tongue. "His name continues before the sun," because the name of the deity and his majesty, without any beginning, came before every created thing. "All the tribes of the earth are blessed in him,"[175] because all those that were subject to the curse of the first parent, until [the time of] Christ himself, have deserved through him to be blessed and saved. "All nations magnify him,"[176] certainly all, surely all, all whatsoever magnify him, except the Jew. For the Jew, since he is not among the number of these nations, and since he has been excluded from the blessing of all the tribes of the earth, and since he does not deserve to magnify him with all the nations, has been rejected. Because these verses cannot be understood in any other way, because the true Scripture can only stand upon this interpretation, it is necessary that you, O Jews, change your blaspheming tongue, it is necessary that you, pressed by so many proof-texts and such powerful proof-texts, confess now not only that Christ is man but even that he is true God. Or do so many proof-texts and such powerful proof-texts not suffice for you to confess that our Christ is the Son of God, and to confess that he is God? It could already seem superfluous to present the many other examples that still remain from the law or from the prophets.

But if your own testimonies seem worthless to you or if foreign testimonies please you more, then listen even to the Sibyl who prophesied from the midst of the nations so that the spirit of God might strike the enemies of God even through the speech of a Gentile woman. For this same spirit of God sometimes is accustomed to act and to present prophetic or divine things in a Gentile tongue. He did this through Job the just,

173. Ps 71.11.   174. Ps 71.17.
175. Ibid.   176. Ibid.

not a Jew but an Idumean, and he did this through the impious Balaam, who, among the others who foretold the future, also offered up a solemn and well-known prophecy about Christ: "I will see him," he said, "but not now, I will perceive him, but not near. A star will arise from Jacob and a rod rise up from Israel."[177] And after some other verses: "Alas, who will live, when God will do these things?"[178]

What, then, did the Sibyl say about Christ? What kind of testimony did she offer to Christ's deity?[179] Hear the names of the false gods that were execrated by a woman, admit the deity of Christ that she continuously and openly confessed. Speaking of the Passion of Christ, she said this, among the many other things that she had said prophetically:

He will come later into the hands of the unbelievers. They will lay a blow upon God with defiled hands, and they will spew poisonous spittle from an impure mouth. He will simply offer a holy back to the blows. And, while receiving the blows he will remain silent, so that no one will know that Word or whence it comes, to speak to the lower regions and to be crowned with a crown of thorns. They gave him bile as food and vinegar for his thirst. They will show this table of inhospitality. Thinking this to be foolish, you have not understood it to refer to your God; but ridiculing him with the minds of mortal men, you crowned him with thorns and mixed in a filthy bile. The veil of the temple will be rent, and in the middle of the day it will be exceedingly dark for three hours, and for three days he will die the death, having taken up sleep, and then, having returned from hell he will come to the light as the first of the resurrection, the beginning [of which] has been revealed to those who have been recalled.

The Sibyl said these things about Christ long before the time of Christ. You cannot say that her words should not be accepted, because even though she did not derive her fleshly lineage from the people of God, nonetheless she perceived and professed the same things that the law of God contains and confesses.

177. Nm 24.17.
178. Nm 24.23.
179. A reference to a collection of Sibylline oracles. Some Christians viewed the Sibyl as a pagan prophetess who predicted the advent of Jesus. See Arnaldo Momigliano, "Sibylline Oracles," in the *Encyclopedia of Religion,* ed. Mircea Eliade (New York: MacMillan Publishing Co., 1987), 13: 305–8; *Encyclopedia Judaica* 14: 1490–91.

Therefore, wretched people, will you dare one by one to deny that Christ is God when you hear that he is called God not only once but a thousand times by your own prophets and through the mouths of Gentiles who so clearly, so lucidly, so brightly, do not worship idols but the one God? Will you deny that God is born and already commands heaven and earth when before he was born, when many ages before, so many truthful witnesses time and time again confessed that he is God? Will you deny that God, whom, in the Gospel of the Christians and in the profane temples of the pagans, even the demons—than whom now you have become worse in comparison—have been compelled by divine power to confess to be God?

CHAPTER THREE

That, unlike what the Jews think, Christ is not a temporal king but the eternal and celestial King

UT BECAUSE THIS can be enough for now concerning these matters, in the third part of the division mentioned above let the discussion (*sermo*) of divine wisdom proceed against another inspiration for your very foolish error, and in this part let it show you how foolish you are. Now, because you hear from the prophets that Christ is called a king, because you read in the Scriptures that he has a kingdom, you think that he will be a temporal king and that he will reign in time in the manner of David or Solomon, or of the other kings of Jerusalem, Judaea, or the Galilee. You imagine that he will sit upon David's earthly throne, that he will rule over all or almost all the nations, that he will liberate the Jews from such a long-lasting captivity, that he will recall and gather them up again from all places and nations and that he will lead you back, wherever you are gathered, to your land of ancient promise for which you alone, you brutish men, always yearn. For this, you propose for yourselves countless examples from the Scriptures, and whatever is said there about these matters you, who are deprived of sense and overwhelmed by a love of earthly things, twist in a bestial manner that is far removed from every other meaning to whatever you alone are wont to desire. You feed your unhappy souls on a vain hope and, since you pertinaciously aspire to earthly and perishable goods, you cast aside the celestial and eternal goods that are promised and given by Christ unremittingly to all nations, without cease, except to you. Every day others seize the kingdom of heaven,[1] while you, taught to love always only carnal filth,[2] await an earthly kingdom in vain.

This is why you strive to adapt to your vain hope the things foretold by prophetic voices concerning the eternal kingdom of Christ, like this one from Jeremiah: "Behold, the days will come, says the Lord, and I will raise up the just seed of David, and a king will reign, and he will be wise and he will execute judgment and justice in the earth."[3] And, a few passages later, he says with respect to leading you out of your captivity again: "And they will not say any more, 'The Lord lives, who led the children of Israel from the land of Egypt,' but, 'The Lord lives, who has led and brought forth the seed of the house of Israel from the land of the north and from all'" the places in which they were dispersed, "'and they will live in their own land.'"[4] Indeed, you propose these passages from Jeremiah. But you can propose something like them from Ezekiel also. "Behold," says the Lord, "I will raise up the children of Israel from the midst of the nations to which they have gone forth, and I will gather them up on every side and will bring them to their own land. And I will make them one nation in the land on the mountains of Israel, and one king shall be king over them all."[5] And below that: "And I will save them from all their crimes with which they sinned, and I will cleanse them. And they will be my people, and I will be their God. And my servant David will be king over them, and they will have one shepherd."[6]

These and many other passages like them that could have illuminated you with their splendor have blinded you instead—you who are undeserving because of your crimes—bringing no spiritual light to your carnal eyes. For how long, O Jews, will this bovine intellect possess your hearts so that you will be unable, regardless of effort, to see the Scriptures of God, or to know Christ, or to be turned from falsehood, or to be converted to the truth. Therefore, if you believe me, cast aside that corpo-

---

1. Cf. Mt 11.12.
2. "Carnal filth": *feces ... carnales.* A more scatological reading could support, as an alternative, "carnal excrement."
3. Jer 23.5.   4. Jer 23.7–8; cf. 30.11.
5. Ezek 37.21–22.   6. Ezek 37.23–24.

real understanding (*sensus*) by which you will always appear not wise but imprudent, and take up that spiritual understanding (*intellectus*) with which to know the truth, to receive Christ, with which you deserve to obtain not the kind of king and kingdom you perceive, but the kind that the Scriptures perceive. If you choose not to do this but instead decide to remain in your customary insanity, and if you prefer to adapt the Scriptures to your corporeal understanding rather than to bend your corporeal understanding to the Scriptures, then listen to those passages that stand against you and that propose what is contrary to your perverse understanding (*intellectus*).

And first proceed, you most sagacious disputant, whoever you are, and go forth among these profane men, and show forth your power to the God that is speaking, if you can. Clearly, you want Christ to be a carnal king, you prefer that the kingdom of Christ be an earthly kingdom. Answer, then, the God that speaks through the prophet: "Tell the daughter of Zion: Behold, your meek king comes to you."[7] Who is this king? Perhaps it is David, perhaps Solomon, perhaps one of the former kings of Judah or Israel? But you cannot say this, O Jew. Why? Because the prophet's time frame prevents this. And who is this prophet? Zechariah. And when was this Zechariah? After all the kings of Judah, after all the kings of Israel in time past. For in the time of Darius the "word of the Lord came"[8] to him, just as his series of prophecies reports. This Darius was the one who, along with Cyrus, overthrew the Chaldean kingdom and ended the Jewish captivity that had been established by Nebuchadnezzar.[9] All the kings of Israel or Judah reigned before that Babylonian captivity. It follows, then, that "Behold, your meek king comes to you"[10] was not said about any of those who had already preceded him and already had died.

But if you use Aristobolus[11] to contradict me, who placed

---

7. Zec 9.9 LXX; cf. Mt 21.5.   8. Zec 1.1.

9. Cf. Dn 5.31.   10. Zec 9.9 LXX; cf. Mt 21.5.

11. After the death of his father, John Hyrcanus, Aristobolus (whose wife was Queen Salome) became king. After his death, Queen Salome proclaimed his brother, Jannaeus Alexander, king in 103 BCE. See Solomon Zeitlin, "Queen Salome and King Jannaeus Alexander: A Chapter in the History of the Second Jewish Commonwealth," *The Jewish Quarterly Review*, n.s. 51.1 (1960): 1–33.

upon himself the diadem of the Jewish kingdom a long time
after the prophet Zechariah, I reply that the prophet was not
thinking of one who assumed the diadem and the priesthood
against God's law and precept and who invaded the kingdom.
But because he was unworthy of it, he possessed it for barely
one year.[12] Nor was one who had deserved to be condemned by
God for something so illicit able to rule for long. Whereas if you
propose Herod instead, it is clear that this was not said about
him either. In fact, the prophet spoke in this way: "Behold, your
meek king comes to you."[13] But Herod was not a Jew but a for-
eigner, and he was not meek, but rather he was harsh, ferocious,
cruel, and it is certain from Josephus's historical chronicle of
the Jews that he was, in addition, the murderer of his sons and
his wife.[14] If you throw up against me his other sons, Archelaus,
Herod, or the other tetrarchs of the father's kingdom, it is well
known from a report of the chronicle already mentioned that
Archelaus was a stupid king who was expelled from his kingdom
by Augustus, and who grew old at Vienna.[15] Moreover, Herod
[Antipas] was condemned by Gaius [Caligula], the third successor of Augustus, with his [wife] Herodias to an unhappy life
in exile in Spanish regions, where he died a miserable death.[16]
And it is well known that the others, who did not rule the entire
kingdom of the Jews but only parts of it, lasted barely until the
destruction of Jerusalem and of the entire Jerusalemite king-

12. Cf. Josephus, *Bellum Iudaicum* 1.6.120–41, in *The Jewish War. Books I–III*,
trans. H. St. J. Thackeray (Cambridge, MA: Harvard University Press, 1956),
57–65.

13. Zec 9.9 LXX; cf. Mt 5.21.

14. Cf. Josephus, *Bellum Iudaicum* 1.22.1.431–44 and 2.6.2.84–86, in *The Jewish War. Books I–III*, trans. H. St. J. Thackeray, 204–11 and 355.

15. Cf. Josephus, *Bellum Iudaicum* 2.7.3.3.111–13, *The Jewish War. Books I–III*,
trans. H. St. J. Thackeray, 365. When Herod the Great died in 4 BCE, popular rebellions broke out, which the Romans subdued. They divided Herod's
kingdom among his sons. Archelaus was a son of Herod the Great. He became
ethnarch of Judea, Samaria, and Idumæa. Herod Antipas (4 BCE–39CE) was
tetrarch over Galilee and Perea. According to Lk 3.1, when Pontius Pilate was
governor of Judea, Herod [Antipas] was tetrarch of Galilee, his brother Philip
was tetrarch of Iturea and Trachonitis, and Lysanias was tetrarch of Abilina.

16. Josephus, *Bellum Iudaicum* 2.9.6.182–84, in *The Jewish War. Books I–III*,
trans. H. St. J. Thackeray, 393–95.

dom, and that finally they perished by different fates as Vespasian and Titus were devastating the entire land.

But perhaps—in order to give the whole world some new reason to laugh at you, moreover—you will say that this prophecy was fulfilled by that asinine king of our age who rose up in rebellion (in fact, from Morocco) in parts of Africa, against a recently named king. Because of the wickedness of that abominable, damned (*perditus*) race (that is, of the Mohammedan sect), he gathered around himself an infinite multitude, although previously he was a very vulgar man, [and] gradually he acquired more and more wicked profit, and very often, when fighting with the already mentioned king, he frequently became the victor in battle. And since he was accustomed from his very first days to ride on an ass (in order to attract the foolish people more easily with a feigned humility), he was commonly called the king of asses. When the Jews had received this report about him, they immediately raised their spirits in hope, and many of them said that their king had come who the already-mentioned prophet had said would ride upon an ass.[17]

17. Cf. Zec 9.9. For this king, see M. Drouard-Ada, "Elements historiques dans un traité de polemique anti-juive: 'L'Adversus Judaeos' de Pierre le Vénérable (Pierre de Cluny)," *Archives juives* 8 (1972): 2–4. The author acknowledges a temptation to identify this "king" with a false messiah—or, rather, a precursor who proclaimed the messiah—mentioned by Maimonides, who arose in Fez in 1127. For this figure, Moses al-Dari, see Maimonides' *Epistle to Yemen* in *A Maimonides Reader*, ed. Isidore Twersky (New York: Behrman House, Inc., 1972), 458–60. Possibly too, this description could refer to Muhammad ibn Tūmart (d. 1130), a Berber from Morocco who was acclaimed the Mahdi and founded the movement of the Almohads, who sought to purify Islam and whose successors brought devastation to Jewish communities of Spain, causing the family of Maimonides to flee to Fez ca. 1159, while some other Jews converted, or feigned conversion. (For a fuller account of his career, see J. F. P. Hopkins, "Ibn Tūmart," in the *Encyclopaedia of Islam*, ed. P. Bearman, Th. Bianquis, C. E. Bosworth, E. van Donzel, and W. P. Heinrichs [Brill, 2007], accessed at Brill Online, Oxford University libraries, 30 August 2007, http://www.brillonline.nl/subscriber/entry?entry=islam_SIM-3395). Muhammad ibn Tūmart was well known for riding a donkey, perhaps just as two centuries earlier the Khārijite Abū Yazīd Mukhallad ibn Kayrād (who led a briefly successful rebellion against Fatimid rulers in present-day Tunisia and Algeria ca. CE 944) rode a donkey as a sign of his humility, and was therefore known as the "man on the donkey." [For a discussion of his career, see Heinz Halm, *The Empire of the Mahdi: The*

What are you doing, O Jew? Are you not embarrassed? Do you not confuse the words uttered by your own prophets? Such is your hope, so ridiculous is the expectation of the Jews—so vain, so foolish. Who will properly be able to deride an insanity so profound of men that are damned (*perditus*)? The Jews have understood that deceitful, cruel man of damnable error—a murderer not only of some men but of many peoples—to be that meek king, that gentle king, that kind king. Why did they not pay attention to the fact that he came neither from the land nor the kingdom that once belonged to the Jews, nor did he even stem from that ancient stock of the Jews? Surely you see how far men of this sort have been cast away from the face of God, men who so easily follow what is false that they do not believe what is true despite anyone's effort. And since I have inserted these things only to put such unnatural men on display, let the following come next.

Now, after having excluded all of these, it follows that what God said through the prophet to the "daughter of Zion"—that is, to the Jews—"Behold, your meek king comes to you riding upon an ass,"[18] does not apply to any of them. Whom do you

---

Rise of the Fatimids, trans. Michael Bonner (Leiden: Brill, 1996), 298–309 and 312–24]. A precise identification based on Peter's information is not possible. Nonetheless, the editor of this text, Yvonne Friedman, suggests that the reference is to either ibn Tūmart or his successor Abd al-Mumin. In fact, it is this story in part that leads to the suggestion that this chapter in the larger text must have been written before 1146/7, since after this time the Almohads began serious attacks on the Jews of Morocco, and after that date "Moroccan Jews could no longer have viewed the 'king of the ass' as the messiah" (p. lxiii). Nonetheless, other possibilities remain. From Peter's text it is only certain that this false messiah hailed from Morocco. It is not clear that he attracted Muslim followers, but only that because of the alleged wickedness of the Muslims he attracted a large multitude. Other messianic pretenders active in the early twelfth century excited Jewish imagination, including Solomon b. Rūjī, who promised to gather Jews into Jerusalem ca. 1121. For this figure, evidently active in Kurdistan, see Norman Golb, "The Messianic Pretender Solomon ibn al-Ruji and his Son Menahem (the so-called David al-Roy)," at http://oi.uchicago.edu/pdf/false_messiah-1.pdf, and idem, *Jewish Proselytism—a Phenomenon in the Religious History of Early Medieval Europe,* Tenth Annual Rabbi Louis Feinberg Memorial Lecture (Cincinnati: University of Cincinnati, 1988), 27–28.

18. Zec 9.9 LXX.

understand, or whom can you understand, this promised king to be except Christ? For, after having excluded all of the kings mentioned, no other king remains except Christ, of whom it can be demonstrated that that prophecy was spoken. Therefore, it is necessary for you to agree to the unvanquished truth, and that this was said to the daughter of Zion about no other king but Christ: "Behold, your meek king comes."[19] But, as was set forth above, you want Christ to be a carnal, temporal king, sitting on a raised throne in the fashion of great kings, resplendent with purple, gems, and gold, abundant with riches, subjugating his enemies with arms and men, ruling over a wider area than all the kings of the Jews or of the Gentiles. But Christ the king is not like this, nor is the kingdom of Christ said to be like this by the prophet.

How is this? Listen, as soon as the prophet proclaimed: "Behold, your meek king comes," he added: "He is poor, and riding upon an ass, and upon a colt, the foal of an ass."[20] Pay attention, Jew, wake up, understand your prophet. What does he say? "He is poor, and riding upon an ass, and upon a colt the foal of an ass."[21] Who is he that is both a king and poor? Who is he that is both a king and riding upon an ass? Who is he that is both a king and riding upon the foal of an ass? What is the relationship between a king and poverty? What is the relationship between a king and an ass? Explain how the king who, according to you, is very rich may be said by the prophet to be poor, and how it may be written that he will ride not upon a proud horse that is frothing at the mouth but upon an ass and upon a colt, the foal of an ass. It belongs to kings and potentates to be carried on horses or at least on mules or burros, but it belongs to paupers or the indigent to be carried on he-asses or she-asses. Tell me then, speak, according to your understanding link a king and poverty, abundance and penury, sublimity and lowliness. But you cannot.

Proceed, then, and read the following: "I will destroy the chariot out of Ephraim, and the horse out of Jerusalem, and the bow for war will be broken."[22] Who is this king who is so

19. Ibid.   20. Zec 9.9 LXX; cf. Mt 5.21.
21. Zec 9.9 LXX.   22. Zec 9.10.

poor that his great poverty compels him to ride upon an ass and an ass's colt, yet who is so peaceful that at his arrival God will destroy a chariot from Ephraim and a horse from Jerusalem and will break the bow for war? A king that you will be able to find flourishing and so secure in his kingdom that, for the great security of the peace, he will repudiate chariots and horses and will reject the bow of war, that is, all warlike instruments? This peace does not exist, this peace does not exist for any earthly king or kingdom. Read again about the time period of Solomon himself, and you will discover that he not only failed to repudiate chariots, horses, and the arms of war that he found in Jerusalem and Israel, but rather he increased them in great measure. Must one believe, then, that what so peaceful a king did not do in his time in a kingdom at peace can be done at some other time by any earthly king?[23] But follow along further: "And he will speak of peace to the Gentiles, and his power [will extend] from sea to sea and from the rivers to the ends of the earth."[24] What do you say to this? Compare again the poverty of the king already mentioned and what you read about his power. "This pauper," he said, "will rule from sea to sea and from the rivers to the ends of the earth."[25] And why is this poverty so extraordinary (*monstruosa*) that he who rules from sea to sea is called a pauper because of it? Why is this power so prodigious that the one ruling from sea to sea will be like a pauper, so that he will be compelled to ride upon an ass and an ass colt? But why do I repeat so many times what is so very clear? It is not surprising. I am speaking to a Jew, I am speaking to one who is deaf, I am speaking to one who is as hard as rock. Therefore, Jew, either find for me the poor king, find for me the one ruling from sea to sea and riding upon an ass and upon the ass colt because of extreme poverty—which you cannot do—or accept that our Christ is the king and that he rules from sea to sea, because he is God all powerful, and accept that he is a pauper and riding on an ass and an ass colt because he is a true man, which is all you can do. Although he is God, he was not only made a man for the sake of men, but he was made a poor man for their sake.

23. Cf. 1 Chr 22.9. 24. Zec 9.10.
25. Conflates Zec 9.10 and Ps 71.8.

Read our Gospel, and through it you will be able to prove literally (*absque involucris*) that your prophecy was truthful: How he rides upon an ass, how, sitting upon it or its colt, he will come to "the daughter of Zion"[26]—that is, to your Jerusalem at that time, to suffer soon.[27]

But perhaps while fleeing from the light and seeking the darkness, in your customary fashion, while unwilling to distinguish truth from error, choosing instead, by a demonic instinct on the basis of which you act, to be implicated in a falsehood, you will say: Why do you bother me over a king and an ass? Why do you throw a king and an ass colt against me? Are there not many powerful men, are there not many rich men that we read are carried on he-asses or she-asses or on the foals of he-asses or she-asses? Doesn't the Book of Judges report that Jair the Gileadite, "who judged Israel for seventy-two years,"[28] had "thirty sons sitting upon thirty ass colts"?[29] Does one not read that, from among the judges, "Abdon the son of Hillel the Pirathonite" had "forty sons and thirty grandsons mounted upon seventy ass colts"?[30] You cannot deny that the sons or grandsons of such great judges, who judged the entire Israelite people and ruled them before the kings or in place of kings, were rich, nor that from compelling need they used ass colts to make a journey. If this is the case, then your objection, which you urge against us—that one cannot accept on the basis of the prophet's words that there was any earthly king who also rode upon an ass colt—has no force.

To which I reply: do not complain that you have been particularly pressed by me on these matters. I press, clearly I press, rather, even I especially press you, to notice that your understanding is far from the prophetic meaning, since you are looking for a temporal king and you do not disavow that he will sit on an ass and a foal. The one hundred you enumerated, the sons or grandsons of the judges of Israel whom you adduced

26. Zec 9.9.
27. Cf. Mt 21.2–4; Mk 11.1–10; Lk 19.29–38; Jn 12.14–16.
28. Cf. Jgs 10.3, although the Vulg. and some of the manuscript variants to this text read "twenty-two years."
29. Jgs 10.4.
30. Jgs 12.13–14.

for this purpose, cannot help you to show both that they were rich and that they were mounted on the foals of asses as was fitting, nor do you prove to be true what we intend to prove concerning our king. And I know as well, nor am I forgetful of sacred Scripture or of human practice, that there were many powerful and rich men that were mounted or could have been mounted on asses or their colts. I recall surely that one reads that your great father Abraham was rich and saddled his ass.[31] For the fact that he was rich we have the testimony of his servant, whose name was Damascus Eliezer.[32] These are the words he spoke to Laban and to the rest of the clan from Abraham's race: "I am the servant of Abraham," he said, "and the Lord blessed my master wonderfully. And he is become great, and he has given him sheep and oxen, silver and gold, men-servants and women-servants, camels and asses."[33] These things that he reported, I say, show that he was rich. But from this same Book of Genesis from which these words were excerpted I heard also that he saddled an ass for himself. For when his faith was tested by God to sacrifice his son, one reads: "So Abraham, rising up in the night, saddled his ass, and took with him two young men, and Isaac his son."[34] I knew these things, O Jew, even before I engaged you concerning them. I knew, too, that while sitting on an ass, Achsah,[35] the daughter of the rich man Caleb, sighed and said to her father: "You have given me a dry southern land; give me also a watery land."[36] But neither the objections you raise nor those that I contribute to your objection support you in any way whatsoever. You object that the sons of the judges were rich and that they nevertheless rode on asses. And I add, as if taking your side, that the rich man Abraham saddled his ass, that the daughter of a rich man rode upon an ass, but none of the examples you have proposed has established anything that is consonant with your interpretation. Of none of these does one read, of none is it written that he was a king, that he was a poor man who, because of his great poverty, was compelled to make a journey mounted upon an ass or its foal. That is one thing, but

31. Cf. Gn 24.35; 22.3.   32. Cf. Gn 15.2.
33. Gn 24.34–35.   34. Gn 22.3.
35. Cf. Jgs 1.14.   36. Jgs 1.14–15.

it is clearly something different if one of these rich men of old often (or even occasionally) chose to ride on an ass, either from the custom of the time or because of a fortuitous choice, who, like one dependent on the fat of riches, was wont to be familiar with riches. It is another thing entirely whether there be any ancient or contemporary king who is also a pauper at one and the same time, who can be understood to be compelled, as was said, to use such conveyances from poverty. Whatever way you turn, there appears to be no exit. In fact, either you will confess that he is a king and delete "poor," or if you grant that he is poor you will not be able to call him a king. But in order to confess both truthfully and to be in agreement with the meaning of heavenly Scripture, cast aside a Jewish spirit (*animus*), close your blasphemous mouth, and, having accepted the Christian interpretation, for the sake of justice believe in your heart and for the sake of salvation confess with your mouth that Christ is both an eternal king from his deity, and a poor man from the humanity that he assumed for the sake of mankind.

But from here let us return again to Isaiah. Hear what he said that is a parallel case: "Behold," he said, "my servant will understand, and he will be saved and extolled and will be exceedingly high."[37] Who is speaking through the prophet? Certainly, it is God. "Behold," he says, "my servant will understand."[38] But he has many servants. He differentiated this one from all the others, however, when he said: "he will be exalted and extolled and will be exceedingly high."[39] But many were exalted and extolled and made exceedingly high by God. How, then, is this servant of God distinguished from the many others? Keep reading: "Just as many have been astonished at you, so his visage" will be "inglorious among men, and his form among the sons of men."[40] How will you respond to a prophet so great, O Jew? You dare not think that he is false. Therefore, what he says is true. You

---

37. Is 52.13. The Vulg. reads *ecce intelleget servus meus exaltabitur et elevabitur et sublimis erit valde*—"Behold my servant will understand, he will be exalted, and extolled, and will be exceedingly high." Subsequent occurrences of this passage as quoted here conform to the Vulgate.

38. Ibid.   39. Ibid.

40. Is 52.14.

should reply: Clearly it is true. Who, then, is this servant of God who has been exalted, extolled, and who is exceedingly high, whose visage among men is, contrariwise, inglorious, whose form is without glory among the sons of men? Seek, struggle, speak if you can [say anything]. Nevertheless, read on: "He will sprinkle many nations. Kings will shut their mouth at him."[41] Again, who is this one that is said to sprinkle many nations, and at whom kings are said to shut their mouth? Certainly he is the same one that is said to be "exalted and extolled and" made "exceedingly high."[42] And who is such a one, one so powerful, one so great that "he will sprinkle many nations, and kings will shut their mouth at him"?[43] Plainly he is not only great but the greatest, not only powerful but the most powerful, for, trembling at his magnitude, marveling at his power, kings shut their mouths, they dare not speak, they await his will as if of one who is greater than they, they bear his command as if of one who rules. Nonetheless, this is he whose visage is said to be inglorious among men, whose form is predicted to be despised among the sons of men.

Perhaps you look to see how you should reply, and you labor over how to lie and how the heavenly oracle can be interpreted in a perverse manner. But no approach is open to you to avoid these difficulties, nor can a heavenly light be obscured or darkened by the darkness of the Egyptians.[44] To which kings, to which princes will you be able to apply things that are so different, so contrary? Whom among them all are you able to imagine as both "exalted" and "inglorious"? "Extolled" and "inglorious"? "Exceedingly high" and "inglorious"?[45] Who is so great, so awesome, that kings dare not speak before him, whose form, nevertheless, the sons of men condemn? And because I know that you will find nothing beyond these sacred passages that will enable you in a rational manner to pervert their meaning, you will be compelled by the power of reason to return to us and to inquire who is the one about whom things so contrary are written. Many have been rightly astonished at the one about

41. Is 52.15.   42. Is 52.13.
43. Is 52.15.   44. Cf. Jos 24.7.
45. Cf. Is 52.13–15.

whom such different things have been pronounced, just as is written among these prophetic passages, but not everyone has remained incredulous, as you have. Many have been astonished at this singular miracle, but many, although not all, have been converted from their stupor to God's Christ and to his salvation. They have understood that there is none other, that it is clearly our Christ and none other who has been exalted, extolled, and made exceedingly high and again whose visage is inglorious among men and whose form is contemptible among the sons of men. Exalted, extolled, and exceedingly high because, as our apostle says: "God exalted him" in the man that he had assumed "and gave him a name that is above every name, so that in the name of Jesus every knee should bow, of those that are in heaven, on earth, and under the earth." His visage is inglorious, and his form made contemptible among the sons of men because, as the same apostle set forth earlier, he was made "obedient unto death, the death on the cross. At him kings shut their mouth"[46] because the highest kings or princes of the earth shut their mouths to remain silent, but when they open their ears to hear, they hear him as the Prince of princes, they submit to him as the King of kings, they make obeisance to him as the Lord of lords. Therefore, because these things cannot be said of any mortal, because contraries such as these cannot be found in any man, it is necessary that you perceive, acknowledge, and accept our Christ in these words.

Nor can you object perhaps that it could escape our attention that there were many kings or princes that were initially great and high, and then later fell from the power of government or from the glory of the kingdom because of various chance events. But remember that the discussion is about the Christ, who you contend will never be wretched but who will be blessed, who never will be subdued but who will rule, who never will be inglorious but rather who will be glorious. But these [contraries] have been proposed to preclude the interpretation of a temporal and not an eternal kingdom in Christ, so that not human but divine glory is attributed to him. Now, I do not be-

---

46. Conflating Phil 2.8–10 and Is 52.13–15.

lieve that you are so insane as to attempt to explain these prophetic passages with reference to any of the kings of Judah or to
any Gentile king from the prophet's own time period.

But perhaps with Jewish cleverness you will attempt to apply
these passages either to King Manasseh, the son of Hezekiah,[47]
who was held captive and then later restored to his kingdom, or
to Josiah,[48] who was slain by the Egyptians, or to Jehoiakim[49] or
Zedekiah,[50] who were led into Babylon. In fact, of the kings of
Judah, only these seem to have fallen from the glory of the kingdom after the time period when the prophet was speaking. But
you will attempt this in vain. Was the impious King Manasseh
ever called "God's servant"? In fact, this is what was set forth first:
"Behold, my servant will understand."[51] Was an idolater, was a
profane man, was he who, as one reads, "filled Jerusalem up to
the mouth with too much innocent blood"[52] said to be a servant
of God? And indeed elsewhere, for contending against impious
nations Nebuchadnezzar, the very worst king, is called a servant
of God, not because he was good but because he served God's
intention, even though not praising that intention.[53] But God's
Scripture does not call Manasseh a servant of God even though
he repented, nor does it report that he engaged in a military
struggle for God's sake.[54] Therefore, Manasseh was not called
a servant of God. Thus it appears that this passage of Scripture
was not offered on his behalf. But words so sublime, so solemnly offered up and repeated so often neither befit him, nor Josiah, nor the rest of the kings, neither to call them exalted, nor
extolled, nor exceedingly high. For although they were kings,
these prophetic words surpass their greatness, surpass their
high position. Nor does what follows apply to any of them: "Just
as many were astonished at him."[55] Who will be astonished by a
king that is first exalted but later humbled, extolled and then

---

47. Cf. 2 Chr 33.11–13.
48. Cf. 2 Chr 35.20–24; 2 Kgs 23.29.
49. Cf. 2 Kgs 23.36, 24.1; 2 Chr 36.6.
50. Cf. 2 Chr 36.11–18; 2 Kgs 24.18–20 and 25.7.
51. Is 52.13.   52. Cf. 2 Kgs 21.16.
53. Cf. Jer 25.9.   54. Cf. 2 Chr 33.12–13.
55. Is 52.14.

dejected, placed on high and then cast down from that high position? In fact, this is quite usual, quite customary among kings and among the powerful. Moreover, people are not wont to be astonished by what is customary. Therefore, what, according to the prophet, astonished many people had to be a singular, atypical miracle. If this is true, then it was not said about captives, or those who were slain, or about kings suffering some misfortune, or about men of any rank whatsoever. But is there anyone who does not see that "he will sprinkle many nations" and "kings will shut their mouth at him"[56] do not apply to any of the kings of the Jews?

And in order that things that are clear not be obscured by frequent repetition, I say in summary: if this scriptural passage cannot be understood to apply to any of the kings of Israel or Judah, if it does not apply to any of the Jews who have lived up until our age, then it cannot be understood to apply to anyone other than the Christ already mentioned by the prophets. But it has been proved, I think, that it can be applied to no one else.

It remains, then, that these prophetic claims (*voces*) be understood to apply only to Christ. Not, however, to the Christ as falsely explained by you, but to the Christ truly understood by us. Not of a Christ ruling in time, but of a Christ ruling eternally. Not of a Christ reigning like kings on earth, but of a Christ presiding like God over all things that are in earth and in the heavens. Who, the prophet wrote, is a "servant of God" because "he emptied himself taking the form of a servant"[57] and is "exceedingly high"[58] presiding over every creature, and who is inglorious for submitting freely to the ignominious passion. "Who sprinkles many nations,"[59] that he commands everywhere to be baptized by the sacred water of baptism. "At whom kings shut their mouths"[60] because everywhere the pride not only of others but even of kings themselves obeys him.

Pay attention, then, Jew, to what is said, and understand the Scripture that is read, believe in the Christ that is proclaimed. Blush at your incredulity, imitate the faith of the Gentiles, of

56. Is 52.15.   57. Phil 2.7.
58. Is 52.15.   59. Ibid.
60. Ibid.

whom the same prophet adds next: "for they to whom it was not told of him, will see, and they that heard not, have beheld."[61] Turn quickly to those passages that follow, and although those that have already been presented show it plainly, acknowledge from the passages that follow that the kingdom of Christ was not once nor will it be again a carnal or temporal kingdom. And in order to avoid the tedium of a prolix demonstration, to the extent permitted by the material already added, I propose to you everything that one reads in Isaiah from the verse that begins: "Who has believed our report,"[62] up to the one that begins: "Give praise, barren one that does not bear."[63]

I believe that you will perceive that many of these passages were pronounced of none other than Christ. To whom but to Christ can one apply what the prophet said: "To whom is the arm of the Lord revealed"?[64] To whom does "Who will declare his generation" apply if not Christ?[65] To whom can one apply: "But he has done no iniquity, nor has there been deceit in his mouth,"[66] if not to Christ? To whom can one adapt: "The just one will justify my many servants and bear their iniquities,"[67] if not to Christ? Of whom can one believe that "he was offered because it was his own will, and he opened not his mouth,"[68] except of Christ? Who will not see that the only one of whom such great things are said is not found among the common number of men at all, but is above every man? Give me, if you can, anyone other than Christ who ought to be called "the arm of the Lord"—that is, the power of the Lord—give me someone whose generation can either hardly be told or not told at all, give me a man who "has done no iniquity, nor has there been deceit in his mouth,"[69] give me someone who is himself just so that he will justify many others and bear their iniquities. If you have him, give me one who "was offered because it was his own

---

61. Ibid. The Vulg. reads "have seen" (*viderunt*) rather than "will see" (*videbunt*).

62. Is 53.1.   63. Is 54.1.

64. Is 53.1.   65. Is 53.8.

66. Is 53.9.

67. Is 53.11.The Vulg. reads *iustificabit ipse iustus servus meus multos,* rather than *iustificabit ipse iustus servos meos multos.*

68. Is 53.7.   69. Is 53.9.

will, and he opened not his mouth."⁷⁰ Now, although you understand your Christ only to be a man, nevertheless these things
are said on behalf of one that is above man. In fact, see and
judge—not in a Jewish fashion, but justly—whether the "arm of
the Lord"—that is, the power of the Lord—can be understood
to be a man and only a man. Now, God is said to be the power
of man; man is not said to be the power of God. Clearly, this
is the voice of man to God: "In your power, O Lord, the king
will rejoice."⁷¹ But if a king, who surpasses others in power and
rank, is not the power of God, but instead himself rejoices in
the power of the Lord, then it is clear that the one who is said
to be the arm of the Lord rules not only over those inferior to
him but even over kings themselves. Therefore, when you hear,
"Who will declare his generation,"⁷² do you not understand
that it distinguishes his generation from a human and common
generation? Indeed, how a human body is fashioned from the
material that has been received in a mother's womb is known
to God alone, but it is still clear to everyone how carnal generation proceeds. But the prophet treats as singular and indescribable what everyone knows, what can be concealed from no one.
Does it not seem to you, then, that one whose generation is so
far distinguished from the human that it is even said to be indescribable, is not merely a man but is also more than man? If one
truly understands this prophetic statement, moreover, to concern that more sublime and eternal generation of God the Son
from God the Father, all the more will that prove that Christ is
not merely man but more than man. For generation from the
Father is far more astonishing, far more indescribable than is
generation from a virgin. What do you infer, what do you think,
when you hear the prophet saying, concerning this same one:
"That he has done no iniquity, nor has there been deceit in his
mouth"?⁷³ Or do you not recall his words: there is no one on
earth cleansed from sin, not even an infant of one day?⁷⁴ Does
it not seem to you, then, that one who has done no iniquity, in
whose mouth there was no deceit, has surpassed man, and does

70. Is 53.7.   71. Ps 20.2.
72. Is 53.8.   73. Is 53.9.
74. Cf. Jb 15.14.

it not seem to you that he is more than man? Pay attention to this as well: "The just one will justify my many servants and bear their iniquities."[75] The one who is called just, who, it is written, justifies many, who is proclaimed to bear their iniquities, which belongs to God alone—see if this one can be understood, believed, or accepted to be a mere man and not, justly, more than man. One to whom this is obscure is not a man but rather a beast, which no wise person will contradict.

Also, when you read, "He was offered because it was his will"[76] —does that not exceed the common number of men? For what man dies of his own free will, what man willingly is slain? I have presented these things so that one believe that whatever the prophet says in the already mentioned series of verses can only be understood of Christ. In fact, this follows because they are said about a man. But one gathers from what has already been said that it is necessary for that man to be more than man. Moreover, there is no man other than Christ who is found to be more than man. And since you, Jew, confirm that no man can be greater than the Christ, and because your prophet forces you to confess that there is one man greater than others, then it is necessary for you to understand that only Christ is greater than all others. Therefore, all these things are said about Christ.

And because all these things are said about Christ, it remains to prove what was proposed, namely, whether one should think that the kingdom of Christ is an earthly and temporal kingdom, as you think, Jew. Run through the prophecy. "There is no beauty in him, nor comeliness. And we have seen him, and there was no sightliness. And we were desirous of him, despised, and the most abject of men, a man of sorrows, and acquainted with infirmity. And his look was, as it were, hidden and despised. Whereupon we esteemed him not."[77] Does this sound as if it has anything to do with kings? Does this appear to be regal? Where is the gold? Where is the purple? Where the bejeweled crown? Where the throne of silver? Where is the power and haughtiness of a ruler? There is no beauty or comeliness in him, there is no sightliness. Desired yet despised, the most abject of men, a

75. Is 53.11.   76. Is 53.6.
77. Is 53.2–3.

man of sorrows, his look was hidden, nor was he esteemed. For the sake of brevity, do not examine all, but excerpt just certain passages: "And we have thought him as it were a leper, and as one struck by God and afflicted, but he was wounded for our iniquities, he was bruised for our sins."[78] And a little further on: "He will be led as a sheep to slaughter."[79] And, after having interjected a few more words: "Because he is cut off out of the land of the living."[80] And finally: "He delivered his soul unto death and was reputed with the wicked."[81] What do you say, Jew? Are you not astonished? By the power of reason you have been forced already to understand that this concerns Christ. Where, among all these, do you find his temporal kingdom? Where do you see the glory of the ruler? Does suffering illnesses and bearing grief have anything to do with ruling? Does it have anything to do with ruling to be thought to be a leper, to be thought to be struck by God, to be thought to be afflicted? Does it have anything to do with ruling to be wounded, slain, handed over to death, to be reputed with the wicked? I remain silent concerning the rest. What are you doing? Do you not yet recognize that the kingdom of Christ cannot be a temporal or earthly kingdom? Clearly you recognize this, if you are human.

And because this is clear, one ought not tarry long over things that are clear. Hear, then, in these reproaches that he is appointed to these wounds, led to this murder, having handed himself over to death. "My kingdom," he said, "is not of this world. If my kingdom were of this world, my servants would certainly strive that I should not be delivered to the Jews."[82] Stop thinking, then, that Christ is a temporal king, that his kingdom is an earthly kingdom. For grandeur and dejection, glory and ignominy, power and weakness, a kingdom and death, cannot exist at the same time; they do not go together. Understand that Christ does not reign in the customary manner of kings, but commands heaven and earth and every creature not merely as a king but as God and as Lord. Acknowledge that his kingdom exists not merely for a few years, but that it enjoys the blessed infinitude of every

78. Is 53.4–5.   79. Is 53.7.
80. Is 53.8.   81. Is 53.12.
82. Jn 18.36.

age, [a kingdom] from which the Jew who denies him is always excluded, but to which the Christian confessing Christ is always admitted.

By no means am I ignorant of how the ancient serpent whispers into the ears of the damned in the synagogues of Satan,[83] nor is it hidden from me how wicked teachers, oppressed by the narrow paths of a truth so bright, pour poisons into their listeners. In fact, I have heard from some people that they say that their Christ was born at the time of Vespasian and was transferred (by what art I do not know) to Rome.[84] There he hid in crypts or subterranean caves, there he was torn and gnawed to pieces by dogs, and he endured the pain and wounds of that gnawing for Jewish sins or iniquities, and this is why it is said: "He was wounded for our iniquities; he was bruised for our sins."[85] Moreover, he will live and endure these pains in the bowels of the earth until he will go forth from there, at a time determined by God, and, gathering up the Jews from all the world, he will return them anew to the first place of the land promised to them. Then all things will be fulfilled that were foretold by the prophets concerning the future felicity of the Jews; then their Christ will rule over many nations; then there will be peace without fear of any disturbance; then, they affirm, they will live in the utmost delight and with glory. They attest that he appeared to one of their great sages in the guise of a beggar and a wretch. And when the one to whom he appeared detested the vileness and deformity of his appearance, he suddenly changed his form into the beauty of a man, and exchanged his exceedingly vile vestments for precious garments. They also propose that as soon as he held up a sapphire stone in one hand, in the other there was a precious stone of jasper, and he said to the one to whom he had appeared: Why are you surprised? Am I not, am I not your Christ, for whom you have waited so long that the time is nigh for me to come, the time is nigh for me to appear? I will lead you out from all the nations, I will gather you

83. Cf. Rv 2.9.

84. Cf. B.T. *Sanhedrin* 98a and Amulo, *Epistula, seu Liber contra Iudaeos* 12 (PL 116: 148).

85. Is 53.5.

up from all the earth, and I will conduct you to your own land. Then there will be fulfilled in your Jerusalem what Isaiah wrote: "O poor little one, tossed with tempest, without all comfort, behold I will lay your stones in order, and will lay your foundations with sapphires, and I will make your bulwarks of jasper."[86] It is sapphire on which Jerusalem must be founded, or jasper on which the bulwarks of your city have to be built.

O consolation, O hope that must be embraced, O felicity that must be awaited without scruple! O dregs[87] (*feces*) of the human race, do such things appease you, do such things mollify you, do such things persuade you to wait for Antichrist rather than for Christ? In truth, Satan is having some fun with you just as men have fun with apes; he drags you wherever he wants like the lowliest beast of burden with a bridle of foolishness; he promises you many things indeed like the father of lies, only to take them all away;[88] he gives you dreams to remove the reality; he feeds on fables those that he defrauds of Christ, who is the bread of angels and men.

And what should I say? Words are inadequate to refute a foolishness so profound of men so senseless. Behold, you present us a dog-Christ, and you who are embarrassed by the fact that he was slain by Jews blame this on dogs. We do not disagree with that. In truth, as you say, Christ was gnawed by dogs, by ones unclean, by ones who barked at him, and, as we confess, Christ was slain. Let Christ be heard in the psalm: "For many dogs have encompassed me, the council of the malignant has besieged me. They have dug my hands and my feet."[89] Were you not the dogs when, like dogs, you thirsted after blood and licked it almost like a rabid dog, saying: "His blood be upon us and upon our children"?[90] Did you not bark when you cried out time and

---

86. Is 54.11–12.   87. Dregs; or, possibly, excrement.
88. Cf. Jn 8.44.

89. Ps 21.17. For this passage see especially James H. Marrow, "*Circumdederunt me canes multi:* Christ's Tormentors in Northern European Art of the Late Middle Ages and Early Renaissance," *Art Bulletin* 59.2 (1977): 167–81. It was not uncommon for either Jews or Christians to depict the other as a "dog" in the religious polemics of the age. See my *Marks of Distinction*, 148–51; and Kenneth Stow, *Jewish Dogs: An Image and its Interpreters,* Stanford Studies in Jewish History and Culture (Palo Alto: Stanford University Press, 2006).

90. Mt 27.25.

time again to the judge who condemned your wickedness and attempted to turn it aside, "Crucify him, crucify him"?[91] But let me ask about those dogs on which the analogy to your rabid madness is based: can anyone be led to death by dogs? For Isaiah said of Christ: "He will be led just as a sheep to the slaughter."[92] To lead one to death pertains to men, not dogs; to lead one to death pertains to men, not beasts; to lead one to death pertains to rational and not irrational creatures. It is clear, then, that the prophet predicted that Christ would be led to his death not by dogs of this sort but by Jews, who are far worse than dogs. And since it is almost the same thing either for someone to rush against such useless fables as soon as they are heard by disputing such contemptible things, or to wear out one's strength by applying powerful blows one after another to thin air, let what has been said suffice. Let the discussion return to the topic, on account of the fact that it has been taken up from Jewish fables that are more abundant than all human errors. Moreover, this is what this discussion intended to prove—or, rather, that it has already proved both with proof-texts and by reason (*ratio*)—that one should not understand Christ to be a temporal king, that it is unnecessary for the kingdom of Christ to be understood to be an earthly kingdom that must come to an end.

What has already been set forth can suffice to provide every man with certainty in this matter. But because my discussion is with a Jew—I do not know whether he is a human—still other things must be added. Surely I do not know whether a Jew, who does not submit to human reason nor acquiesce to proof-texts that are both divine and his own, is a human. I do not know, I say, whether one is human from whose flesh a heart of stone has not yet been removed, to whom a heart of flesh has not yet been granted, within whom the divine spirit has not yet been placed,[93] without which a Jew can never be converted to Christ. Return to the contest then, Jew, and observe that Christ cannot be a temporal king, that Christ's kingdom cannot be an earthly or transitory kingdom, based on your own authorities and not those that belong to others.

91. Lk 23.21; Jn 19.6.
92. Is 53.7.
93. Cf. Ezek 36.26.

"His power," Daniel said, "is an everlasting power that will not be taken away; and his kingdom that will not be destroyed."[94] Whose? Is it not Christ's? If you are in doubt, pay attention to what came before that: "I beheld until thrones were placed, and the Ancient of Days sat. His garment was white as snow, and the hair of his head like clean wool. His throne like a flame of fire, the wheels of it like a burning fire. A swift stream of fire issued forth from before him. Thousands of thousands ministered to him."[95] And after a few more passages placed in between: "I beheld therefore in the vision of the night, and lo, one like a son of man came with the clouds of heaven. And he came even to the Ancient of Days, and they presented him before him. And he gave him power, and glory, and a kingdom; and all peoples, tribes, and tongues will serve him."[96] And just after what I have set down, he added: "His power is an everlasting power," and the rest.[97]

Who is this "Ancient of Days"? Who is the one who "like a son of man came with the clouds of heaven"? Who is the one who "came even to the Ancient of Days" and was presented "before him" and to whom were given the things already mentioned? Tell me, Jew, if you have anything to say. Or will you be able to imagine that the "Ancient of Days" is other than God? Or will you be able to offer anyone at all other than God to whom "thousands upon thousands minister," before whom "ten thousand times a hundred thousand stand"?[98] Again, whom do you understand to be the one coming "like a son of man" with the clouds of heaven, if not Christ? Who came to the "Ancient of Days" and was presented "before him," if not Christ? Who was given power, glory, and kingdom, and all the rest that follow, if not Christ? Examine the infinite mass of the human race, one individual man after another, and see who of all the sons of men can be understood to be as great, as high as the "son of man." And since it is necessary to understand this as referring to a "son of man," then pay attention to whether any son of man can be described in this way and can be said to be as great,

94. Dn 7.14.
96. Dn 7.13–14.
98. Dn 7.10.

95. Dn 7.9–10.
97. Dn 7.14.

other than Christ. Remember, too, what you conceded above, that none of the sons of men can be greater than the Christ. And pay attention to the fact, too, that if you think that these prophetic passages refer to someone other than the Christ, you will already admit that there is one greater than the Christ. Indeed, it is necessary that the man on whom God conferred so much glory be believed to be greater than every man. If you want to escape this inconvenience, you will be forced to confess that these passages have been said of Christ alone, once the others have been excluded. It seems to me, then, that it has been proved that no one ought to think that this son of man is anyone other than Christ. Moreover, that Christ—according to us the Redeemer and our Savior, whereas according to you he is [merely] Jesus—is the one whom, as already mentioned, your fathers have dreamed of in vain and the one whom your silly expectation awaits in vain.

This is said about this Christ, then: "His power is an everlasting power that will not be taken away; and his kingdom that will not be destroyed."[99] But an everlasting power, a kingdom that is never destroyed, cannot exist on earth. Listen to your psalm that says to God: "In the beginning, O Lord, you established the earth, and the heavens are the works of your hands. They will perish."[100] Therefore, if the heaven will perish, if the earth will perish, then where will Christ reign as a temporal and earthly king? If the earth passes away, then how can the power of an earthly king be everlasting? If, according to your interpretation, the earth on which he will reign comes to an end, how will his kingdom not be destroyed? Either bring it to pass that the earth not perish, so that the kingdom of your Christ last forever, or if his kingdom perishes when the earth perishes, know that you are far removed from the understanding of the prophet who said of the Christ: "His power is an everlasting power that will not be taken away; and his kingdom that will not be destroyed."[101]

Hear once more Ezekiel saying much the same thing: "They will dwell," he said, "upon the land that I gave to my servant

99. Dn 7.14.   100. Ps 101.26–27.
101. Dn 7.14.

Jacob in which your fathers dwelled. And they will dwell in it forever, they and their children and their children's children, and David my servant will be their prince forever. And I will strike a covenant of peace with them; it will be an everlasting covenant for them."[102] What do you say to this? Explain David to me, explain to me also David's everlasting government. Do you not read that David's death occurred almost 500 years before these words were uttered?[103] How, then, will he be said to reign in the future, to rule, whose kingdom has already passed away, who brought it to an end with death? Now, in the same series of passages from the same prophet, the one who is now said to be prince was called a king a little earlier. "And they will be my people," he said, "and I will be their God, and my servant David will be king over them, and there will be one shepherd for them all."[104] Who is this, who is this David that the prophet, born many years after David's death, says will be the future prince and king and the one shepherd of the Jewish kingdom? But I know that Jewish perversity, no matter how great, cannot interpret this to refer to anyone other than the Christ. Actually, the Christ had to be borne from the root, or rather from the very household and family of David, because like David he is called David and it is written that he will be a prince over his people, although he had to rule longer than David and differently than David, in judgment and justice and total fairness upon his people, whom he saves from sin and from all enemies. Therefore, even Jeremiah said: "Strangers will no more rule over him, but they will serve the Lord their God and David their king whom I will raise over them."[105] But how will this be everlasting? How will this be forever? In fact, just as I said, it is written there: "David my servant will be their prince forever."[106] And I continue: "And I will strike a covenant of peace with them; it will be an everlasting covenant."[107] If you understand this kingdom carnally, if you await an earthly government, tell me how David will be able to rule in a land that is not everlasting, in a world that must come to an end. In fact, hear another prophet say that the pres-

102. Ezek 37.25–26.
104. Ezek 37.23–24.
106. Ezek 37.25.
103. Cf. 1 Kgs 2.10.
105. Jer 30.8–9.
107. Ezek 37.26.

ent has to come to an end, that it cannot be everlasting: "And the former things shall not be in remembrance, and they shall not come upon the heart," he said.[108] But if "they shall not be in remembrance," if they "shall not come upon the heart," then certainly earthly kingdoms, certainly the government of mortals not only will not endure, not only will not remain, but they will not even exist in remembrance nor come upon the heart. Since this cannot be questioned, since these things cannot be contradicted because the invincible argument (*ratio*) of truth prevents it, I am surprised if henceforth the thought of a temporal kingdom, if at length an expectation for an earthly government, insofar as it applies to Christ, will come upon your heart, if it will be able to prevent you from understanding the true and everlasting kingdom of Christ.

And, in order that the Jewish heart that is overcome with multiple arguments cease its foolishness and begin to understand, tell me whether you believe in the resurrection of human flesh, whether you confess it. But I know that you believe this, I know that you confess this. Actually, you have received this from your sages both ancient and modern, and the clear and many-layered authority of divine Scripture compels you to believe this. Thus you have in the Psalms: "My flesh also shall rest in hope."[109] But if in hope, then surely either in the hope of resurrection or in some other hope. But in what other hope can the flesh rest if not the hope of resurrection? In fact, what else can the dead flesh hope for but to live again? What else but the animation of the lifeless flesh? For what does that flesh that has already died hope if not resurrection? Therefore, human flesh rests in the hope for resurrection. And you have this from Isaiah: "And all flesh shall come to adore before my face, says the Lord."[110] Read that part of the book of the prophet in which this is written, and you will find that there the prophet also understood the resurrection of the flesh. This is why after a few words he added this, concerning the wicked: "and they shall be a loathsome sight to all flesh."[111] The wicked can only be a "loathsome sight to all flesh" if all flesh will live again, if all

108. Is 65.17.   109. Ps 15.9.
110. Is 66.23.   111. Is 66.24.

flesh will be [re]animated, if it will have the power of seeing the torments of the wicked even with the eyes of the flesh. And you have also in Ezekiel: "Behold, I will open your graves, and will bring you out of your sepulchers, O my people, and will bring you into the land of Israel."[112] And in Job: "In the last day," he said, "I shall rise out of the earth, [. . .] and in my flesh I will see God."[113]

From this point on, I know that you will be unable to repudiate the resurrection of the flesh. But death (*casus*) precedes that resurrection, death (*mors*) comes before new life, lifelessness exists before that [re]animation of bodies. Since you cannot deny this, especially since you witness this every day, tell them, how will your messiah, a carnal king, command all those who are already dead; tell them, how will one that is himself already dead rule over the dead? Tell them, over whom will he reign when he himself and all the others have died at the end of the world; tell them, I say, whom will he govern then? In fact, since his kingdom is everlasting, it is necessary that his government be everlasting, just as you heard from the prophets. Avoid these difficulties if you can; remove your foot from this snare if you are able. Actually, either show us what is everlasting in the earthly kingdom of your messiah—without any interpolation— or, if you cannot deny that there is an end to the world and the corruption of corporeal things along with humans themselves, then along with us you should understand that the everlasting kingdom of Christ is not on earth but rather somewhere else. I will not allow you to escape to what comes after the resurrection of the flesh, to dare to dream that the future kingdom of your messiah be found there. So long as you understand his kingdom to be a carnal one, by the authority of sacred Scripture you will be excluded from his kingdom—both present and future. What beast can be found to be as foolish as the Jew who thinks that after the resurrection of the flesh there will be a carnal life, a carnal king, a carnal kingdom? In saying this, I do not deprive human flesh of its true essence, but I prove that the future condition of the flesh is entirely different. If you who have been

112. Ezek 37.12.
113. Jb 19.25–26.

nourished on the filth (*faex*) of flesh and blood, who have made "flesh your arm,"[114] if you are unable to grasp this, what is it to me?

Listen to Scripture and attend to its judgment, and not to mine. Listen, pay attention, lest you suspect that after the universal restoration of human flesh the kingdom of Christ be wont to exist like that of other kings. Isaiah says: "You will no more have the sun for your light by day, neither will the brightness of the moon enlighten you: but the Lord" your God "will be for you an everlasting light."[115] And elsewhere: "The eye has not seen, O God, besides you, what you have prepared for those that love you."[116] And Zechariah says: "The Lord my God shall come, and all the saints with him. And it shall come to pass in that day, that there shall be no light, but cold and frost. And there shall be one day, which is known to the Lord, not day or night."[117] What will you say to these things? Make something up, if you can. Show how your Christ's carnal empire, a kingdom of the earthly Jerusalem, will be without sun or moon, without day or night. Tell us whether you will be able to understand what has been said to apply to a kingdom understood in that way: "The eye has not seen, O God, besides you, what you have prepared for those that love you."[118] If none but a divine eye has been able to see what has been prepared for those that love God, will yours? Or your fathers'? Or anyone's? You see, then, how quickly, how lucidly, he condemns every notion of a carnal king, of an earthly empire, of worldly glory. In fact, with these few words he proclaims that not only are the earthly Jerusalem, Judea, and the Galilee excluded, and, what is more, all of Syria, in which region the Jewish kingdom flourished in the past, but even all of the lands of the earth, so that neither the kingdom of Christ nor the glorification of the saints can be understood to exist anywhere on earth. Now, if you are unable to find the

114. Jer 17.5.

115. Is 60.19.

116. Is 64.4. Peter's text departs from the Vulgate, and reads "those who love you"—*hiis qui diligunt te*—rather than "those who await you"—*expectantibus te*. Cf. 1 Cor 2.9.

117. Zec 14.5–7.

118. Is 64.4. See n. 116, above.

kingdom of your Christ (as you are wont to understand it) in this life, which must come to an end, nor in that everlasting life that follows after it, then soften your inveterate hardness, cast aside your stony heart, take up a heart of flesh, and know that our Christ reigns in this world by means of the invisible power of deity, by faith and grace, and reigns in the future life with manifest glory.

Surely, if my discussion is with a man and not with a beast, then pay careful attention, and, if God's grace will assist, consider that the final purpose of the law, of the prophets, and of your entire canon is nothing but the blessed eternity it promised to the saints. What else? Do you think that God performed so many acts and such great acts, acts so unusual and so wondrous, acts that had to be proclaimed, only for a brief, wretched life subject to countless deaths? Was Egypt struck by the well-known ten plagues,[119] was Pharaoh drowned with his [troops],[120] did it rain manna each day for forty years,[121] was there a column of smoke by day and fire by night,[122] a fleshy shower of quail,[123] water from rocks,[124] the dividing of the Jordan and the obedient return of the sun,[125] the raising of the dead[126]—were such solemn miracles and so many similar things that were attached to the oracles of the prophets, were all these, I say, performed for such a trivial life that is so wretched and carnal or, rather, that is no life at all? Were they done merely so that you, O Jew, might stuff your belly with various foods and meats? Were they done merely so that you might become drunk, and, once drunk, so that you might snore? Were they done merely so that you might devote yourself to your passions, so that you might indulge yourself in desires? Were they all done merely so that you might abound in riches, so that you might fill your chests with gold and silver and many treasures, so that you might raise yourself up with the arrogant pride of one who rules despotically over his subjects? Let this thought be far away, let it be far removed

---

119. Cf. Ex 7.17–12.29.   120. Cf. Ex 14.21–28.
121. Cf. Ex 16.4–35.   122. Cf. Ex 13.21.22.
123. Cf. Ex 16.13.   124. Cf. Nm 20.11.
125. Cf. Jos 3.14–16 and 10.12–13.
126. Cf. 1 Kgs 17.22; 2 Kgs 4.32–35; 2 Kgs 13.21.

from human minds, let it be far removed from souls with a capacity for reason, let it draw far away from all those who know
God. Reason does not accept and justice itself contradicts the
notion that the human, who was preferred by the Creator to
all irrational creatures—although this may not be the case for
some humans—be compared across the whole of his genus "to
senseless beasts, and become like unto them."[127] For if this were
so, if God only bestowed these carnal goods upon man, what
more would wretched man possess than does a cow, than an ass,
than any of the most vile vermin? In fact, he was created from
everlasting to everlasting, although he deservedly lost that for a
time due to his guilt; nevertheless he did not lose the hope of
recovering it. Hence it is that God, nursing you like an infant[128]
on carnal benefits for spiritual ones, nourishing you little by
little on temporal benefits for eternal ones, bestowed transitory
goods upon you at the beginning, so that, encouraged by these,
you would learn to guard God's law, and then, moving up from
them, you would pass on to hoping for and loving heavenly and
eternal goods.

This eternity was the cause of their miracles so sublime, so that
this unruly people—enticed by benefits on the one hand and, on
the other, encouraged by acts so wondrous—would become accustomed to obeying the Creator and, by obeying, return to that
blessed eternity of which it had been deprived because it was will-
fully disobedient. And because not all things had to be lavished
at one and the same time on new people who arose at the beginning of this world and were altogether ignorant of divine things,
one reads about this eternity more rarely in the Pentateuch or
the Heptateuch, whereas it is commended more frequently by
the prophets, and it is proclaimed most frequently—rather most
assiduously—by the Gospel of Christ. But until you acquiesce
to the Gospel, it is not reasonable to produce a reasonable argument against you from the Gospel. But hear your own texts,
which you cannot refuse to hear. Hear Jacob himself, your great
father and patriarch, hear him blessing his son Joseph: "The
blessings of your father are strengthened with the blessings of his

127. Ps 48.13.
128. Cf. Hos 11.1; Nm 11.12.

fathers, until the desire of the everlasting hills should come,"[129] he said. Also hear Moses himself, who spoke in a similar fashion, when blessing the tribe of Joseph: "Of the blessing of the Lord be his land."[130] And, after an intervening few words, he added, "Of the tops of the ancient mountains, of the fruits of the everlasting hills."[131] What are these everlasting hills? This earth of ours does not have everlasting hills or everlasting mountains. In fact, if this earth will perish, as the argument written above understands, how can its hills be everlasting? If this whole earth should perish, how will a part of it endure? When this earth perishes, then the hills will perish too. Thus it happens that its hills cannot be called everlasting.

What, then, are the everlasting hills? As long as you are earthbound, so long as you seek everlasting hills on earth, you will not find them. Lift up your minds, seek them above the heavens. There you will find not only everlasting hills but even mountains that endure forever. The psalmist said of them: "You enlighten wonderfully from the everlasting mountains."[132] It is not for me to teach which these are. I am dealing with an enemy, not instructing a student. But if you believe, you will understand.[133] If not, then you will not know either these or the other mysteries (*sacramenta*) of God. Remember, too, what David said about this eternity: "I thought upon the days of old, and I had in my mind the eternal years."[134] But, just as I said concerning the hills, you will be unable to find "eternal years" by restricting them to time. Speaking to God in another place, he himself indicates that time must come to an end, that the years of men will fail: "But you are always the selfsame, and your years will not fail."[135] He would not say this, he would not present this as something unique, if he knew that human years would not fail. And the preceding passages by which he had shown that things human will perish, by which he added that things divine will endure forever, indicate this.

Listen also to Isaiah concerning this eternity—that it will not

129. Gn 49.26.   130. Dt 33.13.
131. Dt 33.15.   132. Ps 75.5.
133. Cf. Is 7.9 LXX.   134. Ps 76.6.
135. Ps 101.28.

be within this heaven and this earth: "For as the new heavens, and the new earth, which I will make to stand before me, says the Lord: so will your seed stand, and your name."[136] These words teach both that this heaven and this earth will pass away, and they designate the new state of the world to come with the name of a new heaven and a new earth. God makes these to stand before him, because after the end of the world all things will obtain this condition such that they will not lose it, as they did once already, but so that they will hang onto it steadfastly and without end. Run through all of the prophets, and you will find that this eternity is often proclaimed, and solemnly commended. Turn the mind away, then, from things that pass away, withdraw the heart from things that will perish, and believe in our Christ, the author and king of this blessed eternity, and labor in this his eternal kingdom with Christian faith and with acts ascribed to faith. For we Christians understand Christ to be such a king, we believe in one such as this, we adore one such as this, and we hasten to reach such a kingdom as this by grace and vigorous efforts. And we invite Jews to this kingdom by the same means.

But they themselves, so far as they can, reject us and all those who arise from the Gentile nations. In fact, they say that God spoke only to them, gave a law only to them, sent prophets only to them and, moreover, that the Christ has yet to be sent after all of the prophets, and they assert that his kingdom pertains only to the Jews. But just as it was foolish to think that God performed such great and wondrous acts only for the sake of matters that belong to the present and are subject to decay, so it is not less foolish to think, it is in fact bestial to think, that the Author of all the world cared only about the Jews, having treated the Gentiles as of secondary importance, and that he gave the hope of breathing life anew only to them. God did not think in this way, since he cares for all, nor did he confine his compassion to such strict limits that, choosing a small number of the people that is troublesome and ungrateful to him, he would cast aside the endless number of the Gentiles, even as he would allow those not

136. Is 66.22.

reaching out to him to descend forevermore through the byways of error to the depths of perdition. In fact, it was fitting that the One who created every race of mortals would show compassion to all at the appropriate time, and would call all of the nations to salvation by a generous bounty, once the Jews had been rejected owing to their own wickedness.[137]

If according to your wont, Jew, you presume to murmur against these things, and you bandy about that you are a special people called by God, then pay attention once again to your Scripture, and learn that it is not the case that you alone have been chosen and called by God.[138] Read once more the verse of your psalm that addresses God: "All the nations you have made will come and adore before you, O Lord."[139] After this, will you continue to bandy about that God cares only for you? It proclaims that the nations will adore God. Not only this one, but all the nations. And, so that no nation could be excluded from this understanding, even though it should suffice that it says "all nations"—it added "'that you have made." It is certain, however, that God made all nations, and none can be found that were not made by him. Therefore, all nations will come; no nation is excluded; all nations, it is written, will come to adore God. This is why you have this in the psalm: "All the ends of the earth will remember, and will be converted to the Lord. And all the families of nations will adore in his sight."[140]

Is the witness of this psalm alone insufficient, apart from others, to demonstrate the vocation of the nations? Then pay attention to the many similar things that God said through Isaiah: "They have sought me that before asked not for me, they have found me that sought me not, and I said: Behold me, behold me, to a nation that did not call upon my name."[141] What will you say? You see God hurrying to cross over to a people not calling upon him. In fact, these are the words of one hurrying, of one vigorously hastening: "Behold me, behold me." And, indeed, this has already been done; this has actually already been fulfilled. The Jew calling upon God merely with his voice has

137. Cf. Rom 11.25.   138. Cf. Is 51.16; Zec 13.9.
139. Ps 85.9.   140. Ps 21.28.
141. Is 65.1.

been condemned, while a Gentile people ignorant of God has been chosen. Pay attention to both, I say, pay attention to both, and hear very clearly through Malachi that the Jews are condemned and the Gentiles are chosen: "I have no pleasure in you, says the Lord of hosts, and I will not receive a gift from your hand. For from the rising of the sun even to its going down, my name is great among the Gentiles, and in every place there is sacrifice, and there is offered to my name a clean oblation."[142] But this was not the case in Malachi's age. For then all the world, except for a few Jews, served not the Creator but the creation, sacrificed not to God but to idols.[143] But what was not fulfilled at that time had to be fulfilled at another time. Indeed, one reads the present tense in the prophet, but understands a future tense. If you had even a little learning, you would know that this is customary for your Scriptures. What is demonstrated not to have occurred at the time when the prophet was preaching, then, is known to have been fulfilled in these days of Christian faith. Clearly now it is great, truly the name of God and his Christ is great among the Gentiles, and from the rising of the sun until its setting, "every tongue confesses that the Lord Jesus Christ is in the glory of God the Father."[144]

But what shall I say also about what is added there: "and in every place there is sacrifice, and there is offered to my name a clean oblation"?[145] What shall I say also about this: "I will not receive a gift from your hands"?[146] In fact where—or when—does God receive a gift from your hands? Was not your temple already destroyed from old? Was not your altar buried? Were not the sacrifices withdrawn? Were not the burnt offerings removed? Here certainly the Jewish polemic fails, here actually your obstinate stiff neck gives way. You see, Jew, that you cannot deny it, you see that you cannot prevail by interpreting this first one way and then another, as is your custom. See this as well, then, that in every place a clean oblation is offered to God. See that across the entire world churches of Christ are constructed, altars are consecrated in every place, and the Lamb of God,

142. Mal 1.10–11.   143. Cf. Rom 1.25.
144. Phil 2.11.   145. Mal 1.11.
146. Mal 1.10.

whom you slew on the Cross, is offered without end upon the same altars in these same churches to the Father Almighty for the salvation of the world. You will discern that these prophetic words have been fulfilled in them all, that is: "I will not receive a gift from your hands,"[147] and "in every place there is offered to my name a clean oblation."[148]

Now cease, then, to rage so foolishly as if you are out of your mind, cease to say that you alone—the others having been spurned—are chosen, to think that you alone have been taken up and others have been cast off, when elsewhere you hear that he has chosen others after having spurned you, that he has summoned others after having rejected you, that he has taken up others after having cast you off. In order to bring this chapter to its conclusion: either discard those Scriptures that deny the temporal kingdom of the Christ, or if you dare not, then accept the everlasting kingdom of our Christ.

147. Ibid.
148. Mal 1.11.

CHAPTER FOUR

In which it is demonstrated that
the Christ is not still to come, as the Jews
foolishly think, but rather that he has come
at a sure and preordained time for
the salvation of the world

T REMAINS for me to pursue a fourth and penultimate battle against you, O Jew, a battle in which (so I think) the one who conferred an easy palm of victory upon me in the earlier battles will do so once more. I will not be without the sword of Goliath to destroy you, as I hope to do if you do not want to live, a sword that I will use against you while you lie prostrate in your complete ruin, and I will cut off once again a blasphemous head with that blade's edge with which you, girded up, had advanced against God. Once this last battle that alone remains has been finished, you will cease to draw another breath; once this battle has been concluded, you will never again dare to murmur [against God].

Furthermore, this is the cause for which this last clash must be fought: I say that the Christ predicted by the prophets has already come; you deny this, and you say that he has not come but is still to come. I say, he has come; you say, he will come. It is incumbent upon me, then, to test what I have proposed. And in order not to delay too long, in order not to hold you in suspense too long, hear this. Hear, I say, not just any of the prophets but that great father of prophets, the great prophet—rather, patriarch—Jacob. Hear him, in whose lineage and name you pride yourselves, from whom you are called Israel—would that you were called after him both in reality just as in name "a man who sees God."[1] If, then, you are a man who sees, then see, understand, and pay attention to what he says: "The scepter will not be taken away from Judah, nor a ruler from his thigh, until he come that is to be sent. And he will be the expectation of nations."[2] Alas, what more evasions do you seek? What subterfuges? There is nothing here to offer you any escape. In fact, if this is said about the Christ, then either show me the royal scepter of Judah or the ruler from the thigh of Judah, or concede that the Christ has already come. No Jew, in my estimation, will contradict that this is said about the Christ.[3] At one time I had a conversation about this passage with some Jews who said that they thought that this had been proclaimed of none other than the Christ and that all Jews agreed in this view. But if anyone from among the number of the perfidious [Jews], overcome by the fruitless task of leading others astray, gives up hope that he can resist such powerful evidence in the prophetic passage, which he would prefer be interpreted in some other manner, he will fail. Of whom, other than Christ, can these words, which are so specific, so solemn, be understood to apply? Of which of the prophets other than Christ, of which of the kings other than Christ can this passage be understood: "until he come that is to be sent."[4] Other than Christ, of whom can it be understood that "he shall be the expectation of nations"?[5] Although all the prophets were sent by God, of whom, other than Christ, was it said specifically: "until he come that is to be sent"?[6] Surely the holy patriarch knew that this title of one that is sent was shared by all the prophets. Therefore, what he knew was common to all, he indicated applies to this one in a particular way. He would not have indicated that sending (*missio*) as specifically unique unless it was greater than that of the prophets, who were sent.

Because he indicated it specifically, he showed that the one he said had to be sent was greater than all those already sent or

1. Jerome, *Liber interpretationis hebraicorum nominum,* ed. P. de Lagarde, CC SL 72 (Turnholt: Brepols, 1959), pp. 13, 21; 63, 22; 74, 15; 76, 20; idem, *Liber quaestionum Hebraicarum in Genesim* 32.28, ed. P. de Lagarde, CC SL 72 (Turnholt: Brepols, 1959), p. 52.

2. Gn 49.10.   3. Cf. B.T. *Sanhedrin* 98b.
4. Gn 49.10.   5. Ibid.
6. Ibid.

to be sent. You also, Jew, confess that the Christ is greater than all mortal men. It follows, then, that one must accept that what was said about one who is greater than all, whom even you profess to be greater, was said only of the Christ. Truly, who except Christ could be called the "expectation of nations"? That which is proclaimed is not insignificant; the one of whom something so great is proclaimed is not insignificant. Necessarily, then, that one who is said to be awaited by the nations is great, the one who is proclaimed to be the future expectation of the nations is greater than all the rest. Plainly, this does not have to do with the common crowd nor with the common assemblage of men, in which both the collapse of Jewish government and the expectation that the nations should be saved takes its start. See then, Jew, whether the one that is called by the patriarch the "expectation of the nations" and that the prophet writes stands as an "ensign of the people"[7] is not one and the same person.

Indeed, here are the words of Isaiah: "In that day the root of David, who stands for an ensign of the people, him the nations will beseech."[8] Therefore, the one whom Jacob said that the nations must await, Isaiah said must be adored by the same nations.[9] Examine the entire text of divine Scripture and show me where such things, or similar things, were said of any ruler of the Jews or of the Gentile nations. But I know that you will fail, I know that you will find none but Christ with whom these things are in agreement. And because this is so clear, return to the subject at hand, you who assert that Christ has not yet come; show me who is the "scepter from Judah" or the "ruler from his thigh" according to the judgment of your patriarch. Indeed, the prophetic voice compels you to do so. In fact, either, as has been said, you will confess along with us that the Christ has come, or, if you deny that he has come, you are compelled to reveal a king or prince of the tribe of Judah. Actually, as you know, the king of kings alone is customarily indicated by a "scepter" on the right hand side, while by the word "duke" (*dux*)[10] a prince

7. Is 11.10.
8. The Vulg. reads "in that day the root of Jesse ..."
9. Cf. Is 66.23.
10. Cf. Gn 36.15–31.

of lower dignity is indicated, and by "the thigh of Judah" his lineage is denoted. Therefore, produce for me a king from the line of Judah, or, if you cannot do so, at least show me a duke.

But I do not propose to accept that the king be one that some of you confess is from the city of Narbonne in Gaul, or others confess is at Rouen, which is ridiculous.[11] I say I will not accept as king of the Jews any Jew who dwells in France, any Jew who dwells in Germany, any Jew who dwells in Italy, or any Jew who dwells in the remote parts of the East, of Africa, or in the remote parts of the North, or who lives somewhere else. I will not accept any Jew as king of the Jews except one who lives and rules in the kingdom of the Jews.[12] You are not unaware that the ancient kingdom of the Jews is where David, where Solomon, and where the other kings of the Jews once ruled, a kingdom for which now you yearn with a stubborn plaintive sigh, and from which with unceasing lamentation you lament that you are in exile. I reject the empty name of a king that you put forward; I reject it even if he will have arisen from the very tribe of Judah,

11. See Aryeh Graboïs, "La dynastie des 'rois juifs' de Narbonne (XIIe–XIIIe siècle)," *Narbonne. Archéologie et histoire*, vol. 2: *Narbonne au moyen âge* (Montpelier: Fédération historique du Languedoc méditerranéen et du Roussillon, 1973): 49–54. Graboïs demonstrates that by the middle of the twelfth century both Jewish and Christian sources attest that a Jewish communal leader in Narbonne had assumed the title *Nasi* ("prince") and traced his—and his family's— lineage back to King David; it was commonly accepted that Charlemagne had confirmed the family in this "royal" title. Cf. Aryeh Graboïs, "Une Principauté Juive dans la France du Midi à l'Époque Carolingienne," in his *Civilisation et société dans l'Occident médiéval* (London: Variorum, 1983), XV: 191–202. Although the title "king" of the Jews—attested in diplomatic sources—implied only seigneurial rank, among some non-Jews it became a source of complaint. This was the case not only for Peter the Venerable, but also for Thomas of Monmouth. See his *The Life and Miracles of St. William of Norwich by Thomas of Monmouth* 2.11, ed. M. R. James, 94. For further discussion especially of a *rex judaeorum* at Rouen, see Norman Golb, *The Jews in Medieval Normandy: A Social and Intellectual History* (Cambridge: Cambridge University Press, 1998), 202–7; and see my *Marks of Distinction*, 198 n. 85.

12. That medieval Jews may have attempted to blunt the Christian exegesis of this text by alleging the existence of Jewish rulers elsewhere, after the destruction of the Second Temple, is amply demonstrated in the *Tractatus contra Judaeos* by Fulbert of Chartres (d. 1029), which is concerned exclusively with a treatment of Gn 49.10. Fulbert's text will be found in PL 141: 305–18.

whichever one of yours you throw against me. I reject one that
is king in name alone and is without the power of a king, even
if he is from the same stock. And, O souls that, deluded by the
phantasms of Satan, only take pride in the empty names of real
things because they cannot take pride in real things. They pursue the shadows of bodies, holding nothing solid before their
hands, and when like dogs they snatch at fleeting images, they
lose the meal they were able to chew that was already held between their teeth while rashly opening their mouths wide.[13]

Must I accept a slave as a king, a wretch as one who is blessed,
a captive as one who is native-born? Show me even one—I do
not say a king or a duke—but even one Jew in the entire world
who is not disgraced with servitude. What nations do not rule
over the Jews? What peoples do the Jews not serve? What race of
men[14] does not tread upon them as the vilest of slaves? In truth,
just as God threatened them in the past in Deuteronomy, when,
with respect to religion, they were at the head of all peoples,
now they have been transformed into "the tail" of all the nations.[15] Thinking that there is no safety for them anywhere and
fearful of what should not be feared, and in a state of anxious
uncertainty for all the things that have occurred, they are "a fugitive and vagabond [. . .] upon the earth," like Cain, the murderer of his brother.[16] He should consider carefully what was
written in the book already mentioned: "And their life is before
their eyes and, made to tremble by the powerful force of dread,
they do not trust their life."[17] Will you provide for me a king, O
Jew, from among the number of such as these? Will you offer

13. The story of the dog that loses its meal when it sees its own reflection in
the water was well known, and can be traced back as far as Aesop's *Fables*. For medieval transmission see, for example, the Aberdeen Bestiary (Aberdeen University Library MS 24), fols. 19v–20r (http://www.abdn.ac.uk/bestiary/translat/20r
.hti, accessed December 26, 2012).

14. Reading *genus hominum* for *genus hominem*.

15. Cf. Dt 28.13, 44.

16. Gn 4.12.

17. Cf. Dt 28.66–67. The Vulg. reads "et erit vita tua quasi pendens ante te;
timebis nocte et die et non credes vitae tuae" (Dt 28.66)—"And your life shall
be as it were hanging before you. You shall fear night and day, neither shall you
trust your life."

an exile for a king? Will you produce a servant as a king? Will you propose a slave for a leader? Will you say that among such as these there endures still the prophecy: "the scepter shall not be taken away from Judah, nor a ruler from his thigh"?[18] And since it is clear that it is childish and foolish to take pride in the title of king that is empty, without royal dignity, if you do not want to confess that the Christ has already come, then show me a king with both the royal title and royal power. If you cannot, at least show me a duke from among the Jews. But since the glory of the kingdom and ducal power actually perished among the Jews once the Christ had come, then understand that Christ has come, the one that had to be sent by Jacob,[19] the one that we believe and we say was sent by God a long time ago already.

And indeed I have already taught that he has been sent, but up to this point I have not actually proved it. But the already cited prophecy demonstrates this very clearly. It said that the messiah had to be sent at that very moment when Jewish rule would be taken away, once the kings or leaders had been removed. Investigate with me, then, the sequence of the generations of Judah, and when you recognize that kingdom or leadership has ceased for the tribes of Judah, then know that the messiah has come, then adore him, then accept him. Moreover, although when he lived Judah was of greater dignity than his brothers, and although Scripture is not silent concerning the fact that his tribe was distinguished more than the others with certain privileges,[20] nonetheless it took its kingdom or rule especially from David, and it endured up to the era of the messiah.

Begin, then, to reckon the tribes of Judah from David, the first king, and recognize that from that point "the scepter shall not be absent from Judah, nor a ruler from his thigh."[21] Run through the individual kings and, numbered from Solomon, Rehoboam, Abijah, and Asa,[22] through those that follow after them before the Babylonian captivity as far as Joachim or Ze-

---

18. Gn 49.10.   19. Cf. Nm 24.17.
20. Cf. 1 Chr 5.2.
21. Gn 49.10: "sceptrum de Iuda vel dux de femore eius non defecerit." Cf. Vulg.: "non auferetur sceptrum de Iuda et dux de femoribus eius . . ."
22. Cf. 1 Chr 3.10.

dekiah, to reach the last king of the tribe of Judah. And then continue the course from there through Shealtiel and his son Zerubbabel,[23] the one who rebuilt the temple of God and was the first leader from the tribe of Judah after the royal dignity, and from them, the ones that Josephus, the historian of Jewish antiquity—and himself a Jew—described,[24] continue up to King Herod. And once you have identified all those leaders from among the Jewish people who ruled for that entire time period, who drew their line of descent from the tribe of Judah, see, then, that not only the kingdom but even leadership had passed from that same tribe in the time of the already mentioned Herod.[25] If you have read, then remember; if you have not read, then read and learn that for the entire period from Zerubbabel until Herod there was a mediator that held the Jewish government while bearing the title of leader (*dux*) in some cases and of kings in others, but more often actually bearing the title of the priests, descending from the aforementioned tribe of Judah.[26]

But if you say that those who ruled from Zerubbabel until Herod cannot clearly be demonstrated from the chronicles to have taken their origin from the tribe of Judah, I reply that although this cannot be clearly gathered from the chronicles, nonetheless it is clearly demonstrated from that already mentioned prophecy which is superior to all chronicles of that sort. For even though the chronicles of Josephus or of other historians do not explicitly identify by name the Jewish tribe from which the aforementioned kings drew their lineage, yet even though they do not affirm this, nonetheless neither do they deny it. The prophecy, then, completely fills in what is lacking in the chronicles, because the Spirit of God that speaks in the prophet is far more worthy of faith than any writer describing in a human manner the things that he saw. That about which the writer of a chronicle is silent, the Spirit described, [and] what

23. Cf. 1 Esdras 3.2.
24. Cf. Josephus, *Antiquitates, Books 12–14*, 14.5.1.80–84, trans. Ralph Marcus, 487–91.
25. The Maccabean kings were not from the tribe of Judah.
26. The priests were from the tribe of Levi. Cf. Lv 21.1, 10.

he lacked God filled in. Therefore, as was said, from Zerubbabel up to Herod, princes were set over the Jews who drew their lineage from the tribe of Judah, bearing the title of kings in some cases or of priests in other cases.

Those who ambitiously but illicitly seized possession of the priesthood, which under the law belonged to the sons of Levi, nevertheless ruled the Jews for the entire period with this or that title of rank. In fact, when they were unable to use the royal title or rank (*fastus*), because the title had been forbidden by the Persians or the Macedonians to whose rule they were subject, they ruled over the Jews as a simple leader or with the rank of priest. If you want to know their names, then listen: Zerubbabel succeeded as governor of Judah, while one reads in the prophecy of Haggai that Joachim the son of the high priest Joshua succeeded to the rank of priest.[27]

Elias(h)ib succeeded to him, Joiada to Elias(h)ib, John to Joiada, Judah to John, Onias [I][28] to Judah, Eleazar to Onias [I], Onias II to Eleazar, Symon to Onias [II], Onias III[29] to Symon, Judah Maccabee[30] to Onias as governor without the priesthood, his brother Jonathan[31] to Judah both as governor with the priesthood, his brother Symon[32] to Jonathan in both, John[33] to Symon, [and] Aristobolus to Johannes.[34] This was the first one after Zedekiah that assumed the diadem of kings, and, keeping

27. Cf. Hg 1.1, which identifies Joshua as son of the High Priest Josedech. Josephus, at *Antiquitates* 11.5.1.120, pp. 372–73, identifies Joachim (Joakeimos) as the son of Joshua (Jesus).

28. The high priest Onias I lived at the end of the fourth century BCE. Cf. 1 Mc 12.20–23.

29. A high priest deposed by the Hellenistic ruler Antiochus IV in 174 BCE.

30. Hasmonean ruler from 165–160 BCE.

31. Ruled from 160–142 BCE.

32. Ruled from 142–134 BCE.

33. Viz., John Hyrcanus, Simon's son, who ruled from 134–104 BCE.

34. The names in Peter's list show a number of variants as they move from Hebrew to Greek to Latin. His Elias = Elias(h)ib (see Josephus, *Antiquitates* 11.5.5.158, pp. 390–91). He was succeeded by Joiada (see Josephus, *Antiquitates* 11.5.7.1.297, pp. 456–57), and Joiada was succeeded by John. John was then succeeded by his son Jaddus (see Josephus, *Antiquitates* 11.5.7.2.304, p. 461), or Judah in Peter's text. Cf. Jerome, *Commentarii in Danielem* 3.9, ed. F. Glorie, CC SL 75A (Turnholt: Brepols, 1964).

for himself the priestly dignity, he ruled over the people for only
one year, as was mentioned above. Alexander[35] succeeded Aristobolus[36] as both king and priest at the same time. Moreover,
after him his wife Alexandra ruled. After the two already mentioned sons of Alexandra and Alexander, Hyrcanus succeeded
in the pontificate and Aristobolus in the kingdom. Once Aristobolus was conquered by the Roman consul Pompey and was
sent bound in chains to Rome, Herod, who was actually foreign
to Judah or to the race of the Jews, obtained the kingdom of
the Jews at the order of the Roman senate after Hyrcanus the
brother of Aristobolus had already been slain. Give credence to
your own Josephus, who wrote that Herod was begotten from
an Idumean father named Antipater and an Arabian mother
called Cypris.[37] Once Herod obtained the Jewish kingdom, it
was not only the Gospel voice that proclaimed that Christ was
born,[38] but also the already mentioned chronicle of Josephus
and the sure report of many Christians as well as pagans that
declared Christ was born.[39]

From that age of Herod, then, until this year 1144, in which
I have written this, show me if you can, after having applied all
your effort, even one leader, let alone a king, either from the
tribe of Judah or from any of the tribes of the Jews. Did not
your Josephus report that, after the first Herod died, his son
Archelaus succeeded him in the government of the entire Jewish kingdom at the direction of the Roman Caesar? And once
he was removed, did not other sons or close blood relations of
this same Herod succeed to the same kingdom through the tet-
rarchy or multiple divisions?[40] And did not all of them rule a

35. Presumably Alexander Jannaeus, who succeeded Aristobolus and ruled
from 103–76 BCE.
36. Presumably the Hasmonean ruler, the son of John Hyrcanus (ruled 104–
103 BCE).
37. Cf. Josephus, *Antiquitates* 14.1.3.8–9, pp. 452–53; for Cypros/Cypris, cf.
Josephus, *Antiquitates* 14.7.3.121, pp. 510–11.
38. Cf. Mt 2.1.
39. Cf. Josephus, *Antiquitates* 18.3.3.63, trans. Louis H. Feldman, 48–49; Augustine, *De civitate dei* 18.46.1, ed. Bernhard Dombart and Alfons Kalb, CC SL
48 (Turnholt: Brepols, 1955), 643–44.
40. Cf. Josephus, *Antiquitates* 17.11.4.318, trans. Ralph Marcus, 312–13.

mere sixty years from the birth of Christ to the devastation and
final destruction of the city of Jerusalem and of the whole of
the Jewish kingdom? And from that time forth, after that land,
which in the past had been given to the Jews by God, spewed
forth all the Jews just like useless vomit, spreading them across
the entire world, and exposed them to be trodden under the
feet of all the Gentiles, you know that not only were they unable
to aspire to any government or kingdom but they were unable
in any fashion even to recover from ignominious servitude.

What, then, is left? Clearly, this: actually, as has already been
said, either you will show that the scepter of kings or the dignity of leadership from the line of Judah still endures, or you
will confess that, since "the scepter of Judah or a ruler from his
thigh"[41] [has been taken away], Christ has already come. Nor
just that alone. For either it is necessary for you to disprove, rationally, all I have disclosed from divine books or true chronicles, or, if you are unable to do so, it is necessary that you confess that Christ was born under King Herod. But in truth, even
as is clear to all who have bleary or blinded eyes, no Jewish perversity, no insanity of any error whatsoever can resist a truth so
robust. Therefore, let the stiff neck bend, let the blasphemous
tongue be silent, and let it await Christ, the Savior of the world,
not as if he has not yet come but is yet to come, but rather let
it adore him just as one that has already filled the world while
irradiating it with the clear light of his coming. What seems to
you, Jew, to be the case concerning all these matters? Or has the
Jewish heart in you not yet been buried under this bulwark of
divine statements? Or does something of [your] damnable perfidy still remain? Perhaps I have spoken more extensively than is
appropriate about this, because I seem perhaps to suspect your
obduracy more than others.

Let this discourse, then, tend toward an end, and let it conclude the matter already so long discussed in the last of the
prophets. You, Daniel, who are inferior to none of the preceding
prophets, come, then, after the others, and let there be revealed
to me what God revealed to you through Gabriel, concerning
Christ's advent. Expound all those things that are hidden, de-

41. Gn 49.10.

clare those that are obscure, and unlock those that are closed. Compel the Jews to confess what they deny, and do not explain to them merely that Christ is about to come, but even expound for them that time when he has [already] come. And lest some path of escape remain open for their obstinate evasion or there exist any place for effecting it, enumerate for them those years from the time of the vision revealed to you up to [the time of] Christ. Hear then, O Jews, the prophet of God, and, using pebbles or the fingers on your hands, calculate the prophetic years from Daniel to Christ. Do not investigate the time beyond and after the Christ, [but] grasp the year of his advent that is the most certain.

Listen, then, to Gabriel speaking to Daniel:

Daniel, mark the word, and understand the vision. Seventy weeks are shortened upon your people, and upon your holy city, that transgression may be finished, and sin may have an end, and iniquity may be abolished, and everlasting justice may be brought, and vision and prophecy may be fulfilled, and the saint of saints may be anointed. Know therefore, and take notice, that from the going forth of the word, to build up Jerusalem again, until Christ the prince (*dux*), there will be seven weeks, and sixty-two weeks. And the street will be built again, and the walls in straitness of times. And after sixty-two weeks Christ will be slain, and the people that will deny him will not be his. And a people with their leader that will come, will destroy the city and the sanctuary, and the end thereof shall be devastation. And after the end of the war there will be appointed desolation. And he will confirm the covenant with many, in one week, and in the half of the week the victim and the sacrifice will fall, and there will be in the temple the abomination of desolation. And the desolation will continue even to the consummation, and to the end.[42]

What are you doing, Jews? See that your prophet described not only the year of the advent of Christ but even the time for his Passion and death. And not only that, but also what happened to you from that time on. He did not fail to proclaim or describe what happens to your city, to your sanctuary, and to the entire Jewish stock even until today. Return, then, to the number of years, and understand not only the period of time from Daniel's vision until Christ but even the very year in which he was born. But lest perhaps the words of a modern reporter

42. Dn 9.23–27.

are worthless for us, receive the same number not from a modern but from the ancient and most learned man Tertullian.[43] You will be unable not to believe him, even though he is one of ours, since you will be compelled to accede to the truth calculated by him from the time of the princes and the confidence (*fides*) in true chronicles.

Listen, then, to him. He says,

How do we prove that Christ comes within seventy weeks? Count from the first year of [the reign of] Darius, since it was then that the vision was revealed to Daniel. In fact he [Gabriel] said to him: Understand and conclude that I reply these things to you from prophesying the word. Whence we have to compute from the first year of [the reign of] Darius, when Daniel saw this vision. Let us see how the years are fulfilled until the advent of Christ: Darius reigned nineteen years.[44] Artaxerxes [reigned] sixty-one years.[45] Ochus[46] and also Cyrus [reigned] twenty-four years, and Argus one year. A second Darius, who is called the Mede, [reigned] twenty-two years. Alexander of Macedon twelve years. Then after Alexander, who had ruled both the Medes and the Persians, whom he had conquered, and who had consolidated his rule in Alexandria, at which time he even called [the city] by his own name, there reigned in Alexandria Sother, for thirty-five years. Philadelphus succeeded him, reigning for thirty-eight years. After him Evergetes reigned for twenty-five years. Then Philopater ruled for seventeen years. After him Epiphanes [ruled] for twenty-four years. Likewise, a second Evergetes [ruled] for twenty-seven years. Then Sother for thirty-eight years and Ptolemy for thirty-eight years. Cleopatra [ruled] for twenty years and five months. Then Cleopatra ruled jointly with Augustus for thirteen years. After Cleopatra, Augustus ruled [as emperor] for forty-two more years. Now, the entire duration of Augustus's imperial reign numbered fifty-six years. Moreover, we see that in the forty-first year of the reign of Augustus, who ruled after the death of Cleopatra, Christ was born. Moreover, this same Augustus lived fifteen years after the time when Christ was born. And the remaining period of time from the day of Christ's birth, in the forty-first year of Augustus, after the death of Cleopatra, [was] four hundred thirty-eight years and five months. Thus sixty-two and one-half weeks were completed which produce four hundred thirty-seven years and six months until the day of Christ's birth.

43. As Yvonne Friedman suggests (see CC CM 58, 75n), Peter is in fact not following Tertullian here but rather Jerome, who cites Tertullian. See Jerome, *In Dan* 3.9, ln. 483, CC SL 75A.

44. Darius I, reigned 522–486 BCE.

45. Actually Artaxerxes reigned from 465–424 BCE.

46. Presumably Darius II Ochus, who reigned 423–404 BCE.

And thus eternal justice is revealed and the anointing of the Saint of saints—that is, of Christ—and the vision and the prophecies have been sealed, and sins are dismissed, which things are bestowed by means of faith in Christ's name upon all those who believe in him.[47] What does it mean, moreover, that the vision and the prophecy are sealed? Since all the prophets announced him, [it means] that he would come and would have to suffer. Thus, since the prophecy has been fulfilled by his advent, he also said that the vision and the prophecy are sealed, since he is himself the seal of all the prophets fulfilling all those things that the prophets announced previously. After his advent and his Passion, moreover, no more is there a vision or a prophet to announce that Christ will come.

And a little later he said:[48] "Let us see," he said,

how the other seven and one-half weeks that are separated from the previous weeks will be fulfilled. In fact, they are completed after Augustus, who lived for fifteen years beyond the birth of Christ. Tiberius Caesar succeeded him and possessed the *imperium* for twenty-two years, seven months, and twenty-eight days. In the nineteenth year of his rule Christ suffered, being almost thirty-three years old when he suffered [death]. Then Gaius Caesar, who is also known as Caligula, ruled for three years, seven months, and thirteen days. Tiberius Claudius ruled for thirteen years, seven months, and twenty days. Nero ruled for eight years, nine months, and thirteen days. Galba ruled for seven months and twenty-nine days. Otho ruled for three months and five days. Vitellius ruled for eight months, nineteen days. Vespasian, in the first year of his rule, made war against the Jews, and this was in the fifty-second year plus six months.[49] He ruled for ten years. And thus on the day of his assault against the Jews they completed the seventy weeks predicted by Daniel.

And thus [wrote] Tertullian.

What else, O Jews, remains concerning your error, what else of your nefarious obstinacy, rather of your damnable insanity? Behold, from this truthful and learned man explaining and distinguishing the number of the years you will perceive that from the year that this vision was revealed to the prophet, up until the final destruction of your city and your kingdom, there

47. Cf. Dn 9.24; Dn 8.26.
48. Cf. Jerome, *In Dan.*, p. 884, lns. 533–885, ln. 535.
49. As indicated below, fifty-two years (which equal seven and one-half weeks) pass from the birth of Christ to the completion of the seventy weeks indicated in the Book of Daniel.

were seventy weeks, that is, four hundred and ninety years, "that transgression may be finished; and sin may have an end; and iniquity may be abolished; and everlasting justice may be brought; and vision and prophecy may be fulfilled; and the Saint of saints may be anointed."[50] How is this? Reveal what you understand in any way you can, and show when or how or by whom things so wondrous, so cherished, will be fulfilled within the prescribed time period. Explain how transgression will be finished, how sin will be brought to an end, how iniquity will be abolished, how everlasting justice will be brought forth within the same time period, how the vision and the prophecy will be fulfilled, and finally show who will be the one who is proclaimed as the Anointed, the Saint of saints, at the same time.[51]

And, as was mentioned above as the cause of another opinion, there were some from those days who perhaps also attributed to themselves a royal anointing with the diadem that they assumed. First there was Aristobolus, and after him his successor Alexander, and then again a second Aristobolus and then Herod or Archelaus. But was Aristobolus the Saint of saints? Was Alexander the Saint of saints? Was Archelaus the Saint of saints? Did not, as the aforementioned Josephus often relates, a bad development and a worse end follow the wicked beginnings of all of them? Therefore, none of these is the Saint of saints. Therefore, the angel did not say to the prophet that any of these would be anointed the Saint of saints. Therefore, it is necessary for you to find someone else within these seventy weeks who may possibly be understood to be "anointed as the Saint of saints." It is also necessary for you to show how at this same time "sin will have an end," and how "everlasting justice will be brought" and how "the vision and the prophecy will be

50. Dn 9.24.
51. For the interpretation of these verses in medieval Jewish-Christian polemics, see especially Robert Chazan, "Daniel 9:24–27: Exegesis and Polemics," in *Contra Iudaeos. Ancient and Medieval Polemics Between Christians and Jews*, ed. Ora Limor and Guy G. Stroumsa (Tübingen: J. C. B. Mohr, 1996), 143–59. For a fifteenth-century Jewish reply to Christian exegesis of this text, see R. Yom Tov Lippmann Mühlhausen, *Disputatio adversus Christianos ad Jeremie, Ezechielis, Psalmorum et Danielis libros institute*, trans. M. Sebaldus Snellius (Altdorf: Typis Viduae Balthasaris Scherffi, 1645), 1290–91.

fulfilled," or, if you cannot do this, inquire from among others how this will be done. Nothing else is left except for you to understand that Christ our Lord is the anointed Saint of saints, who is "anointed" as man by the Father Almighty with the "oil of gladness" and is the "Saint of saints" because he is "above his fellows."[52]

Nor did he "give him the Spirit by measure"[53] so that he would become merely a saint like the other saints, but instead the entire Spirit was poured out upon him so that he would become the Saint of saints. Nor only so that he would be the Saint of saints, but even so that he would sanctify all those being sanctified by that same Spirit with which he was infused. When will you be able to accept truly that "sin has come to an end," when will you be able to accept that "iniquity has been abolished" within the period of the aforementioned weeks, unless or when the sins of all those that are baptized or of those being baptized have been loosed by him through his baptism, or he said to the disciples: "Receive the Holy Spirit. Whose sins you shall forgive, they are forgiven them."[54] What will you say about such a clear foreshadowing of the Passion and death of Christ? In fact, does the death of Christ appear more clearly as the evangelist reports it than as the prophet proclaims it? He said, "After sixty-two weeks Christ shall be slain."[55] O wretched deafness of the perfidious, O detestable blindness of the impious! Why do you not scatter at so thunderous a sound of the prophetic voice? Why do you not open your eyes at such a brilliant light of the angelic sun? Do you hear the angel speaking, do you see the prophet writing: "After sixty-two weeks Christ shall be slain"?[56] What will you do? What will you say? Behold, both the angel said and the prophet wrote that after sixty-two weeks Christ had to be slain, so that no unrestrained opportunity (*excursus*) to wander is given to you through seventy weeks of years, that is, through four hundred and ninety years.

Now, after sixty-two weeks have passed, how many of the seventy weeks remain? Just eight. Therefore, the prophetic voice

52. Heb 1.9; cf. Ps 44.8.
53. Jn 3.34.
54. Jn 20.22–23.
55. Dn 9.26.
56. Ibid.

urges you to confess that within those eight weeks Christ suffered, and Christ was slain. But according to the calculations
of the authority already named, half a week from those eight
weeks had already been completed on the very day of Christ's
birth. Therefore, seven and one-half weeks remain. Four weeks
will be completed from their declaration, taken from the beginning of this same birth of Christ, once five and one-half years
have been added to the fifth week—that is, once thirty-three and
one-half years have been added, representing Christ's age at the
time of his Passion.[57] Therefore, there remain one and one-half
years from this fifth week, once Christ's Passion has been accomplished. Once one and one-half years are added to the two
weeks that remain from the seven weeks described above, there
will be fifteen and one-half years left. When the one-half week,
containing three and one-half years, that remained of the seven
weeks is added to these fifteen and one-half years, there will be
nineteen years left. From this it is clear that the [total] number
of these seven and one-half weeks has been completed and that
Christ suffered within these same weeks, with nineteen years following after his Passion. If, then, we count these seven and one-
half weeks within which we have proved that Christ suffered,
which we said have their beginning on the day of Christ's birth,
if, I say, we count these seven and one-half weeks along with the
sixty-two and one-half others that preceded the birth of Christ,
then the sum of the seventy weeks predicted by the angel Gabriel
or the prophet Daniel will be completed. Within them, according to the differentiation of the ages already presented, "transgression is finished, and sin has an end, and iniquity is abolished;
and everlasting justice is brought forth; and vision and prophecy
are fulfilled; and the Saint of saints is anointed."[58] Within them,
moreover, the Saint of saints who is said to be anointed, that is,
Christ, has been slain, and the Jewish people who denied him
with a blaspheming mouth has been condemned by him.

57. That is, since one week represents seven years, the 33.5 years from
Christ's birth to his death will be represented by four weeks plus 5.5 years. After
subtracting 5.5 years from the fifth week, then, only 1.5 weeks will remain of that
fifth week.
58. Dn 9.24.

If this seems obscure to you, then listen to the same one when he speaks more openly: As has been said, from the year of this prophetic vision up to the birth of Christ sixty-two and one-half weeks have been completed, so will not seven and one-half weeks of the numbered seventy weeks still remain? You cannot deny that. And how many years are indicated by seven and one-half weeks? Certainly, fifty-two and one-half [years]. In fact, just as it is certain that a week of days is always reckoned by the number seven, so, too, in this prophetic vision a week of years is reckoned by the number seven. Therefore, the sum of seven and one-half weeks completes fifty-two and one-half years. These fifty-two and one-half years remain, then, from the day of Christ's birth until the perfect completion of seventy weeks. Therefore, count as precisely as you can, Jew, and you will find that within these fifty-two and one-half years, after thirty-three and one-half years elapsed, Christ suffered, or rather, as your prophet says, was slain. Subtract thirty-three and one-half years from fifty-two and one-half years, and nineteen years remain. Once these nineteen years have been completed after the Passion or death of Christ, then the entire number of seventy weeks predicted by Daniel is found, and within these it is declared that "the Saint of saints is anointed" and within these [weeks] the same "anointed" one—that is, Christ— was slain; within them it is proclaimed, gleaming more brilliantly than the sun, that "iniquity is abolished, and everlasting justice is revealed, and vision and prophecy are fulfilled."

But if you are so learned in history that you object that Tertullian was altogether silent concerning the years of Claudius Caesar and that he counted fewer years for the other caesars than some of the historians do, I answer: this has nothing to do with the argument. They disagree over the number of years from the Passion of the Lord, as is fitting for historians, although it follows that it is clearly proved, according to the oft-mentioned prophecy of Daniel, that Christ was born within the seventy weeks, that Christ suffered, that "iniquity is abolished," that "everlasting justice" has appeared, and that in fact the universal mysteries (*sacramenta*) of human salvation were completed in him and by him. But though I say this, although, as I once read, a certain false copy excerpted from Tertullian's principal book is silent concerning the years of Claudius Caesar among the years of the caesars, nonetheless the actual book of the author, from which no caesar is passed over from Augustus to Vespasian and Titus, just as it omits none of them when counting those that have succeeded one another, carefully describes the entire span of years during which they ruled over the empire. And when investigating the truth one ought to believe a painstaking author more than someone who heedlessly excerpts material copied from someone else, because the water of the source is always purer than that of the river.

Therefore, O Jews, in order to reach more quickly the appropriate conclusion to the statements that have been proposed, it behooves you, it is necessary that you either reveal some other anointed one, some other saint of saints, some other that is plainly the Christ that was slain during the period of weeks already mentioned, during this same year of weeks, or to receive along with us our anointed one, our Saint of saints, our Christ, who was crucified not just by anyone whatsoever but by your fathers during those very same days and who was slain by the torment of the cross, even though he was their Redeemer and Savior. And because it has been proved that Christ was slain after sixty-two weeks but before the seventieth week, because that very week has been revealed in which it is written that he was slain, and because that year in which he was slain has been declared, do not, do not—if you properly understand things— seek further for another christ, do not wait for another.

Turn your attention to what follows in the prophecy, and read what indeed is predicted in it but which is most clearly fulfilled in you: "The people that deny him will not be his."[59] In truth now you are not his; in truth so long as that inveterate madness persists in you, you will not be his. "You will not be his," as formerly you belonged to him, but you belong and will belong to another, just as God says about you in the psalm: "The children that are strangers have lied to me; children that are strangers have been hardened, and have halted from their paths."[60] And also there is fulfilled in you what was threatened

59. Dn 9.26.
60. Ps 17.46.

in our Gospel for such as these: "But he that will deny me before men, I will also deny him before the angels of God."[61] You denied him when you slew him, you denied him when "you reproved the stone that is become the head of the corner,"[62] you denied him when you replied, "We have no king but Caesar," to the judge who asked, "Shall I crucify your king?"[63] Know that this was predicted for you by the angel, spoken by the prophet: "The people that deny him will not be his."[64]

Nor should what he added next escape you: "And a people with their leader that will come, will destroy the city and the sanctuary, and its end is devastation, and after the end of the war the appointed desolation."[65] Did not your fathers experience all of these things? Did they not see all these things with their own eyes? As soon as these seventy weeks had come to an end, did not the Roman people, coming with their leader Vespasian and his son Titus, destroy the Jewish kingdom? Did it not destroy all the cities? Did it not lay waste to Jerusalem itself, the capital (*caput*) of your kingdom, and its sanctuary? Did it not set it afire? Did it not tear it down even to the ground?[66] Did it not condemn the entire population of Jews to a different outcome of diverse misfortunes? During the siege in your principal city of Jerusalem, did it not slay or take captive thirty times a hundred thousand, in addition to the countless others it found there?[67] This devastation was the end of your city, it was the end of your sanctuary. "The appointed desolation,"[68] according to the prophetic passage, followed this end to the war. But perhaps this desolation will be brief, perhaps the desolation will last only a few years? It will not, it will not. And why do I say it will not? Hear the prophet himself, hear the angel speaking to the prophet: "The desolation shall continue even to the consummation, and to the end."[69] It will not be brief, he said, nor

---

61. Peter conflates here Lk 12.9 and Mt 10.33 from the Vulg.
62. Peter conflates the Vulg. Ps 117.12 and Acts 4.11.
63. Jn 19.15.   64. Dn 9.26.
65. Ibid.   66. Cf. Na 2.6.
67. Cf. Josephus, *Bellum Iudaicum* 6.9.3, pp. 420–22.
68. Dn 9.26.
69. Dn 9.27.

will it last for a short time, nor will it be like other desolations. It will not be like the Egyptian bondage, it will not be like the Babylonian captivity, it will not be like subjugation under the Assyrians or the Macedonians or any of the other nations. In each of these cases, some relief appeared not much later. After eleven hundred years, however, now not even the slightest consolation has appeared following this last desolation. And why do I say it has not appeared after it? I say even more—that never at any time will it appear. Listen intently to the prophet: "The desolation will continue even to the consummation, and to the end."[70] Until what consummation? Until what end? Certainly until the consummation of [all] things, until the end of the world.[71] Why, then, do you still dream of some fantastic christ? Why do you still hope for a false christ—nay, for one that is no christ? Why do you still expect that your earthly freedom will be restored to you? Why do you still await your return to the old land of ancient promise? Hear, understand, attend to what Gabriel spoke and Daniel wrote: "The desolation will continue even to the consummation, and to the end."[72]

Therefore, O Jews, it has been proved by this four-part division,[73] as I see it, that it is necessary to understand that Christ was predicted or proclaimed many times by the prophets to be the Son of God. He is not the Son of God in the manner of certain human beings who, on account of some grace given to them by God, are said to be sons of God, but rather he is the Son of God by virtue of a generation that is itself natural from the essence of the Father. Thus it has been proved that the Son of God is also God. He does not belong to the number of those gods of whom

70. Ibid.

71. For the more aggressive claim, emerging in the twelfth century among Christian polemicists, that Jews *qua* Jews had *no* hope for future redemption or restoration to the Holy Land (in contrast to Jews themselves, who expected eventual redemption), see Robert Chazan, "Undermining the Jewish Sense of Future," in *Christians, Muslims, and Jews in Medieval and Early Modern Spain: Interaction and Cultural Change,* ed. Mark D. Meyerson and Edward D. English, Notre Dame Conferences in Medieval Studies, no. 8 (Notre Dame, IN: University of Notre Dame Press, 2000): 179–94.

72. Dn 9.27.

73. I.e., by these four chapters.

one reads: "The Lord has spoken [as] God of gods," but in fact, "just as light from light, so too God from true God."[74] It has been proved that Christ must not be understood in any sense to be an earthly or carnal king, nor may his kingdom be believed to be a temporal kingdom. In fact, it has been shown that an earthly kingdom does not befit God, nor are created and eternal compatible.[75] It has been proved that Christ has already come, that he who has already come is not to be awaited by the Jews or anyone else as if he had not come.

Since all of these things have been proved, O Jews, both with scriptural authorities and invincible arguments, which will you support? If you place your faith in your Scriptures, then accede to authority. If you would be rational or reasonable, then acquiesce to argument (*ratio*). If you are still anxious, then believe the miracles that confirm all these things, because according to our apostle, "The Jews require signs."[76] "Lift not up your horn on high; speak not iniquity against God."[77] Do not glory in the miracles performed in the era of your Law, nor prefer it to the Gospel of Christ for that reason or for some other reason. The miracles of the Jewish law were many and great, but the deeds of Christian faith are far greater and incomparably more wondrous.

In fact, who will treat the miracle workers that have performed miracles from the beginning of Christian grace until our times, so that I may remain silent concerning those miracles whose number is beyond comprehension? Who will treat such great and numerous miracle workers that spread across the world from the very [first] days of the Lord Christ, who have trod upon the proud neck of the world with divine and wondrous deeds and caused it to submit to the humility of Christian faith? Compare your Moses, O Jew, I do not say to Christ, but, if you dare, merely to his apostle Peter, and you will see which one ought to be set above the other in such things, which one will prevail

74. Cf. The Nicene Creed, *Symbolum Nicaenum* (Mansi 2, p. 667).

75. *Paritura et aeterna* cannot modify *principatus,* leaving unclear what it is they modify. The apparatus indicates that the manuscript tradition also offers *eterno,* but this is little help. In sum, the sense here is elusive.

76. 1 Cor 1.22.

77. Ps 74.6.

over the other with powerful miracles. The one, at God's command, divided the Red Sea,[78] caused manna to rain down from
the heavens,[79] brought water forth from a rock,[80] and performed
such things as these that were great, but few in number. But how
do these compare to Peter? I will remain silent about the fact
that Peter commanded demons, that he raised the dead, that
he often cured every kind of illness not only with a command
but even merely by the shadow of his body,[81] that he performed
every kind of miracle whatsoever he willed both as he willed and
when he willed. Whose memory can recall, whose tongue will
be able to proclaim merely those miracles that he performed
through the countless disciples sent to diverse parts of the world
for the sake of sowing the faith?[82] In fact, when will I be able to
make known adequately not the few I do mention, nor the many
I do not mention, but even the people I do mention that have
themselves been freed from various diseases, cured of diverse illnesses, raised from the dead after not only three or four days,
but even after forty days by the power of Peter's disciples; when
will I be able to make known adequately that the sun has been
fixed in place, the mountains moved, the seas divided, the waves
trodden upon, the elements conquered?[83] But perhaps you will
think that among the apostles only Peter was conspicuous with
these signs. But this was not said about Peter alone, but instead
was enjoined by Christ upon all eleven of his co-apostles: "Heal
the sick," he said, "raise the dead, cleanse the lepers, cast out
devils."[84] And again, "Behold, I have given you power to tread
upon serpents and scorpions, and upon all the power of the enemy."[85] And further down: "Rejoice not that spirits are subject to
you."[86] And elsewhere: "If you have faith as a grain of mustard
seed and you say to this mountain, 'Go into the sea,' it will go."[87]
Nor was so sublime or so great a power to perform miracles
given only to the twelve apostles or to those who in mortal life

78. Cf. Ex 14.16.

79. Cf. Ex 16.30–35.

80. Cf. Nm 20.11.

81. Cf. Acts 5.15.

82. Reading *efferre* for *effari*.

83. Cf. Mt 14.22–23.

84. Mt 10.8.

85. Lk 10.19.

86. Lk 10.20.

87. Peter conflates elements from the Vulg. Mt 17.19 and Lk 17.6.

(*mortaliter*) were associated with him in the flesh. Hear what was said by Christ after he had already suffered, died, and was raised again for all those that truly believed: "And these signs shall follow them that believe: In my name they will cast out devils, they will speak with new tongues. They will take up serpents. And if they drink any deadly thing, it will not hurt them: they will lay their hands upon the sick, and they will recover."[88]

Is not, O Jew, the number of Christian signs deserving of wonder, and is not the number of deeds of Christian faith deserving of wonder? The number of deeds is clearly infinite, [and] the number of those performing them is infinite. Your law has but a few who are distinguished by wondrous deeds, beyond Moses, Joshua, Gideon, Samson, Samuel, Isaiah, Elijah, Elisha, [and] Jonah, whereas the Christian faith has and has had countless miracle workers. Why, then, do you continue to mutter? Why do you grumble? At last give, give your hand to the Christ that you have demonstrated already to have come at the definite time foretold so long ago, to be the Son of God, to be God, to be the eternal King, by so many sacred authorities, with so many indubitable arguments, [and] by so many and such great signs of wonders.

Do not complain any longer that the Mosaic Law was changed by Christ, because, just as God is the one who gave it, so God is the one who commanded that the Gospel be embraced. There is not one God and another God, one who gave the one and another who gave the other, but Christ is himself one and the same God who bestowed that [law] on the Jews earlier, before he appeared to men in the flesh; he is himself the one already made man, who commanded all the Jews as well as the Gentiles to observe this second, new, final [law]. If he is God, then certainly what he commanded ought to be embraced. But it has been demonstrated by scriptural authorities, by arguments, and by miracles that he is God. It follows, then, that what he said should be considered valid, that what he commanded should be guarded as God's command. If, then, contrariwise you seek God,[89] it is necessary for you to accept the commands of the

---

88. Mk 16.17–18.   89. Reading *contrarie* for *contraire*.

Christ-God, it is necessary for you to bend your necks, which have been proud for so long, to his sweet yoke, as he says himself.[90] If you recognize that Christ is God, you will no longer pose for us the stubborn question or the old complaint that the Christian rejects circumcision, that he condemns the Sabbath, that he does not guard the legal sacrifices, as if your law were spurned.

You will see, and you will understand that it was permissible for God to arrange things appropriate to specific times, to arrange them first for some times and then for others, first for specific times and then for many and then for all, for the sake of persons, causes, and times known in their original state to him alone. If you have examined things properly, you will observe that God commanded new things not only at the time of Christian grace, since you know that he often did similar things from the very beginning of human creation, as your Scriptures attest. Did he not say new things that he had not said previously when, to punish the guilt of sinful man, he said: "Cursed is the earth in your work; with labor and toil you will eat thereof all the days of your life,"[91] and the rest?

Did he not make new concessions and ones that one does not read that he allowed previously when, after the world had been destroyed by the flood, he said to Noah: "All the fishes of the sea are delivered into your hand, and everything that moves and lives will be food for you." And immediately after that: "Even as the green herbs have I delivered them all to you, except that flesh with blood you will not eat"?[92] Who, when promulgating as well a new law of which he had been silent until that time, added: "For I will require the blood of your lives at the hand of every beast, and at the hand of man. At the hand of [every] man, and of his brother, will I require the life of man. Whosoever will shed man's blood, his blood will be shed. For man was made to the image of God."[93]

Did he not command something new, concerning which he had actually kept silent earlier, when he enjoined this upon Abraham, your father according to the flesh but ours accord-

90. Cf. Mt 11.29–30.   91. Gn 3.17.
92. Gn 9.2–4.   93. Gn 9.5–6.

ing to faith, saying: "This is my covenant which all will observe, between me and you, and your seed after you: All the males among you will be circumcised and you will circumcise the flesh of your foreskin, that it may be a sign of the covenant between me and you,"[94] and the rest that follows?

Did he not command something new and something that he had concealed throughout so many ages when through Moses he gave to your fathers, both orally and in writing, the Sabbath, when he gave them the first days of months,[95] when he gave them the many solemnities,[96] when he gave them the various sacrifices and, to bring many examples to a conclusion in brief, when he gave them the whole body of the law, from which you are more accustomed to take pride than to be instructed? And who will easily be able to enumerate all those that, mindful of the salvation of humankind, divinity commanded should be safeguarded by many [people] not all at once but gradually, whether universally or individually, not at the same time but at different times? If, then, God often commanded new and different commandments for people before Christ [became] man, why is it surprising if the same Christ, both man and God in one and the same person, commanded what he has deemed more appropriate for mortal men in these days?

But perhaps you will say: indeed you have proved that God often commanded new things, but you have not proved nor can you prove that the law that was finally given through Moses should be changed or should expire. I say, I do prove it. First, I offer this from Isaiah: "To what purpose do you offer me the multitude of your victims? says the Lord. I am full. I desire not holocausts of rams, and fat of fatlings, and blood of calves, and lambs, and buck goats."[97] And just below, "Incense is an abomi-

94. Gn 17.10–11.

95. "First days of months": *initia mensium,* a reference, presumably, to the kalends. Cf. the Venerable Bede, *In Ezram et Neemiam libri iii,* 1, ln. 1109, ed. D. Hurst, CC SL 119A (Turnholt: Brepols, 1969): "Kalendas autem uocat initia mensium, id est ortum lunae nascentis a quo semper hebraei menses incipiebant . . ." Peter may also intend an allusion to Is 1.13–14, which he quotes just below, in which the Lord rejects sacrifices, the new moons, festivals, and the Sabbath.

96. Cf. Is 1.14, and below.

97. Is 1.11.

nation to me. The new moons, and the Sabbaths, and other festivals I will not abide. Your assemblies are wicked. My soul hates
your new moons and your solemnities."[98]

But perhaps you will say that these are the words of an angry and indignant God, and you will contend that he condemns
all those things only because at that time the people was sinful.
But hear him speaking in the psalm, with no previous basis for
anger: "I will not accept calves out of your house nor he-goats
out of your flocks."[99] And a few verses later: "Shall I eat the flesh
of bullocks or shall I drink the blood of goats?"[100] After having
condemned these sacrifices, he added what he would rather
have or what he prefers over them: "Offer to God the sacrifice
of praise,"[101] and what follows that. Hear also the testimony of
Malachi that I had offered above for another reason:[102] "I have
no pleasure in you, said the Lord of hosts, and I will not receive
a gift of your hand."[103]

Hear, too, something to which you will be unable to make
any reply and which, once presented, will force you to be silent.
Hear God promising that he would surely give new commandments and that he would exchange the new and eternal testament of Christ for the Old Testament, the Mosaic testament:
"Behold, the days are coming, says the Lord, and I will make a
[new] testament with the house of Judah, not according to the
testament which I made with their fathers, when I took them
by the hand to bring them out of the land of Egypt. But this is
the new testament that I will make with them, giving my laws
into their mind, and in their hearts will I write them."[104] Both
humbling and confounding that pride of yours that finds glory
in such things, he said through Ezekiel: "I also gave them stat-
utes that were not good, and judgments, in which they will not
live, and I polluted them in my gifts, when they will offer all that
opens the womb, for their sins."[105] What then? Has it not very
clearly been proved for all time that God frequently bestowed

---

98. Is 1.13–14.   99. Ps 49.9.
100. Ps 49.13.   101. Ps 49.14.
102. *Supra*, chap. 3, p. 135.   103. Mal 1.10.
104. Peter conflates passages from Jer 31.31–32 and Heb 8.10.
105. Ezek 20.25–26.

new commandments on the world and that he foretold that even the Law of Moses would be changed?

But so that you will see more keenly that the Jewish quiver has been emptied of arrows, produce now another one and, as you long for death, loose it against us with as much strength as you can. What, you ask, about what God repeats so often in the law that was given us, that he so often reiterates—that at no time will that law ever come to an end, that the law that he commands with diverse cultic sacrifices and with every ritual described there for us has to be everlasting? Surely this is the case for the words of God that one reads in Exodus commanding the sacrifice of the lamb: "And this day shall be for a memorial to you, and you shall keep it a feast to the Lord in your generations with an everlasting observance"?[106] What about what is written nearby in the same book, concerning the same matter: "You will keep this word as a law for you and your children forever"?[107] Did not the Book of Leviticus assert the same thing? In fact, while relating and proclaiming distinctly God's numerous commandments concerning different types of sacrifices, it inserts these words: "The priest will take a handful of the flour that is tempered with oil, and all the frankincense that is put upon the flour, and he will burn it on the altar for a memorial of most sweet odor to the Lord."[108] And, after other verses have been interposed, it adds: "It will be an everlasting ordinance in your generations concerning the sacrifices of the Lord."[109] Again, after others, it adds: "You will not drink wine or anything that may make drunk, you nor your sons, when you enter into the tabernacle of the testimony, lest you die because it is an everlasting precept through your generations."[110] In the same way, when it concerns the offering of firstfruits to God, the same Book of Leviticus adds: "And on the same day that the sheaf is consecrated, a lamb without blemish of the first year shall be killed for a holocaust to the Lord, and the libations shall be offered with it, two tenths of flour tempered with oil for a burnt offering of the Lord, and a most sweet odor, libations also of wine,

106. Ex 12.14.
108. Lv 6.15.
110. Lv 10.9.

107. Ex 12.24.
109. Lv 6.18.

the fourth part of a hin."[111] And after an intervening verse: "It is
a precept," he said, "forever throughout your generations, and
all your dwellings."[112] And after a few more verses, he said: "You
shall offer also a buck goat for sin, and two lambs of the first
year for sacrifices of peace offerings. And when the priest has
lifted them up with the loaves of the firstfruits before the Lord,
they shall fall to his use."[113] And immediately after that, "And
you will call this day most solemn, and most holy. You will do no
servile work on it. This will be an everlasting ordinance in all
your dwellings and generations." Following this book, the Book
of Numbers adds something similar pertaining to the eternity
of our law: "And on the sabbath day you will offer two lambs of a
year old without blemish, and two tenths of flour tempered with
oil in sacrifice, and the libations, which regularly are poured out
every sabbath for the perpetual holocaust."[114] Not many verses
later, it said this concerning the sacrifices of the first day of the
seventh month: "And you will offer a buck goat for sin, which is
offered for the expiation of the people, besides the holocaust of
the first day of the month (*Kalendae*) with its sacrifices. And you
will offer the perpetual holocaust with the accustomed libations
with the same ceremonies for a most sweet odor to the Lord."[115]
Since, then, the eternal nature of our law is commended time
and time again, how do you assert that it has been changed,
how do you affirm that it was foretold that it would be changed?
But hear the more explicit testimony of the Book of Deuteronomy, and from it understand at least that at no time does it have
to be changed or did it have to be changed. For Moses, when
speaking to our fathers in the aforementioned book, said: "Lay
up these my words in your hearts and minds, and hang them for
a sign on your hands, and place them between your eyes. Teach
your children to meditate on them."[116] And after a few more
passages, he said: "That your days may be multiplied, and the
days of your children in the land that the Lord swore to your fathers, that he would give them as long as the heaven hangs over
the earth."[117] What can be said to demonstrate the everlasting

111. Lv 23.12–13.   112. Lv 23.14.
113. Lv 23.19–20.   114. Nm 28.9.
115. Nm 29.5–6.   116. Dt 11.18–19.
117. Dt 11.21.

nature of our law more clearly than these passages? Also hear from the same Book of Deuteronomy the commandments of our lawgiver, and from them pay attention to whether our law should be changed in the least little thing. He said: "You shall not add to the word that I speak to you, neither shall you take away from it."[118] And elsewhere in the same book this is added, after numerous curses which precede it, as if it is the culmination (*clausula*) of these same curses: "Cursed is he who does not abide in the words of this law, and does not fulfill them in work. And all the people shall say: Amen."[119]

O Jew, as I see it, what our apostle said about you and yours is true, it is clearly true: So long as "Moses is read, the veil is upon their heart."[120] And that also is true that Christ—not yours, but ours—said after light was bestowed upon the man who had been born blind: "For judgment I am come into this world so that they who see not, may see, and they who see, may become blind."[121] In fact, see that your eyes, which once gazed upon God, have been blinded, and the eyes of the Gentiles, which were closed until the time of Christ, have been opened by him. God said, "They that held the law knew me not."[122] Surely the Jew holds the law and does not know God, whereas the Christian reads the same law and from it worships the God he comes to know.

But return to the topic, O Jew. You objected whatever you were able to object most strongly to show that the Mosaic Law is everlasting and to bring to naught as if with an invincible argument anything that had been said concerning its being altered.

But I ask you: were the statements from the Pentateuch that you presented to prove the eternity of your law offered by God or through Moses? You answer, certainly, by God. From there, I follow up: were the statements that I presented from the prophets to prove that your law is to be changed, were they proclaimed through the prophets by God? I think, or rather I know very well, that you will not deny this. If this is the case, it is clear that according to your understanding there are many inconsis-

118. Dt 4.2.
119. Dt 27.26.
120. 2 Cor 3.15.
121. Jn 9.39.
122. Jer 2.8.

tencies among the divine words. And in order to elucidate more
clearly what I am saying concerning the testimonies from sacred
Scripture that you bring against me, let me select one to represent all of them, that is, one in place of all the rest of them:
"And this day shall be for a memorial to you," said God concerning the sacrifice of the paschal lamb, "and you shall keep it
a feast to the Lord in your generations with an everlasting observance."[123] From those that I have proposed on the other side,
I will select one testimony from Jeremiah to represent all the
others: "Behold, the days are coming, says the Lord, and I will
make a [new] testament with the house of Judah, not according to the testament that I made with their fathers, in the day
when I took them by the hand to bring them out of the land of
Egypt. But I will make a new testament for them, giving my laws
into their minds, and in their hearts will I write them."[124] Have
you listened, Jews? Look, pay attention, examine all aspects,
and change whatever you can, whether by reason or by skillful
artifices.[125] You cannot deny—rather, you confess as do I—that
the one [testament] was proclaimed by God through Moses and
that the other was proclaimed by the same God through Jeremiah.

Do it, then, do it, I say, if you can, lest the one that you read is
faithful in his words,[126] of whom often you both read and chant
that "he will destroy all who speak a lie,"[127] lest clearly even he
appear to be made a liar by his words, lest he be associated with
those who speak lies whom he himself is written to destroy. You
seem to sense, even if you do not pay heed to it, that this is
something too nefarious, too blasphemous [to say] about him.
And why do I say that you seem to sense this? More precisely,
you profess this openly when you confess that the same God
who gave this everlasting law also foretold that it would have to
expire.

---

123. Ex 12.14.
124. Jer 31.31–32 and Heb 8.8–10.
125. The numerous variants in the apparatus would indicate that later
scribes also found the Latinity of this passage problematic.
126. Cf. Ps 144.13.
127. Cf. Ps 5.7.

Really, choose, choose which of the two you want. In fact if, according to the Jewish understanding, what he said through Moses concerning the eternal nature of the law is true, then what he foretold through Jeremiah concerning its change is false. If it is true that, according to Jeremiah, it will have to be changed, then it is false that, according to Moses, God commanded it to be everlasting. Because it is impious and detestable to think such as this about God, as you know, then either unravel the difficulty that has been raised by Jewish interpretation, if you can, or, if you cannot—and in truth you cannot—then acquiesce to a sound and truthful Christian understanding. Listen, then, now, and do not be embarrassed to receive instruction, because the most stupid thing of all is to prefer to remain in error rather than to learn, to prefer to be overshadowed by one's own darkness rather than to be bathed by light, even though by another's light. Pay attention to the fact that God was unable to proclaim words by which he contradicted himself or that were in contradiction to one another, in order to say on the one hand that the law which he handed down would be eternal, according to your understanding, or on the other to foretell again that it had to expire. Obviously he did not hand it down to be eternal, but obviously he handed the law down to you and yours so that it would expire.

Clearly how, how would he bestow an eternal law upon the world when, as God surely knew, both it and its time are going to expire with all his own possessions, whether Jews or Gentiles? How, I ask, was a law without end given in a world that is not without end? How is an eternal law given to those who are not eternal, how is it given not only to those who will die little by little, but who at some point will cease to exist altogether? For if, as I set forth far above for a similar purpose,[128] "heaven and earth," in the words of your psalm, "will perish,"[129] for whom does it remain unclear that neither the Jewish sacrifices nor the numerous rites nor, finally, all the things that were commanded or described in the law, will be able to endure?

128. Cf. ch. 3, p. 125.
129. Cf. Ps 101.26–27.

But perhaps you will disagree with that passage; perhaps, as is your custom, you will stick to the literal meaning. You may argue pertinaciously that in that scriptural passage the law is called everlasting, the law is called eternal. But, if you have heard this already, recall—if you have not heard this, then learn—that the eternal is not always understood to exist without limit, the everlasting is not always assumed to exist without end. You will find this in the Second Book of Kings: "But it came to pass that night," it says, "that the word of the Lord came to Nathan, saying: Go, and say to my servant David, thus says the Lord: Will you build me a house to dwell in?"[130] And, after a few other verses have been interposed, it says: "I will raise up your seed after you, which shall proceed out of your bowels, and I will establish his kingdom. He shall build a house to my name, and I will establish the throne of his kingdom forever."[131] And a little further: "Your house will be faithful, and your kingdom forever before my face, and your throne shall be firm forever."[132]

What do you have to say to this? Have you not discovered now something "everlasting" that has a limit; have you not discovered something "eternal" that has an end? He said, "I will establish the throne of his kingdom forever."[133] Whose is it? Clearly, according to your Jewish (that is, carnal) understanding, it is Solomon's, or one of the kings who succeeded him in the Jewish kingdom. Do you see that this "everlasting" throne ended many centuries ago? It ended at the very advent of our Lord Christ, from which and by which was cast down the temporal throne of the sons of David, nor will it ever again be restored, forever.

What will you say concerning the next testimony presented? I say, concerning this testimony: "Your house will be faithful, and your kingdom forever."[134] Did David's house—that is, the lineage of David's sons—remain faithful to God after him, even "forever"? Is not the unfaithfulness and perversity of some of the kings well known even while the kingdom of David's stock in Judah still flourished, so that a true scriptural passage attests

130. 2 Sm 7.4–5.
132. 2 Sm 7.16.
134. 2 Sm 7.16.

131. 2 Sm 7.12–13.
133. 2 Sm 7.13.

to some of them: for as many years as this one or that reigned,[135] "he did what was evil in the sight of the Lord"?[136] Was Jehoram faithful to God?[137] Was Ahaz faithful?[138] Was Zedekiah faithful?[139] Did the house of David or its kingdom remain faithful to God by despising the idolater Manasseh, the profane son of Hezekiah?[140] So where now is that "eternity" of yours that concerns me? For if eternal, how—I do not say merely at some time, but how—was it so quickly brought to an end? What more will you demand? Do you hear the "throne of David" must be established "forever," when it ceased to exist a thousand years ago? Do you hear "his house" will be "faithful forever,"[141] when, to pass over things already mentioned, that faithfulness lapsed when Solomon, his own son, was worshiping idols?[142] And in order to convince you with numerous proof-texts not from foreign books but from your own that "eternity" is often substituted for a finite time period, hear something similar that even David himself sings to God concerning the same matter. For when introducing God speaking about him, he says this: "I will make his seed to endure forevermore and his throne as the days of heaven."[143] And just below, after a few other verses: "Once have I sworn by my holiness, if I lie to David: His seed shall endure forever."[144] And just after this: "And his throne as the sun before me and as the moon [will be] perfect forever."[145] And why is it necessary to make note of these one after another? In fact, it is certain, it is patently obvious, one cannot deny that these words that one reads—"I will make his seed to endure forevermore,"[146] or these: "His seed shall endure forever,"[147] or even these: "His throne as the sun before me and as the moon [will be] perfect forever"[148]—never signify an infinite eternity, which we see is finite with respect to the part and which we know has to expire with respect to the whole. With respect to the part,

135. Cf. 1 Kgs 14.22; 2 Kgs 8.18, 27; 2 Kgs 21.2, 20; 23.32; 24.9–19.
136. 1 Kgs 14.22.   137. Cf. 2 Kgs 8.16–18.
138. Cf. 2 Kgs 16.2.   139. Cf. 2 Kgs 24.18–19.
140. Cf. 2 Kgs 21.2–7.   141. 2 Sm 7.16.
142. Cf. 1 Kgs 11.4–6.   143. Ps 88.30.
144. Ps 88.36–37.   145. Ps 88.38.
146. Ps 88.30.   147. Ps 88.37.
148. Ps 88.38.

we see that it is finite because we perceive that, as was said already, the kingdom and temporal throne of David's sons was overthrown a long time ago, and there is no one who doubts that his seed—that is, David's line of succession—will come to an end at least with the end of the world itself.

And with a Christian interpretation we understand these examples that I have presented from the Book of Kings and from the Psalms to prove that the "finite eternity" of David's seed, of the throne of David's seed, refers to Christ, and according to that interpretation we deny that his throne—that is, kingdom—is earthly, and in this way we affirm that it is eternal, not in a temporal fashion but entirely without end. But because I am dealing with you, and you are far removed from this interpretation, I concede your interpretation, and I show you that an infinite eternity cannot be understood in those words. In fact, a kingdom that has already perished cannot be said to be eternal, that is, infinite; David's seed—that is, the lineage of kings following David—which no longer exists, cannot be said to be everlasting. Do you still want more testimonies than these, Jew, to show that eternity is not always eternal, so to speak? Then, after what you have already heard, listen to what your Moses, or rather ours, commands concerning a Hebrew sold into slavery. Now, passing over certain things that I pass over because they are not relevant to what concerns us now, he adds: "But if he say: I will not depart, because he loves you, and your house, and finds that he is well with you, you will take an awl, and bore through his ear in the door of your house, and he will serve you forever (*in aeternum*)."[149] Listen also to another text from the same Book of Deuteronomy, from which the preceding text also has been drawn. In fact, when Moses wrote to distinguish the priests from the people and from those who offer sacrificial victims, he added: "For the Lord your God has chosen him of all your tribes," he said, "to stand and to minister to the name of the Lord, him and his sons forever (*in sempiternum*)."[150] You will also find something akin to this in the First Book of Chronicles: "Aaron was separated," he

149. Dt 15.16–17.
150. Dt 18.5.

said, "to minister in the holy of holies, he and his sons forever (*in sempiternum*), to burn incense before the Lord, according to his ceremonies, and to bless his name forever (*in perpetuum*)."[151]

But will it always be necessary for me, time and time again, either to unlock things that have been revealed or to illuminate things that are clear? How is what I said true? Certainly it seems surprising, but it is true. In fact, what is patently obvious to everyone else is closed to you alone. The things that are clear to everyone else, are obscure to you alone. Actually it is clear to everyone, it is well known to everyone, that a Hebrew servant who was pierced in the ear or wounded in the ear by his lord was unable to serve him forever, and neither was a priest chosen by God nor were his sons able to minister to God forever. For it was necessary that when the servant died his service would die too, so to speak, and when a priest or his sons ceased [to live], then of necessity the ministry would have to cease too. From all these instances, infer, observe, understand that these words—"eternal" (*aeternus*), "everlasting" (*perpetuus*), and "forever" (*sempiternus*)—are not always intended to denote something infinite, but sometimes instead are intended to indicate something temporal and finite.

It follows from this that if you will be able either to oppose this or to turn it into the opposite, then in reality everything that is understood sanely you will be able to interpret insanely. Listen, then, to the canticle of Moses, of Aaron, of Mary, and of your entire people called Israel. The canticle is known not only to you and yours, but to the entire world. After having crossed the Red Sea, after Pharaoh was drowned, after the Egyptians were killed, the singers added this to divine praises: "The Lord," they said, "shall reign forever and ever."[152] Is this "forever" (*aeternum*) understood to denote an infinite? If it is understood to denote an infinite, then why is "and ever" (*ultra*) added? How can anything be added to an infinite eternity? Clearly how, how is there anything beyond it (*ultra illam*)? So either remove this "beyond" (*ultra*) and understand here an infinite "eternity," or, if you are unwilling to remove the "beyond," then understand

151. 1 Chr 23.13.
152. Ex 15.18.

that when one reads "forever" (*aeternus*) there, it nevertheless refers to a finite period, even though a very long time. Since, then, you can avoid this in no other way, because in no other way will you be able to remove a foot from the snare, then recognize that the "forever" referred to there was written for a vast although nonetheless finite period of time, but that when "beyond" was added to it, then it must be understood to mean forever (*sempiternus*) without end or limit.

Besides these sacred texts and in addition to the proof-texts indicated above, it is not only the divine, but even a human and common manner of speaking, in which not an infinite but a greater or lesser period of time is denoted. You will observe that this mode is employed by everyone almost constantly, even if you bend your ear heedlessly to those who are speaking. In fact, who does not frequently repeat this mode of speaking in the words: "I have always loved you," "I will always love you," "I have always hated him," "I will always hate him," that one will "always be a pauper," and this one "always rich," this one "always speaks the truth," that one "always lies," this one "always speaks," that one is "always silent," and in a thousand other instances? And when I say "always" (*semper*), understood in its proper signification, it denotes nothing less than an eternal infinite; nonetheless, those who utter it do not understand anything infinite by it, but rather, as I said above, a period of time that is longer or shorter, but that is nevertheless a finite measure of time. On this our Latin proverb rests:

He will be a slave forever (*aeternum*) who does not know how to make do with little.[153]

And on this rests his proverb:

Unhappy Theseus sits, and he will sit forever (*aeternum*).[154]

From the end of the verse to the beginning of the next verse, although the author (*prolator*) understands that some misfortunes are eternal (that is, without end), nonetheless he does not think that he is in any way immortal (*aeternus*), that is, that

153. Horace, *Ep.* 1.10.41.
154. Vergil, *Aeneid* 6.618.

he will sit without end. Thus that great man among the Latins also [said]:

As soon as the horizon of Sicily sank from view, the happy ones raised sail and clove the spume of salty air. But Juno, harboring an everlasting wound in her breast, mused: "Must I, defeated, fail of what I will . . . ?"[155]

And the same one said again:

Was Jupiter able to ordain so vast a shock of arms should come between nations destined to perpetual peace?[156]

But the author of these verses did not think that the wound in the breast of Juno, who was angry with the Trojans, was eternal without end, nor that the nations would remain in the future in eternal, that is infinite, peace, which he knew could not happen. There are many other examples besides these, but I think these will suffice. All of these, Jew, have proved that you have produced in vain so many terms for eternity to prove the infinite character of your law, since it follows, both from the sacred proof-texts and from the examples drawn from human usage, that it is not always the case that infinite realities are denoted by the term "eternity," but that sometimes it even denotes finite realities.

But perhaps you will respond: indeed you prove from the foregoing that the term "eternity" sometimes is understood to refer to a finite time period, but you do not deny that sometimes it can be understood to refer to the infinite. I do not deny it, I say, but in fact I affirm it. Therefore, you say, you will concede both: that is, that the term "eternity" is sometimes understood to refer to a finite time period, and also that sometimes it stands for an infinite one. It is true, I say. If, then, it is true, you say, that the term "eternity" is often employed to denote both, that is a finite or an infinite period, then how do you conclude, how do you prove that the testimonies previously presented, in order to show the infinite character of the Jewish law, have to be more finite than infinite? I do prove it, I say, and I will compel you to agree to that with a necessary argument. In order to bring this about more quickly and with greater clarity, let us present again

155. Vergil, *Aeneid* 1.34–37.
156. *Aeneid* 12.503–504.

those two examples that were introduced above, the one by me
and the other by you. By me, Jeremiah's words; by you, Moses'
words. These are Jeremiah's: "Behold, the days are coming, says
the Lord, and I will make a [new] testament with the house of
Judah, not according to the testament that I made with their
fathers, when I took them by the hand to bring them out of the
land of Egypt. But this is the new testament that I will make with
them, giving my laws into their minds, and in their hearts will I
write them."[157] These are Moses': "And this day," God said, with
respect to the sacrifice of the paschal lamb, "shall be for a memorial to you, and you shall keep it a feast to the Lord in your
generations with an everlasting observance."[158] As I said, according to your interpretation these two are completely contrary to
one another, standing on opposite sides, and they are opposed
to one another. In fact, what one of these two sentences affirms,
the other denies. For Moses affirms that the law is eternal, that
is, according to you, that it will never be brought to an end. Jeremiah affirms that it will be changed, that is, that another one
will be given, and not according to the manner or in the fashion of the previous one. Do you see that no other alternative to
these two can stand? Unless you understand things differently,
do you see that either Moses or Jeremiah is deceitful? Thus, so
that religious and well-known ministers of the truth not appear
to be liars, it is necessary either for Jeremiah to be exposed as
one such as this, so that the infinite character of the law be revealed in accord with your opinion, or for Moses' words to be
understood in such a way that what Jeremiah proclaimed with
respect to a change in the law be proved true. But what Jewish intellect, what powerfully perspicacious Christian intellect
and sharp eye, so to speak, can discover anything different from
what was said in Jeremiah's words? What else can one think
but that they report without a cloud, without a cloak, without
a mask of metaphors? Surely they report this, they clearly indicate this: that God will not draw up another testament like the
testament given by God to the fathers. Clearly he calls that a
new testament, because an old one preceded it. What else then,

157. Peter conflates passages from Jer 31.31–32 and Heb 8.10.
158. Ex 12.14.

obviously, what else will you be able to understand by "old testament" except the Jewish law that preceded, and what else will you be able to understand by "new testament" but the Christian one that had to follow it? Since this is the case, since nothing else can be understood from Jeremiah's words other than what has been said, nor with some Jewish cleverness can some part of it be twisted in some other way, you, O Jew, will be compelled to transcend the statements of Moses and to understand just as I do that the terms "eternity" or "perpetuity" that were set forth were not intended to stand for an infinite period but rather for a finite period of time. This is the way to understand, then, that statement that you presented concerning the paschal lamb, and concerning the many diverse sacrifices, and concerning the observance of the Sabbath, and concerning that circumcision that as our Lord says "is not of Moses, but of the fathers."[159]

Wherever you find the term "eternity" written in similar places in your law, understand it in this way, I say, understand it in this way. And when you understand "eternal" to stand there for a finite period of time, then you will find that Moses does not contradict Jeremiah, nor does Jeremiah contradict Moses, and you will recognize that that law is finite that Jeremiah foretold must be brought to an end.

I say it is finite, just as one of our great men said is the case with respect to a symbolic precept, but not with respect to a moral precept.[160] In fact, as far as pertains to a moral precept, what the old law commands for the Jews the Gospel also commands for Christians, and each one of them struggles to guard it by grace and with his own strength. In fact, "You shall love the Lord your God with your whole heart [. . .] and your neighbor as yourself,"[161] and, "You shall not have strange gods before me,"[162] and, "Honor your father and your mother,"[163] and, "You shall not kill, you shall not commit adultery, you shall not steal, you shall not bear false witness against your neighbor," and,

---

159. Jn 7.22.

160. "non quantum ad modum agendae vitae, sed quantum ad modum significandae vitae." Cf. Augustine, *Contra Faustum* 6.2, ed. Joseph Zycha, CSEL 25 (Vienna: F. Tempsky, 1891), 285.

161. Lk 10.27; cf. Dt 6.5; Lv 19.18.   162. Ex 20.3.

163. Ex 20.12.

"You shall not covet your neighbor's house, nor shall you desire his wife, or his servant, or his handmaid, or his ox, or his
ass, or any thing that is his"[164] and the like; just as they were
commanded to the Jew as in accord with a correct faith, hon-
est practices, and a holy life, so too are they commanded to the
Christian. Thus, as far as concerns a moral precept, the law that
concerns one there is not finite. Whereas, it is actually finite
when it concerns a symbolic precept. For the carnal circumcision that foreshadows the spiritual one, the Sabbath rest that
hints at another rest, the sacrifices of four-footed animals, flying creatures, fine wheaten flour, wine, oil, and the like, which
foreshadow the unique and supreme sacrifice of Christians just
as a shadow does a body, have ceased, just like something that
symbolizes what is symbolized. Thus, as was said, all those things
that weigh upon the neck of a stiff-necked people are permitted
to a free people and, so that now it not be burdened with an unnecessary yoke, they were brought to an end entirely by the one
who said, "My yoke is sweet and my burden light."[165]

But if this discussion concerning the word "eternity" amus-
es you so much that you still struggle to prove that your law is
without end, change the signification, and you will find your
"eternal" without end. Change the signification, I say, and confess concerning the old testament what I confess concerning
the new testament. I say that the testament given by Christ is
new and eternal. New, I say, because yours is the more ancient.
How is it eternal? How is the baptism that Christ instituted eternal? How is the sacrifice eternal that he bestowed upon those
who are his own? How are the other sacraments also bestowed
upon Christians eternal? How can the many other Gospel commandments be eternal? They are not eternal because they must
come to an end when the world does, just as I said yours must,
yet nonetheless they are eternal because they prepare one for
eternal things. They are brought to an end, but nonetheless the
eternal life to which they lead does not come to an end. Speak
then, but speak from faith,[166] believe for justice, confess for your
salvation in a way such that the law can be understood to be

164. Ex 20.13–17.   165. Mt 11.30.
166. Cf. Rom 4.16.

eternal, because it exists as a foreshadow and forerunner of this Christian grace, which in truth alone leads to blessed and eternal life through Christ. Only in this sense can your law, with which you have been concerned, be understood to be eternal without end, and in every other sense it can be understood to have an end.

But so that none of your objections remain unaddressed or unresolved, understand our reply to apply to your final objection as well. For you set Moses against us when he spoke to your patriarchs, [saying] among other things: "That your days may be multiplied," he said, "and the days of your children in the land which the Lord swore to your fathers, that he would give them as long as the heaven hangs over the earth."[167] To this I say: according to your interpretation the possession of that land was promised to the Jewish stock "as long as the heaven hangs over the earth," the land that was distributed in part to these first Jews by Moses, and was distributed in part by Joshua. But the heaven still hangs over the earth, and yet that land was taken away from the Jews a long time ago already. But you will say: indeed, this is because they neglected the commandments handed down to them by God. And what difference, I say, does this make to me? In fact, I confess that because they neglected the commandments of God—rather, because they have always been opponents and rebels against God—and because they were idolaters, profaners, slayers of the prophets, and because, to fill up the measure of their fathers,[168] they were the ones to crucify his Christ the very Savior of the world, and because they were his most wicked accusers,[169] they were cast out from that land by God as well as excluded both from all worldly prosperity and from eternal blessedness.

Now, with respect to what you added, that Moses commanded: "You shall not add to the word that I speak to you, neither shall you take away from it,"[170] is it not surprising, is it not actually astounding that you throw this against us as if it worked on

167. Dt 11.21.
168. Cf. Mt 23.21–32.
169. Reading *condempnatores* for *condempnatoris.*
170. Dt 4.2.

your behalf? For which of us ever added a word to your law, who ever removed a word? Instead, we safeguard the books intact, we guard them uncorrupted both as they were written by Moses and as they entered the languages of all the Gentiles, translated from the Hebrew and conserved, so to speak, by faithful translators; nothing is added to them, nothing is removed from them. I, a Latin, have, a Greek has, a Barbarian has, everything in those books that you have, O Jew. We copy what you copy, we read what you read, but on the whole we do not interpret the texts written or read in the way that you interpret them, nor on the whole do we understand them as you understand them. You sometimes follow in them the "letter that kills," whereas I always follow in them the "vivifying spirit."[171] You chew on the bark, whereas I eat the pith.

I do not cast aside the covering of the letter where there is one, nor do I reject the mystery of salvation that is concealed by the letter. In this way, while accepting the letter but following more its author, [namely,] the letter's spirit, I add nothing, as I said, to a word of your law, and I remove nothing, but I argue that the Jew neither follows the letter of his law more nor recognizes the divine spirit in the letter, and I condemn and reprove the one who is unwilling to acquiesce to the truth.

After these two matters have been resolved in this way, you threaten us last with a third [objection] and you struggle to show with the three of them that unless we become Jews we will be subject to a divine curse. You say, "Cursed be he that does not abide in the words of this law, and does not fulfill them in work, and all the people shall say: Amen."[172] This curse, O Jews, does not rest upon us but rather upon you and your children.[173] For we Christians came from the Gentiles, not from the Jews, and the yoke of the Jewish law was not imposed on us. The necks of a stiff-necked people, who otherwise could not be subdued to serve God, were made subject to the precepts of the Law of Moses, whereas the neck of Christian faith was raised

171. Cf. 2 Cor 3.6.
172. Dt 27.26. Cf. Hermannus Iudaeus, *Opusc. de conversione sua*, c. 3 (ed. G. Niemeyer, p. 78).
173. Cf. Mt 27.25.

up by our Christ into a freedom appropriate to the age. And
for this reason, the Christian does not understand the Jewish
curse to refer to him, because he knows that, just as times have
changed, so too the precepts have been changed. But because
according to the manner in which the law was distinguished
above, we believe that your moral or symbolic law is ours, we
call it ours, it is necessary for us to be careful of its curses and to
desire its blessings. We take care against, or rather we completely avoid its curses, if we live life according to its decrees, that is,
by not coveting, killing, stealing, and bringing false witness, and
by observing the remaining precepts like these, which your old
scripture commanded and which the Gospel of a new grace has
commanded us to embrace even more. We avoid its curses if we
observe not the symbol but what is symbolized, that is, if we do
not observe a carnal circumcision, if we do not observe a carnal
Sabbath, if we do not observe carnal sacrifices, but rather the
spiritual virtues that are indicated by the carnal sacraments. In
neither way, then, either by doing those that were commanded
unconcealed, or by fulfilling those that were signified under
the veil of sacraments, is the Christian subject to the curse of
the law, and this demonstrates that it is a false Jew that assaults
him who declares that he remains within the words of the law
in these ways. Therefore, the curse that you threw against him
does not affect him in the least way, Jew, but rather it turns back
upon you, it rushes whole against you, you who neither remain
within the words of your law in the spirit of freedom as Christians do, nor fulfill them to the greatest extent in work, like the
first Jews, in a servile and carnal condition.

Pay attention, then, [to the fact] that it is not the Christian
that is subject to the curse, as already indicated, but instead
you are subject to the curse that you threw against him, concerning which Moses said: "Cursed be he that does not abide
in the words of this law, and does not fulfill them in work, and
all the people shall say: Amen."[174] With all these [examples] the
matter reaches this conclusion, that you dare not continue to
believe that the law given to Moses is everlasting, according to

174. Dt 27.26.

the interpretation you held earlier, nor dare to proclaim that it is eternal. Recognize, Jew, that this was accomplished through Christian faith, fulfilled through the evangelical law, and finally that the Old Testament that passes away flourished until a new and eternal one arrived. Recognize, Jew, that this was accomplished by Christ, I say, who, as author of the new and eternal testament, enlarged, removed, and changed many things in it, beyond what ancient usage had contemplated. He enlarged it when he said: "Unless your justice abound more than that of the scribes and Pharisees, you shall not enter into the kingdom of heaven."[175] And he added: "You have heard that it was said to them of old: You shall not kill. And whosoever shall kill shall be in danger of the judgment. But I say to you, that whosoever is angry with his brother, shall be in danger of the judgment,"[176] and what follows. And again: "You have heard that it was said to them of old: You shall not commit adultery. But I say to you, that whosoever shall look on a woman to lust after her, has already committed adultery with her in his heart."[177] And next: "You have heard that it was said to them of old: You shall not perjure yourself [. . .] But I say to you not to swear at all."[178] And afterward: "You have heard that it has been said: An eye for an eye, and a tooth for a tooth. But I say to you not to resist evil. But if one strike you on your right cheek, turn to him also the other,"[179] and the rest that our gospel reading indicates. "You have heard that it has been said: You shall love your neighbor, and hate your enemy. But I say to you, Love your enemies, do good to them that hate you, and pray for them that persecute and calumniate you,"[180] and the rest that that heavenly Scripture recites. When Christ commanded these things, certainly he expanded a good bit the precepts of the old law.

To be sure, he removed [commandments] when he established through his apostles, in whom he spoke, what is written below. Indeed, their epistle reports in this way: "The apostles and elder brethren, to the brethren of the Gentiles that are at Antioch, and in Syria and Cilicia, greeting."[181] And, following

175. Mt 5.20.
176. Mt 5.21–22.
177. Mt 5.27–28.
178. Mt 5.33–34.
179. Mt 5.38–39.
180. Mt 5.43–44.
181. Acts 15.23.

after another verse: "For it has seemed good to the Holy Spirit and to us," they said, "to lay no further burden upon you than these necessary things, that you abstain from things sacrificed to idols, and from blood, and from things strangled, and from fornication. From which things keeping yourselves, you shall do well."[182] When he commanded that these few commandments be guarded, he eliminated many from the multiplicity of legal precepts. Moreover, when he substituted baptism for circumcision, when he substituted rest from sin for Sabbath leisure, when he substituted the pure, innocent, immaculate Lamb of God alone for the countless sacrifices of bread, flour, wine, four-footed animals, and flying creatures, he determined thereby that he himself be offered each day to God Almighty for the salvation of all. And because he has been proved to be God, he commanded these things, and he ordered what he willed by divine authority, and he eliminated the questions of doubting unbelievers concerning his commandments. Among other things, he answered the astonished Jews and those who very foolishly complained that by healing many people with a word he did things that were unsuitable on the Sabbath: "The Son of man is Lord also of the Sabbath."[183] Indeed, God is certainly he who is Lord of the Sabbath. Only God can be Lord of the Sabbath. Whence it follows that he who is Lord and God of the Sabbath is Lord and God of circumcision, Lord and God of the sacrifices, or rather he is Lord of all things. Just as it was fitting for the Lord and God of all things whatsoever to create the things that exist when he willed, to change those that have been created into other things and other species, so was it fitting for him to set forth laws not yet given to man because the causes of justice were arcane and known to him alone, [to give laws] to whom he willed and at the time when he willed, and again to expand, reduce, or change them for those he willed, and when he willed.

Cease then, Jew, from being scandalized over changes to Moses' Law through Christ, because one and the same God who appeared to men through Christ the man promulgated, when he willed, legal precepts that did not exist earlier, and changed

182. Acts 15.28–29.   183. Lk 6.5; Mt 12.8.

those that had already been handed down, when he willed. Next, it is not the case that, as you assert, anyone could be justified through that old and already expired law since you find that many people are called just [in the time] before it existed, and they are called just apart from it during its age, and even after it. And, to return to ages long past, did not the innocence of Abel's heart and the purity of his simple sacrifice please God without circumcision, without the observance of the Sabbath, and without any ritual of your law having been imposed on him?[184] And is it not the case that "Enoch walked with God [. . .] and was seen no more because God took him"[185] even without circumcision, without the observance of the Sabbath, and without the manifold burden of your law? Was it not written concerning that great man, Noah, that even without circumcision, without the observance of the Sabbath, and without the manifold burden of your law, "Noah was a just and perfect man in his generation, and he walked with God"?[186] Did not God even say to him: "You I have seen as just before me in this generation"?[187] What shall I say of father Abraham, in whom you are particularly wont to glory? Was it not said that "Abraham believed God, and it was reputed to him unto justice"[188] before there was circumcision and apart from all those already presented—the Sabbath, the legal precepts? And what of his lineage: Isaac or Jacob and the rest, down to Moses? Did they not please God with circumcision alone, and especially with the observance of justice, without all the rest of the decrees of the law given later, and did not these two merit the extraordinary and glorious title of the patriarchs along with Abraham who preceded them? And indeed this was before the Law. Once the law had already been given or shortly before being given, I see that Job—not a Jew, but almost a stranger from the race of the Jews—without circumcision and without Sabbath observance and without all the legal precepts having been instituted, is called by the divine voice a simple, righteous, God-fearing man avoiding evil.[189] And I see that Balaam—without circumcision and without Sabbath

184. Cf. Gn 4.4.   185. Gn 5.22, 24.
186. Gn 6.9.   187. Gn 7.1.
188. Gn 15.6; Rom 4.3.   189. Cf. Jb 1.1.

observance and without the many precepts of Moses—spoke
to God, obeyed God, and by divine inspiration foretold many
things that would be useful for human salvation. Although he
fell, although he foresaw and predicted his fall, because he re-
counts his fall, he declares that he had abided [in justice] before this fall.[190] Thus, although he did not remain firm in justice, the one who heard the words of the Lord only deserved to
live on account of some of justice's merit. I also see that many
kings, I perceive that not merely a few foreign nations during
the time of the law worshiped God and eagerly pursued justice
and were justified by this same dedication to justice, without
circumcision, without Sabbath observance, without the Mosaic
precepts that have been instituted. Although one does not read
about them in the Jewish canon, nonetheless reliable histories
have proved that there have been men such as this.

But what is the point of these examples? So that when you
see how many people pleased God before the law and under
the law without the works of the law, you will cease to brag about
your law as if it is something unique, and put aside the old
boasting pride that you took from it. Not for this reason alone,
but also so that you observe that just as you perceive that before
the law and under the law many people were honored with the
title of justice without the legal observances, so too you will understand that after the law not just many people but everyone
can be justified by the grace of the Christian gospel alone. This
is indeed that new covenant (*testamentum*) of which you have
already heard God and the prophet say: "Behold, the days are
coming, says the Lord, and I will make a [new] covenant with
the house of Judah not according to the covenant which I made
with their fathers, when I led them out of the land of Egypt."[191]
Therefore, either show us another covenant that was given by
God different from that old covenant given by him, or accept
that this covenant of our gospel was truly given by him. Actually,
it is different from it, because it is more than it is. It is different
from it because the one is earthly and the other is heavenly. It
is different from it because the one is temporal and the other

190. Cf. Nm 31.8; cf. *infra*, ch. 5.1.
191. Jer 31.31–32.

is without doubt in reality everlasting. Not because the sacred Scripture of the Gospel given by Christ or what was commanded in it have to endure forever, but because the glory notwithstanding that Christ promised to those guarding the Gospel reasonably will endure forever.

I also conclude all the things that were said above about Christ in a more diffuse manner with a similar argument: in fact, either it is necessary for you to produce someone else about whom all those things truthfully can be understood, or it is necessary to agree with us that they were all said about our Christ.

But perhaps you may object: although I am unable to produce anyone else to whom the prophetic statements quoted above can apply, with what argument can you force me to understand that these prophetic statements refer to your Christ rather than to someone else? With a powerful one. I force you, I say, to understand this with a powerful argument. But let a proof-text precede the argument that is presented, which the argument will cap off later in its order. You ask why I think all those passages quoted above apply more to our Christ than to anyone else, and why I will force you to accept them too. Obviously I understand and I advocate that one must understand that our Christ and no one else is represented in all these prophetic statements, because I recognize that those words referred to him and to no one else.

And, in order to excerpt an example from the countless passages that pertain to him, what your prophet said and what our Church frequently repeats can be understood to refer to none other than he: "Behold, a virgin shall conceive, and bear a son, and his name shall be called Emmanuel."[192] For no virgin has conceived or will conceive, has given birth or will give birth to a son, except the supercelestial and ever-virgin Mary to Jesus Christ our Lord.

Of none other than of him can this be understood: "A star will rise out of Jacob, and a man will come forth from Israel."[193] In fact, it is not said to be a comet that changes kingdoms, or

192. Is 7.14.
193. Nm 24.17; cf. Vulg.: "orietur stella ex Iacob et consurget virga de Israhel."

some very bright constellation that has risen when our Christ was coming forth from Israel according to the flesh, but rather a star shone forth more splendid than all the constellations and comparable to the brightness of the sun itself, presaging the birth not merely of any person whatsoever but of him alone.

This can be understood to refer to no man other than to him: "I will pour upon you clean water, and you shall be cleansed from all your filthiness."[194] For only he and no other poured upon all clean water cleansing all the filth from sinners, when he commanded his disciples: "Teach all nations; baptizing them in the name of the Father, and of the Son, and of the Holy Spirit."[195]

To no age other than his can this apply: "Then shall the eyes of the blind be opened, and the ears of the deaf shall be unstopped; then shall the lame man leap as a hart, and the tongue of the dumb shall be free."[196] In fact, during his age, by his power, by his command, both through him and through countless others receiving this same gift from him, sight was restored to the blind, hearing to the deaf, the ability to walk to the lame, and speech to the mute, and countless other miracles of every kind and every type were performed.

This can apply to none other than to him: "He was wounded for our iniquities [. . .] and by his bruises we are healed."[197] For no one but he is found to have been wounded on account of the iniquities of man; only his bruises made men hale again. No one but he "was offered because he willed,"[198] no one but he "was led like a sheep to the slaughter"[199] "because he willed."

This can apply to none other than to him: "You will not give your holy one to see corruption."[200] In fact, as Peter our apostle said when speaking (just as I do) to Jews, not even David, who uttered these words, nor any other man nor even one of the saints who had been buried could escape the corruption of the flesh, except our Christ.[201]

This can apply to none other than to him: "He will revive us after two days: on the third day he will raise us up."[202] For no

194. Ezek 36.25.
196. Is 35.5–6.
198. Is 53.7.
200. Ps 15.10.
202. Hos 6.3.

195. Mt 28.19.
197. Is 53.5.
199. Is 53.7; Acts 8.32.
201. Cf. Acts 2.29.

dead person other than he lay for three days in the grave, rose up on the third day with the resurrection of his own flesh, and then raised up many of the saints, and, at the end of the age, will raise up all, both the good and the wicked equally, either to life or to everlasting death. But neither did the same prophet add this about anyone else: "His going forth is prepared as the morning light."[203] His going forth was like the morning light from the grave to immortal life, because he rose up "before the sun"[204] at the very beginning of light, as both our Gospel and he himself said in the Psalms: "I will arise with the morning light."[205] He not only added the everlasting nature of his resurrection to the transitory nature of light, but with it he also illuminated the long-lasting darkness of mortals.[206]

This can apply to none other than to him: Ascending "on high," he led "captivity" captive, he gave "gifts to men."[207] Deity alone cannot properly be said to ascend on high, because it is always on high, just as it is down low and in every other place. But according to the words of our apostle this was said of him: "he ascended" because "he also descended first into the lower parts of the earth," and from there, having assumed human flesh, "he who descended is the same also that ascended above all the heavens, that he might fill all things."[208]

This can apply to none other than to him: He will be "a root of Jesse and he that will rise up to rule the Gentiles, in him the Gentiles will hope."[209] You can observe this best by seeing it with your own eyes rather than by listening to prophetic texts. In fact, the Gentiles place their hope in him, they pray to him, they worship him, our Christ, who arose from the root of Jesse, as all the world declares to you.

This can be said of none other than of him: "I know that my Redeemer lives, and in the last day I shall rise out of the earth [. . .] and in my flesh I will see God."[210] Now, only one who redeems can be called the Redeemer. Actually, no one redeemed

203. Ibid.
205. Ps 56.9.
207. Cf. Ps 67.19.
209. Rom 15.12; cf. Is 11.10 LXX.

204. Cf. Ps 71.17.
206. Cf. Jn 1.5.
208. Eph 4.9–10.
210. Jb 19.25–26.

Job; the only one going to redeem was Christ, the Son of God, to whom this passage refers. Foreknowing that he will give the price of his own body and blood for his own redemption and for that of the world, he [Job] calls him his Redeemer, names him as God, and affirms that on the last day he [Job] will see him again, once he has been raised up in his own flesh.

We believe that all these and the many similar things said about him can be understood to refer only to our Christ, in whom and by whom we know all things are fulfilled, with the exception of that one last thing that remains to be fulfilled at the end of the world, and we exhort the unbelieving Jews to believe and understand the same things.

You have heard, O Jew, the proof-text, or rather the proof-texts, on account of which the Christian believes and understands that all the ones that have been presented have referred to no one else but Christ; now hear also with what argument the Jew may be compelled—willingly or unwillingly—to yield to him. And what greater argument will be able to persuade you other than those divine and boundless miracles I already mentioned? In fact, who will not see, so long as human intelligence flourishes in him, that so many and such great miracles performed by Christ and through Christians could only be performed by divine power? And he acknowledged that he is the Son of God, that he is God, that he is the eternal king, that he is the Christ who was foretold by the prophets. But if these were false, not only would no signs attend him, no power to perform miracles accompany him, but rather, as is wicked to believe, he would be condemned as a liar, a blasphemer, and impious. But since he foretold all these things about himself, since he made those believing in him capable of performing miracles as if they were omnipotent, just as he himself said, "All things are possible to him that believes,"[211] then it is clear, it is perfectly evident that whatever he taught should be believed concerning him, without any doubt whatsoever ought to be believed, whatever he commanded should be done ought to be safeguarded without any question.

But so that you can raise some objection, let me raise an

211. Mk 9.22.

objection against myself. Perhaps you will say either that there were no miracles or that they were acts of magic.[212] If you say that there were no miracles, if you say that we fabricated them, I respond quickly to you and I agree with your claim: If you assert that the miracles said to have been performed by Christ or through Christians either did not happen or were fictions, because we did not see them, then we assert as well that those that are read to have been performed by Moses, Joshua, or the rest of the Jews either did not happen or were fictions, because you did not see them. You can impart no greater certitude to the Jewish miracles than we can to the Christian ones. In fact, just as you have Jewish books in which they are recorded, so too we have Christian books in which they are reported, as well as Jewish books in which they were foretold. For this reason, then, either reject the Christian miracles and we will reject the Jewish ones, or admit the Christian miracles and we will acknowledge the Jewish ones. But because you put faith in signs (even though they have not been seen) solely based on the reading of books handed down from the fathers, you are urged to agree to put faith in the books handed down to us by our elders even as we do, and moreover because we offer assent to yours, you should offer assent to ours. We believe in your prophets; believe, then, in our apostles. Believe also for the reason that whatever they said would happen concerning Christ and events pertaining to Christ, they showed have been fulfilled in this world without any diminution. Therefore, you will be unable to prove in this way that there were no miracles of Christ; you will be unable to prove in this way that we fabricated them.

But, again, how else will you be able to prove that there were none or that they were fictions when you see that not just some parts of the world but almost the entire world is itself subject to Christian laws? Now the world's pride falls in surrender to Christ, and all the contemptible arrogance of worldly glory serves the ignominy of the one crucified and condemned by men. It worships his cross, which earlier it looked upon with

212. This common Jewish criticism is treated extensively in one of Peter the Venerable's sources, Petrus Alfonsi's *Dialogue Against the Jews*. See Petrus Alfonsi, *Dialogue Against the Jews*, trans. Resnick, 106, 232–35.

horror; and that which previously it thought to be foolishness, now it does not doubt to be far wiser than all its wisdom.²¹³ It recognizes that its power, with which it was accustomed to conquer all earthly things, is weak before the one acknowledged to be Christ, who is the power of God, and judging its own wisdom by him, who is the wisdom of God, it condemns it as foolishness. How, then, will it have freely subjected its wisdom to Christian foolishness, so to speak, its strength to weakness, its nobility to ignobility, its glory to ignominy, unless it was persuaded to do this by miraculous, wondrous, and previously unknown deeds? It follows, then, that your objection—that Christian miracles were not miracles or were fictions—is false.

But perhaps, seeking out Jewish subterfuges, you oppose us still. Why do you want to urge that, were it not for miracles, the world would have been unable to believe in Christ, when before Christ almost the entire world—actually the whole world, for some time—served idolatry, and was not converted to that idolatry by any signs but by its own error? I agree, I say, that the world sometimes submitted to idolatry without signs, except certain vain and demonic ones by which sometimes, although rarely, the error conceived in the hearts of foolish men was incubated, but the world began to surrender to despicable worship at that time when it was cast off as an exile from the face of God in the persons of the first parents, who had been thrown out by God from paradise into this vale of error and blindness. When, as a result of its own iniquity, it became gradually forgetful of its founder, nevertheless, thanks to the power of innate reason, having no doubt that divinity exists somewhere but still ignorant of where it ought to look, it looked for it either in praiseworthy men or in their images or in beautiful creatures and their proper uses, and thus became accustomed to worship instead of the Creator those things that he had created, with the worship that belonged to the deity.²¹⁴ And "when he was in the honor" of a human nature, [the human being] "did not understand," but rather "he is compared to senseless beasts, and is become like to them,"²¹⁵ both in terms of divine understanding

213. Cf. 1 Cor 3.19.					214. Cf. Rom 1.25.
215. Ps 48.13.

and in his own conduct. If only you were a careful investigator of your own Scriptures, you would know that what I say is true, that there was no cause of such great error other than that reason had been put to sleep in him and there was none who could resuscitate his reason, [and] the law having been given, hitherto "he said" like "a fool in his heart, there is no God."[216] Wherefore it was not surprising if at that time a part of the world, or even the whole world, was easily able to be deceived. But conversely, the age of Christ and of Christians was already an enlightened age, the Jewish law had already been given almost 2000 years earlier, philosophical schools everywhere were eager to study matters both human and divine, and with the vigor of human genius or knowledge flourishing again both in natural law as well as in written laws, it was impossible for men to be deceived and to submit generally to Christian faith and to change their faith, customs, and life into something different and opposite [to what they had had] at the command of one man without unlimited prodigies and signs. Therefore, the objection you proposed cannot stand.

But I fear the obduracy, well known to all, of a hardened countenance, lest your customary impudence proceed further and say: If the already enlightened Christian age was unable to be deceived or to believe without miracles, how is it that, when five hundred years had passed after Christ, the Mohammedan heresy arose, and that without any miracles a sect as nefarious as this infected such large parts of the world?[217] Was this age not enlightened, and nevertheless, such enlightenment notwithstanding, did it not fall before so great an error? I respond to this, first: it is one thing for parts of the world to fall into some error, and something else for the entire world to fall into it, and for that reason one ought to judge in one way concerning a particular error and in another way concerning a universal one. For there was no time in the past—except at the very beginning

216. Ps 13.1.
217. A reference to the claim that Mohammad performed no miracles. For further development of this argument, see Petrus Alfonsi, *Dialogue Against the Jews*, trans. Resnick, 154.

of the human race, which I touched on above—nor will there be any time in the future when darkness is not mixed with light, when truth is not mixed with error. And even though, according to our Gospel, "the light shines in darkness, and the darkness does not comprehend it,"[218] even if they are not the same, they are closely related. Therefore, as was said, some error can infect some parts of the world, but it cannot infect the entire world. Therefore, just like many other errors, it was able to infect some parts of the world, but it was unable to seize all of it.

In fact, the Christian faith did not bring under its sway little bits or parts of the world in the manner of [these] errors, but like a truth derived from the highest truth, which is Christ, it subjected the entire world to itself. I said the entire world, because even though the heathens (*gentiles*) or the Saracens exercise dominion over some parts of it, even though the Jews lurk among the Christians and the heathens (*ethnici*), there is still no part of the earth, not even a small part, neither the islands of the Tyrrhenian sea[219] nor even of the most distant ocean, that is not inhabited by Christians that either rule or are subjects there, so that what Scripture says about Christ appears to be true: "And he shall rule from sea to sea, and from the river unto the ends of the earth."[220] And also what our apostle said, that "in the name of Jesus every knee should bow."[221] If Mohammedan error corrupted some part of the world, then, after the law was given by Christ, what does that have to do with anything? In fact, many heresies arose among the Jewish people after the Law of Moses, many arose in the Christian world after the Gospel of Christ. Therefore, even though the age in which this heresy arose was an enlightened one, nonetheless that plague grew strong not throughout the entire world but only in a part of it, and, as I already said, like other heresies it infected a member of a large body as if with a corrupt humor. Thus there is no comparison between this diabolical falsehood and the divine

218. Jn 1.5.
219. An extension of the Mediterranean between the western coast of Italy and Corsica, Sardinia, and Sicily.
220. Ps 71.8.
221. Phil 2.10.

truth of the Gospel, since even though the former has obtained some—even many—[parts of the world], the latter has acquired all of it in the manner already described.

But you state in contradiction that those that were deceived in this Christian age believed the vile deceiver without miracles, and you aver this in order to cancel out our miracles. You infer, then, by analogy that in this enlightened age Christians could have been deceived without miracles just as in this same enlightened age the Saracens have been deceived so wretchedly without miracles. But this inference is not valid, and actually the analogy is weak. For I prove from this same enlightened age both that the Saracens have fallen into error without miracles and that necessarily Christians did not believe in Christ without miracles. For it was impossible either that those whom this discussion concerns, or any others, could be converted to things new and unfamiliar in this learned age, or that they could be turned away from a stubborn and ingrained practice without an obvious cause attracting or compelling them.

No other enticing or compelling cause exists, however, unless I am mistaken, but authority, reason, miracles, power, or pleasure, or a combination of all or some of these at one and the same time. But let no one be surprised that I placed miracles before reason above, [but] now I separate reason from miracles. In fact, there I said that miracles possess the power of reason, since just as reason draws the rational mind to believe something, so too miracles compel it to where they direct the attention, in place of reason. Here I separate one from the other, however, and I restore to each one what properly belongs to it, so that both by the term "reason" the rational intellect either will perceive what is implied to the mind or is explicit in words, and by the term "miracles" will be expressed the remarkable power to perform wondrous deeds. Therefore, once these two have been understood in this way, and once they have been added to the three already mentioned, there are five, as already indicated: authority, reason, miracles, power, and pleasure. Investigate which of these causes was able to attract or compel those that are condemned to receive a new error.

Eliminate, then, first those things that, as they themselves at-

CHAPTER FOUR 193

test, were not a cause of their error. In fact, they themselves attest that no reason (*ratio*) seduced them, [but] the witness and teacher of this very error did. For he said in his book, while not naming God, but introducing God as the one speaking to him: "If anyone would argue with you, say that you have turned your face and that of your followers to God, thanks to which both those knowledgeable in the law and those who are illiterate will follow a good law. But it is for you only to reveal my precepts to the nations . . ."[222] Again: "If someone would engage you in debate about the law, tell him that anathema and God's wrath threaten only such as these."[223] And once more: "Do not debate with those who have the law. For it is better for you to agree than to argue."[224] And many others like these.[225]

Again as if the voice of God spoke to him, he said that truly he did not challenge them with any miracles: "Indeed, you will never come to them with God's clearly manifest miracles, since they reject them as if they were odious and contrary."[226] Also: "we would give you signs and wonders, except that we know that they will not believe you just as they did not believe others."[227]And he repeated the same thing often. These two [that is, reason and miracles] are necessarily eliminated, then, because the one just like the others is confessed to be the author of their heresy, as was said.[228]

Therefore, the causes that remain by which they are shown to be deceived are authority, power, and pleasure. I do not call that an "authority" that could be divine, but rather one that the lying and deceitful author fabricated to be divine and that a foolish people, seduced by the lying and deceiving author,

222. Qur'an 3.18–19, according to the trans. of Robert of Ketton. Cf. J. Kritzeck, "Peter the Venerable and the Toledan Collection," 196–97. See *supra*, pp. 9–10, n. 17.
223. Qur'an 3.61, according to the trans. of Robert of Ketton.
224. Qur'an 29.45; and cf. al-Kindi in Kritzeck, "Peter the Venerable and the Toledan Collection," 196–97.
225. Cf. Qur'an, 2.187; 2.214, according to the trans. of Robert of Ketton.
226. Qur'an 6.4–5, according to the trans. of Robert of Ketton.
227. Qur'an 17.61.
228. This passage is troubling, since the referents for the intensive pronouns—*ipsum* and *ipsi*—remain vague and unclear.

received from him as if it were divine. I call "power" what the same presumptuous author indicated in the already mentioned book: "Only in the power of the sword have I been sent."[229] And once more to his own followers: "Be plunderers and conquerors, and to the extent that you are such as these, you will become more powerful than all. And unless you confess that I am a prophet sent by God, I will take away all your substance, and I will subject your wife and your sons and daughters to captivity, and I will slay you."[230] And [he said] many other things in the same manner. Now since we read that the successors of his government and that he himself, while he lived, did just this, and observed this as if it had been enjoined upon them by divine command, they subjected those whom they could through the violence of arms and the military force of the nefarious sect.

I call that "pleasure" whose restraints the especially wicked deceiver loosed, and in which the wretched race particularly engages, as is well known to all. Thereupon we read many things that were written by him, including these: "God," he said, "deals lightly with you, seeing that" in the faith of the Saracens "there is nothing but serenity and rest and God does not want from you what is difficult, but what is easy."[231] And again: "you will eat and you will drink and you will lie down then for the entire night until such time as a white thread can be distinguished from a black one."[232] And again: "You may have at least four wives. And as many concubines as you can."[233] And a thousand [more statements] such as these. Therefore, with books and deeds openly proclaiming [such things], they have been enticed or they have been forced to accept the name of that execrable sect by their authority, by power, and by pleasure, but they are not [enticed or forced] by reason or miracles.

Do you see, Jew, that in this enlightened age that race has

229. From al-Kindi; see Kritzeck, "Peter the Venerable and the Toledan Collection," 193.

230. From al-Kindi; see Kritzeck, "Peter the Venerable and the Toledan Collection," 194.

231. Qur'an 2.181; cf. Mt 11.30.

232. Qur'an 2.183, according to al-Kindi. Cf. B.T. *Berakhoth* 9b. See also Petrus Alfonsi, *Dialogue Against the Jews*, trans. Resnick, 147–48.

233. Qur'an 4.3, and 70.29–30. Cf. Petrus Alfonsi, *Dialogue Against the Jews*, trans. Resnick, 161.

been seduced by other causes, but not by miracles? See, too, that on account of what you introduced as if as an analogy, the Christian world was not converted to Christ without boundless miracles. In fact, I will demonstrate this not only with a probable but even with a necessary argument. I propose to you, then, those causes that I proposed earlier, and I prove Christian miracles from them necessarily. Let authority, reason, miracles, power, and pleasure be set before us again. All, or only some, of these enticed or forced the whole world to receive the Christian faith. But just as we did above, let us eliminate those that neither enticed nor forced the world to accept the name "Christian."

It was not enticed by authority, because although now Mosaic or prophetic authority is revered as if truly divine, nevertheless the world did not revere it as such before it believed in Christ. Indeed, after it was converted to Christian faith, it acknowledged everything that was foretold by the authority of those Scriptures that it perceived was fulfilled in Christ or in his Church, but before it was converted, it was ignorant of what was foretold by the prophetic spirit. Seeing that the Scriptures were foreign, it did not assent to them, nor did it think that anything belonging to the law of the Jews applied to it. Therefore, it did not come to pass that it believed in Christ first by the authority of those texts; but rather because it first believed in Christ, it accepted the authority of the same Scriptures. But it was not converted to this faith by paternal tradition nor by the authority of their elders, a faith from which ancient error always recalled it, so long as it yielded, under great pressure, to books, threats, and punishments. It is evident from this that the world was not converted to Christ by any authority whatsoever.

But neither was it converted by reason, because, as Christian doctrine itself says, although the merit of faith is great, faith does not derive merit where human reason provides proof. And indeed, some doctrines in it seem to follow human reason, which is why he says to his apostles: "Be ready always" to render, "to everyone that asks you, a reason for that hope which is in you,"[234] but many doctrines are so far removed [from reason] that they cannot be grasped through mental contemplation nor

234. 1 Pt 3.15.

penetrated with the tenaciousness of human modes of thought. With these, certain great teachers of secular philosophy have examined the unseen things of God that have been created, and almost all that the Christian foretells concerning the divine majesty, the curious philosopher investigates. In this way, one of ours says: "In the beginning was the Word, and the Word was with God, and the Word was God,"[235] and the other things that follow just as the evangelist and philosopher writes, but no mental acuity grasps "the Word was made flesh."[236] For the proud mind does not know how to grasp that supreme humility with which the Word of God deigned to be made flesh. Only the devotion of those that are humble understands that, being instructed by the grace of God's spirit. Whence these, too, are the words of our Savior speaking to God the Father: "You have hid these things from the wise and prudent, and revealed them to the little ones."[237] Thence, too, come the words of our great apostle, who, perceiving that the Jews were condemned and that the Gentiles were chosen by Christ, and wanting but unable to know the cause for this, exclaimed: "O the depth of the riches of the wisdom and of the knowledge of God; how incomprehensible are his judgments, and how unsearchable his ways."[238] It follows then, Jew, that the world was not converted to Christian faith by human reason, as Christ himself and his apostles confess.

But did anyone force it by power to accept that same faith of Christ? Clearly, we need not delay here any longer. We need not, I say, delay here any longer to show that people have not been forced to accept the Christian religion (lex). Not only were they not forced to accept it, but in a thousand ways they are shown to have been forced not to accept it. On account of it they suffered terrors, torments, prison, fire, and the sword, and yet those who suffered every kind of death were unable to be deterred or drawn away from it. The unbelieving world has long been witness, vainly employing all the forces of its malice against them, and even the earth itself is witness, stained everywhere with Christian blood and covered by the sacred bodies of the martyrs of Christ. There-

235. Jn 1.1.
237. Mt 11.25.
236. Jn 1.14.
238. Rom 11.33.

fore no power forced the world to accept the faith of Christ.
But has it been enticed by pleasure? And what pleasure
is there, O Jew, in the religion (*lex*) of Christ? Did he himself
not say to his own [disciples]: "In the world you shall have distress"?[239] Did not his apostle say: "And all that desire to live godly in Christ Jesus suffer persecution"?[240] Does not the Christian
sword cut off everywhere whatever it can that pertains to pleasure? Many examples of evangelical law stem from this that I
pass over, in order not to bore the readers, and for the sake of
brevity I select only some from that large number. For the sake
of pleasure a carnal man wants to feast to excess, and for the
sake of pleasure he wants to drink to excess and become inebri-
ated. Christ contradicts him and says: "See lest your hearts be
overcharged with surfeiting and drunkenness."[241] And his apostle [says]: "not in rioting and drunkenness [. . .]."[242] The carnal
man wants to live pleasurably and wantonly, not only for a pleasurable act but even for a pleasurable thought. Christ opposes
him, saying: "Whosoever shall look on a woman to lust after her,
has already committed adultery with her in his heart."[243] And
elsewhere: "There are eunuchs, who have castrated themselves
for the kingdom of heaven."[244] And while admonishing them in
another spot: "Let your loins be girt."[245] And the Apostle said:
"not in chambering and impurities."[246] And he also said: "But
fornication, and all uncleanness [. . .] let it not so much as be
named among you."[247] With spiritual pleasure the carnal man
wants to be revenged against an enemy. Christ resists him and
says: "But I say to you not to resist evil."[248] Drawn by the pleasure
of owning possessions the carnal man greedily wants to amass
wealth. Christ puts fear into him and says: "You cannot serve
God and mammon."[249] And again he says: "Lay not up treasures
for yourselves on earth."[250] And in another place: "He who does
not renounce all that he possesses, cannot be my disciple."[251]

239. Jn 16.33.
241. Lk 21.34.
243. Mt 5.28.
245. Lk 12.35.
247. Eph 5.3.
249. Mt 6.24.
251. Lk 14.13.

240. 2 Tm 3.12.
242. Rom 13.13.
244. Mt 19.12.
246. Rom 13.13.
248. Mt 5.39.
250. Mt 6.19.

The carnal man, with a desire for glory, proudly wants to place himself above others. Christ admonishes him and says: "He that is the greater among you, let him become as the younger; and he that is the leader, as he that serves."[252] And again he threatens: "Every one that exalts himself shall be humbled."[253] And, "I saw Satan like lightning falling from heaven."[254] Because of an appetite for life or an ill-considered fear of punishment, the carnal man wants to escape death and avoid torments, while offending against justice. Christ exhorts him and says: "Blessed are you when they will revile you, and persecute you, and speak all that is evil against you, untruly."[255] And on the same matter: "Be not afraid of them who kill the body, and after that have no more that they can do."[256] It is clear, then, that the world was not enticed to believe in Christ by any pleasure found in mortal life or [temporal] objects.

Therefore, miracles remain, which were placed in the middle of the [list of] aforementioned causes. If it is true that a race can only be forced or enticed to embrace what is new and unfamiliar by authority or reason or miracles or power or pleasure, then it is certain that the Christian world could only be enticed or forced to embrace the religion (*lex*) of Christ, which was new and unfamiliar to it, by one of these causes. But it is true that no race could be enticed or forced to accept new things except by one of these. It follows, then, that the Christian world was neither enticed nor forced to believe in Christ except by one of these. But again it has been proved that it was not converted to Christ by authority, nor by reason, power, or pleasure. It is clear, then, that only by miracles was it challenged to accept the faith of Christ, only by the grace of the Spirit.

But lest my responses be thought not to answer your objections in their own order, I will briefly reprise your objections. In fact, you said: the miracles that you say converted the world to the faith of Christ either are not miracles or they are magic. But it has already been proved false that they were not miracles; instead it has been proved that it is perfectly true that many mira-

252. Lk 22.26.
254. Lk 10.18.
256. Lk 12.4; Mt 10.28.

253. Lk 14.11.
255. Mt 5.11.

cles and in fact great miracles have already occurred, so I think. It remains to be proved that they were not magic. Actually, the miracles of Christ and of his disciples could in no way be magic, as will become clear from what follows. You demand of me then, Jew, to show this as well. I show, I say, that they could not have been magic but that they were divine acts. In fact, only someone literate and learned has been wont to teach or transmit magic. But the apostles and Christ's first disciples were entirely illiterate and unlearned, insofar as pertains to the arts or liberal or magic disciplines. Thus, concerning these elder disciples, among us one reads: The Jews, "seeing the constancy of Peter and of John, understanding that they were illiterate and ignorant men [. . .] knew them, that they had been with Jesus."[257] This reveals, too, their type of employment, since they led a poor life. For four of these apostles—that is, the two already mentioned plus Andrew and James—were fishermen, another was a tax collector, and the remainder from other vile types of employment were selected by Christ, who chose "the base things of the world,"[258] to destroy the proud. Therefore, it is clear that magic, which cannot or can barely be transmitted or learned without letters, was not received by them nor by Christ, nor was it transmitted to others by them. But lest perhaps you throw up against me the illiterate stage-players or mimes of our day, who are accustomed to deceive the eyes of the audience with certain illusions, I add that magic—whether transmitted with [the knowledge of] letters or without letters—requires not just a brief time but rather a long time to learn. It demands not only days or months, but very often even a period of many years, owing to its difficulty, during which period the unskilled disciple of Satan can slowly be initiated into its disciplines and finally, as one that has been instructed, avoid its worst effect. Where will you be able to find among Christ's disciples, O Jew, this protracted time period necessary for this nefarious art? In fact, a period of many years, months, or at least days was unnecessary for them to learn from Christ how to perform wondrous acts, so that they could perform them at will by the power of the eternal Word (which he

257. Acts 4.13.
258. 1 Cor 1.28.

was himself), but instead he instructed them suddenly and as if in a blink of an eye. This is written about in our Gospel, even though you do not accept it: Jesus "having called his twelve disciples together, gave them power over unclean spirits, to cast them out, and to heal all disease and all infirmity."[259] And again he said to them: "Heal the sick, raise the dead, cleanse the lepers, cast out demons."[260] And what commands are more succinct than these? How brief was the time in which so few words were set forth? Does this not only not require years, as was said, or even months, but not even a week, a day, or even an entire hour? It follows, then, that the magic art—which is so laborious, demands so much study, such protracted effort—could not be learned by the disciples nor transmitted by Christ in so little time. If perhaps you contend that, because one reads this in the Gospel, it is not true but that rather it is an invention, look, consider, observe that if the magic art had been transmitted by Christ to Christians either in written or verbal instructions, in no way could one have concealed this from so large a multitude of Christians across the entire world. Nor could the nefarious art be concealed for so long by universal consent, nor could Christian men of so many diverse races and tongues with such great religious learning and who are so God-fearing deceive themselves for so long a period of time with the diabolical art, and have desired what the heathens themselves execrated. To the arguments already presented I add only two more, by which I will show necessarily that Christian miracles not only probably were not magic, but really were not magic.

As the first, I propose that magical portents are always false and deceiving. They display nothing of truth, they present nothing solid, they deceive human senses and by demonic administration they feign that what does not exist does exist, that what is not seen is seen, that what is not heard is heard. They imitate their author, and, just as he is "a liar, and the father thereof,"[261] so too the magical progeny engendered by him present nothing that is true but all things false. Deceiving the human senses with occult tricks in this way, he produces not men but false images

259. Mt 10.1.   260. Mt 10.8.
261. Jn 8.44.

of men, not quadrupeds or flying creatures but false images of quadrupeds or flying creatures, not creeping things but false images of creeping things. From this source, with magic power he presents to human sight phantasms of springs, of rivers, of trees, and of all things. In these ways, Satan vies with the Author of nature with haughty envy, as is his custom, to create new things that he wills and to transform things already created into other substances or species as he wills, and in this way that author of deceit, because he cannot truly create, merely fashions false likenesses of things created to deceive fools. The ephemeral character of the invented phantasms reveals the emptiness of such tricks, which, as soon as they appear, immediately fade away like clouds or like smoke that swiftly dissipates, and, in this way, when suddenly removed from sight, they demonstrate that even when they were visible they were as nothing.

But contrariwise the miracles of Christ, innocent of diabolical falsehood, show that they are divine, not from fashioning empty and false things, but by presenting ones solid and real. For Christ trod on foot not over an imaginary sea but over a real sea without a boat as an instrumental medium;[262] he changed water not into imaginary wine, but into real and good wine;[263] he restored or bestowed not imaginary but real eyes upon the blind;[264] he conferred not a simulated but a natural power to hear upon the deaf,[265] not a simulated but a real power of speech upon the mute; he cured lepers not deceitfully but truly; he expelled demons from human bodies not deceitfully but truly;[266] not deceitfully but truly he cured all the diseases of men; he raised again the dead as it pleased him to do;[267] and finally, not like some prophet and not like some magician, but as God and Lord of all creation, "All the Lord willed he has done, in heaven, in earth, in the sea, and in all the deeps."[268] Not only did he do these things, but he also conferred this same power to perform miracles upon all those that truly believed in him, which only God can do.

262. Cf. Mt 14.25–27.
264. Cf. Mt 9.30.
266. Cf. Mt 8.16.
268. Ps 134.6.

263. Cf. Jn 2.3–9.
265. Cf. Mk 7.32–36.
267. Cf. Mt 9.25.

Now all those that one reads, believes, or avows to have performed any wondrous deeds whatsoever either before or after
him, employed not their own but another's power to do these
things; these deeds were accomplished not by human but by divine power. This is why they always offered up prayers to God
when they were intending to do these things, and once they had
obtained with these same prayers the miracles for which they
became famous, they performed them. Thus although you read
that Moses was silent before he divided the Red Sea, before he
drowned Pharaoh, God said: "Why do you cry out to me?"[269] You
read, too, that before Elijah raised the dead,[270] or consumed the
sacrifices offered to God with celestial fire,[271] or washed the dry
[offering] three times with rain water, he prayed, he bent his
knee, and that he performed none of these things except what
he had already set forth in prayer. So too for the rest. For not
one of them was able to perform any of these deeds by himself,
but when he performed them, he begged that they be done by
God. But if he was able to do nothing of himself, surely he did
not have the power to influence others to do anything. If in fact
you object that Elisha said to Elijah: I beg that "your double
spirit may reside in me,"[272] recall what Elijah replied to him, and
you will recognize that he was able to produce nothing by himself. Now when he said: "If you see me when I am taken from
you, you will have what you requested; but if you do not see me,
you will not have it,"[273] it shows that it belonged to another and
not to him to bestow on anyone the power to perform acts such
as this, or that the power to perform miracles belonged to God
and was not his own. But unlike Moses, unlike Elijah, unlike
any of the prophets who performed miracles not with their own
power but by having sent forth prayers, Christ effected miracles
as God and even as man, and effected them when he willed with
the power of his own deity, and with divine bounty he bestowed
upon whomever he willed the power to do the same things. And
to all those by whom the world was converted to Christian faith,
the miracles of Christ do not appear, O Jew, to be magic, or

269. Ex 14.15.   270. Cf. 1 Kgs 17.20.
271. Cf. 1 Kgs 18.36–37.   272. 2 Kgs 2.9.
273. 2 Kgs 2.10.

imaginary, or false and empty, but rather divine, true, concrete, and useful.

Again, pay careful attention to the fact that I say "useful," however. It is the last of the two [arguments] that I presented above, and by which I prove not only with a probable argument but with the necessary argument I had promised that Christ's miracles are not magic or false, but divine and real. The usefulness alone of Christ's miracles would suffice for proving this, even if all the rest mentioned above were lacking. In their usefulness is in fact the clear, certain, indubitable proof of miraculous acts, and it clearly demonstrates whether or not they come from God, even to those who do not pay careful attention. Now, everything of this sort that comes from God occurs on earth to serve the salvation of men; whatever like things come from Satan serve vain curiosity. Their human usefulness actually distinguishes and separates divine miracles from diabolical fictions, which usefulness the tricks of the devil always lack but which alone the miracles of Christ always serve. In fact, what benefit is there for the present circumstances of mortals—I do not say for eternal circumstances—in the airborne flights of magicians, the imaginary courses of rivers, the laughter of images, the fictions of the ages, the battles of shadows, in defensive ramparts constructed in but a moment of time, in the highest towers that are erected, in huge cities constructed as if in dream-like fancies, and in all the false and deceitful figments of Satan that are similar to these? I want the readers to understand just as I do why I said that magical fictions have been of no benefit for the present circumstances of men. In fact, I have known some magicians or some very deceptive practitioners of demonic tricks that were led to conclude that the occult is often useful, at the time when they disclosed to curious or covetous men what they learned from demons, from the secrets of nature, or from very long practice, or satisfied their eyes with wisp-like images, and very often obtained many things either for themselves or for those by whom they were urged to do these things. I am not concerned with these instances, nor do I even count lucre of this sort to be among the present things useful for human salvation. These are in fact more injurious than profitable, and lead more often to destruction than to salvation. I am not concerned, I say, with the wicked and abhorrent arts of magicians or stage players, or with the empty arts of those that approve of them in relation to useful ones, but rather I am concerned with those miracles that either serve the eternal salvation of souls or at least by whose remedies human bodies are healed. For what sick person was ever healed by the false and deceiving fictions of Satan? What wretch has been cured with such remedies? For what are such things fit except popular ridicule? What do they satisfy but the eyes of foolish people?

But you will mention to me the Egyptian magicians, and you will propose that they performed signs before Pharaoh similar to Moses' signs.[274] But recall that the miracles of Moses were true and not imaginary, as were those of the magicians, and remember that they served useful purposes for God's people that the magical figments actually failed to do. Moses performed signs, he introduced plagues to the Egyptians by divine command both so that a people in rebellion against God would be justly punished along with its perfidious king, and so that the race then chosen by God would be saved in his mercy. But the cause behind the portents was not the same, or even similar. There was no intention in them for human benefit because they were not performed for salvation or for any useful purpose whatsoever, but instead they were fashioned to imitate sacred signs and to display skill in a detestable art. The magical tricks lacked the useful purpose of divine signs; divine miracles are entirely different from the damnable vanity of curious men. Do you see now, Jew, the difference between signs and signs, miracles and miracles, wonders and wonders?

Separate now what perhaps previously you did not know how to separate, and acknowledge that there are false signs that you know have nothing to do with human salvation, and recognize that there are divine ones that you learn contribute to it. Are you not aware that not one blind person, deaf person, mute, nor any person suffering from disease has ever been healed—not to mention raised from the dead—by even the most skilled magician? Both the demonic power and the will are equally entirely

274. Cf. Ex 7.11; 8.7.

lacking for that, because the will to care for mortals was ever absent from them, as well as the power to restore whatever is broken or to heal those that have been corrupted. But Christ and the Christian faith transmitted to the world through him, actually intended nothing else, nothing else but these and countless other wondrous deeds; he employed so great a deed for no other purpose than to heal bodies here, to justify souls, and later at a time preordained by him before all creation, to unite to everlasting angelic blessedness a whole and complete man that has been snatched from every death, corruption, or misfortune. And because you are hemmed in on all sides by truth, Jew, because it has been clearly proved that Christian miracles only serve human salvation, you cannot deny that it follows that they are not false but true, not magic but divine. Acknowledge, then, that I have responded fully to the twin objections you posed above. In fact, it follows that what you said—that Christ's miracles are not miracles or that they are fictions—is false because it has been proved that there were many miracles. It has been revealed that what you said is not true—that they are magic—because it has been proved that they were wholly divine.

But how do I convince you from Christ's miracles, which occurred in the past, that our Redeemer is in truth Christ and God, when from the wondrous deeds of my own age I am unable very easily to convince someone who denies this or to provide corroboration to someone who confesses it? I pass over the countless and lofty miracles that occurred throughout the first thousand years of Christ and then of the apostles or other disciples who cleaved to him while still alive in a mortal body; I lay aside the countless legions of martyrs of Christ throughout the entire world, the multitude of confessors and priests of each order, the herds of monks, the hosts of hermits, not a few of whom glowed with heavenly signs while they still lived; I lay them aside, I say, I pass over them all, and I omit whatever wondrous deeds they performed while still living in a mortal body. I come to their tombs or sepulchers, and I show from their sacred ashes what blessedness or glory their spirits possess in the interim in the presence of their almighty and benevolent Author.

Reconsider, Jew, and reread intently all the books of the old

and sacred canon handed down to you in the past, and show
us, with the exception of the bones of Elisha[275] and of a certain other prophet, any miraculous acts that were performed by
any dead man of the Jewish law, however holy he was, until the
time of the Passion and death of our Christ. Because you cannot do this, turn your eyes away from the dead laws, so to speak,
and gaze upon the evangelical dead to see how much Christ has
accomplished through the cadavers of his Christians or those
that are already almost completely reduced to ash. Observe the
peoples of the earth rushing to the sepulcher of some Christian
who previously was viewed with contempt and often petitioning
those who in the past were slain with the most atrocious torments, for aid in danger and for remedies for every illness. Observe how much more quickly the dead hear them than the living hear them, and how frequently they are heard favorably by
the dead and carry away the benefits they wished for from the
temples and shelters of their Christ. I do not want you to work
too hard. Merely open your eyes and see those who entered
the sacred places blind and left seeing, deaf and left hearing,
crippled and left walking, mute and returned with their speech
restored, and last look at all the sick that rejoice at having put
off the illness that afflicted them. Look upon the eternal virgin Mother of Christ, more splendid than the sun itself, who is
superior to the heavens, whom you have always despised with
a special hatred, look even if with an envious eye upon the sal-
vific Cross of Christ, which hitherto you particularly detested.
Acknowledge that the places dedicated in their honor or memory are the more familiar and very often they become more established or greater, so that the more particularly you are confounded by that the more you are scandalized, and so that those
that you vilify as if with greater ignominy are distinguished with
a glory greater than others. Burned by an offensive and horrify-
ing fire, they rush to the same places as the countless number
affected with various afflictions, and filling the churches with
their multitude, within a short period of time not only two or
three or four, but often even fifty or one hundred are cured.

I myself saw someone rejoice who formerly,[276] during a noc-

275. Cf. 2 Kgs 13.21.
276. Reading *quondam* for *quandam*.

turnal vision, had recovered a healthy nose, a nose that previously had wasted away from that pestilential fire as far as the face's underlying surface.[277] I saw some people as well who had been blind for a long time or who had always been blind, according to the testimony of many reliable witnesses, who saw again, the light having been restored to their eyes. I saw other things too. But how many are they, in comparison to those that have been received from truthful men who are worthy of trust, or from those who have had sight restored, or from those who learned about them from those who saw them?

Among these, there was even the pilgrim of the apostle James[278] slain by his own hand thanks to a demonic delusion, who was raised up again by the same apostle only a few days after death, and who also reported what he had seen when he was outside the body and reported that he had been restored to his body by the merits of the saint.[279] The many miracles of Christ that have occurred in the modern age elude the mind and they are so numerous that even if there were no ancient miracles, these would provide sufficient support for the Christian faith.

But perhaps you will say that you will not accept the testimony of Christians concerning Christ. I ask the reason. You will reply that every sect engages in self-promotion and can deceive or be deceived by such reports or ones like them. I add to these [reasons]. If someone is so evil as to deceive others, can he be so wicked that he wants to deceive himself? In fact, they deceive themselves who bustle about saying that they have seen miracles of Christ that they have not seen, that they have heard what they have not heard, either in this way to strengthen their own Christian faith or to rouse others to the same faith with a marvelous fiction. That type of deception neither could nor ever will be able to exist among all those crying out with me against it. Moreover, I do not think that even Satan wants to deceive himself, even though he is the author and father of falsehood.[280] If

277. Presumably St. Elmo's Fire. See Peter's *De miraculis* 25.1 (CC CM 83).
278. A pilgrim to the shrine of St. James of Compostella, whose shrine had become more important in the twelfth century.
279. Cf. Peter the Venerable, *Sermo de transfiguratione Domini* (PL 189: 957).
280. Cf. Jn 8.44.

the father of falsehood and lies does not want to be deceived, even though he always desires to deceive, how much less does one of his offspring want to be deceived by someone else or deceived by himself. In addition to this, whosoever lies or deceives either lies or deceives from fear of losing what he has and cherishes, or from a hope of acquiring what he does not have and cherish. But those who have said that they themselves saw or heard miracles of Christ performed in our age, have never been afraid to lose anything or hoped to gain some profit thereby because they said that. It is clear, then, that they only spoke the truth.

But how do I work to set forth for a Jew one after another all the astonishing deeds of Christ that have been performed throughout various parts of the world, when they are beyond number, but when I know far fewer than the majority of them? Obviously, the number of miracles unknown to me is much larger than the number that is known. Nonetheless, how large a volume or how big a book could contain those that I consider with certitude to be beyond doubt? But let those be set down, and let them be saved for their own age or volume.

I propose for you, Jew, only at the end of [this] work the one divine and public act of Christ that you cannot deny, that, with the whole world crying out, you are forced to confess so that your silence not condemn you. You have heard of the miracles of Christ's disciples, you have heard of the miracles of Christ's mother, you have heard of the miracles of Christ's cross; hear, then, as well of the sublime miracle of Christ's sepulcher. You cannot claim that Christians fabricated this, when it has heathens and Saracens as its witnesses. For there is no Christian almost anywhere in all the world, no heathen, no pagan to whom that lies hidden, who could be ignorant of this because of the distance, no matter how remote, of his dwelling place. Christ visits his sepulcher with a light sent each year from heaven and illuminates it with a supernal brightness, not just on any day whatsoever but on that very day when he lay in it.[281] He reveals life by his death, he shows that an eternal light has illuminated

---

281. See William of Malmesbury, *De gestis regum Anglorum* 4.367, ed. William Stubbs, *Rerum Britannicarum medii ævi scriptores,* 2 vols. (Wiesbaden: Kraus Re-

the world from the darkness of his cave, so that the perfidious Jew who spurns his death will be confounded and the faithful Christian who places all his hope in this same thing will be saved. Fifty years ago the enemies of Christ occupied the temple and sepulcher of Christ along with the divine and royal Jerusalem, and they ruled it with a nefarious government. A few of the eastern Christians kept guard over this same sepulcher of the Lord, and, with the rare westerners mixed in, they attended to the grotto of salvation while patiently bearing the very harsh yoke of the impious [Saracens], for the love of the Savior. The violent custody of those Saracens menaced this most sacred place, and with torments and blows the cruelty of the perfidious ones extorted what it could, not only from the compliant but also from the pilgrims who arrived after much effort, drawn to the sepulcher of the Redeemer by their desire and fervor. Even then the heavenly light did not cease to penetrate the darkness of the impious, and from on high it irradiated the sepulcher of the Savior with a visible fire, shining upon earth on the Holy Saturday preceding the Easter Sunday of the Resurrection. The Egyptians bent the Persian bows, and the Ethiopians, either as a joke or in seriousness, threatened to pierce the angel (as they called him) who carries the divine fire with arrows that they loosed.[282] Surely the evidence of a miracle so sublime so prevailed over the minds of the unbelievers that they confirmed, even if by wicked undertakings, what they could not deny. If you have denied then, Jew, what Christians confess concerning a miracle as great as this, how will you be able to deny what the heathens and Saracens of the entire East and the South confirm for you concerning that?

In the past, God sent fire down upon the offerings of the just man, Abel, but did not send fire down upon the sacrifice of the ungodly Cain.[283] He sent fire from heaven down upon the burnt

---

print, 1964), 2: 423. For a list of sources pertaining to the miracle of the Holy Fire, see *supra*, p. 44, n. 151.

282. See Sāwīrus ibn al-Mukaffa, *History of the Patriarchs of the Egyptian Church*, ed. and trans. Y. Abd al-Massih and O. H. S. Khs. Burmester, 4 vols. (Cairo: Société d'archéologie copte, 1943–74), 3: 398.

283. Cf. Gn 4. 4–5 and Lv 9.24.

offering of the great Elijah,[284] but did not send it down upon the sacrifices prepared for the demon Baal. Thus plainly, O Jew, thus the same God distinguishes in this our age between the prayers and sacrifices of Christians and of Jews. He condemns your sacrifices that for a long time already he has not permitted to exist, but receives the Christian burnt offering when that Lamb, who offered himself as an immaculate offering to God, honors that place in which he once lay dead with such great miracles of divine fire that recur each year.

Therefore, O Jew, in order to summarize briefly what was said more extensively with the manifold authority of the Scriptures as well as with the visible proof (*ratio*) of miracles, acknowledge that it has been demonstrated, embrace it as certain that Christ our Lord is not the adoptive but the essential Son of God, is God not in a metaphorical sense but is true God, that he is not a temporal but the eternal King, not as one who is awaited who has not yet come, but rather as one who has already come at the prescribed time to be received and worshiped.

284. Cf. 1 Kgs 18.38; cf. Peter the Venerable, *De laude Domini sepulchri,* ed. Giles Constable, 252.

CHAPTER FIVE

On the ridiculous and very foolish fables
of the Jews

IT SEEMS TO ME, O Jew, that with so many proof-texts and with so many arguments (*rationes*) I have satisfied every human being, I think, on those matters pertaining to the question proposed. But if I have satisfied every human being, then I have satisfied you too, if, nonetheless, you are human. In fact, I do not dare avow that you are human, lest perhaps I lie, because I recognize that that rational faculty that separates a human from the other animals or wild beasts and gives precedence over them is extinct or, rather, buried in you. Even your psalm provides evidence of these things to me, where it deplores that a man is turned into a wild beast. It says, "Man when he was in honor did not understand; he has been compared to senseless beasts, and made like unto them."[1] Although, according to a certain understanding, this can be understood to have been said of all humanity (that is, of the human race), nonetheless you cannot deny that it is said of you specifically, of you individually, in whom all reason has been eclipsed. Now why should you not be called a wild animal, why not a beast, why not a beast of burden? Consider the cow, or, if you prefer, an ass (since there is none that is more stupid among the herd animals), and listen together with it to whatever they can hear. What difference will there be between your hearing and that of the ass, what distinction? The ass hears but does not understand; the Jew hears but does not understand. Now, am I the first to say this? Was not this same thing said many centuries

1. Ps 48.21.

ago? Did not your sublime prophet claim the same thing? He said, "With the ear you shall hear, and shall not understand; and seeing you shall see, and shall not perceive."[2] Whence, although it has been fully proved by these sacred authorities that you are a beast of burden or a wild animal, although I have made this sufficiently evident in the preceding four chapters (even if you were not moved by them), nonetheless let, then, a fifth chapter be added from which, once it has been brought to light, let it become clear not only to Christians but even to the whole world that you are truly a beast of burden and that when I affirm this I have not exceeded the limit of truth nor gone the least bit too far.

I lead, then, the monstrous beast out from its lair, and push it laughing onto the stage of the whole world, in the view of all peoples. I display that book of yours to you in the presence of all, O Jew, O wild beast, that book, I say, that is your Talmud, that egregious teaching of yours that you prefer to the books of the prophets and to all authentic judgments. But do you wonder, since I am not a Jew, how this name became known to me; whence it assailed my ears; who revealed to me the Jewish secrets; who laid bare your intimate and most hidden secrets? It is he, he, I say, the Christ whom you deny; it is the Truth that has laid bare your falsehood, unveiled your ignominy, which says: "For nothing is covered that shall not be revealed: nor hid, that shall not be known."[3] Certainly it will be shown from that book of yours, it will be revealed clearly from it how you have been given by God's just judgment over "to a reprobate sense,"[4] since you want to approach the clearest truth without the labor of human studies, and so are easily satisfied with the darkest falsehood. In you and your like are fulfilled the words of our apostle, who said: "Therefore God shall send them the operation of error, to believe lying; that all may be judged who have not believed the truth, but have consented to iniquity."[5] Plainly it is a surprise and almost incredibly a surprise that men do not believe, as was said, a credible and fully revealed truth, and believe an incredible falsehood. But conversely it is not surprising if

---

2. Acts 28.26; cf. Is 6.9 LXX.
4. Rom 1.28.

3. Mt 10.26; cf. Lk 12.2.
5. 2 Thes 2.10–11.

the once dense darkness of the Egyptians that was driven out of Egypt, while every vestige of light withdrew, seizes Jewish hearts, because according to a true Scripture "there is no concord between Christ and Belial, nor any fellowship between light and darkness."[6] But now this darkness must be stripped away, and your chosen text,[7] the Talmud, must be brought to the fore. According to you and to your like, it is so great and has such great dignity and loftiness that "God does nothing in heaven but read that text continually and confer over it with the wise Jews who composed it."[8]

But what shall I do? If I begin to respond to this insanity or to others like it, I myself will also appear practically insane. Will not he be thought insane who replies to a man that suffers either from madness or from a demon's furious assault, when he says strange or terribly absurd things? Will not he seem crazy who strives to debate reasonably with a man of a sort in whom the whole of reason has been buried, and who offers up nothing but vain and foolish things? Plainly one could believe this of me as well were it not for the fact that an unerring reason (*ratio*) protects me from this foolishness. That unerring reason is that even if I am unable to benefit all Jews with this disputation of mine, nonetheless perhaps I will be able to achieve something with some of them. Actually, although at present they have been cast aside by God properly for their iniquity and, according to the prophet, they will not be recalled to him until the multitude of the Gentiles has gone first, at which time a remnant of Israel will be saved, nonetheless supernal compassion sometimes gathers up some in the interim and separates others—albeit few— from the mass that has perished, for whom this, my response or disputation, will perhaps not lack some useful effect. Those among the Jews who have been tainted for a long time already by the aforementioned impurities will be able to be more completely cleansed once they cross over to the church of Christ, and once they have been relieved by such an antidote, than those that are tainted by that ruinous text. Hear then, O Jew,

6. Cf. 2 Cor 6.15, 14.
7. "text": *scriptura.*
8. Midrash *Gen. Rabbah* 64.4; B.T. *Ber.* 8a, *Abodah Zarah* 3b.

of your insanity and the insanity of your people and, what is worse, of your blasphemy. Now, the punishment for the sin I touched on above is the insanity of madmen, but it is not the sin. In fact, blasphemy is not only an intolerable sin, but, insofar as it pertains to your case, the punishment is for sins that went before. Now, had you not foolishly acted so wickedly, you would not have deserved this for your previous sins or crimes and for those of your fathers.

"God," you say, "does nothing in heaven but read continually that text, the Talmud, and confer over it with the wise Jews who composed it." And first I ask: Why does God read in heaven? To become more learned and to learn what earlier he did not know, or to recall those things he had forgotten? For every reader reads for these reasons: either to learn what previously he did not know, or to recall things he had forgotten, or to instruct someone else from that reading, or to entertain, or to argue, even if there are other things that pertain to the special character of reading. But to pose the question I posed earlier, does God read in order to learn? Or is he lacking some knowledge or wisdom? Does one not read not only of his magnitude but also of his wisdom: "Great is our Lord, and great is his power, and of his wisdom there is no number"?[9] Did not the prophet say to him in the same [Book of] Psalms, "You made all things in wisdom"?[10] Did not the same prophet say again to the same God, "Behold, Lord, you have known all things new and old."[11] Since he knows all things new and old—that is, all that are last and all that are first—certainly he is not ignorant of those that are in between. In fact, what follows next concerns them: "Your eyes did see my imperfect being, and in your book all will be written."[12] But lest you think that this book belonging to God is your Talmud, tell me, if you can, whether all men who have existed or who exist now or who will exist have been written in that book of yours. These are actually the words of the psalm: "In your book all will be written." But it is certain that you will not be able to show with any cunning, and with any effort, that all have been written in that book of yours that concerns us

9. Ps 146.5.   10. Ps 103.24.
11. Ps 138.5.   12. Ps 138.16.

here. That book cannot be the Jewish Talmud, then, of which it is said: "In your book all will be written." Hear, too, the good woman Susannah, who, although she is not part of your canon, was nonetheless from your people.[13] Hear from her whether God can be ignorant of anything, proclaiming in her own prayer: Lord, she said, "who has known all things before they exist."[14] Clearly if he knew all things before they exist, then he is not ignorant of them after they have been made. Therefore, it is not the case that God reads the Talmud to learn something.

But neither does he read the Talmud to be reminded of anything. Hear your prophet: "Can a woman," God said, "forget the infants of her womb? And if she will have forgotten them, nonetheless I will not forget you."[15] Recall, too, that verse you seem to have forgotten: "If I forget you, O Jerusalem, let my right hand be forgotten."[16] But perhaps you will object: God said this because he was moved by such great love for our fathers. I do not deny this, O Jew. But if love for the ancient Jews caused him to say this, it did not do so—as even you concede—so as to make him a liar. It is true, then, that he could not forget your fathers, and it is true that he could not forget your city Jerusalem. But could he forget anything else, besides the Jews? Did not Job, who is in your canon, say to God: "Although you conceal these things in your heart, yet I know that you remember all things"?[17] He who conceals the memory of all things in his heart certainly is forgetful of none, and clearly continually remembers all things. In fact, if at some moment of time the memory of all things should be lost to him, he would not conceal that memory in his heart because it would be lost for an interval of time. For no one is said to conceal what does not exist, but only what does exist. Therefore, it is clear not merely to the understanding of some but to all, that by no means can God forget any human beings or any things.

13. Peter alludes to the fact that the Hebrew text of the Book of Daniel ends with Chapter Twelve and therefore does not contain Chapters Thirteen and Fourteen found in the Vulgate and some other Christian Bibles. The passage he quotes next—Dn 13.42—which relates the story of Susannah, is absent, then, from Jewish sources.

14. Dn 13.42.   15. Cf. Is 49.15.
16. Ps 136.5.   17. Jb 10.13.

But you object: "Therefore, God remembered Noah and all those that were in the ark with him, and God caused a wind to pass over the earth, and the water subsided."[18] And you also object with this: "He remembered that they are but flesh, a wind that passes and does not return."[19] And then you add, What, then, does it mean when it says, "God remembered Noah," and, "He remembered that they are but flesh," if God neither forgets nor remembers anything? And I ask: Had God forgotten Noah, and had he forgotten all those who were with him in the ark before he brought a wind and caused the waters to subside upon the earth? Had he forgotten him whose ark he piloted among immense storms, among gusts of raging winds, among elements fiercely battling one another, ripped away from the law of nature, under violent rainstorms falling beyond measure, upon the immense sea of the abyss, among all these, I say, without a helmsman, without sails, without rudders, without the support of any human skill for almost an entire year? It seems to me, O Jew, that what is greater doubtless follows for me and doubtless follows for all who are not Jews, namely, that God could in no way forget those whom he declared he had not forgotten with such clear indications. See for yourself, see and judge if [you can do so] properly, whether Noah's ark could float over even one sea in the whole world, among so many and such great obstacles to navigation, without a divine hand, without human skill, when a small boat is unable to sail or cross even a narrow channel without great effort from the sailors. If what is obscure to no one but you is now clear to you, then you are compelled to confess that Scripture did not say that God had remembered Noah because he had forgotten him even for a minute, but rather that sacred Scripture was guarding the human manner of speaking when after it had stated several things concerning the character of the flood already associated with Noah's name, it appropriately recalled how he was snatched from such great dangers by God. Therefore, confess, as reason compels you, that at no time did God forget Noah or those who were with him in the ark. And confess this, too: that when it is said: "He

18. Gn 8.1.
19. Ps 77.39.

remembered that they are but flesh, a wind that passes and does not return,"[20] this does not indicate that God is forgetful but instead commends his compassion. Indeed, how can one believe that he had forgotten his people, whom he illuminated not only with sublime and frequent miracles but also with continuous signs and benefits? I say nothing of the Red Sea that he divided for them, nothing of the water he produced from a rock, nothing of the fact that he glorified them with certain other signs that he performed but once. Did he not feed them for forty years on heavenly manna flowing down from the supernal regions every day but the Sabbath, "when Israel went forth from Egypt, the house of Jacob from a people of strange language,"[21] as far as the Jordan River, which was divided;[22] with a pillar of cloud during the day and a column of fire at night, did he not continuously show them when they should pitch the tents, when they should march the measure and distance of the entire journey without going astray, through impassable places and deserts? Therefore, he cannot be said at all to have forgotten those whom he revealed that he had constantly remembered, not merely with intermittent signs but, what is greater, with continuous signs. Thus it is not the case that God in heaven reads or did read your Talmud, O Jew, to recall some things that he had forgotten. As a result, it is clear that God does not need to read it or anything else to learn or to remember. But neither does he do so to instruct students as a teacher does, nor to entertain people as the tragedians or comedians do, nor even, as satiric critics do, to prove profane matters. But why do I speak of these matters? For these are ridiculous things and should not be repeated except that with your profound stupidity, O Jew, you compel me unwillingly to address what I tremble even to contemplate. Let the rest, therefore, follow.

"God," you say, "reads the book of the Talmud in heaven." But what type of book is this? If it is of a kind such as the others we have in use for daily reading, is it bound together at any rate

20. Ps 77.39.
21. Ps 113.1.
22. "Jordan River, which was divided": *divisum Iordanem*. Perhaps an allusion to Ps 113.3, which explains that the Jordan was "turned back." Also Jos 3.

from the skins of rams, goats, or cows, or made from papyrus or rushes from eastern marshes or from the scrapings of old cloths or perhaps from some other even more vile material, and is it written by quills or marsh reeds and stained with some ink? And, O wretch, have you subjected the wisdom of the Almighty to a need so great that it is necessary for him to consult your most vile pages to learn or to remember some things and to beg for understanding from the skins or papyri? How could he who gave the Law to the Jews written on stone tablets with his finger—that is, by his Spirit—learn anything from the books of the Jews? What could he learn from any book of the Jews, when he is himself the author and promulgator of their law? Once again I am loath to respond to such abject foolishness, but because you who are so wise believe such things, I cannot remain silent.

You say, "God does nothing else in heaven than read the text (*scriptura*), the Talmud." This has already been discussed. And what follows next? "And to confer over it with the wise Jews who composed it." Clearly, such great dignity have the Jews, such excellence, that God deigns to read in the heavens a book composed by them and to confer over it with the wise Jews. But why does God confer with the wise Jews over that text? In order to teach, or in order to learn? In fact, it is the nature of human speech that one who confers with another over some matter either teaches or is taught, or else is made better trained, keener, or less inclined to do something. Therefore, when conferring with the Jews on the book already mentioned, does God become either better instructed by their conversation, better trained, keener, or less inclined [to do something]? Answer as you prefer. If from their conversation he becomes more learned, better instructed, or keener, you contradict your prophet, who says: "Who has known the mind of the Lord, or who has been his counselor?"[23] And you contradict the one who said: "Whom have you desired to teach? was it not he that made life?"[24] See then, consider, and take into account that that conversation in heaven between God and the Jews will be in vain, or rather that it never will exist, since God cannot have a counselor, since he

23. Rom 11.34; Is 40.13 LXX.
24. Jb 26.4.

cannot have a teacher. In fact when it says, "who has been his counselor?" this question was not asked to show who it is, but rather to show that there is none. Also when it says: "Whom have you desired to teach? was it not he that made life?"[25] it shows unsurprisingly that God cannot accept any teaching from anyone since it is he himself that has created the life of all living beings. How, then, will someone be able to teach God, without whom he cannot live? How will he teach wisdom to God, without whom he could not have life itself? How will he confer wisdom upon God, if he could not have life without God? Therefore, with the whole world as judge, it is false that God reads in the heavens without interruption that text, the Talmud, and confers with wise Jews over it. But now let that admirable text composed by wise Jews be brought before us, and let one see how much the very God of the universe ought to admire its wisdom.

"Sometimes," says the Talmud,

a certain question arises for the Jews conferring with God over this same text, regarding the different kinds of leprosy that are found in the book of Moses, and concerning allopecia and certain other illnesses.[26] Where, although God said that allopecia is leprosy, they, however, in opposition deny this and while energetically disputing it they contradict him and can in no way agree with him, and after long arguments and very serious quarrels they agreed on this: that whatever Rabbi Nehemiah said about this should be considered true. Furthermore, Rabbi Nehemiah, whom the Jews assert to be the great and most holy of all their teachers, was still living at that time. Therefore, God commanded an avenging angel to conduct his soul, bringing it quickly into heaven. When he came upon him, the angel found him reading the Talmud

(namely, the aforementioned text that the Jews call holy because no one can die while reading it).

Therefore, as soon as Rabbi Nehemiah saw the angel of death, he asked him why he had come. He told him that he had come for his soul. But he, since he was terrified and feared death, adjured him terribly in the

25. Ibid.

26. "Allopecia," or alopecia: for medieval medical writers, a type of leprosy arising from corrupt blood and marked by hair loss, but not to be confused with modern allopecia. See Roger Frugard's *Chirurgia* 4.19, in *Anglo-Norman Medicine,* ed. Tony Hunt (Cambridge: D. S. Brewer, 1994), 1: 86–87; and Bartholomaeus Anglicus, *De rerum proprietatibus* 7.64 (Frankfurt, 1601; reprint, Frankfurt on Main: Minerva, 1964), 351–54.

name of God himself and in the name of the holy text of the Talmud that he was reading, not to put a hand on him, because in no way did he want to die yet. When the angel, however, said that it was better for him to be in heaven with God and with the holy Jews and to delight in celestial things and that he should allow him to lead his soul away, in no way did he acquiesce, but read the Talmud without interruption so that he could not be killed. Thus, the angel returned and reported this to God, saying that Rabbi Nehemiah was utterly unwilling to die and read the Talmud without interruption, so that he could do nothing at all to him. God said, "I will give you advice. Return to him quickly and create in the air over his head a mighty wind and a storm of hail and rock, as it were, so that when, terrified, he averts his eyes from the Talmud, then you can seize his soul and bring it here." So the angel returned and did as God had commanded. As soon, however, as Rabbi Nehemiah's soul had been led away to heaven and he saw God sitting on his throne debating the aforementioned question with the Jews, he began to cry out in a great voice: "It is clean, it is clean."[27]

That is, you have been vanquished by the Jews concerning this question, O God, because allopecia is not leprosy, just as you had said, but is rather a clean illness.

Then God, being somewhat embarrassed and not daring to say anything to contradict the testimony of so great a man, thus replied in a jesting manner to the Jews who were debating with him: "Nazahvni Benai,"[28]

that is, "My sons have vanquished me."

For now I am not dealing with you, O Jew. I do not have sufficient strength, I do not have the power, I do not find words appropriate to confute such great madness. Your prophet, although actually not yours but *our* Isaiah, takes my place against you. What do you say against the Jews, greatest of prophets? He says, "Hear, O Heavens, and give ear, O Earth, for the Lord has spoken. 'Sons have I reared and brought up, but they have rebelled against me. The ox knew its master, and the ass its master's crib.'" Nevertheless, "'Israel has not known, and my people has not understood'" me. "Woe, sinful nation, a people laden with iniquity, offspring of evildoers, corrupt sons. They have forsaken the Lord, they have blasphemed against the Holy One of Israel, they are utterly estranged."[29] Since you said such things in

27. Cf. B.T. *Baba Mezia* 86a.   28. Cf. B.T. *Baba Mezia* 59b.
29. Is 1.2–4.

God's name against the Jews of your time, O prophet, since you
inveighed so harshly, since you declared so sublimely against
the impious Jews while as yet the greater number of the Jews
still believed rightly in God, while they [still] confessed him,
while they continually immolated sacrificial victims, what would
you say about them if you should hear that the Jews assert that
God debates with dead Jews in the heavens just as if with equals?
What would you say if you should hear that God maintains one
judgment concerning the types of leprosy and the Jews another
judgment, that God asserts that allopecia is leprosy and that the
Jews in opposition deny this, and while debating with him they
ardently contradict God? What would you say if you should hear
about this matter in the heavens, after the Jews' protracted arguments and weighty debates with God, that Rabbi Nehemiah
was selected as an arbiter with each side's agreement to pro-
mulgate a definitive judgment on this question between God
and the Jews for the purpose of resolving the argument? What
would you say if you should hear that God commanded an angel to bring him the soul of the living Nehemiah that was still in
the flesh to render this judgment, and that he defended himself
by reading the Talmud uninterruptedly so that the angel could
not compel his death? What would you say if you should hear
that his soul was finally seized and borne off to heaven by a divine trick, at which time he offended God sitting on the throne
and still debating with the Jews over the aforementioned question, when he immediately began to cry out that God was deceived in his premise, and had been overpowered by the Jews?
What would you say should you hear that God blushed, having
been overcome by Nehemiah's judgment, or if you should hear
that he dared say nothing against the judgment of such a great
judge, or if you should hear that he even confessed this Jewish
victory with his own mouth, saying: "My sons have vanquished
me"? I do not believe that you could patiently bear to hear God
called foolish, to be called deceived, to be instructed by men,
to be subdued by the judgments of men, [and] to hear that human souls escape from bodies by trickery, and to hear so many
things that are inappropriate not only with respect to God but
even with respect to any wise or good man, or to hear unworthy

things asserted about God. You hear how he is called foolish by the Jews when they say that he lacked the knowledge to discriminate between different types of human illnesses, and you hear how they deny to God Almighty what they grant to every physician. Clearly they call him foolish because of the knowledge they snatch from him.

What do you say about this? Certainly, I hear you resisting the opinion of the Jews in your customary unfettered speech, when you say: "The Lord is God everlasting who created the ends of the earth and will not grow faint or labor, nor is his understanding searchable."[30] I also hear Job: "Hell is naked before him, and there is no covering for perdition."[31] Now, if God's wisdom is as great as you say, such that there will be no searching it out, that is, so that it cannot be searched out by anyone, then it is certain that nothing is hidden from him. That if nothing is hidden from him, then neither is any type of illness hidden from him. But according to your judgment (which it is wicked not to believe), nothing is hidden from him. Therefore, the Jew is deceived who says that whether or not the already mentioned type of disease was leprosy was hidden from God. Again, if "Hell is naked before him," and if "there is no covering for perdition before him,"[32] then what the Jew says was hidden from him could not be hidden from him. Actually, if hell—that is, if all those are laid bare before his gaze who exist now or will exist within the infernal regions, can any of those that exist or will exist on earth be concealed from his eyes? If he sees the demonic spirits and human souls that are confined in the infernal regions and sees the things that are done to them, will he not know the people still placed on earth and living in the flesh and the things that are done among them or against them? Because this cannot happen, because clearly it cannot happen that any creature that has been created should be hidden from its Creator among created things, because the Maker cannot be ignorant of what he has made, again I say that you [Isaiah] affirm the same as I: that the Jew is deceived who has dared to say that there is anything of which God is ignorant. And what else shall

30. Is 40.28.   31. Jb 26.6.
32. Jb 26.6.

I say? Earlier I was interested in addressing the Jew, but now I am interested in addressing you, O holy prophet. Why? Because I am confounded speaking to the deaf, speaking to the insane, speaking to a beast of burden. But it helps me to deal with you concerning these matters, if you do not object, since I know that while you lived you always acted in similar matters against the Jews, even if in ones not so insane. Since you were filled with the Spirit of God, you despised their madness, although their perfidy, coming long after your age with its zeal for God, is more despicable than I can execrate in words. Or is what I mentioned previously not execrable beyond all measure? Those that they add now are not less deserving of being despised with every curse. A single blasphemy does not suffice for them, but rather they have filled large volumes with an infinite number of blasphemies against God. After so many thousands of years among false hearts,[33] they have collected a vast sea of impieties, and, gathering wicked things little by little that have been poisoned by the mouth of the poisonous serpent over so much time, they pour them out daily against God so much as they can, so much as they dare. They have said that God is foolish, and they call him a liar. Do they not call him a liar when they confess that he has said what is not the case and denied what is the case concerning the illness written about above?

But reason overthrows this, authority overthrows this, and the wisdom that speaks through Solomon overthrows this: "My mouth shall meditate upon truth, and my lips shall hate wickedness. All my words are just, there is nothing wicked nor perverse in them. They are right to them that understand, and just to them that find knowledge."[34] And what is this wisdom that speaks through Solomon? Is it not God himself? It is clearly God himself. Actually, it is not the case that God is one thing and his wisdom another, just as Solomon was one thing and his wisdom another. For even if there were a Solomon without wisdom, nonetheless Solomon would exist. God cannot exist without wisdom, however, because he is not one thing and his

33. "Among false hearts": *in condempnatis pectoribus*. According to the apparatus, other MSS offer *peccatoribus* (i.e., "sinners") for *pectoribus*.

34. Prv 8.7–9.

wisdom something else, but rather what God is, so too is his wisdom. Thus it is one and the same thing if God is mentioned or his wisdom named, because God is wisdom and wisdom is God. Therefore, God says: "My mouth shall meditate upon truth, and my lips shall hate wickedness."[35] God's mouth meditates upon truth and not falsehood, then, while God's lips despise the impious and not the just, but none more correctly than you, O lying Jews, who strive to assert that God's wisdom is false. And because, moreover, a just, truthful man oftentimes is deceived—even if not from injustice, nonetheless from ignorance—and because sometimes he is deceived by being unaware of injustice, Scripture adds: "All my words are just, there is nothing wicked nor perverse in them."[36] If, then, not just some but all the words of God are just, if there is nothing wicked in them, if there is nothing perverse in them, then what the Jew said is false, O prophet, when he called God a liar. And there follows next: "They are right to them that understand, and just to them that find knowledge."[37] Thus it is not surprising if not all God's words are right to the Jews, because they are not right to those who do not understand. Nor is it surprising if they are not just to these very same Jews, because they are not just to those who do not find knowledge. Thus, because the Jews do not understand, because they do not find knowledge, all God's words cannot appear right to them. "You will destroy all that speak a lie,"[38] says the psalm. Pay attention, O you wretches, since I am compelled to turn to you again from the prophet's discourse; pay attention, I say, O you wretches, to how far down you cast yourselves into the abyss when you called God a liar by means of that wicked text in which you believe. In fact, if God will destroy all those who speak a lie, and God himself speaks a lie, then certainly God will destroy himself. Who will bear this? Who will tolerate it? Who will endure it?

And since, if I have tarried too long over things that are so clear, I will seem to flog the air in vain, let me proceed to the things that follow. O Jew, has not your already mentioned fable, after it imposed upon God a mark of foolishness, after

35. Prv 8.7.
37. Prv 8.9.
36. Prv 8.8.
38. Ps 5.7.

it imposed a mark of falsehood, when it said that he learned from Nehemiah what previously he did not know, has it not also subjected him to discipleship under human instruction? These things are unnatural and cause more astonishment than all ghostly appearances. I am surprised, I remain amazed (it is not enough to be surprised), at how a human mind could fabricate these things, how a human hand could write them, how a human mouth could or dared produce them. I myself fear to speak such things even while contradicting them, and yet do you not fear to speak such things while asserting them? I am afraid to propose such things even for the sake of instruction, and do you not fear to contemplate them, to write them, to speak them for the perdition of you and your people? Let the discussion that began be pursued nonetheless.

As I said, you say that God is instructed by men, that the eternal One borrows wisdom from mortals, that heaven borrows from things of the earth, and that the highest wisdom borrows from fools. Hear whether all your texts—not the profane ones but the sacred—oppose or concede such a perverse opinion. I counter profane texts with the sacred, I oppose impious texts with texts divine. Above, you heard the testimony of the just man, Job, concerning a similar matter when he defended God against this wicked opinion of yours, when he said: "Whom have you desired to teach? was it not he that made life?"[39] Hear also a similar example from the Psalms, where the Spirit of God inveighs against you and yours, where he despises this unheard of opinion against God: "Understand," he says, "you senseless among the people, and you fools, be wise at last."[40] Could he indicate more forcibly than with these words the mood of someone who is angry and indignant? "You senseless," he says, "understand, and you fools, be wise at last."[41] What next? "He that planted the ear, shall he not hear? or he that formed the eye, does he not consider?" What next? "He that corrects the nations, shall he not rebuke, or he that teaches man knowledge,"[42] shall he not rebuke? Have you heard this last [passage], Jews? According to your psalm, God teaches man knowledge,

39. Jb 26.4.   40. Ps 93.8.
41. Ibid.   42. Ps 93.9–10.

man does not teach God knowledge. And let me employ the divine words against you: "Understand, you senseless among the people, and you fools, be wise at last."[43] What do I want you to understand? What do I want you to know? I say again that man does not teach God knowledge, but God teaches man knowledge. If this is true, then your Nehemiah, who you admit was a man, did not teach God knowledge, nor have the Jews, also men themselves, taught God knowledge. Having set aside the infinite number of other passages affirming the same testimony, does this prophetic passage alone not suffice, O Jew, to prove that God cannot be taught by man? I have learned that it is sufficient.

But hear this, too: "All wisdom," says a certain text of yours, "is from the Lord God, and it has been always with him, and is before all time."[44] But if "all wisdom is from the Lord God" then the wisdom or knowledge of the Jews by which they knew that allopecia is not leprosy was from him. But if it was from him, then certainly it was his. If what they knew was his, he could not be ignorant of it. But you cannot deny that this is so. What you thought, then, is false, and what you believed is incredible. But lest perhaps you object (if you even know enough to make this objection) that the passage just cited is not from the highest part of the canon of the Jewish texts, then return to the Psalms, and see what they express in another place on a similar matter.[45] The prophet says, "Your knowledge is become wonderful for me, it is fortified, and I cannot reach to it."[46] To whom does he speak? To God. What does he say? "Your knowledge is become wonderful for me"; it says "for me" (*ex me*) according to the Hebrew language, "beyond me" (*supra me*) according to the Latin interpretation.[47] That is, "Your knowledge is become wonderful," more than I could understand, more than I could grasp. And what else? It also explains what it said and adds what it did

43. Ps 93.8.

44. Sir 1.1.

45. Peter refers to the fact that the book of Ecclesiasticus (Sirach) is a deutero-canonical book absent from the Hebrew Bible.

46. "is fortified": *confortata est* (Vulg.: *excelsior*). Ps 138.6.

47. Cf. Augustine, *Enarrationes in Psalmos* 138.9, ed. Eligius Dekkers and J. Fraipont, CC SL 40 (Turnholt: Brepols, 1956), p. 1997.

not say: "it is fortified, and I cannot reach to it." See then, Jew, when so great a man, so great a king, so great a prophet pronounces that God's wonderful knowledge is beyond him, when he affirms that it is high, when he affirms that he cannot reach it, will the knowledge of your Nehemiah not only transcend the knowledge of David but also surpass the knowledge of God himself? I do not believe that you will dare to compare this Nehemiah to King David, let alone prefer him to David. But if you do not dare to compare him to your king, how will you prefer him to your God? Abandon irrationality, and cast this ridiculous madness from your heart. Are you not embarrassed to assert so many wicked things? Are you not embarrassed to prefer the aforementioned judge Nehemiah to God? Are you not embarrassed to submit to human judgments him who is called "a just judge"[48] by the prophet, who "judges the entire world in justice and [its] peoples in his truth"?[49] If you have human eyes, eyes not of the body but of the soul, then pay attention, look inward, turn this way, because if the prophetic claim is true that says that God "will judge the entire world and [its] peoples in justice and truth,"[50] then it is false that he has invoked human judgment, and false that he has submitted himself to it.

But perhaps you will object that when the prophet said "he will judge," and not "he judges," he established this for a future time, not for time present. Thus when the prophet said that, since that judgment was still a future judgment, in the interim he could be judged by man. But if you say this, if by the term "future time" you want to eliminate this difficulty, then hear that God is also the judge of time present, hear that he is the judge of time past, hear that he is at the same time the judge of time future. When God drew nigh to destroy the Sodomites and those of Gomorrah, Abraham approached him and said: "Will you destroy the just with the wicked? ... Far be it from you to do this thing, and to slay the just with the wicked, and for the just to be in like case as the wicked. This is not seemly for you.

48. Ps 7.12.
49. Cf. Ps 9.9; also Pss 95.13b and 97.9, both of which read "will judge" (*iudicabit*) in the Vulg.
50. Cf. Pss 9.9, 95.13b, and 97.9.

Will you who judge all the earth, not make this judgment"?[51] Do
you recognize, O Jew, Abraham's name? I know that you recognize it, and, I reckon, you keep it in mind tenaciously above all
the names of men. Will you prefer your Talmud, then, to the
words of Abraham? What did Abraham say? "Will you who judge
all the earth, not make this judgment?"[52] See that Abraham establishes the present tense when he says: "You who judge all the
earth." Nonetheless, the present tense contains within it an understanding of times past and future. In fact, Abraham sensed
this when he said: "you who judge all the earth," that God judges the whole earth at every time. Such is the sense, too, in the
Psalms: "You that sit upon the cherubim,"[53] and, "You who make
your angels spirits,"[54] and, "Keep in mind, O you who rule Israel,"[55] and, "The Lord rules over me,"[56] and in many similar
instances.

And God did not sit upon the cherubim[57] or make his angels spirits or rule over Israel or rule over David only at the time
when this was said, and not also before then and after, but rather
at that time and before and after. David perceived this when he
made those statements. Abraham perceived this when he said:
"You who judge all the earth." Therefore, this passage which concerns us in this instance is in the present tense, but past, present,
and future are understood. If what Abraham said is true, namely,
that God judges the whole earth at every time, then what the
fable invents—that at some time he is subject to the judgment of
earthbound man—is false. But I believe that you will be afraid to
say that Abraham is a liar. If you are afraid to say this, if you are
unwilling to call him a liar, then certainly you will deny that God
is bound by human judgments.

Do you want something still to be added to the foregoing?
Let it be as you wish, although it is superfluous. Let it be the
case that your Nehemiah was great, wise, and learned, or rather,
as you claim, a teacher of the law. Was he greater than the one
of whom another text in your canon says: "Behold, God is high

51. Gn 18.23, 25.
52. Gn 18.25.
53. Ps 79.2.
54. Ps 103.4.
55. Ps 79.2.
56. Ps 22.1.
57. Cf. Ps 17.11.

in his strength, and none is like him among the lawgivers"?[58] And the text adds, after a few verses that come in between: "Behold, God the great overcomes our knowledge; the number of his years is inestimable."[59] Do you see, then, that although, according to you, Nehemiah is a great teacher of the law, nonetheless he is not greater than God nor is he on a par with him, because "none is like him among the lawgivers." You also see that although, according to your claim, Nehemiah was wise, nonetheless he was not greater in knowledge than God or on a par with him because, as a true text says: "God the great overcomes our knowledge,"[60] that is, all human wisdom.

Now, who can tolerate what that wicked text falsely has dared to state, that with acts of trickery God snatched away Nehemiah's soul, which otherwise he could not have done while Nehemiah resisted by reading the Talmud, and that an angel carried it off to the heavens to render a judgment between him and the Jews? And first, who besides Satan could teach, and who besides the Jew could listen to (not to say believe) a thing so absurd as that reading the Talmud could be prejudicial to God's power or as that the ridiculous recitation of an infernal book could withstand the will or command of God? In reality, O Jew, is that book of yours more sacred than the five books of Moses? Is it more sacred than the books of the prophets? Is it better? Is it more worthy? And nonetheless Moses, the giver and reader of the law, is dead, and the prophets (the writers of their books) and their readers are dead. Was reading these books that are so sacred able to save no one from death, and was the reading of the Talmud able to block God's judgment so that Nehemiah would not die? In truth, preeminent is the power of a book that has the power to exempt anyone reading it from the common condition of all things, since it was said to all men through one man, "You are earth, and you will return to earth."[61] But because it follows that this is entirely absurd, I turn to the divine tricks.

When the angel returned to God and said that Nehemiah was utterly unwilling to die and that for that reason he read the Talmud without

58. Jb 36.22.
60. Ibid.

59. Jb 36.26.
61. Cf. Gn 3.19.

interruption, so that he could do nothing at all to him, God said, "I will give you advice. Return to him quickly, and create in the air over his head a mighty wind and a storm of hail and rock, as it were, so that when, terrified, he averts his eyes from the Talmud, then you can seize his soul and bring it here." So the angel returned and did as God had commanded.

O divine counsel, O counsel apart from which the deity of counsels was unable to find any better. Would it not have been more fitting to await the human body's inevitable needs that would compel him to pause from reading the Talmud, than to take refuge in laughable tricks, and is it not, I would add, somewhat ludicrous to offer God better advice than he himself offered? For however tenacious he was disposed to be in reading, after two or three [days] the need for eating or at least sleeping, even if there were no other needs, would turn even a dumb beast (*mutum*) completely away from reading. In that period of time the angel sent to slay him could carry off I do not say only his one soul and bear it away as he wished, but he could snatch a thousand or more human souls from their bodies. In the past, the angel of God who struck the Egyptians did this, even slaying thousands beyond number of the firstborn in barely one hour of the night.[62] He did also something akin to this under the Assyrian king, when he slew 185,000 in his camp in a brief moment of time during the night, while they were sleeping and lying awake.[63] He could have done the same thing when Nehemiah struggled against God by the aforementioned reading [of the Talmud], lest he die. Clearly it would have been more fitting to carry off the soul of a person that was eating or sleeping than to distract a very stubborn reader from a reading that is so holy and so very sacred by a storm of hail or stones.

But perhaps God could not endure delay and hastened to bring to an end so weighty a debate of the question that had been proposed by the impetuous judgment of human wisdom. In fact, there was a great need to bring peace to celestial disputes lest perhaps, if they dragged out longer, with the passing of time there would arise even greater ones and these would incite against God public enemies in the heavens themselves. So

62. Cf. Ex 12.29–30.
63. Cf. 2 Kgs 19.35.

that this not happen, the precaution was taken to summon Nehemiah quickly by some stratagem, and through him the peace lost between God and the Jews would be restored. Nonetheless, I do not think that God would call in such a judge from earth to the heavens if his judgment defined him as the inferior one, and if it established the Jews as the superior ones in the protracted dispute. For Nehemiah did not spare him, he did not fawn upon him, but rather as soon as he was snatched from the body and ascended to the heavens and gazed upon God sitting upon the throne, clearly steadfast and a lover of truth, "acknowledging no difference of persons,"[64] he proposed a condemnatory judgment of God, saying how God had said of the type of illness that he thought it was leprosy, while he contended: "It is clean, it is clean." The repetition of the phrase bears this sense: It is certain, it is firmly established in your statement, O God, that you have been vanquished by the Jews, because it follows that if they spoke the truth, you were deceived.

What, then, remains, O Jew? Since you have found a man wiser than God, since you have passed judgment on the Judge of all things, let God descend from the throne, let him cede it to the better, let him cede it to the one that is wiser. I say that this is necessary. Indeed, if anyone is found to be wiser than God, then certainly the one who was thought to be God was not, nor is, God. But it is not enough that God is condemned with Nehemiah's judgment, unless he is condemned even by his own admission. "Once the judgment was given," it said, "God blushed and he replied, laughing, that he dared not contradict the testimony of so great a man: Nezahvni Benai";[65] that is: My sons have vanquished me. What else? Overcome by human judgment, overcome with embarrassment, overcome by his own admission, why does God tarry on the throne of omnipotent wisdom? God has been deposed by the Jews; not omnipotent, he has been cast down by the Jews, and he is proved not to be omniscient by the elders and by Jews wiser than he.

And indeed I know that these words, which are more than mad or demonic, ought not be refuted by authority or by rea-

64. Cf. Dt 1.17.
65. B.T. *Baba Mezia* 59b; *supra*, p. 220.

son, but spit out, if it can be done, with a fitting mocking gesture and curse. But since you believe, speak, and write down
these things, O ruined race and race deserving of destruction,
who shall be silent? Who may restrain his hands, much less his
words? Indeed, since for 1100 years already you have moaned
in sorrow under the feet of Christians, whom you hate above
all others, having been made a mockery not only to them but
also even to the Saracens and to all races and demons at one
and the same time, what will restrain our hand from spilling
your blood if not the commandment of the one who cast you
off and elected us, the commandment of God saying through
your prophet: "Slay them not"?[66] Actually, he does not want you
to be preserved for honor but for opprobrium, not for your advantage but as a spectacle for the world; he wants you to be preserved like the fratricide Cain. Cain, who said to God when the
latter upbraided him for spilling his brother's blood, "All who
find me will slay me," heard, "Never will this be so."[67] But, "You
will be cursed upon the earth,"[68] and, "You will be a fugitive and
wanderer upon it."[69] Thus are you cursed, thus are you fugitives,
thus were you made insecure upon the earth after you spilled
the blood of Christ, your brother with respect to the flesh but
your Lord with respect to deity, so that, in what is worse than
death, for the duration of the present age you are made a reproach among men, while for the future forevermore you will
be a mockery among the demons. Certainly your wicked heart
deserves all these things, and your blasphemous mouth, which
not only continuously vomits curses against men but even pours
out impious and wicked things against God himself, deserves
them. For what is as impious, what is as wicked as what you
say: God is a liar, God has been vanquished, God blushed with
shame, God has admitted that he has been vanquished.

---

66. Ps 58.12. At *De civitate Dei* 18.46, ed. B. Dombart and A. Kalb, CC SL 48,
644–45, Augustine cites this same passage from the Psalms to demonstrate that
God has chosen not to kill the Jews, but to tolerate their existence as a sign or
witness for those who come after them. For the importance of Augustine's interpretation in the formulation of a medieval policy of toleration toward Jews, see
especially Jeremy Cohen, *Living Letters of the Law,* 29–41.

67. Gn 4.14–15.   68. Gn 4.11.
69. Gn 4.12.

But it was proved above that he is not a liar. Other than to you, to whom is it unclear that he cannot blush with shame? For whosoever blushes with shame seems to admit a certain guilt, a certain error, a certain excess. For unless these or causes like these have been present earlier, it is impossible for anyone to blush. Do you see, my prize-fighter, how you have spoken, how proudly, how wickedly, how stupidly you have set your mouth against heaven?[70] To ascribe guilt, error, or excess to God—what is this if not to rage in madness? "Have you thought iniquitously," said God, "that I will be one like unto you? I will reprove you and set [myself] against your face."[71] He who seems to speak to only one Jew actually reproves all the Jews at the same time when he adds: "Consider these [things], you who have forgotten God, lest he carry [you] off, and there be none to deliver [you]."[72] In this verse, in fact, he struck down the already mentioned fable of your Nehemiah—rather, what is greater, he destroyed it. For you said that God wanted to carry off Nehemiah's soul by an angelic minister, but that Nehemiah resisted him by reading the Talmud so that he could not carry it off. In this way, then, he upbraids you, in this way he demonstrates that your legend is utterly false. "Consider these [things]," he said, "you who have forgotten God." What is more true? Have you not forgotten God, when you think such unworthy things concerning God? Certainly of you it is said: "Consider these [things], you who have forgotten God." But how does he exhort you to consider? "Lest he carry [you] off, and there be none to deliver [you],"[73] he says. Do not be deceived, he says, do not be seduced, do not think that Nehemiah or anyone else can oppose him when he has decided to carry off souls. He confirms the same thing with another verse from another psalm. When he said: "Promise and return gifts to your Lord God," to which he added, to him that is a "terrible" God.[74] And immediately after that: "And to him who will bear off the spirits of princes."[75] But perhaps he bears off only the spirits of princes, and no others? Hear Job, then, speaking to God not only of princes but even of all: "You know that I have done

70. Cf. Ps. 72.9.
72. Ps 49.22.
74. Ps 75.12.

71. Ps 49.12.
73. Ibid.
75. Ps 75.13.

nothing wicked, although there will be no one who can deliver
me from your hand."[76] Not only can this one or that not deliver
from your hand, but no one can deliver from your hand. Therefore, it is clear that the oft-repeated statement that your teacher
delivered his soul from the hand of God by some stratagem is
false. But as I said above, O Jew, when you say that God blushed
with shame, you confess that he incurred either some guilt, or
error, or excess. If I intend to defend him with some proof-texts
or by reasoned arguments, I may appear perhaps [to do some-
thing] superfluous or excessive. For who really thinks that God
can incur guilt, error, or excess, except perhaps "the fool who
said in his heart, there is no God"?[77] I fear even that what Job
replied to a friend was said even to me: "Whose helper are you?
Is it of him that is weak? And do you sustain the arm of him who
is not strong?"[78] It is almost the same to labor over things so clear
as for a finger to point out to clear and watchful eyes the sun's
orb shining with brilliant rays on a calm day. Certainly things
that are perfectly clear ought to be passed over with only a very
brief reply or even with no reply at all, even if the Jew objects
to them. Those, and what contains the conclusion of the fable,
number among these, when it asserts that God is vanquished,
when it invents that he has himself admitted with his own mouth
that he has been vanquished, when it lies that he said: My sons
have vanquished me.

Actually, who but a Jew would fail to recognize that this needs
no contradiction? Certainly, what everyone knows to be false by a
self-evident truth needs no contradiction. In fact, for whom can
it be uncertain that God cannot be vanquished by any power or
wisdom when the entire world, when all have heard him saying
from antiquity: "To whom have you likened me, and made me
equal, and compared me, and made me like?"[79] And a few lines
later: "Remember the former age, for I am God, and there is no
God beside, neither is there the like to me proclaiming from the
beginning the things that shall be at last, and from ancient times
the things that as yet are not done, saying: My counsel shall

76. Jb 10.7.   77. Ps 13.1; 52.1.
78. Jb 26.2.   79. Is 46.5.

stand, and all my will shall be done."[80] And although, as was said, it may seem superfluous to defend God from these inept scoffers, the reason is so that the discourse will openly produce their other errors on a similar matter, lest someone think that the Jews have erred only once, or blasphemed only once, which would be more tolerable. For the reader easily will be able to observe in their countless blasphemies just how far they who have been able to believe or perceive so many unworthy, so many absurd things concerning the most sublime and incomprehensible majesty of God Almighty have been cast away from the face of God. For in addition to the things that have been mentioned, in their own synagogues of Satan they also say and teach that "when God made the firmament" that is visible to our eyes, "he did not perfect it as a whole, but left unfinished a space with a certain large aperture in its northern region."[81] They represent the purpose for which he will have done this as both very fitting and reasonable. They assert that he did this according to his providence, "so that if, as time passes, one should arise and say that he is God and equal to God, God may present him with the aforementioned imperfection in the firmament, saying: If you are God, as I am, create at least in the region that I, also [a creator], made. I made the larger parts of the firmament, so you, also [a creator], should make this part which I left unfinished, if you can."[82]

How shall I complain further, O Jews, that you do not know spiritual things with a spiritual eye, when you do not even know corporeal things with a corporeal eye? Certainly the firmament is corporeal, and the eyes of your own flesh are corporeal. Why, then, is this concealed from the Jews alone, when it is clear to the eyes of the whole world, except yours? Plainly no eye except yours sees an imperfection in the north, or in the south, or in any part of it, but sees the firmament complete in all its parts. The northern axis that is always glowing with a golden color over the earth and which, being opposite the southern axis that is never visible to human view, reveals to all eyes except to the

80. Is 46.9–10.
81. Cf. Petrus Alfonsi, *Dialogue Against the Jews*, trans. Resnick, 90–91.
82. Ibid., p. 91.

eyes of the Jews nothing imperfect in that region of the heaven, [and] refutes the entire fiction of your lie.

Because this is very well known, with the world as judge, let us move on to far more ludicrous blasphemies. For you claim that "God becomes angry once each day"[83] and you also strive to confirm this with what you think is the robust testimony of the psalm: "God is a just judge, strong and patient: he is angry every day."[84] And, no longer pursuing the literal sense of your Scriptures, which alone you seem to follow, O beasts, is this presented in an affirmative or declarative manner and not rather in an interrogative fashion while denying [the statement]? In fact, it was said in this way: "Is he angry every day?" as if to say: He is not angry each day. Reread your Hebrew language text, and you will discover (if Jewish blindness does not prevent it) that this is the meaning of this text. Now even though we are Latin readers, nonetheless nothing could conceal the truth of your Scriptures from us, whom the abundant erudition of many men skilled in both languages has instructed. I remain silent over how foolishly you think that God grows angry, in human fashion.

If you think this, then certainly you affirm that he is mutable. For if, according to the usual practice of men, he grows angry at one moment, at another he is subdued, at another he rejoices, at another he is saddened, at another he forgets, at another he remembers, and either he performs or experiences other similar things in a manner analogous to our own, then your prophet is lying who, debating the mutability of the heaven and earth and the stability of God, says to God: "These,"—that is, the heavens and earth—"will perish, whereas you remain always." And a few words further on, "You will change them, and they will be changed. You, however, are always the same."[85] If God remains, if he is not changed, then certainly he is changed neither in essence nor in affect. You could perhaps object that God is not changed in essence but changed in affect. That he is not changed naturally but changed accidentally. But even if you deny it a thousand times Scripture removes both and excludes both when it says: "whereas

83. B.T. *Ber.* 7a; cf. Petrus Alfonsi, *Dialogue Against the Jews,* trans. Resnick, 66.
84. Ps 7.12.
85. Ps 101.27–28.

you remain," and when it says, "You, however, are the same."[86] Therefore, God does not at one moment grow angry according to our practice, nor at another is he subdued. You add, beyond those things already mentioned, that "he grows angry at the first hour of the day, and the cause of his anger," you propose, is such as this: "that at that hour, that is, the first hour, the kings of iniquity arise and place the diadems upon themselves and worship the sun."[87]

You add that "no one ever knew the minute of that hour when he grows angry, except Balaam, son of Beor."[88] You add to that, and provide a fitting associate for him in this knowledge— namely, the "cock," who, you affirm, "alone, with Balaam, knew the minute of the aforementioned hour."[89] What shall I say? As I admitted above, I do not know whether it is more appropriate to reply to such inept foolishness or to remain silent. While it seems superfluous to reply, it seems inappropriate to remain silent. Superfluous, because the matter proposed reveals itself clearly to be stupid.[90] Inappropriate, because it is not expedient to remain silent when one ought to reply to the things that have been proposed. And, as you have placed it first, let the first discussion present itself—which authority has taught, which argument has persuaded you to believe that God grows angry and grows angry each day and grows angry at the first hour of the day? In fact, what genuine legislator said this, what prophet wrote it, which among those read in your entire divine canon taught this? Present anyone from the multitude of the saints of old who either wrote this or taught this or even thought it, and I will concede. If that authority has abandoned you, you cannot defend what you have said on its strength; or, defend such a prodigious fable with some [rational] argument. But if you do not have that, what remains? What remains, I say, except that with their insulting fables the proof will be displayed to heaven and to earth and to angels and to men that you are the most stupid people?

86. Ibid.
87. Cf. Petrus Alfonsi, *Dialogue Against the Jews,* trans. Resnick, 66.
88. Cf. Petrus Alfonsi, *Dialogue Against the Jews,* trans. Resnick, 67.
89. Ibid.
90. "Clearly": *absque tegmine,* lit., "without a covering."

Who will not see that you cannot establish the effect once the cause has been removed? But it is incumbent upon me to state what I should name as the cause and what I should call the effect. For, if I am able to remove the cause, I will equally be able to remove the effect. I call that the cause, O Jews, that you yourselves propose, namely, that "as the kings of iniquity arise at the first hour of the day, they place the diadems upon themselves and worship the sun."[91] The effect is that God, seeing the things that are done at the first hour of the day, grows angry at the first hour of the day, and because he sees that that occurs daily at the same hour, he grows angry each day at the same hour. Who are these kings of iniquity that place the diadems upon themselves and worship the sun, never at the third hour of the day, nor the fourth, nor the fifth, nor the sixth, nor the seventh, nor at any other hour, but always at the first hour of the day? In truth, they are most zealous and peculiar worshipers of iniquity who cannot be distracted by any of the business of their kingdoms nor by any impediments, but who each day, and at the very same hour, both place upon themselves the diadems and worship the sun. What peaceable kings and most subdued kingdoms they are that tremble at no adversity, that are buffeted by no domestic or civil or external upheavals, that enjoy the most quiet leisure, and that insist upon a ceaseless, profane worship. Clearly, as was said already, these are golden ages that make available to their kings such desirable and extended leisure that, having put aside force of arms, having put aside cares, the devotees zealously serve their own religion to the extent that, over a long period of time, they miss neither one day nor miss even the same hour of the day. And indeed I have heard that at one time the kings of the East worshiped the sun, but I never knew that it was every day or always at the first hour of the day. But I should say more correctly that I know that they did not do so daily, nor always at the first hour of the day. Actually, they were quite warlike, and almost always under arms, whence they were able neither to observe cursed rites every day, nor were they able always to guard the same hour of the day, as reason itself teaches.

91. Petrus Alfonsi, *Dialogue Against the Jews*, trans. Resnick, 66.

But why am I speaking of the ancient errors and rites of kings, when the Jewish fable describes this not only for time past but even for time present and future? In fact, the fable does not speak of ages past but of the present time, saying that the kings of iniquity arise each day at the first hour of the day to place upon themselves the diadems and to worship the sun.

One paying even scant attention observes how un-circumspect it is to think this, how incorrect it is to say this, for our time. For there is no longer a king in the East, nor in the West, nor in the South, nor in the North (the four regions that encompass the entire globe), who worships the sun—not, I say, at the first or the sixth or at any other hour of the day or night—nor is there one who offers up worship to something created by the Creator. In fact, it is certain that not one of the Christian kings or the Saracen kings (which Christians or Saracens rule almost the entire world), not one of these, I say, worships the sun, and this is even unheard of for the few others who still govern certain pagan peoples. From this it follows that it has already been adequately proved that none of the kings of our time worships the sun. Because this is true, the Jewish fable lies that had said that each day at the first hour of the day the sun is worshiped by some kings of iniquity. In fact, if none of the kings at any time worships the sun, then it is certain that none of them worships it each day or at the first hour of the day. So, if no king worships the sun on any day, at any hour, then what the Jew had added is false, namely, that Balaam or the cock knew that God was accustomed to grow angry at the minute of the first hour. In fact, neither Balaam nor the cock could know the minute of that hour which does not exist, nor can the hour of that day be indicated that does not exist in any passage of time. Therefore, once the cause is excluded the effect is excluded, because God does not have a reason to grow angry, since none of the kings throughout the earth is discovered to be a worshiper of the sun. Therefore, all those are false that were proposed in contradiction, either that God grows angry each day or that the kings of iniquity place upon themselves the diadems and worship the sun.

Now I am amazed and I ask, O Jews, why Balaam and the cock have deserved so much attention from you, more than the other men and birds of God. I ask, I say, why have they deserved so much from you, so that you wanted to bestow on only these two—and none but these two—the knowledge of divine anger and of the very hour when you say God grows angry. Clearly, this is a great prerogative, the greatest privilege for Balaam and the cock, with which the one stands above all men and the other stands above all birds. Certainly, it is surprising to us, it is surprising to everyone except you (since you cannot be surprised at all, seeing that all that you say is surprising) if Balaam is preferred to Moses, to David, to Solomon, to Isaiah, if he is preferred above all the prophets of God, if, finally, he is preferred above all the wise and divine men in the knowledge of the oft-mentioned hour. Is it not surprising that Balaam is preferred over the one of whom God said to Aaron and Miriam: "If there be among you a prophet of the Lord, I will appear to him in a vision, or I will speak to him in a dream. But it is not so with my servant Moses. . . . For I speak to him mouth to mouth, and plainly, and not by riddles and figures does he see the Lord"?[92] Is it not surprising that he is preferred over the one who said to God, "The uncertain and hidden things of your wisdom you have made manifest to me."[93] Is it not surprising if he is preferred over the one to whom God said: "I have given you a wise and understanding heart, so much so that there has been no one like you before you, nor shall arise after you"?[94] Is it not surprising if, with respect to knowing the secrets of God, Balaam is preferred over one who could perceive "the Lord sitting upon a throne high and elevated" and "the seraphim standing upon" the temple, veiling the face and the feet of God with their wings, and who could hear them cry out, "Holy, Holy, Holy"?[95] But perhaps it seems to you that he ought to be preferred over all of them because he predicted some true things and because he conversed with his ass. But did he predict things more heavenly, more divine, more numerous than the prophets did? Just because one time an ass spoke to the man with human speech, is that to be preferred to all the wondrous signs that Moses worked? But so that I may satisfy you in some way, lest perhaps you plead that

92. Nm 12.6–8.
93. Ps 50.8.
94. 1 Kgs 3.12.
95. Cf. Is 6.1–3.

I am always an enemy, I concede that Balaam, a prophet or a divine or a soothsayer of lesser merit, deserved some specific gift beyond that of other men, even though they had greater merit. Therefore, he had this gift—to know the hour or minute of divine wrath. He had this gift, but only so long as he pleased God. But how about after he displeased him? Did he have this gift after he displeased God, after an angel of God said to him, "Your way is perverse, and contrary to me,"[96] and when, after returning to his people, he gave perverse counsel against the people of God,[97] so that afterward he was not honored by your fathers, O Jews, as a prophet of God but was slain instead as a wicked opponent of God, and even as a public enemy?[98] I do not believe that you are so foolish, that you so lack human reason as to believe that wicked men, especially after death, take part in the secrets and counsels of God. If this is true, then it is false that Balaam could know the daily hour or minute of divine anger.

Now, let the world see, let the whole of the earth judge that you admit the cock to divine counsels, that you say it is aware of God's secrets. Let it see and let it judge whether a cock should be admitted to the knowledge of divine secrets or acts to which hardly any man has ever been admitted. But because it is always Jewish practice to misuse the Scriptures, just as you have misused the verse in the aforementioned psalm to show that God is angry each day, namely, "God is a just judge, strong and patient: he is angry every day,"[99] perhaps you will misuse also the passage in the Book of Job in order to demonstrate the singular wisdom of your cock, which says: "Who has put wisdom in the hearts of men, or who has given intelligence to the cock?"[100] Perhaps you have established your defense here. You presume that this seemingly very strong tower of Jewish interpretation cannot be breached. Based on this, you give preference to the intelligence of a cock surpassing all human intellects. But if on that basis the cock is to be preferred to all birds, cattle, and to the intellects of men,[101] because one reads of it, "Who has given intelligence to

96. Nm 22.32.
97. Cf. Nm 31.16.
98. Cf. Nm 31.8.
99. Ps 7.12.
100. Jb 38.36.
101. Reading *hominum intellectibus* for *hominem intellectibus*.

the cock," then what do you think of the wit of an ox, what do
you think of the intellect of the ass, of which the prophet wrote,
"The ox knows his owner, and the ass his master's crib"?[102] What
will you say of the wondrous ingenuity of certain birds, of which
another prophet says: "the turtledove, and the swallow, and the
stork have observed the time of their coming"?[103] Why should I
remain silent concerning the diverse and wondrous intellects
of the larger animals; what, I ask you, do you say of the little
bee whose wise labor and industry makes honey; what do you
think of the ant which, although it barely has a body, your Solomon proclaimed, so that he sent men to it to learn even its wisdom? What did he write about it? "Go to the ant, O sluggard,
and consider her ways, and learn wisdom,"[104] and the rest. But
what is this intelligence of your cock? Would that I might pass
over the spiritual intellect that does not belong to you, to whom
there is not "given knowledge of the mystery of the kingdom
of God."[105] This plainly is the intelligence of the cock, of which
Scripture speaks, which we all perceive, which we see continually, so that, by a certain natural and ingrained vivacity of intellect, it will announce with its songs (either long intermittent
songs or songs very often repeated in the intensity of nocturnal darkness) that it senses the imminent arrival of the light? Is
it because it can do this, because it understands this, that you
will immediately admit it to knowledge of the counsels of God,
will immediately admit it to the hour of divine anger that is unknown to all mortals, will immediately prefer the intelligence
of the cock not only to that of all men, but even to the wisdom
of the angels themselves? In the same way, the flying creatures
that I remarked upon above as an example, namely, the turtledove, the swallow, and the stork, let them be preferred to all of
them; let the ox and the ass be preferred; let the bees and the
ants be preferred; and the other animals that seem to have an
intelligence bestowed upon them that is beyond the others, that
pertains specially to their own nature. Let them be admitted
and immediately taken up as far as the third heaven, to which

102. Is 1.3.   103. Jer 8.7.
104. Prv 6.6.   105. Lk 8.10; Mk 4.11.

our apostle, in whom you do not believe, was taken up,[106] nor let anything among the divine mysteries be concealed further from the flying creature or quadruped, after something of any intelligence whatsoever has been able to lay claim for itself to a property beyond the others by a law of nature. But I believe that there is no rational creature, not only in the heavens nor only on earth, but even in the lower regions, who will not reject, not mock, not condemn this Jewish interpretation.

Let these things suffice concerning these matters, and let there be a quick transition, as your prophet says, "to see far greater blasphemies" and abominations of words "than these,"[107] since it is offensive to tarry long over so many wicked things. You say and you read in that heavenly and truest text, your Talmud, that "every day God cries once a day, producing two tears from his eyes that drip down into a great sea, and," you assert, "these [tears] are the lightning flash that seems to fall from the stars at night time."[108] You also say that "his weeping," which you ascribe to God, "is because of the Jews' captivity." Moreover, "on account of that grief he roars like a lion three times each day, and," you claim, "for the same reason he beats the heaven with his feet like someone treading in a wine press. Moreover, he makes a sound like a cooing dove and also shakes his head and says in a voice of lament: 'Woe is me, woe is me! I have reduced my dwelling-place to a desert, and burned my temple, and transferred my people to the Gentiles! Woe to the father who has transferred his children, and woe to the children who have been transferred from their father's table.'"[109] You add, too, that "therefore in a certain ruined place some of your sages heard this voice and that he rubs his feet together as if they were itching and claps his hands like someone who is grieving, and that he prays daily that his

106. Cf. 2 Cor 12.2–4.
107. Ezek 8.13.
108. Peter, following Petrus Alfonsi, seems to be describing shooting stars. Cf. Petrus Alfonsi, *Dialogue Against the Jews*, trans. Resnick, 67.
109. Ibid., 68. See also Michael Fishbane, "'The Holy One Sits and Roars': Mythopoesis and the Midrashic Imagination," in *The Midrashic Imagination: Jewish Exegesis, Thought, and History*, ed. Michael Fishbane (Albany: SUNY Press, 1993): 60–77.

compassion surpass his anger and that he go among his people in compassion."[110]

What are you waiting for, reader? What do you expect? Do you think that I will speak out against the Jews concerning these things? Far be it from me to speak out against them concerning such things, far be it from me to reply to impudent dogs and the foulest pigs as if to those with a capacity for reason and to indicate that they are worthy of any reply whatsoever concerning these things. Are they worthy of my response or of any response at all who, as if they were born only to blaspheme God, are given over as fodder for an eternal fire? Those who, even if I have called them dogs or pigs, I have not gone too far. For although carnal impurity is customarily signified in the sacred Scriptures by these animals, nonetheless does not such a great and oft-repeated blasphemy surpass carnal evils?

Thus I am unwilling to be contemptuous of the words of my Lord by casting divine pearls before such beasts, to be trampled underfoot.[111] Although I appear to have done that above, it was nonetheless for the reason that I mentioned myself, so that this text of mine might be beneficial, if not for all and if not for many, at least for the few who we see are sometimes converted to God, who were either infected with this disease or could have been infected. But seeing that intolerable things follow upon unheard-of things, it is not worthwhile to deal with those speaking them as if with men using reason. There is also an infinite number of their fables and traditions that are actually foreign to God's law, concerning which the Lord said to the Pharisees in the Gospel: "You have abandoned the commandment of God," he said, "for the sake of your traditions."[112] But far more tolerable are those [traditions and fables] that nonetheless do not touch upon divine things, thus preserving them unharmed, even if they express many absurd things about people or human things. But actually those that burst forth in such great madness as to proclaim boldly of God that which human ears barely tolerate ought to be condemned, they ought in no way to be tolerated. And that is what is repeated in a number of

110. Ibid., 69.   111. Cf. Mt 7.6.
112. Cf. Mk 7.8; Mt 15.3.

their traditions. Who, then, ought to reply to or to deem worthy those speaking these things? Who should deign to reply to the blasphemous, foolish, and impious voice that says, "Every day God cries once a day, that his two tears drip into a great sea, that he roars like a lion three times a day, that like one that is angry—almost raging—he strikes the heaven with his feet with resounding blows, that he moans like a dove, that he moves his head with indignation, that he sharply rubs his hands and feet against one another anxiously, to say, like one grieving wretchedly, 'Woe is me, woe is me.'"[113]

Nonetheless, I will respond, as I did above, if they should have a sound understanding in all of these instances or even in a few of them, if they should explain either the weeping or the roaring or the moaning or the grief, which dreadful blasphemy they ascribe to God in a literal sense, if, I say, they should expound any of them according to the meaning of sacred Scripture. For although I do not ever remember having read in the Old Testament of divine weeping, although I do not ever remember having read that God moans like a dove, nonetheless I do read that God roars, I do read that God grieves, I do read that God cries out, and, what may be more surprising if a sound understanding is lacking, I read that God whispers, I read that God screeches. I read that God roars in Amos: "The Lord will roar from Zion, and utter his voice from Jerusalem."[114] He grieves, as in the Book of Judges: "And the children of Israel cried out to the Lord, who grieved over their miseries."[115] He cries out, as in Isaiah: "He shall shout and cry out, he shall prevail against his enemies."[116] He whispers, in the same book: "The Lord shall whisper for the fly that is in the uttermost parts of the rivers of Egypt, and for the bee that is in the land of Assyria."[117] And he screeches, as in Amos: "I will screech under you as a wain screeches that is laden with hay."[118]

If in any of these or those like them—for many like these are found that are attributed to God in the sacred texts—if,

113. Cf. Petrus Alfonsi, *Dialogue Against the Jews,* trans. Resnick, 69.
114. Am 1.2. 115. Cf. Jgs 10.10, 16.
116. Is 42.13. 117. Is 7.18.
118. Am 2.13.

plainly, in any of these the Jewish meaning should be in harmony with the Christian or, if they abhor that, in harmony with a rational understanding, let me reply again to the Jews, as I did before, that I do not disdain to speak with them concerning such things. But when the Jews are unwilling to accept either metaphor or allegory or any of the common and multiple modes of speaking by means of which all of these are appropriately adapted to God, but understand them instead only according to the letter that kills, what shall I say?[119] How shall I excuse God from foolish weeping, from an insane roar, from wretched moaning, from the remaining monstrous and mad movements that are vainly attributed to him? In fact what wise man does not know—or even merely a person who is not wholly devoid of understanding—the correct meaning of the weeping, roaring, and moaning, and does not know that the rest, which have already been described as monstrous, cannot be referred to God, and that the divine nature is actually unrelated to all of these? Who is ignorant of the fact that the incorporeal, simple, uncircumscribed nature that is far removed from every complexion or composition of the corporeal elements, a nature for which there exists neither likeness nor unlikeness to the head, body, or any other human members, is devoid of all those characteristics that despicable Jewish error imparts to him? For who weeps without eyes? Who roars without a voice? Who rubs hands and feet, if he does not have any? Who, finally, exercises the functions of the members when he is without the instruments of any members whatsoever? I remain silent concerning the rage of one that grows angry, the sadness of one that grieves, the wretchedness of one who cries out, "Woe is me, woe is me!"[120] I remain silent over the fact that Jewish wisdom has rendered the Omnipotent One impotent, which, even should it wish to do so, cannot end the long lasting captivity of the Jews, so that for that reason he may weep, for that reason he may roar, for that reason he may moan, for that reason he may rub together hands and feet. For who else has ever dared to think that God says, "Woe is me"; who has dared to assert this except the Jew? I

119. Cf. 2 Cor 3.6.
120. Cf. Petrus Alfonsi, *Dialogue Against the Jews,* trans. Resnick, 68.

read indeed that he says through the prophet: "Woe! I will comfort myself over my adversaries, and I will be revenged of my enemies."[121] But although this "woe" is proclaimed by God, it is not applied to God but to men; it does not apply to God but to his enemies. Therefore, let God's enemies see how absurd the things are that they impute to God's majesty.

In fact, to say, "Woe is me," applies only to the wretched; to say, "Woe is me," is only to bewail one's own wretchedness. Therefore, when the Jew says that God says, "Woe is me," clearly he says that God is wretched. But who but the Jew, however, will not be horrified even to think that God is wretched, much less to call him so? And truly this is a wretched race of men, truly this is a race that has been transformed from the head into the tail of all races,[122] one that invents that God is like a human with respect to the essence of his deity, that differentiates him according to the division of human members, that distributes to them human functions as if to human members, that ascribes to God not only human but even bestial acts, roars, and moans. Moses did not think this of their God, he did not say this, he did not leave this after him written in the last book of his Pentateuch. He said to the Jews, "You saw not any similitude in the day when God spoke to you in Horeb from the midst of the fire, lest perhaps being deceived you might make for yourselves a graven image . . . of any beasts that are upon the earth, or of birds that fly under heaven, or of creeping things that move on the earth, or of fishes that move in the waters under the earth, lest perhaps lifting up your eyes to heaven, you see the sun and the moon, and all the stars of heaven, and, being deceived by error, you adore and serve them, which the Lord your God created for service to all the nations that are under heaven."[123] And how could he speak more clearly to a people so foolish that it is always prepared to think and to believe every wickedness? How could he warn these men more clearly not to become idolaters,

121. Is 1.24.

122. Cf. Dt 28.13, where God establishes the people as the head, and not the tail, if they will obey the commandments.

123. Dt 4.15–19. Cf. Petrus Alfonsi, *Dialogue Against the Jews,* trans. Resnick, 73.

not to believe that there is in God's nature any image or likeness of either male or female, of beasts or birds, of things that
creep or of fish, of the sun or the moon or of the stars. Clearly
he denied it with these words, nor did he allow God to be understood as masculine or feminine, as a beast or bird, as a thing
that creeps or as a fish, as the sun, the moon, or a star. Moses
would not have forbidden the Jews, however, to make a graven
image or likeness of these things if he knew such a truth of the
divine nature. Because he forbade it, he understood that God's
nature is not like the natures of any of these animals or of living things, or the sun, the moon, or the stars. What authority
or reason (*ratio*) is there for the Jew to fashion man as God, to
the extent that, as has already been said, he regards the nature
of God, to ascribe human members to him, to assign human or
bestial acts or emotions to him, to say that he roars like a lion or
moans like a dove?

Let these wretches recall that it was for this same reason that
God commanded the artisans of the tabernacle under Moses or
the artisans of the temple under Solomon not to weave, sculpt,
cast, paint, or fashion any likeness of any animal, either in the
tabernacle or in the temple or in the tabernacle and temple
both, with the exception of the two seraphim that were made
into a likeness for the sake of men, but as a remembrance of
and from respect for the angels, so that, once admonished by
this sight, the hardhearted Jews would understand that they
ought to prefer God not only to earthly men but even to celestial powers.[124] Let them also recall the bronze serpent fashioned by Moses at divine command and preserved for a long
time afterwards, that was broken by the good king Hezekiah lest
the Jews, who believed almost no truths, who thought almost
all falsehoods to be true, should believe at any time that the
serpent was God, which they had already believed for some time
to be God, and to which they had offered up sacrifices as if to
God.[125]

Therefore, having excluded every body and every corporeal
likeness from God, I believe that the proposed Jewish fable has

124. Cf. Ex 25.18–22; 1 Kgs 6.23–27.
125. Cf. Nm 21.8–9; 2 Kgs 18.4.

been dispatched in its entirety. Indeed, that nature which has nothing in common with corporeal things, to which one cannot ascribe impotence, grief, and misery, is free from all the remaining feelings (*affectiones*) of corporeal things. Therefore, whatever the blasphemous Jews proposed above concerning such things is false.

But now from a dialogue with the reader I return to the Jew, since although I was unwilling to deal with him when he tossed about blasphemies concerning God because it seemed unworthy, yet will I deal with him in the customary manner nonetheless concerning serious errors, although these do not pertain to the nature of God. Tell me then, Jews: Do you think that what your Talmud relates concerning Og, king of Bashan, is true? I know not only that you think it is, but even that you believe it to be truer than the legal or prophetic texts. Whatsoever sort it may be, let it be brought before us, and let it become apparent whether it shines with the clearest truth.

The Talmud says:

Og king of Bashan, seeing the enormous army of Israel, 604,500 men thirty years old or more, and in addition women and children who could not be numbered, lifted a stone of unheard-of size onto his head and wanted to crush the entire force with it. While he was contemplating this, a very small hoopoe bird perched on that stone and dug at it with his beak for a long time, until, after the bird had created a large hole about the size of this same king's head, the stone, passing by the head, fell down upon the king's shoulders. Once this had been done and with the same stone resting upon the king's shoulders and his head sticking up above the stone, his teeth suddenly grew extremely long and prevented him from lifting it off. When Moses saw this, whose body was 10 cubits tall and who had a rod of the same length, he lifted himself up 10 cubits off the earth like a high-jumper, in order to strike him with the rod somewhere on his body. Although he was lifted up off the earth by such a great leap, nonetheless the length of the rod with which he intended to strike him was unable to reach further than his ankle, by which the leg is joined to the foot and which in the vulgar tongue is called the *cavilla*. When Moses had struck King Og there, he died immediately as he fell.[126]

126. Petrus Alfonsi, *Dialogue Against the Jews,* trans. Resnick, 92. Details of this tale are largely found in B.T. *Ber.* 54b, although there it is an army of ants, and not the hoopoe, that gnaws a hole in this rock mass. For the hoopoe, see Louis Ginzberg, *The Legends of the Jews,* trans. Henrietta Szold, 7 vols. (Philadelphia:

This is surely your noble fable. But see how much more foolish or how much wiser you are than all the Gentiles. Many of
the ancient Gentiles, indeed, invented many and various fables
concerning diverse matters, as Aesop did among the Greeks
and Ovid did among the Latins. In truth they invented many
that ought to be laughed at, but the authors of these fables did
not mean for them to be understood in the manner in which
they wrote them, but instead wanted them to be adapted to natural objects or to human manners. This is why they said that Atlas[127] supports the heaven, that the giant and hundred-handed
Typhoeus,[128] that is, having 100 hands, stacked mountain upon
mountain and, from their summit, made war against heaven
and Jupiter. After a protracted war against the heavenly gods,
they asserted that he was laid low although not slain by the lightning bolts of Cyclops hurled by Jupiter, and was deposited on
the large island of Sicily, lest he be able to rise again to resume
his battles with the gods, and they asserted that he often caused
an earthquake to occur on the island as he struggled to rise up
again to fight the gods. Thus, too, Orpheus compelled broad
rivers to stand still and forests to move after him with his wondrous songs and melodies never before heard on the *cithera*,[129]
[and] they wrote that Hercules did battle against the many-
headed Hydra but that in place of each head cut off by him
100 other heads grew in its place, and, finally, that he burned
up entirely that monster with the Greek fire sent when he re-
sided in the Lerna swamp. And in texts they handed down that
Phaeton, the son of the sun, while driving the paternal chariots
badly, almost burned up the world,[130] that Circe, the daughter
of this same sun, with herbs and songs changed the compan-
ions of Ulysses into wolves, lions, tigers, and various types of

---

1909–28; repr., Hildesheim: Georg Olms Verlag, 2000), 6: 120. This legend of
Og became a staple in subsequent Christian polemics or disputations. See, for
example, Nicholas Donin's remark from the Parisian disputation of 1240, in
Hyam Maccoby's *Judaism on Trial: Jewish-Christian Disputations in the Middle Ages*
(London: Littman Library of Jewish Civilization, 1993), 161–62.

   127. Ovid, *Met.* 2.296–97.
   128. Ovid, *Met.* 3.303–306; Horace, *Carmen* 2.17.14.
   129. Ovid, *Met.* 11.1–2. The *cithara* was a stringed instrument similar to a lute.
   130. Ovid, *Met.* 2.47–234.

beasts,[131] that a watchful dragon was guarding the golden fleece
of a ram,[132] that men [were changed] into gods, women into
stars, and that foxes, chickens, hares, geese, and the remaining beasts or birds spoke to one another with human language,
as well as many other things in this fashion worthy of ridicule.
But although they said these things, although they wrote them,
they meant them and wanted them to be understood and interpreted by others far differently than was said. In fact, they
were rational men, and, although they were far removed from
the divine worship that the world could not yet comprehend,
they were wise men. I would explicate clearly their meaning in
such fables by individual examples, except that more properly
I should avoid dragging out this work and I see that this does
not pertain to the task proposed. Thus it would not be especially surprising if even you, Jews, should have fables and transform their meaning into something true and useful. For the
true and holy page has itself the characteristic that sometimes
it narrates something whose text is false when taken literally but
whose meaning is true and necessary. Thus in your book called
Judges you read that the trees went forth to anoint a king over
them, and that they spoke to the olive tree and the fig and the
vine and the bramble.[133] Everyone knows that that is not literally
true; everyone knows that trees cannot speak. Whoever turns
nonetheless to the truth of the matter, which is drawn out by a
certain analogy to insensible fruit-bearing trees, does not doubt
that the use of such a locution is frequent in Scripture. From
this, one who has been instructed in these matters understands
the sons of Gideon by the vine and the olive and the fig, which
are fruit-bearing trees, whereas the fratricide Abimelech is signified by the bitter bramble that bears no fruit. This meaning
is also found often in other parables contained in your divine
canon, as in the one that the prophet Nathan proposed to him
after David had committed adultery with the wife of Uriah.[134] In
fact, what he said to him was not literally true, either what he
said about the rich man and his 100 sheep, or about the pauper
and his one sheep, or that the rich man spared his 100 sheep

131. Ovid, *Met.* 14.245–297.   132. Ovid, *Met.* 7.149–51.
133. Cf. Jgs 9.8–16.   134. Cf. 2 Kgs 12.1–8.

and that he had prepared a dinner for his guest with the one sheep that had been taken violently from the pauper. Nonetheless, what the prophet meant by these words was true. David was the rich man, Uriah was the poor man in comparison to the king, his wife was his one sheep, the king's concupiscence the foreign guest, the dinner prepared from the sheep for the guest was the woman prostituted to illicit desire. There are many analogies like this.

If you would interpret your fables in this way, O Jews, if you would understand them wisely in this way, if you would explicate them in this way in a useful manner, I would not be surprised, even if I would not lavish praise upon you. I would not praise you, because I do not approve of anything that you have received or receive as authentic outside your sacred canon. I would not be surprised, if I should see that you approve some things outside the law, outside the prophets, even though cloaked in the mantle of a fable, that is, other divine books handed down to you from antiquity for some useful instruction. But since your fables lack all these things, since actually nothing useful is concealed in them, but the whole [of the Talmud] appears to be foolish, the whole impious, the whole blasphemous, there is no reason my pen ought to spare you because not even God himself spares you. In fact, the Jewish fables surpass all the fables of the ages because the Talmud, the sacred text of Jewish fables, relates what has not been heard by the ages. O how astonishing is the aversion of the Jewish people for God, who think that they serve him under this divine worship, who think about the Creator and his nature what idol worshipers themselves were never able to believe or invent. O lost race, what the apostle, our nature, our doctrine, said of such as these, is fulfilled in and for you: "For there shall be a time, when they will not endure sound doctrine; but, according to their own desires, they will heap to themselves teachers, having itching ears. And they will indeed turn away their hearing from the truth, but will be turned unto fables."[135] Behold, truly we perceive now the time when this apostolic judgment has been fulfilled; behold, the time when we see that you do not support sound doctrine. Will you say that you

135. 2 Tm 4.3–4.

support sound doctrine, you who after having cast aside the law of God and his prophets, prefer strange foolish tales to celestial words? But the itching of your ears causes this when, loathing useful things, you desire useless ones, and having brushed aside the teachers of the ancients you have gathered new teachers for yourselves. In truth, you have gathered new teachers, you have created a great multitude of teachers, so that almost no number of old ones seems to compare to the number of new teachers. But teachers of what? Certainly not of salvation but of perdition, not of truth but of falsehood. Whence there follows what the apostle said: "And they will indeed turn away their hearing from the truth, but will be turned unto fables."[136] Is it not so? Truly, it is. With the entire world as witness, you have turned your hearing away from truth, whereas you have turned toward fables, as I said.

Among them ought to be considered the one that I presented earlier, namely, concerning Og, king of Bashan. What can be said to be more fabulous, more erroneous, more laughable than that you read and that you believe that the sole of his foot alone was 30 cubits high? How is this so? "Because," you claim, "the length of Moses' body was 10 cubits, the length of his rod 10 cubits, and when Moses struck the giant with the tip of the rod at the joint of the leg and the foot, he had lifted himself off the ground with a leap of 10 cubits."[137] And for this reason, when the 10 cubits of Moses' body, the 10 cubits of Moses' rod, and the 10 cubits of Moses' leap are added together, they make 30 cubits, leaving aside the length of his extended arm, which can be measured as between his head and the lower tip of the rod that he held in his hand. If this is true, then according to the usual proportion of the human body, his leg alone, from his foot to the beginning of his calf, was at least, I would say, 150 cubits. Thus there is no doubt that the same calf, which is longer than the leg from the knee to the femoral joint, will be, as I said, at least 200 cubits according to the body's natural measurement. From there, if a proper measurement proceeds to the top of the spine that is joined to the neck, you will find

136. 2 Tm 4.4.
137. Petrus Alfonsi, *Dialogue Against the Jews,* trans. Resnick, 93.

that it is more than 230 cubits. And this is in addition to the size of the neck and the head, which you will find to be not less than 80 cubits. When all these are added together, they produce [not] less than 710 cubits. You see, then, Jews, that according to this—not according to our measurement but to yours—the height of Og king of Bashan passed 690 cubits in length. According to this calculation, moreover, his girth will approach 120 cubits. Who, then, besides you, has ever been able to find such a monster? Who, I ask, besides you, could claim that there is a man 690 cubits high and 120 cubits wide?

I propose only one thing against your insanity, which ought not to be the subject of debate any longer but which ought instead to be laughed at, since it is so clear that it does not lie hidden from blind men. Do you believe Moses? I know that you believe him. Since you believe Moses, therefore, why have you been able to believe something so absurd, so contrary to the words of Moses? For indeed he himself wrote in the Book of Deuteronomy, which book you must know, if you are Jews. He said, "For only Og king of Bashan remained of the race of the giants. His bed of iron is shown, which is in Rabbath of the children of Ammon, being nine cubits long, and four broad after the measure of the cubit of a man's hand."[138] A bed always is customarily larger in length and breadth than the one lying on it. Since, then, he said that the bed of this giant was nine cubits long and four cubits wide, certainly he showed that he had to have been somewhat less than the bed in terms of height and width. Therefore, it is clear that that king was not nine full cubits in length, nor was he four full cubits in width. But I concede that he did not fall [far] short of nine cubits in length, nor of four cubits in width.

Was he, then, longer and wider than his own bed? I believe that here the Jewish argument is put to rest. What you said is false, then, that the man was of such great height. That you said that Moses was himself 10 cubits in height is equally false. For he did not write that the bed of the giant Og was nine cubits, as if for a very rare monster. If he himself was 10 cubits, on what basis (*ratio*) would it appear surprising for a man's bed to be 9

138. Dt 3.11.

cubits? It would seem that rightly it ought to be more surprising that he was himself a man of 10 cubits rather than that another man's bed was 9 cubits.

In truth, lest I drag this out longer than is necessary, I conclude in this way: if you believe that the bed of Og king of Bashan was only 9 cubits, as Moses says, I believe that you will say that he could not have been larger than his bed. But as I already said, I know that you believe Moses in this case. Therefore, you should be certain thenceforth that the oft-mentioned giant's height was not 680 cubits, but 9 cubits at most.

And, to connect this to what comes next in the fable, how could he, even though the size of his body be greater than ours, place on his head a stone of a size so unaccustomed and never previously seen, such that he thought that with his throw he could bring down 604,500 men-at-arms of the Jewish army, excluding the women and countless small children? In order to accomplish this, if I may provide an analogy for your fables, either [Mount] Olympus would have to be lifted up into the air, or our own Mount Jupiter[139] would have to be placed on his head, although insofar as it exists across the sea from him, either the Taurus of Cilicia[140] or one of the mountains of Armenia, which was closest to him, would without a doubt have to be completely uprooted. Although he had placed hope of victory on that stone, he had brought forth in vain such a great army to do battle against Moses and the people of God. For Moses said of this army: "Og the king of Bashan came against them with all his people, to fight in Edrei."[141] But behold a stone so great, behold one so large, placed upon the head of the king.

What next? What does this most excellent text say next? It says, "A hoopoe, the smallest bird, perched on that stone and dug at it with his beak for a long time, until, after the bird had created a large hole about the size of the same king's head, the stone, passing by the head, rested upon the shoulders of the

139. Montjoux, near Grenoble, France.

140. I.e., the Taurus or Toros mountain range in southern Turkey, whose pass known as the Cilician Gates (*pylae Ciliciae*) was mentioned by Greek geographers. Cf. *Dictionary of Greek and Roman Geography*, ed. William Smith (London: John Murray, 1878), 2: 618.

141. Nm 21.33.

king."[142] I find nothing that surprises me more among wonders beyond description. What should surprise me more, or less: that a small hoopoe bird with its even smaller beak attacked so large a stone for so long as to pierce it, until it made a hole in it capable of passing over the giant's head, or should I find it more surprising that this man's patience or strength supported so large a stone resting upon his head for so long, until little by little this modest bird with a short beak penetrated with weak blows such a hard mass of a body so enormous? And for this reason, once the hole had been made to the size of the king's head, the stone, being unable to rest upon his head, once having fallen by its natural weight onto the broad shoulders of the wretched man, whose breadth it was unable to pass beyond because of the narrowness of the hole, was stopped there, lest it fall further.

And what follows? Once this was done, with the stone resting upon his shoulders and with the king's head sticking up above the stone, his teeth, having suddenly grown very long, prevented him from removing it. And indeed I read not a Jewish but a pagan fable that invented that a dragon's teeth were sown from which the Theban people sprang forth, not unarmed but armed, arrayed with helmets, cuirasses, shields, swords, and every military armament.[143] But as I said above, the pagans did not doubt that in these and in others like them they have written fables and not accounts of real events, nor did they believe or, at the same time, teach that they are true, but rather that they symbolize some real events. In fact, when they said that the already mentioned people arose from the dragon's teeth, they wanted a stubborn people and one weakened by malice to be understood by the analogy to a poisonous and savage living being. By the fact that it proceeded out of the ground already armed, they indicated that it is warlike and will always be under arms.

If they had indicated such a thing as your giant's teeth after the stone fell upon his shoulders, O Jews, it would certainly have to be reported just as I presented it above. And what shall I say this fable contains either at its core or in its marrow, when it contains nothing mystical in divine [matters], when it contains

142. Petrus Alfonsi, *Dialogue Against the Jews,* trans. Resnick, 93.
143. Ovid, *Met.* 3.101–110.

nothing meaningful in human matters, just as your other fables fail to do? What shall I say upon seeing a man, whom you, overcome by a dream of profound foolishness, have dreamed bears a stone—rather, a large region—upon the shoulders, with teeth of immense size extending further from the prominent head than in the case of a boar, unable to remove the stone either because the shoulders prevent it from below or because the teeth block it from above?

But why was Moses silent concerning what were, according to you, such great miracles? Why was he silent concerning such great miracles who, although he described many miracles, and great ones, nonetheless also described many lesser ones? Why was he silent over the fact that the oft-mentioned little hoopoe bird penetrated such a thick, hard stone with its fragile beak? Why was he silent over the giant's teeth that grew so? Why was he silent over the fact that he alone assaulted him, that he was lifted up off the ground by a stupendous leap, and that he cast him down to the ground, prostrated him, and killed him by a rod's light touch? It is amazing that he, who by divine power changed the same rod into a serpent before Pharaoh,[144] who turned the waters of Egypt into blood with the same rod, who divided the [Red] sea,[145] and produced water from a rock,[146] was so noticeably silent concerning such a distinguished miracle. Certainly he was not silent regarding this as if he were unwilling to write down what happened, but he was silent like one who is unwilling to write down what never happened. He was not silent to avoid writing down what is true, but because he was unwilling to write down what is false. And why do I say "being unwilling"? Rather that he was unable to write down what was never heard, what had never happened. And because no language properly suffices to abhor this in individual instances, let the discussion hasten to things similar.

Let our people hear your secrets (*sacramenta*), O Jews, let them penetrate your profound mysteries to reveal your wisdom

144. Correctly, it was Aaron who turned the rod into a serpent. Cf. Ex 7.9–11, 19–20.
145. Cf. Ex 14.21.
146. Cf. Ex 17.6; Nm 20.11.

to all. Let them hear the following from your precious book, the Talmud:

There was among the Jews a certain man called among them Iozahben Levi, whom we call Joshua the son of Levi,[147] "a religious and God-fearing man," as they say, "who applied himself to this book from his infancy to old age, so that in this way he could escape death. When the Lord, who wished to carry off his soul, saw this, he ordered an avenging angel to go to him and to bear off his soul in order to congratulate him with the Jewish friends of the Lord for studying the Talmud all their lives. The angel, rejoicing, obeyed the Lord's command immediately. He came to the roof of his home and stood not far from him. Once, however, Joshua raised his eyes, as soon as he saw him, he knew at once that he had come to bear away his soul. And he said: "What do you seek?" "The Lord sent me for your soul," he said. But the other one said: "The Lord sent you in vain, since I am meditating upon and reading the Talmud. And I swear to you by that book that you do not have the power of bearing off my soul." Once the angel had returned to the Lord he reported this, however. The Lord said to him, "Go back and tell him to come, to rejoice, to feast with us, and to acknowledge that it will be better for him here than there." The angel returned and proclaimed what the Lord commanded. Joshua, however, responded to the angel reporting this that he would obey the Lord's command only if he was willing to concede to him, under a binding contract, a request he demanded of him. When the angel reported this to the Lord, he agreed somewhat unwillingly to what he sought. The angel, however, reported that the Lord had agreed quickly. When he heard that, Joshua said that he wanted to peer into the halls of hell and of paradise while still in this life. "Climb onto me," said the angel, "and I will take you where you want to go." "I will not climb on nor go with you," said Joshua, "unless you give me a sword, for I am afraid that you will slay me on the way." At once, then, he gave him a sword. And when he had climbed onto him, the angel said: "Where do you want me to take you?" He replied: "To the halls of hell, so that afterward I may take delight in the vision of paradise." Once he was led there, he saw many peoples of every nation under heaven—Christians, Amorites, Jebusites,

147. For the legend of R. Joshua ben Levi, see B. T. *Ketubot* 77b. It was a popular tale in the medieval world, and was included as well in the influential *Alphabet of Ben-Sira*. For a translation, see Moses Gaster, "Hebrew Visions of Hell and Paradise: The Revelation of R. Joshua ben Levi," in *Studies and Texts in Folklore, Magic, Mediaeval Romance, Hebrew Apocrypha and Samaritan Archaeology*, 3 vols. (New York: KTAV, 1971), 1, pp. 144–64, and esp. 144–45. Also see *Rabbinic Fantasies: Imaginative Narratives from Classical Hebrew Literature*, ed. David Stern and Mark Jay Mirsky (Philadelphia and New York: Jewish Publication Society, 1990), 194–95.

Avvim,[148] Hittites, and Perizzites,[149] Moabites, Ammonites, Arabs, and Philistines, also the kings Pharaoh, Sihon, Og, and all the others that were slain by Joshua; Jabin and his general Sisera;[150] [and] Eglon, who was slain by Ehud; Nebuchadnezzar and his general Holofernes. When he inquired of him the reason for the damnation of each, one after another, Joshua said: "Why are the Christians damned?" The angel said, "Don't you know?" He replied, "I know, but I want to hear it from you." He said: "Because they believe in the son of Mary, and they do not observe the law of Moses, and especially because they do not believe in the Talmud. The reason for the damnation of the other peoples or kings takes longer to explain, but this alone is the reason: because they have not believed in the Talmud, or because they have made war against the children of Israel." Moreover, Pharaoh was lying prostrate in hell while holding his head under the threshold of the gate of hell, and his eye became the hinge pin of its gate. Moreover, the gate was turned in each direction upon his eye at the souls' entry. Joshua asked, to be sure, why he suffered such great punishment. To which the angel replied: "Because he afflicted the children of Israel in the land of Egypt and pursued them, after their affliction, as far as the sea." Once Joshua had seen all the torments that occur in hell, he said, "Lead me to paradise." The angel reported, however, that paradise is fortified on all sides by a wall. When he had led him there, he placed him at a spot from which he could hardly see paradise. Joshua said, "Take me higher. My eyes were blinded and my senses weakened by the smoke of hell." The angel led him a little bit higher then. Joshua said to him: "Unless you put me on top of the wall so that I can see the places of delight and the saintly souls, you know that you will not have fulfilled my request." And he placed him on top of the wall. Joshua looked within and saw the many saintly souls of the patriarchs, the prophets, and of others whose deeds during their lives had pleased God. Among others, he saw Pharaoh's daughter sitting on a most exalted throne. Therefore, Joshua asked, "By what act, with what service did she merit such a reward?" And the angel said: "Because she saved Moses from death and nourished him and taught him the wisdom of the Egyptians." A little later, when he saw several others who were honored above the rest, he asked why they had merited such glory. The angel replied: "Because these are the men who discovered and composed the Talmud from memory, and these are their successors, who studied the Talmud." And the angel said that Joshua should come down from the wall. He replied, "I still want to see more." Once he said this, he threw himself with the sword down from the wall, inside paradise. Then the angel cried out to him, "You deceived me!" Joshua replied: "I do not care whether you were deceived or not." And the angel told him to leave very quickly. But Joshua replied

148. Cf. Dt 2.23.   149. Cf. Gn 15.20.
150. Cf. Jgs 4.7–20.

with an oath that thenceforth he would not leave there. When those who inhabited paradise saw him, they were amazed that a clothed, living man had entered paradise with a sword in this way. Since Joshua did not find a seat, he stood, and he approached Pharaoh's daughter. "Rise up," he said, "and go; behold, your father is at the gate." She rose quickly and hastened to the gate. Then Joshua immediately took her seat. And when she did not find her father, she returned and said to Joshua: "Why did you lie to me?" "I did not lie," he said. "For your father is at the gate of hell." "Why," she asked, "have you taken my place away from me?" He said: "Because the Lord has granted it to me, and henceforth it will be mine." Meanwhile, the angel returned to the Lord and reported what had happened. The Lord, however, ordered him to leave there quickly. And when the angel commanded him on God's behalf, Joshua said, "By God himself or by the holy Talmud, I will not leave here again." And when the angel reported his oath to God, God said, "Examine the entire collection of books, and if ever you find that he has sworn falsely in the past, then he will have to leave. If not, then one must allow him to remain there either on account of his religion, or because he always studied the Talmud." The book collection was examined, and the angel did not discover that he had lied or sworn falsely. Thus the Lord agreed that he would not have to leave there again. Then the angel approached Joshua and demanded from him his sword, with which he was accustomed to slay men wherever he found them. And Joshua replied that he would not return the sword to him unless he swore to him that thenceforth he would not slay men with it. Again the angel returned to the Lord and announced what Joshua said. But the Lord agreed to his request, although unwillingly. And Joshua returned the sword to the angel under that condition.[151]

The fable that has been read is long and is one which, through either the eyes of the readers or the ears of the audience, could fill their mouths with laughter or their hearts with derision. For who can contain the laughter, who can repress derision, hearing from men what he could not hear from the demons themselves? Whom has anyone persuaded or striven to persuade that there was ever a mortal who could escape death in this life? To whom has he said: "Read something, say something, do something, and you will not die"? You, O Jews, strive to persuade men of this, and you have already persuaded yourselves of this from the wicked texts already named. In fact, you assert that one that meditates on or reads the text of the book the Talmud cannot be subject

151. For this extended passage treating Joshua ben Levi, cf. Petrus Alfonsi, *Dialogue Against the Jews,* trans. Resnick, 94–95.

to death. And you believe that the one the fable treated, namely,
Joshua son of Levi, is one of that number. But what weariness
shall I bring upon the reader by running through the whole
fable, line by line, with perhaps superfluous prolixity? Therefore, I will not run through it all, but plucking something from
this difficult collection I will cast it with its proof-texts into eternal flame, deservedly to be consumed completely. Thus I think
that one ought to leave to one side the beginning of this fable,
because what one reads there about this Joshua son of Levi is
almost the same, O Jews, as what was set forth against you concerning Rabbi Nehemiah in the first fable of this chapter. Thus
one ought not to repeat exactly, perhaps, the reply that was out-
lined above against similar bits of nonsense. In fact, the fables
are alike insofar as each one resisted God and his angel by reading the Talmud, lest he die. Nonetheless, they are unlike one
another in this respect: that God prevailed by a deception to slay
the latter, whereas the former, as if one more cunning, he was
unable to deceive by many tricks, no matter how excellent. As
was written above, he drew the latter [that is, R. Nehemiah] away
from reading the Talmud with the fear of a storm, and in this
way, in the interval, snatched his soul. Unwillingly he permitted
the other one [that is, Joshua ben Levi] to live, however, who was
a more stubborn reader and circumspect with regard to divine
and angelic traps, since he could do nothing to him while he was
reading the Talmud continuously. Thus he replied as one who
was secure to the avenging angel, who said to him, "The Lord
sent me" to bear off "your soul"; he replied, "The Lord sent you
in vain, since I meditate on and" assiduously "read the Talmud."
Therefore, "I swear by that book that you do not have the power
to carry off my soul." And although God, through the same angel, commanded him again to come, to rejoice, and to feast with
him, because it would be better for him to be with him than to
remain in the world, nonetheless the wise man could not be deceived nor in any way fall for divine tricks. Moreover, knowing
that God was avid for his death, and fearing that he might dupe
him with some clever trick just as he had deceived Nehemiah, he
very cleverly provided for himself a dwelling place in paradise,
with God unwilling to and not taking precaution against the

tricks. He said that he wanted to peer into the halls of hell and of paradise before he die, having extorted from God the condition that he would not obey him in any way with respect to dying unless he grant the petition that he intended to demand of him.

Let the readers see what kind of deed this might be, how he was able to triumph over the infinite wisdom of God with human tricks. Now, I will concern myself no more with this. In fact, to do so would seem to be as vain and superfluous, I think, as to work to show whether God is more powerful, wiser, or better than Joshua. In fact, I do not think that the readers who demanded my discussion on these matters are so crude and foolish as to say that I have to reply to such nonsense.

But I turn to what follows:

"Climb onto me," said the angel, "and I will take you wherever you want." "I will not climb on," said Joshua, "nor go with you unless you give me the sword that you carry. For I am afraid that you will slay me on the way." At once, then, he gave him the sword. And when he had climbed upon the angel, the angel said: "Where do you want me to take you?" He said: "To the halls of hell, so that afterward I may take delight in the vision of paradise."

And what shall I say about this? Where are the shoulders, where is the back, where is the angelic body upon which that man climbed and by which he was carried—as if on a beast of burden—to see the delights of paradise and the terrors of hell? Where, too, are the angelic wings, because you think that they are never without them since you never see them depicted without them? Those that are removed from every nature of the elements, as far as relates to their own essence, who lack all form and lack the complexion of bodies, must they be believed to have bodies or parts of bodies akin to the bodies of terrene animals? Certainly men do not believe this, even if beasts will have thought it. But even if the angel who was prepared to obey God wished to adapt the body that you think he had, O Jews, in order to carry Joshua, nonetheless Joshua was not so heedless as to climb up. Clearly, he was unwilling to climb upon the angel unless he gave him the sword he carried, lest perhaps he slay him on the way. That man was exceedingly careful, as I said, and he was very shrewd at avoiding angelic tricks, fearing that

God might perhaps devise some traps against him through his angel, in contravention of the agreement that God had made with him, and he did not believe him until he received the sword from him. Once he had received it, and secure now that he could not be slain by him, he climbed upon one more noble than a human in a manner that is appropriate to a beast of burden. If they can accept things such as this, let the readers speak, let the audience judge.

But I proceed: he was led to hell on this angelic conveyance, he was led there in order to perceive the delights of paradise. And what happened after these things? "From there," that is, having been led earlier to hell, "he saw many races from every nation that is under heaven, Christians, Amorites, Jebusites, Avvim, Hittites, and Perizzites, Moabites, Ammonites, Arabs, and Philistines, and also the kings Pharaoh, Sihon, Og, and all the others that were slain by Joshua; Jabin and his general Sisera; Eglon, who was slain by Ehud; Nebuchadnezzar and his general Holofernes."

But here I ask you, O Jews: He saw in hell these kings and these peoples that were your enemies in the past and bordered your land; why did he pass over the Gauls, Iberians (*Hyberi*), Africans, Germans, Dacians, Norsemen, Scythians, and, lest I omit the Orientals, the Persians, Indians, and the rest of the peoples of the world? Did he not see a prodigious number of them in hell? Did not your prophet Ezekiel say about such as these: "There is Elam, there is Asur, and all his multitude round about his grave,"[152] as well as many like them? But perhaps he did not have as keen an eye as the prophet, in order to perceive with corporeal eyes all that the prophet saw with a spiritual intelligence. Nor do I disagree with this opinion. But why was he, who was able to see many foreigners there, unable to recognize many of his own people in the same place? Why is it that this observer from the uppermost spot of paradise and hell who spied the Christians there, whom he names among the first, why did he not recognize in hell Dathan and Abiram, the rebel Korah and all his multitude,[153] whom the earth swallowed up, the

152. Ezek 32.24, 22.
153. Nm 16.35.

leading men whom a celestial fire consumed in the desert, the
countless thousands of Jews whom supernal wrath consumed
at various times either for idolatry or for diverse crimes, all of
these men, I say, of his own race, or at least some of them? And
certainly and without any question these were in hell, of whom
sacred Scripture says in the Book of Numbers: "And they went
down alive into hell, the ground closing upon them."[154] Clearly,
what was the reason that he was unable to see there his own na-
tive sons and yet recognized so clearly foreign-born Christians?
But it is unnecessary for the expositor to ask why this was invented by your sages, O Jews.

But the reason for such a harsh condemnation should not
be passed over. "'Why,' Joshua asked the angel, 'have the Christians been condemned?' He said: 'Because they believe in the
son of Mary, and do not keep the law of Moses, and especially
because they do not believe in the Talmud.'" If asked by anyone
why all the Jews from Christian times are in hell, with the exception of those who have believed in Christ, I can reply even more
accurately: Because they do not believe in the Son of Mary and
do not keep his Gospel, and especially because they blaspheme
against him continually. It would not take much work for me to
state these truths to the one that is speaking, nor does it take
much work for you, O Jew, to state these falsehoods for the one
inventing them. I speak the truth easily, you speak falsehood
easily. But I am not concerned here with which of our judgments be truer, because I treated that above. I treated that in
the preceding four chapters, in which I have demonstrated with
countless proof-texts and with reasoned arguments that our
Christ, both Son of God and God, a king not temporal but eternal, is not, as you think, still to come but has already come. And
if these are true as I expressed them—rather, because they are
true—then what you said is false, namely, that your Joshua saw
Christians in hell because they believe in the Son of Mary, do
not observe the law of Moses, and do not believe in the Talmud.

I proceed to the next part of the vision: "Moreover, Pharaoh
was lying prostrate in hell, while holding his head," beneath
"the threshold of the gate of hell. His eye became the hinge pin

154. Nm 16.33.

for the gate to hell. Moreover, the gate was turned in each direction upon his eye at the souls' entry." And, O wretched men, because I hear astonishing things, I am compelled to exclaim or declaim often, wretches, men, I say, do you never perceive anything except in the manner of beasts? Do you believe that nothing can ever exist among those above or below except what you have learned on earth? Why do you not grasp that just as the nature of spirits is far removed from bodies, so too it is necessary that the nature of spiritual things exist far removed from the condition of corporeal ones? In fact, light does not exist there as it does here, darkness does not exist there as it does here, rest does not exist there as it does here, such men do not exist there nearly in the same way as they do here, dwellings do not exist there as they do here, gates do not exist there as they do here, and in fact all things there belong to a different genus and have a different quality than here, with the exception of the truth of the substances. And, to remain silent concerning the rest (which do not pertain to the present task), just as that infernal prison is different from this one, so too is it far removed from this one. Indeed, a human prison is built either from stones or wood or some terrene material. The strongest gates appear in it, so that an entrance appears there for entering but no opportunity for leaving appears to those enclosed within. With respect to the infernal prison, is God afraid that any of those enclosed in it will leave against his will, with the result that he has blocked its entrance with gates for security? Are there souls or angels (whether they be of a good or evil essence) that cannot pass through bodies once they have left behind their bodies? Or, can there be neither free entry to nor exit from those places for souls or demons unless that infernal gate with which you are concerned is opened? Truly, since you have the most impoverished intellect, you are unable to observe with prudent reason that incorporeal beings have an entirely different quality than corporeal ones, that nothing corporeal can stand in the way of spirits, that even when we lie down in our home with the doors closed on every side, it is accessible to spirits through the bodies of the doors, through the walls and their windows, just as there is a pathway through for air for us. Since this is true, since nothing corporeal can block spirits, let it be said of God that "there is none that can deliver out of his hand";[155] let your unnecessary gate be removed from the entrance to hell, and let Pharaoh rise from under the threshold, and let the one who with his eye alone has supported the hinge of a gate so heavy through so many ages, with such horrible torment, be freed by our compassion.

But let us hear the reason for such torment. The angel says, "Because he afflicted the children of Israel in the land of Egypt and pursued them, after their affliction, unto the sea." Based on this, you hardly seem to have examined that text. In fact, it was not only this Pharaoh who perished in the sea that afflicted the children of Israel in the land of Egypt. Actually, there was another Pharaoh who previously had afflicted these same people, of whom that true Scripture says: "Now after a long time the king of Egypt died. And the children of Israel, groaning, cried out because of the works."[156] But perhaps you distinguish the one from the other in this way, because the angel said: "And he pursued them unto the sea."

Now truly, at last, let us leave your hell and come to our paradise. The Talmud says, "Paradise is said to be enclosed by a wall on all sides." And well it should. In fact, it ought to seem so to the inhabitants of paradise, lest perhaps any nation rise up against it just as often nation is accustomed to rise up against nation, and kingdom against kingdom. If this should happen, it must be repelled first at some distance by arms, and then, if in some way it should be able to prevail so as to approach as far as paradise itself, it must be repelled by a wall.

Let, then, the cherubim and the fiery sword be removed that God positioned to guard paradise after Adam had been cast out.[157] In fact, what good will it do there since the wall will be sufficient to defend paradise? But if perhaps it is necessary with the accompaniment of the wall, let it remain and, with at least assistance from the wall, let it free the holy inhabitants of paradise from fear of the enemy. Now we believe that that wall has been removed by the death of Christ and that the fiery sword

155. Cf. Dt 32.39.   156. Ex 2.23.
157. Cf. Gn 3.24.

has already been extinguished by his blood. But what then? Let it return as a guard, and by its circuit let it render the saints resting there more secure. Now, let the fraud that is praised follow, and let the entire world admire that man dwelling in paradise against God's will.

The angel, compelled to be the man's porter by the pact that he had made with God, led him to paradise and at first deposited him at a distance, and then brought him nearer, and then finally deposited him on the wall itself, not knowing to be on guard against the tricks of that shrewd man. And once he had been placed on the wall by the angel, while he posed many questions concerning those who inhabited paradise and those whom he then saw nearby, and while the angel replied to him appropriately concerning the individuals, he duped the angel, who had been distracted from his purpose by this mutual exchange, and suddenly cast himself down from the wall of paradise into paradise with the sword of death that the angel had entrusted to him, but that he had neglected to guard.

O foolish angel, O wise man! Angels were wont to surpass men in wisdom; now men surpass the angels. Why did he believe the man again, one whose trickery he had already experienced once or twice; why did this angel, the most foolish of all the angels, not take care that he not deceive him, so that he not present himself as a laughingstock to the people? Behold, an angel deceived so many times; behold, a man deluding an angel so many times. At last the angel barely recovered his mind once he had been fooled, but lamented and said to the man who already obtained paradise from him against his will, calling out not in a soft voice but loudly, like one sorely moved: "You have deceived me!" From whom he heard a fitting reply: "I do not care whether you have been deceived or not." And the angel added in a commanding voice that he should quickly leave. "He swore, and by the same oath finally he replied that he would not leave. When those who inhabited paradise saw him, they were amazed that a clothed, living man had entered paradise with a sword in this way."

And what shall I say? Let anyone say what he can. I confess that at this point I can say nothing worthwhile concerning these matters. Indeed, I read in the Christian Gospel, in which, O wretches, you do not believe, that "the kingdom of heaven suffers violence, and the violent bear it away."[158] But with arms? With frauds? With deceptions? No. How then? With repentance, humility, continence, and truth. Nonetheless, that stranger who fell into paradise, who possesses paradise, who holds onto paradise, lacks these virtues. How then? With God willing it? No, but unwilling, and actually contradicting him. But perhaps with the angel assenting? No, but grieving, crying out against it, forbidding it with as many cries as he could to prevent it from happening.

Therefore, such a man possesses paradise with God unwilling, with the angels unwilling, and with men unwilling. What kind of deed this may be, let others say. Now I turn quickly to the things that remain. Nonetheless, I say this one thing: that it is not surprising that the inhabitants of paradise were amazed to see that a clothed, living man holding a sword had entered paradise. For since Adam was cast out from there, they had learned that no one could be its inhabitant while living in the flesh, and no one—not even Adam himself before he was cast out—who was clothed in human garments, and no one with a sword. But let the other things come next.

Thus the man occupying paradise, "when he found no seat there," says the Talmud,

stood and approached Pharaoh's daughter. She had merited an exalted throne in paradise because she had saved Moses from death, because she had nourished him, because she had instructed him in all the wisdom of the Egyptians. He approached her and said: "Rise up, go, behold, your father is at the gate." Quickly she rose up and hastened to the gate. Joshua immediately snatched her seat. And when she did not find her father, she returned and said to Joshua: "Why did you lie to me?" "I did not lie," he said. "For your father is at the gate of hell." "Why did you take my place away from me?" she asked. He said: "Because the Lord granted it to me, and henceforth it will be mine."

Who will not deplore this trick? Certainly, I will not deplore it. If the daughter of Pharaoh wishes, let her deplore it. Let her deplore the fact that she was so foolish, so improvident, that,

158. Mt 11.12.

although she taught Moses all the wisdom of the Egyptians, she
allowed herself to be so easily deluded by a man whose wisdom
was so inferior to Moses'—if nonetheless you, O Jews, concede
that—and she lost her seat that had been given to her in paradise with such a facile inducement.

Let me address the things that come next: "Meanwhile, the
angel, having returned to God, reported what had happened.
The Lord, moreover, commanded that he should leave there
quickly. To him the angel replied: He has sworn" by your name
"and by the Talmud that he will not go forth from there. Examine the collection of books, said God. If ever he committed
perjury or deceit, then he will have to leave. If not, however,
then he must be allowed to remain either on account of his religion, or because he always has studied the Talmud. The angel
examined the collection of books and did not find that he had
ever sworn falsely or deceived. Thus, the Lord conceded that he
would not ever have to leave there again."

Perhaps some of the readers who are not instructed in such
matters will be astonished that I speak again and again using an
ironic form of speech. Perhaps, too, they will be surprised that
I do not reply to all these bits of idle nonsense one by one, with
an argument (*ratio*) as it were. And what else can I do? What else
should I do? I have responded above to some fables, and I have
confuted them in part by [an appeal to] a proof-text and in part
by argument. I did so for this reason: lest, if I always use the
ironic form of speech that I often use now, some of the simple
readers might think that I have nothing else to say against the
Jews concerning these matters. In fact, I would never have employed any proof-text against them in this disputation had the
argument (*ratio*) not demanded it. I would have spoken only
in that [ironic] fashion in which I spoke to them by replying
that they are not worthy of a rational response, but deserve only
the highest derision, more than all story-tellers. But the reason
I reply to them ironically more often than is customary, and not
with an argument, is because they have deserved this more than
all other mortals.

Moreover, how one should respond to that type of fable
seems to be outside our hands. For what else but laughter and

derision befits a fable that states that a foolish angel was deluded by a wise man and that after he saw that he was deceived, since at that point the man already possessed paradise against God's will, he returned to God to report what had happened. Clearly, not knowing the events that had transpired, God was ignorant of what had happened. Therefore, it was necessary for the angel sent by him to return to him to report what had happened. Now, perhaps at that time God had forgotten that wisdom of his by which he knows all things even before they occur. But if before they occur, then not also when they occur? That wisdom had perished, of which it is written: "You have made all things in wisdom."[159] And that same wisdom had perished of which it is said: "Who will search out the wisdom of God that encompasses all things? Who has numbered the sand of the sea, and the drops of rain, and the days of the world?"[160] Was he able to be ignorant of the tricks of the one who had stolen his paradise with deceit? For what purpose, then, did the angel report to him what had already happened? But since we have heard how God's wisdom is void of understanding, let us also see how God's power will languish: "Moreover, the Lord," he said, "ordered that he quickly leave." He duped you [the angel] at every turn with deceit, he said, all that he said was spoken with deceit, he cast himself into my paradise with deceit. But nothing that he did will benefit him, he will gain nothing from us with deceit; let the deceitful man leave, let him withdraw, let him leave our paradise to us.

"To him the angel said:" he said that "he swore by" your name (*per temetipsum*) and "by the Talmud that he would not leave there." That is: What is it that you say, O Lord? You command that man to leave paradise. But this is impossible. It is impossible for your word to prevail over his word, for his judgment to be changed by your command. The man has such great power that it is necessary that you give in to him, and he has such great truth that his truth will prevail by right over your truth. For he swore by your name and by the Talmud that he would not leave there. It is necessary, then, for you to oppose yourself and to

159. Ps 103.24.
160. Sir 1.3, 1.2.

prefer his word to your word because he swore by your name. And still more. For he swore also by the Talmud. If you have disdain for yourself, you have to serve the Talmud. If you condemn the fact that he swore by your name, you cannot condemn the fact that he swore by the Talmud. In fact, the Talmud is greater than you are. The Talmud is so much greater than you that even if you command that men die, the Talmud will withstand you; if you send your angels to snatch away the souls of men, the Talmud will withstand you; if you summon anyone to you by any messengers whatsoever, the Talmud will withstand you and will not allow him to come. For these reasons, the Talmud is greater than you. Thus you command in vain to leave paradise the one whom the Talmud commands not to withdraw. What you say, the Lord said to the angel, is true. That man cannot leave paradise—even though I command it—unless the Talmud permits it, unless it agrees that he leave even after my command. But since there is no other suggestion, "let his life be examined in the collection of books. If it be found there that he has ever perjured himself or has lied, it will be necessary for him to leave paradise. If not, however, then it is necessary to agree that he remain either on account of his religion or because he always studied the Talmud."

To these things I reply: is the Jew, who, as I said above, is both God's worst enemy and mine, worthy of my response? For he said previously that God's wisdom is fatuous; now he says that God's power is enfeebled. What is it that Holy Scripture says: "And he shall rule from sea to sea, and from the river unto the ends of the earth"?[161] But perhaps his power has dominion "from sea to sea"—that is, on this earth—but, unknown to us, does not extend as far as his paradise? If truly a question arises in that respect, it can be solved in another respect if paradise is proved to be on earth. But it is proved to be on earth when Scripture says: "The Lord God had planted a paradise of pleasure from the beginning."[162] And, finally, it is on the earth more clearly, rather that it was the earth: "The Lord God brought forth of the ground all manner of trees, fair to behold, and

161. Ps 71.8.
162. Gn 2.8.

pleasant to eat: the tree of life also in the midst of paradise."[163]
But if he produced those trees from the ground, then surely he
produced them from earth. For the ground (*humus*) has only
one other name, that is, earth (*terra*). The earth, however, from
which the trees were produced, is paradise. Therefore, paradise
is both the earth and on the earth. But the psalm says of the
earth: "All the things which God willed he did, in heaven and
on the earth."[164] If, then, paradise is the earth, and God accomplished all that he willed in heaven and on earth, then surely he
accomplished his will in paradise, because it is the earth. Then,
when the Jew says that that man did not obey God's will and
God's command that willed and commanded him to leave paradise, it is false; it is false that he defended himself, lest he be
compelled to leave, by introducing the divine name and, as an
additional factor, the book of the Talmud.

But perhaps what follows is true, namely, that God had commanded that the library of his life be examined so that a dili-
gent reader might search through it to discover whether he
ever committed perjury or told a lie. If he is convicted by that
text to have ever perjured himself or lied, he may be expelled
from paradise. If not, however, he may remain and thereafter
need not be afraid that anyone can expel him from paradise.
The collection of books was examined, and it exonerated him
from perjury and lying. Therefore, this colonist in paradise remained there by right, with God agreeing to it.

God could not remember the deeds without a book, nor
could his fleeting memory recall them without the assistance of
the books or parchments. This is why he issued the edict that
the man's life should be examined in the collection of books.
But if God's memory languished over the acts of one man, how
will it have the strength to retain the deeds of all mortals? What
parchments will suffice? What ages will not be missing? And certainly I know, and I have it from a Jewish book that Solomon
said: "And all things that are done, God will bring into judgment
for every error, whether it be good or evil."[165] But from books?
Will he reread all the things that men have done in books, or

163. Gn 2.9.
164. Ps 134.6.
165. Eccl 12.14.

will he present them from books? Thus has God's memory perished, or will it perish? And who is the one that speaks in one of
your books by means of a certain wisdom: "My memory is unto
everlasting generations."[166] Is it not God? Certainly it is God. I
do not examine the countless and similar judgments giving testimony to God's eternal memory because these alone suffice, if
not for the Jew, for whom nothing suffices, then nonetheless for
every person but the Jew.

What of the remaining things that follow? The collection of
books is reexamined, and because it has been found once again
that he never perjured himself and that he did not lie, it is granted and it is conceded to a man still living in mortal flesh never
to be compelled to leave paradise thereafter, lest he die outside
it. The merit of the man who is doubtlessly to be preferred to
all your patriarchs and prophets is great, a man to whom was
given what David could not merit, concerning whom it is written in your [book of the prophet] Malachi: "David slept with his
fathers."[167] [Even] Moses could not merit this, of whom it is said
in Deuteronomy: "Moses the servant of the Lord died, and" the
Lord "buried him";[168] and [even] Abraham himself could not
merit this, of whom Genesis says: Abraham, "being old and full
of days,"[169] has died. The ancient Jews did not think this way,
and they themselves were not promoters of your impiety. For
when our Savior said to the Jews, your fathers: "Amen, amen
I say to you: If any man keep my word, he shall not see death
forever,"[170] nonetheless they replied quite differently than these
do, or than one with your understanding: "Now we know that
you have a devil. Abraham is dead, and the prophets; and you
say: If any man keep my word, he shall not see death forever.
Are you greater than our father Abraham, who is dead? and the
prophets are dead."[171] Although these men were certainly impious, they despised greatly your understanding by which you
say that with tricks that man extorted from God in order not to
die, that with tricks he extorted from him a perpetual dwelling
in paradise that was granted to him while still living in mortal

166. Sir 24.28.   167. 1 Kgs 2.10.
168. Dt 34.5–6.   169. Gn 35.29.
170. Jn 8.51.   171. Jn 8.52–53.

flesh, even though against God's will. Therefore, may you repent (which nonetheless I say in vain) that you have believed
this, that you have said this, when you hear, when you see, that
your fathers replied so harshly to our God and Redeemer in this
matter, which he nonetheless perceived differently.

Although we have passed over some very astonishing things,
still more astonishing things follow. Actually, that man who obtained paradise from God against his will by such deceit, as was
said, attempted a still greater deceit, because great things had
come neatly to him. For it did not suffice for him to be carried
to paradise by a conveyance more noble than the one that had
carried Elijah up to heaven, since the latter was borne by a fiery
chariot into heaven, while the former was borne by a celestial
angel into paradise; it did not suffice that, having vanquished
God, he would inhabit his paradise as a victor; nor did it suffice
that he had merited this privilege: that he alone among mortals
was able to escape death. Enticed by a most successful outcome
of events, he strove to make all the others immortal. For he responded suddenly to the angel who had bestowed upon him the
sword with which he had been accustomed to slay people wherever he found them, whether on the road or in the meat market, as that urbane text says. What [did he say]? Clearly, Joshua
responded that he would not return the sword to him, unless
he swore to him that he would not slay men with it any more.
Truly, he is a pious man, continually showing compassion for dying mortals and looking out for them with kindness so that they
will not die in the future. For that reason he was unwilling to
return the sword, the instrument of death, and he did not give
ground to the angel that repeatedly and unlawfully desires human death. Repeatedly duped, the angel returned to God, and
reported what Joshua had replied. "But the Lord agreed that
his plea be fulfilled, although unwillingly. And Joshua returned
the sword to the angel under such a condition."

Here, among the many other things that ought to be inves-
tigated, I ask only this one thing: since that angel was so foolish that he was unable to guard against the trick of that shrewd
man who extorted the sword of death from him, why, then, did
he demand it back from him afterward? Was he unable to fash-

ion another one in place of the sword that he lost? Did divine power need it because if it lost something, owing to the stupidity of that foolish messenger, nothing like it could be obtained after that? What necessity compelled him to beg for the sword that had been taken away by a sly, shrewd man when he could have fashioned, I think, many swords? Were the good or bad angels—the slayers of men by divine command—always accustomed to use just the one steel sword? I read that an angel slew the firstborn of the Egyptians on one night so that in the whole of the great Egypt there was not a single dwelling in which death was not present.[172] I read, too, of the 185,000 from the army of the king of Assyria who were slain by divine command in a brief time or moment.[173] I read, too, of certain other cases like these. Were all of these slain by only one and the same sword of God? And what would these angels do who slew so many thousand people at that time if they lost the slayer's sword? Then, once the sword was lost, with what instrument could they slay so many people? It was a proper, sufficient precaution for them before Joshua was born (who snatched away the divine sword) never to slay all those appointed [for death] with the same sword. For if it were snatched away first, then the angel, the minister of death, would be unable to fulfill God's command once the sword had been taken away. After the age of Joshua, with what sword were so many countless thousands of people slain by God's command? By what sword, I ask you, were they cut down after that sword had been lost earlier? Answer here, Jews. Here difficulties constrain you, although not now for the first time, from which you will never be delivered. Either restore the sword to God that your Joshua wrongly took away, so that he can slay people in customary fashion as he wills or, if you do not do this, make mortals immortal and advise them all not to fear death any more.

But so that it not perhaps seem astonishing or false to us that a man, as was said, become immortal in order to dwell in paradise in a manner such as this, you want to cheer us and to encourage [us] to believe with a noble and true example. You say

172. Cf. Ex 12.29–30.
173. 2 Kgs 19.35.

that one ought to believe that Joshua obtained paradise in this way, since Eliezer, Abraham's servant, was likewise snatched away from death to possess heaven, which is even greater. How this happened is described in this way in an oft-cited book, which teaches: "After midday Isaac went out into the field to meet his servant, Eliezer, who was returning with Rebecca from Mesopotamia, where Abraham had sent him. And when Rebecca asked the servant, who is the one he had gone to meet: Here he is, he said, my master Isaac. When Rebecca heard this" (according to our true Scripture) "she quickly covered herself with a linen garment and descended from the camel."[174] According to your false text, "At that descent she lost the sign of virginity. It was time to copulate. Not recognizing the signs of virginity in the spouse, the man attacked the servant to blame him, [saying] that, like a traitor, he had corrupted his wife. But that one, denying it with an oath, said to Isaac: Would that you enjoy the vision of heaven, if what you claim is true. As he said this to Isaac, Eliezer was immediately taken up into heaven."[175] Therefore, who will dare to deny any longer that what you said about Joshua is true, when you invent so much about the servant of Abraham? Because doubtlessly it follows that the immortal Eliezer reached heaven, who will dare to reject your claim, O Jews, that your Joshua inhabits paradise? It should be believed without question because it is proved by an example that is both valid and indestructible.

Also, one should believe what you believe, that what God promised to Abraham in the past is to be fulfilled once the Jews have been gathered up from all the parts of the world and brought together again by your messiah in your land of your promise: "I will multiply your seed as the stars of heaven, and as the sand that is by the seashore."[176] For this to be the case, however, each and every woman will bear one son each day, and thus will she generate

174. Cf. Gn 24.64–65.

175. *Pirkê de Rabbi Eliezer* reports that Eliezer was wrongly accused of having despoiled Rebecca, while the *Derekh Erez Rabbah* adds that Eliezer was admitted to paradise alive (cf. *Encyclopedia Judaica* 6:619). For the suspicion that Eliezer had defiled Rebecca, see *Pirkê de Rabbi Eliezer,* 16, trans. Gerald Friedlander (New York: Hermon Press, 1916; rep. 1970), p. 110 and n. 8.

176. Gn 22.17.

366 sons in the course of only one year.[177] What great fecundity
and quick multiplication of Abraham's seed! It is not, however, as
great as the number of either the stars of heaven or the sands of
the seashore, even if every woman from the first Eve to the last,
who will be born at the end of the world, should give birth to one
infant every day of this age. And truly they will be unhappy wom-
en who give birth if that divine curse imposed on women remains
in force, just as it does on every other day, so that each day they
will be tormented by the severe pain of childbirth. I think that
they would prefer never to conceive than to give birth or to bear
accompanied by pains that are so sharp and frequent. Nonetheless, what will happen to that chapter in the law that commands
that a woman bearing a male child abstain from intercourse with
a man for forty days, and, if bearing a female child, for eighty
days?[178] But I digress. One should not always delay over such matters. Nor have I decided to pass over completely, nonetheless, the
manner in which the Holy Scriptures are given to you, to be interpreted wisely and cautiously. I want to hear from you how you
explicate that verse of your psalm that says: "You have ascended
on high; you have led captivity captive; you have given gifts to
men."[179] "You have ascended on high." Who has ascended? Moses, as you say, ascended into heaven at God's command.

The angels, seeing him, wanted to slay him. Moses, trembling with fear,
cried out to the Lord. Hearing him, the Lord admonished the angels:
"Would you kill my servant?" he said. "You create discord against me."
The angels were ashamed and said: "We do not create discord, but we
deplore the fact that this earthly, polluted man has ascended to heaven."
"He is not," said the Lord, "unclean and polluted, because before he
ascended to heaven we sanctified him from uncleanness." The holy
angels continued to complain not only about this, but also that he gave
the holy and unblemished law to polluted men before giving it to them,
to whom it ought to be given first. And the Lord said: "You struggle
against my precepts foolishly. In fact, here [in heaven] no vices are
perpetrated, no crimes. Therefore, here the law is unnecessary, but it

177. Cf. Petrus Alfonsi, *Dialogue Against the Jews*, trans. Resnick, 124.
178. Cf. Lv 12.1–5. Peter's question asks how a woman can bear every day
of the year, when she is required to abstain from sexual intercourse for forty to
eighty days after childbirth.
179. Ps 67.19.

is necessary for humans, who commit murder and adultery and other wicked acts." Then the angels established peace with Moses and gave him at least half of their wisdom.

"You have taken captivity [captive]"—that is, you have despoiled heaven and the angels of wisdom. "You have given gifts to men"[180]—that is, descending to earth, you have given that wisdom to the children of Israel. "Because they do not believe that the Lord God dwells"—that is, the Gentiles and the Christians do not believe that God dwells in Moses.[181]

How shall I mock that? How shall I ridicule it? How shall I tread it under foot? In themselves these declare sufficiently, or rather very fully, how they should be mocked, how they should be despised, how they should be trodden under foot. And they declare even this, how one should believe teachers who explicate the Holy Scriptures both with subtlety and truthfully.

What shall I say about the keys of Korah? These you have said to have been "so numerous that he had three hundred camels laden with these keys and, because they could hardly bear their immense weight when Moses was the leader of the Hebrews in the desert, they were made not from iron or wood or any other such material but from dried leather in order to be lighter to carry. These keys guarded only the aforementioned Korah's treasures, which had been deposited in hollows or various caves."[182] Richest man of all men, whose wealth could suffice for the entire human race for ages without end. But the loss of so much treasure must be lamented since Korah himself was swallowed up along with Dathan and Abiram and the other rebels, with their sons and daughters and with their tents and all their substance, according to the divine will.[183]

What shall I say when a similar fable has been presented? What shall I say, namely, about this: "When the sons of Jacob carried their dead father to the grave, the sons of Esau, likewise

180. Ps 67.19.
181. Cf. Petrus Alfonsi, *Dialogue Against the Jews,* trans. Resnick, 94. Cf. B.T. *Shabbath* 88b–89a.
182. Cf. Petrus Alfonsi, *Dialogue Against the Jews,* trans. Resnick, 91. For the sources of this legend, see also B.T. *Pesachim* 119a and *Sanhedrin* 110a.
183. Cf. Nm 16.23–33.

carrying their dead father to the same grave, opposed them with a large force, and they engaged in great struggles hither and yon to lay claim to the grave for themselves"?[184] And what about this: that "Dan, the son of Jacob, ascended a mountain and cut off from the mountain a rock as massive in size as the entire army of Esau, which he placed on his head, so that with one throw of the rock he would cast down that entire people"?[185] What shall I say about this: that "returning, when he found both armies at peace, he cast that prodigious millstone into the sea, and the sea, driven back by its size, overflowed its boundaries and destroyed two cities—Pithom and Raamses[186]—with its overflow. Almost four hundred years after their destruction"—here you appear to say something like the truth—"Pharaoh," as you say, "rebuilt these cities, and during their reconstruction he afflicted your fathers with the hardship of making the clay and brick."[187]

If I should wish to pursue similarly foolish tales of the Jews and to report all of them exactly, such fables would be beyond number and cannot be expounded even over a very long period of time. In fact, who could respond with individual arguments or confute so many volumes of nonsense with which men who perished almost 2000 years ago have filled up their book chests? And insofar as it pertains to reason (*ratio*), moreover, could anyone reply to them, someone especially devoid of intelligence would be needed, not just to find the task manageable so much as because there would hardly be sufficient time, and it would not be entirely reasonable to do so. In fact, what rational faculty (*ratio*) permits a discussion about such things to be drawn out beyond measure, which, when each disputant remains silent, every human soul understands to be false, perceives to be deserving of laughter, and knows is fit to be cursed? Therefore, let the pen hasten to an end, and let it not tarry any longer.

Thus, from the immense collection of similar fables cast to the winds like a huge mound of dust, I will reproduce only

184. Cf. Petrus Alfonsi, *Dialogue Against the Jews,* trans. Resnick, 91.
185. Cf. Petrus Alfonsi, *Dialogue Against the Jews,* trans. Resnick, 92.
186. Cf. Ex 1.11.
187. Cf. Petrus Alfonsi, *Dialogue Against the Jews,* trans. Resnick, 92; cf. Ex 1.14.

the one fable of Jeremiah's daughter and his son, and in this
way, by the grace of Christ, I will conclude this Jewish work,
or rather this Christian work against the Jews. But how shall I
speak? What words shall I use? Modesty demands silence, and I
am afraid that by discussing shameful things my words may appear less than decent. One is confounded to present disgrace-
ful things to modest ears that are habituated to hear holy and
heavenly things; one is afraid to pour out things so wicked. But
what then? Let a Christian and more sober speech cast aside
an ill-advised embarrassment and by reproving those who are
shameful and impious, let it compel them at least to blush at
these matters.

[Here the edited text provides two distinct
MSS versions, namely, L and D.]

[L]

It is often the case that God does just this in the first Law,[188]
and in the second he does not remain silent about it.[189] And because he desires to correct men from evils that are hardly fit to
be named, he presented them by prohibiting even more shameful ones. And our apostle did this, as is well known around the
world,[190] and with difficulty he corrected these things in mortals
even though the greatest wickedness he left untouched. Thus
I will not leave that unassailed and untouched in order to confound all the more the enemies of the name Christian, and how
much should they be despised who believe things so deserving of execration even after the matter that is set forth appears
clearer than the sun. "At a certain time," they say,

when it was customary for youths to take baths together, while they
stroked themselves in a sensual manner they poured forth the manly
seed into the water. When the prophet Jeremiah came there because he
was drawn to that place by the demands of travel, and when he saw them
doing such things, he was aghast, and, rebuking them, he cried out
that they were committing a wicked crime. When they heard this, they
exhorted him with words and compelled him by force to do the same
thing himself. Although at first he refused and said that he preferred

188. Cf. Lv 18.6–30.   189. Cf. Mt 15.19.
190. Cf. Rom 1.27; 1 Cor 6.9–10.

death rather than do such a thing, finally, having been compelled by them, he assented and poured out sperm onto the water just as they did. And after it had remained in the water a long time, there approached Jeremiah's daughter, who would be ruined accidentally by these baths and, encountering the sperm by chance, she received it into the woman's receptacle and immediately became pregnant.

[MS D reads]:

In fact, the impious Jews say:

The prophet Jeremiah had a daughter, and his own daughter became pregnant from her father's seed that had been poured out into the water and received in this way into the woman's receptacle.

[Both MSS read:]

Then the time for giving birth came, and she bore a son and called his name Bencera.[191] This one, who began to speak as soon as he was born, begged for warm bread and fatty meat, butter and honey.[192] Since his mother was surprised at this, she said, "Why do you ask for such things, when you ought to take milk?" He said, "Foods like these please me more than your milk." When his mother revealed this to the wisest sages and called them to see the boy, the boy vanquished all of those that were engaged among themselves in several contentious debates. His mother was even more amazed and said: "What is this, my son; what are you doing? From where do you get so much wisdom? How do you know so many modes of disputation when you have not even learned letters?" "I am the son of Jeremiah," he said. He explained how that happened.

What shall I say, reader? Will it be necessary for me to say anything or to open my mouth concerning these things and against them? I hear, O I hear from the Jew what I could not

191. That is, Ben Sira. This tale, too—like that of Jeremiah's daughter—is drawn from the medieval *Alphabet of Ben Sira*. The popular Hebrew and Aramaic collection cannot be securely dated, although it has been suggested that it may have first appeared in the East during the rise of Islam. See Joseph Dan, "Ben Sira, Alphabet of," in *Encyclopaedia Judaica*, ed. Michael Berenbaum and Fred Skolnik, 2d ed. (Detroit: Macmillan Reference USA, 2007), 3: 375–76. Ben Sira's miraculous birth and precocious development are intended to rival Christian claims made on behalf of Jesus. These tales from the *Alphabet of Ben Sira* are made available in translation in *Rabbinic Fantasies: Imaginative Narratives from Classical Hebrew Literature*, ed. David Stern and Mark Jay Mirsky (Philadelphia: Jewish Publication Society, 1990), 169–72.

192. Cf. Is 7.15, where these foods are taken by the son Emmanuel.

hear from the devil. The Jew with his lies surpasses the prince of lies and makes the devil—who is not only a deceiver but is the father and master of lies[193]—almost his son and disciple. The devil is indeed the one who, as our Apocalypse says, is "the accuser of our brethren," who accused them "before our God day and night."[194] Sometimes he accused them truly; sometimes he accused them falsely. But is Satan such a liar in the accusations directed against the brethren as to accuse Jeremiah of fornication in the sight of God, to dare to argue before the highest judge that he is just like a fornicator? But not [to argue this] before men? I do not think so. In fact, how would he dare do so? How, plainly, would he dare call him a fornicator, dare call him unclean, concerning whose cleanness and holiness he heard God say to him: "Before I formed you in the womb, I knew you: and before you came forth out of the womb, I sanctified you"?[195] The devil plainly heard this, although the Jew will not hear it. Certainly the devil knows that no one will believe him in opposition to divine revelation, although if he wished to lie about these things the will to deceive is not lacking, and therefore, lest the liar appear shameless and thus be able to deceive men less, he will prepare his malice in advance even though deceitfully rather than wisely. But not so the Jew, who has so completely consecrated himself to lies that are more than diabolical that no one trusts him in any way whatsoever. Clearly, even if sometimes he proclaims truths, no one now will believe him regarding any of the rest that he himself made up beyond the authentic words [of Scripture]. This is no surprise for one given to so much lying. In fact, which is worse—to allege falsehoods once in courtroom trials, or, once one has been discovered to be a false witness, to be rejected from [legal] actions and to be excluded from [further] testimony. Therefore, should not what happens to someone who lies just once also happen to someone who always lies and, equally, always deceives? And in fact the Jew lies when he affirms what is false. He tricks others when he seduces them with his lies, although this does not happen often. But concerning the matter that this discussion treats, I do not

193. Cf. Jn 8.44.   194. Rv 12.10.
195. Jer 1.5.

believe that a Jew can trick anyone except another Jew, not even the one he inspired with similar dreamlike fables, his former disciple, Mohammad.

He will be unable, however, to trick anyone either to believe or even slightly to suspect that so great a man—so great a prophet of God, who fought until blood was shed, who fought for truth unto death, who fought for justice against liars, who fought against the impious that were none other than the Jews—committed a crime of such turpitude or that he could be forced to perpetrate such a thing from fear or from violence. Previously, he had preferred to endure the Egyptian stones thrown by Jewish hands, and he did not put off suffering what he later suffered on behalf of truth in order to associate himself with unclean youths by some [act of] assent. He had not become so foolish that he who from childhood appeared worthy of conversation with God, now, as a youth or mature adult, would neglect a gift so great and deprive himself of the prerogative of divine friendship with the filth of a crime. No matter the difference in ages, he did not besmirch with any such disfiguring mark one who is clean and innocent of every crime, to whom, when he said, "Behold, I cannot speak, for I am a child,"[196] God replied, "Say not, 'I am a child': for you will go to all that I shall send you to, and whatsoever I shall command, you will speak."[197] And then, "Lo, I have set you this day over the nations, and over the kingdoms, to root up, and pull down, and to waste, and to destroy, and to build, and to plant."[198] Would God send him forth while he was still a child; would he proclaim all the things that he had been commanded to speak; would he be given authority over the Gentiles and the kingdoms, to overthrow and destroy them and then again to plant them and build them, if God should foresee that in the future he would be of the sort that you, O Jews, make him?

But where do you even read that he had a daughter? Therefore, either you reveal from the Holy Scriptures and not from [your] customary nonsense that he had a daughter, or I will reveal from the same divine Scriptures that he had neither a daughter nor a son. I think you will fail. But I will not fail. In-

196. Jer 1.6.   197. Jer 1.7.
198. Jer 1.10.

deed, the Lord said to Jeremiah: And "you will not take a wife, nor have sons and daughters."[199] Reread the book of the prophet himself. There, after you have read this, learn either what you did not know before, or, if you have forgotten it, recall that the prophet Jeremiah had no wife and did not produce sons or daughters. Moreover, a man so great, one so studious, a guardian of the divine precepts, could not neglect a divine command and receive a wife or produce sons and daughters after that prohibition. In fact, who except one who strives to prove that he is unchaste and wicked will dare to assert that he produced a son or a daughter from a woman other than a wife? And I think that no one except a Jew will dare do so. But if Jeremiah neither had intercourse with a wife nor had intercourse at any time with some other woman, then just as certainly he produced neither a son nor a daughter. Let, then, this daughter that you have given to Jeremiah, O Jews, retreat from view, and let her look for another father. But perhaps, in order for him to procreate, sexual union was not necessary, since his seed, according to you, had such great power that it could produce offspring and cause pregnancy even at some distance away from him, as you said happened here. I do not respond by disputing this but by spitting upon your most wicked miracle, namely, the miracle that the seed poured out into the water was unable to be dissolved by the liquid nature of the element or lose generative power.

At this point, it would be inexcusably foolish to want to prove the remaining miracles of the prophetic boy—that he began to speak immediately after birth, that he begged for [and] that he ate warm bread, fatty meat, butter, and honey, that he defeated wise men while debating them; rather, he did none of these things. In fact, why should anyone attempt to prove that he did not say these things or that he did not do them, when it is certain that he never existed?

For that to be considered as certain, I add one more thing relating to that fable: "When Nebuchadnezzar (*Nabugodonosor*) heard of the aforementioned boy's great fame, he sent one thousand armed men to him, each of whom carried one soldier upon the nail of his finger, and since he wanted to know

199. Jer 16.2.

whether what was reported about him was true, he ordered that
he come to him. He [Ben Sira] refused to come, but he sent a
hare to him and whatever he wanted to ask or inquire of him he
wrote on the forehead of the hare. When Nebuchadnezzar saw
this, he knew that he was the wisest of all."[200] Although this fable
is not in the Talmud, nonetheless it is excerpted from a book
that has no less authority than the Talmud among the Jews.

These are your mysteries, O Jews, these are your most intimate secrets, this is the wisdom that you prefer even to all divine
wisdom. Now truly what Isaiah (often mentioned above, now
no longer your prophet but ours) said about you, among many
similar things, seems fulfilled in you: "They have broken the
eggs of asps, and have woven the webs of spiders. He that shall
eat of their eggs shall die, and that which is brought out shall be
hatched into a basilisk. Their webs shall not be for clothing, neither shall they cover themselves with their works."[201] The eggs
that you incubate are not like the eggs of hens that are either
useful themselves as food or so that some fowl would emerge
from them that suits human needs, but they are the eggs of asps
which, once they have been broken by you, infect you with the
deadly poison of impiety, and, in the end, after you have wickedly incubated them for a long time, they will produce the one
who is to come at the end of the world, the Antichrist, the king
of all the ungodly, just as the basilisk is the prince of all poisonous animals.[202] You have incubated the deadly egg for such a
fruit[203] for a long time with the very evil warmth of doctrines
such as these, so that once the egg has burst it will destroy you,
and at the end, as was said, the most noxious fruit of wickedness will burst forth from it upon the entire world. Your webs,
over which you have labored for a long time, are not like the
webs of female weavers[204] or of those who weave so that some

200. Cf. *Alphabet of Ben Sira*, in *Rabbinic Fantasies: Imaginative Narratives from
Classical Hebrew Literature*, 178.

201. Is 59.5–6.

202. For the basilisk as the "prince" and "king" of serpents, see the twelfth-
century *Book of Beasts*, ed. and trans. T. H. White (New York: Dover Publications,
1984), 168–69.

203. Cf. Ezek 17.23.

204. Female weavers: *textrices;* also, possibly, the Fates.

garment or covering can be made from them. Clearly, according to the prophet, they are not like clothing, nor will you be covered by them. Why? Because in all your works, in all your labors, in the entire fabric of impious doctrines, you have accomplished nothing useful to mortal men, because you have woven spider webs.[205] What a truly vain, truly futile labor of so many ages, in which from the time of the prophets (that is, since the time when a prophet has not appeared in Israel) you have woven nothing else, you have been busy at nothing else, you have filled Jewish books with no other instruction but blasphemy and ridiculous and false sacrilege. You have waged battle for so long with diabolical books against divine books, and you have labored to obfuscate heavenly instruction and to cover it with the smoke from the infernal abyss. When you have not netted[206] foolish animals in the nets of your webs, you have struggled to seize un-circumspect birds with clever snares. But the Jewish art of weaving (*textura*) does not have such art or power; it is not such and your design is not such that it could snare a quadruped or even the last bird. You have not spun manly or womanly webs, you have not accomplished manly or womanly things, but rather, according to a prophet who tells only the truth, you have only woven spider webs in the already mentioned fable and in similar fabulous bits of nonsense. These webs, which have been fashioned after long and intense labor, have been unable to deceive or ensnare anyone except a Jew, just like the vilest fly, because of their surpassing fragility.

Therefore, to impose a fitting end at last upon this fifth chapter against you, I will recapitulate briefly what has been presented. First, you strained to assail us with the divine books, and then later with fabulous books. We vanquished you with the divine books. We revealed the fables to be of no importance. What, then, remains to be done? Namely, this: that once you have cast aside the fabulous ones, you will properly understand the divine books in such a way as to believe and worship and glorify in them and from them the Christ who is not a false messiah, as you contend, but the true one, not one who will come

205. Cf. Is 59.6.
206. Reading *iretiti* (MS M) for *irretire*.

in judgment but one who has already come, who has already redeemed, saved, and glorified the world predestined to eternal life from the time of his virgin birth without sin, his dwelling in the world, and by his heavenly preaching, by his divine miracles, by his precious and not, as you think, vile death, by his resurrection, and his ascension. In fact, I believe that by this point you have already been so overwhelmed and confuted by truth itself with such witnesses, with such arguments, that you should resist no more, you should investigate no further.

Here ends the book of Peter, lord Abbot of Cluny, against the Jews.

INDICES

GENERAL INDEX

Aaron, biblical figure, 170–71, 240
Abel, biblical figure, 182, 209
Abija, biblical king, 142
Abiram, biblical figure, 263, 278
Abraham, biblical patriarch, 51,
    62–66, 72, 111, 160, 182, 227–28,
    273, 276–77
Aesop, 250
Africans, 57, 263
Ahab, biblical king, 91
Ahaz, biblical king, 169
Alexander of Hales, 13
Alexander of Macedon, 148
Alexander, king, 145
Alexandra, queen, 145
Alexandria Sother, 148
Alfonso VI, emperor, 5
Alfonso VII, emperor, 5
al-Hakim, caliph, 11
Alphabet of Ben Sira, 29
Ammonites, 259, 263
Amorites, 258, 263
Amos, biblical prophet, 245
Anaclet II, anti-pope, 19, 20
Ancient of Days, 124
Andrew of St. Victor, 36
Andrew, apostle, 199
angels, 59–60, 66, 68–72, 88, 122,
    155, 228, 237, 242, 248, 265,
    267–68, 271, 275, 277–78
Antichrist, 27, 122, 285
Antipater, 145
Apology of [*Ps.*] *Al-Kindi*, 8–9
Arabs, 259, 263
Archelaus, king, 105, 145, 150

Aristobolus, king, 104, 145, 150
Asa, biblical king, 142
Assyria, 245, 275
Atlas, 250
Augustus, emperor, 105, 148–49, 154
Avvim, 259, 263

Babylonian captivity, 142, 156
Balaam, 100, 182, 237, 239–41
Baldwin of Worcester, bishop, 15
Bartholomew of Exeter, bishop, 15
Baruch (ben Neriah), 77
basilisk, 285
Bencera (Ben Sira), 281
Bernard, saint, 3, 13, 18
Bouthillier, Denis, 42
Bruno of Segni, 37

Cain, 23, 141, 209, 232
Caligula, emperor, 149
Chazan, Robert, 26, 150
Christ, Passion of, 100, 116, 147,
    149, 151–53, 206
Christians, 5–6, 8, 12–17, 22–24, 26–
    28, 31, 34–35, 37–38, 40–45, 62,
    87, 90, 100–101, 133, 145, 150,
    156, 175–76, 178–79, 187–88,
    190–92, 200, 206–10, 212, 232,
    239, 258–59, 263–64, 278
Circe, 250
Cleopatra, 148
Cluny, monastery of, 3–7, 15, 19–20,
    29, 36, 49, 287
Cohen, Jeremy, 45
Crusade, First, 8, 12

INDEX OF HOLY SCRIPTURE

New Testament

INDEX OF TALMUDIC CITATIONS

INDEX OF QURANIC CITATIONS